PRISCILLA

PRISCILLA

The Hidden Life

of an Englishwoman

in Wartime France

Nicholas Shakespeare

HARPER

www.harpercollins.com

HarperCollins books may be purchased for educational, business, or sales promotional use. For information, please e-mail the Special Markets Department at SPsales@harpercollins.com.

This book is a work of nonfiction based on the recollections and research of the author. In some limited cases the names of people may have been changed to protect the privacy of others. The author has stated to the original publishers that, except in such minor respects not affecting the substantial accuracy of the work, the contents of this book are true.

Page 425 and the acknowledgements on pages 409–412 consititute a continuation of this copyright page.

This book was originally published in Great Britain in 2013 by Harvill Secker.

FIRST U.S. EDITION PUBLISHED 2014

Library of Congress Cataloging-in-Publication Data has been applied for.

ISBN 978-0-06-229703-7

14   15   16   17   18   OFF/RRD   10 9 8 7 6 5 4 3 2 1

TO LALAGE, IMOGEN, TRACEY AND CARLETON

'Everything is simple in men, and in women, if you look
at them from the outside, and watch them, hesitating and
laughing on the brink of the world. And everything is simple
too, long afterward, when life is over and done with and you
explain them after their death, looking back on lives which
are now only history. It is while it is still unfolding and still
taking place that fate is obscure and sometimes mysterious.'
JEAN D'ORMESSON, *At God's Pleasure*

'Well, there are worse things than fornication.'
ALLAN MASSIE, *A Question of Loyalties*

'Tell all.'
GRAHAM GREENE TO GILLIAN SUTRO

CONTENTS

PRISCILLA

PART ONE

1
THE INTERROGATION: 1943

On the third day the Gestapo appeared with machine guns and drove Priscilla to 11 Rue des Saussaies. She was taken to the basement and stripped. The air was thin, sucked into the cellars by a hand-turned ventilator. Beneath a strong electric bulb a grey-uniformed woman conducted a full and humiliating body search for cyanide pills, and picked through her clothes. Then she was ordered to dress and led upstairs into a large room where a man interrogated her for twelve hours.

Priscilla was accustomed to strangers asking probing questions. In the internment camp at Besançon, she was obliged to fill out forms which demanded to know her family descent, blood group, names of parents, political persuasion, religion. She had to write the answers in duplicate, and it was confusing if you did not speak German. The Commandant had reprimanded one internee for writing 'domestic servant' in the space for religion.

This was more invasive, headier. More personal.

The man talked in French, but it was obvious that he spoke English. It served nothing to lie, his manner said. Where had she been at school? What books did she like reading? He asked about her mother and father, branching off into her marriage and lovers. He checked her replies against the two identity cards which the Gestapo had found on her, and against her previous interrogation by the French police. He was well prepared and ruthless.

When had she first come to France? Why had she stayed? The occupying authorities had released her from Besançon, he noted, because she was expecting a child. What had happened to the baby?

It died, she said.

His eyes looked at her and dropped back to her French carte d'identité no. 40CC92076, in the name of Priscilla Doynel de la Sausserie and registering her as 'sans profession'. This card was no longer valid; it had run out in October the previous year.

He picked up her British passport, flicked through the pages. Mais, Priscilla Rosemary, b. 12 July 1916, Sherborne (England). Height, 5'9". Colour of eyes blue.

The passport – no. 181523 – was issued in London on 10 March 1937, nearly two years before her marriage. She had clung on to it against everyone's advice and not thrown it down the lavatory as her French sister-in-law had urged. But it was fortunate when Priscilla visited Cornet at his hotel that she had stuck to her old identity. If caught with her false French papers, in the name of Simone Vernier, she would have been executed.

Simone Vernier, Priscilla Mais, Vicomtesse Priscilla Doynel de la Sausserie – she was scattered among these identities, left alone by the Germans because of her blue eyes and blonde hair. She remembered her best friend Gillian before the war, sucking in her cheeks: 'La beauté, c'est notre première carte d'identité.'

This last identity was Priscilla's most convincing in Nazi-occupied Paris. Because at some point during the second day her interrogation was broken off: a person of influence with the Gestapo had intervened. In the evening, she was released. She was asked to sign a document with her answers written out, confirming that this was an accurate account. Then she was driven to the nursing home in Saint-Cloud, which she had given as her address.

2.
CHURCH FARM: 1957–66

My aunt Priscilla, my mother's sister, was a figure of unusual glamour and mystery in my childhood. She lived on a mushroom farm on the Sussex coast with her second husband Raymond, a jealous man who never let her far from his sight.

Priscilla invited us for weekends at their home in East Wittering, and whenever her name was mentioned on the journey from London I craned forward in the back of my parents' car. From an early age, I was conscious that my aunt was the sort of woman that men fell for. Both my parents loved her, but were unable to puzzle out the riddle of her relationship with Raymond, one of the most difficult men they had ever met.

Inevitably, as our mauve Singer Gazelle turned into the lane leading to Church Farm, there would be speculation about how late we were going to be, and whether Raymond, a tyrant for punctuality, would – this time – serve mushrooms. The promise of a mushroom is hard to recapture today; mass production has rendered the taste mundane. But to a seven-year-old boy accustomed to the flavour of cod's roe ('the cheapest food we could buy, then,' said my mother), a mushroom in the early 1960s was a fantastic thing – almost as exotic, in its way, as my aunt.

Her home was a red-brick Georgian house built next to a twelfth-century church. There was a courtyard with an injured poplar in it, and stacks of empty fish boxes for growing the mushrooms in. The 'growing rooms' were sinister-looking Nissen sheds, thirty of them side by side, long, low with curved asbestos roofs. I was under firm instructions not to enter. My shoes risked picking up a dangerous virus called 'La France disease', which, if spread, could wipe out Raymond's crop. So I never saw inside a shed. But I do recall buckets of disinfectant and the damp, musty smell of compost.

Church Farm was not a house for a small child. I have memories of foreign housekeepers; cold stone floors with lead-piping between the flagstones; aggressive little dogs with yellow paws, from Raymond's sodium spray; and a swimming pool clouded with dark green algae, so that I was never able to swim in it. The pool water was used to cool the Nissen sheds. Everything circulated back to the forbidden mushrooms, the small, white *Agaricus bisporus* species known as 'champignons de Paris'. Direct sunlight caused them to lose their whiteness – another reason Raymond would not let me enter the sheds. He only ever turned on the lights for watering and picking. For the rest of the time, he kept his mushrooms at a temperature of 64 degrees Fahrenheit, on a diet of horse manure and gypsum, in darkness. 'Kept in the dark and fed on shit' was his formula for a successful flush.

Raymond, with his eagle-beak nose and black-rimmed glasses, was quite terrifying. At Church Farm, he commandeered the whole of the downstairs for his office. Board-meetings took place at the dining-room table, at which Raymond, in cut-off gumboots, liked to sit so that he might monitor his staff. He had a cowbell which he wildly shook when Priscilla was wanted on the telephone, or for meals. A formal lunch, cooked by him, was eaten at 1 p.m. – sharp. Once, his daughter Tracey rang to say that she had a puncture. He ordered her: 'Fix it, but don't be late for lunch.'

Raymond's fag at Harrow had taught him how to cook. Partial to sauces, he was proud of his blanquette de veau; otherwise anything that did not involve mushrooms. It was unbusinesslike to give them away or dish them out to guests, and this extended to relatives. Priscilla had warned us that if we wanted to pick them, Raymond would insist on charging the full market rate of five shillings a punnet. The bad ones he sold at the end of the lane.

Raymond liked to be in charge, doing everything. The few meals he permitted Priscilla to make were steak and kidney pudding, risotto, and stuffed peppers – dishes with which I was already familiar. When my mother married, Priscilla had handed on these recipes, on which my mother soon became entirely dependent. Although I never succeeded in tasting a mushroom during my visits to Church Farm, in another respect I grew up on Priscilla's cooking.

My father was then a poor journalist, earning £500 a year, and he felt a frisson whenever he entered Priscilla's house at the prospect of meeting her smart roguish friends like the Sutros, and going out to expensive restaurants, which Raymond would pay for, and eating his luxurious meals. 'Church Farm was bitterly cold, austere, with rotten furniture. But behind it all there was something romantic.'

Raymond had raced Bugattis at Brooklands before the war. He boasted that Priscilla was a good driver too. Although I never remember my aunt at the wheel, I marvelled that Raymond chauffeured her each time in a different sports car: a black Aston Martin, a second-hand red Ferrari, a green Hotchkiss – and once, a Facel Vega which was supposed to go 100 mph backwards as well as forwards. In excess of this speed, he liked to accelerate us along the Birdham Straight, a long flat stretch between Wittering and Chichester.

In addition to his cars, Raymond owned a succession of motor yachts. Each year, he sailed Priscilla over to France, once taking my father as a crew member. Horse racing was another passion. He never missed Goodwood and, after he died, his daughter Tracey buried his ashes under a tree in the Veuve Clicquot enclosure.

An enthusiastic gambler, Raymond wrote down his bets in a pocketbook, but he was not an automatically good punter; in 1957, the same year that my parents drove me for the first time to Church Farm, his nephew calculated that Raymond spent £210,000 on horses (at least £4 million in today's money) – and won £211,000. Depending on his luck, he was as likely to treat everyone in the vicinity to dinner as to buy Priscilla a silk scarf embroidered with previous Derby winners. Losing was another matter. His nephew recalled once hiding behind the sofa, shaking – 'because that old kitchen door he came through would be slammed shut and he'd come in ranting and raving, throwing books at things, and go to the whisky bottle'.

From my eavesdroppings in the car, I picked up that my uncle was capable of sweeping acts of generosity, but kept his wife on a short leash. Priscilla could sometimes rely on receiving his winnings in France – at which point she would bolt to Hermès and spend an exorbitant sum on an alligator handbag.

Raymond was proud that in sixteen years of marriage he and Priscilla had never spent a night apart; if he had a business meeting, he made sure to return the same evening. None the less, the extent to which Raymond controlled Priscilla was blatant even to me, and I recall feeling that my aunt seemed out of place – a prisoner, almost – at Church Farm, despite her surrendering acceptance. When you enter a room and everyone's talking, you end up being drawn to the silent one. Even though I was only a child and Priscilla a woman in her late forties, I felt protective of her.

'She was an immensely private person,' my father said. 'You felt she was concealing a lot of things.'

Because the main room in the house was Raymond's office and everything had to be perfect for the buyers, the obligation on me was to disappear. On hot days, Priscilla went outside and sunbathed naked in a sheltered part of the walled garden. I was not allowed to see her unless I announced myself, and she quickly covered herself up. I remember her frowning over a book or a crossword, cigarette between fingers – she smoked a lot. And never far away a glass of something with a slice of lemon in it. Most of the time, she vanished upstairs.

Upstairs was Priscilla's domain. She spent long periods on her bed reading, or playing cards, or asleep. She was famed for her ability to sleep, and Raymond contended that she would do so with a pillow over her head, sometimes till noon.

Their bedroom above the kitchen looked out over the courtyard and the lane to the church. Her dressing table was arranged with hairbrushes, combs, mirrors, all enamelled. There she sat, in a nightdress and matching dressing gown, brushing her long blonde hair. 'She liked to brush for a hundred strokes,' said Tracey.

I have a vivid memory of the room because at the foot of the double bed was the first television I laid eyes on. As prosaic now as the taste of mushrooms, it was regarded, then, as the ultimate in luxury to have a television set in your bedroom. The compact, bulbous screen rested on a wooden chest which had a padded top, striped black and white, and it was a special occasion as a boy to be allowed to sit and watch, sometimes with Priscilla. The earliest films I can recall were viewed from my aunt's bed which, even when she was not seated beside me, had the smell of the scent that she always wore, and which I associate with the characters whose dramas I tried to follow on screen. I cannot remember anything about this scent, except that it was strong; but I asked my mother and she said that it was Calèche by Hermès.

For me, the best times were the evenings, after Raymond and Priscilla had taken my parents, together with the Sutros or whoever else was staying, out to dinner at the Bosham Sailing Club: in my memory, I watch them speed off, then go and switch on the television very low, careful not to disturb the French housekeeper in the downstairs wing, or Viking the smelly schnauzer who slept in the bedroom. As soon as I hear the car returning, I scarper back to my room and listen to the disquieting sound of Priscilla stumbling down the passageway.

One of the few paintings I remember at Church Farm was a glassless Peter Scott of flying ducks that hung over the drawing-room fire. Whenever the exposed canvas grew too smoke-blackened, Raymond took it outside and scrubbed it with soap and water from a bucket.

My favourite image of my aunt was a portrait of her as a young woman that hung on the wall at the bottom of the staircase. It was by the Hungarian artist Marcel Vertès and captured Priscilla as she had looked in pre-war Paris.

The gouache was painted in 1939 when Priscilla was twenty-three. It showed her wearing a gold-flecked jacket and green hat designed by Elsa Schiaparelli, for whom she modelled at the time. 'Priscilla had few clothes,' said my mother, who inherited a black corduroy coat from her, 'but they were always smart, couture, and very expensive.'

Although my aunt must have been double the age of the young woman in the portrait, she resembled her: tall, a little less slim, but with her ash-blonde hair falling loose, and the same horizon-blue eyes. The artist had caught a vulnerability which I recognised. The way that she raised her hands to her chin to fasten the straps of her hat was how I had seen people pray in church, with their eyes open.

From the beginning, I am sure of two things. First, her sheer attractiveness. She reminded me of Grace Kelly in one of the films I watched in her bedroom. She laughed, and I remembered my grandfather, his smoky laughter, rising across the South Downs. Her laugh was rejuvenating, and I noticed that my parents changed in her company, perhaps returned to the young man and young woman they were before they had children, when they lived in France.

She transformed their mood, and mine: in a strange way, she was the delicacy that we went to Church Farm always hoping to savour, our champignon de Paris.

The second thing I am sure of was her sadness. She seemed weighed down by a past that I could never work out and nor could my father. 'I suspected she'd had an extraordinary past, but she never spoke about it and one would never ask her.' This aloof, indefinable sadness was her bedrock.

3.
THE ALLIGATOR HANDBAG: 1950

My parents gave me some basic facts.

Priscilla had grown up in Paris, where she had trained as a ballerina.

She had worked in pre-war Paris as a model.

She had lived in France during the Occupation and spent time in a concentration camp, or possibly two. My mother said: 'That's what I was told by her when I was seventeen – at Church Farm. She was captured and tortured by the Germans. I presumed she couldn't have children because she had been raped and caught an infection.'

She had been a vicomtesse; her first husband an aristocratic Frenchman who never ceased to love her.

Most incredible to me, given Raymond's possessive nature, was that Priscilla travelled every year with Raymond to Paris where the couple met up with the Vicomte, her ex-husband. Being a Catholic, the Vicomte still considered Priscilla to be his wife. (In order to marry him, my mother said, Priscilla had to convert to Catholicism.) I loved his nickname for her: 'my little cork' – although why he called her this was not explained.

My mother also told me that Priscilla was at one time engaged to the actor Robert Donat, whom I had seen in *The 39 Steps*, and yet this interested me less than her life in France, even if I did wonder why she had chosen Raymond over Donat.

* * *

Priscilla died in 1982, but her fate obscurely moved me. What had gone on in France? What had she done during the war? Why did she not return to England after getting out of the concentration camp(s)? Why did her father – by then a well-known author and broadcaster – never mention on the airwaves or to my mother the fact that his eldest daughter was isolated throughout the war in Occupied France? I pictured her crouched before an illegal radio-set in a Paris atelier, listening to my grandfather's voice on the BBC, speaking to the troops. Did he ever transmit to Priscilla a personal message that only she could interpret, like one of those mystifying coded messages to the Resistance, such as *Venus has a pretty navel* or *The hippo is not carnivorous*? Could Priscilla have been in the Resistance?

And what was the bond that existed between Priscilla and her first husband which compelled her to keep bobbing back to see him, despite the fact that she had remarried?

Raymond's first wife could not be mentioned. She had run off with his best man at the end of the Second World War, leaving Raymond to bring up their two small children. Raymond never forgave her and he never saw her again.

Priscilla was thirty-one when she married Raymond, and a nervous stepmother to Tracey and Carleton, who were six and four at the time. I knew from my mother how sorely Priscilla had wanted her own children, and how the lack of them was a disappointment. When in my forties, having children of my own, I tried to find out more about her, Tracey let me have Priscilla's haphazardly filled scrapbook. I did not suspect that even more intimate details were to come my way and that the scrapbook was but the first in a trail of unexpected discoveries which would give insight into Priscilla's thoughts and feelings at crucial moments in her life.

On the scrapbook's opening page, scissored out of the *Nursing Times*, was a studio portrait of myself at eighteen months. I had always felt a bond with Priscilla (and the times we sat together watching her television served to deepen it), but not until I saw this photograph did I appreciate how she must have taken an interest in me from early on. Turning the stiff grey pages, I smelled her scent again.

Farmer's wife who escaped Nazis

A woman who led a remarkable life, Mrs. Raymond Thompson, of Church Farm, East Wittering, has died at the age of 65.

Daughter of S.P.B. Mais, broadcaster and author of 200 books, she was born in Sherborne, Dorset.

Educated in Paris she became a ballet student and danced for Anna Pavlova. Osteomylitis ended her ballet career at the age of 16 when she spent a year in hospital. Later she modelled for several Paris fashion houses and was painted by Marcel Vertes.

Before the war she married the late Vicomte Robert Doynel De La Sausserie, and lived in Paris and Normandy.

During the German occupation she was betrayed to the Gestapo and spent some months in a concentration camp before escaping. She spent the rest of the war in hiding with false papers. Later she returned to England and in 1948 married Mr. Raymond Thompson. They started mushroom growing at Church Farm, and the business grew from four mushroom houses to a specialist farm with 30 houses, producing 35,000lb. of mushrooms a week. She was the company secretary.

In the 70s Mrs. Thompson had a further attack of osteomylitis and a major and successful cancer operation.

The funeral was taking place at Chichester Crematorium today. Mrs. Thompson leaves a husband, son, daughter and five grandchildren.

The scrapbook contained articles which intensified Priscilla's mystique. She had 'danced for Anna Pavlova' in the words of an obituary of her. In another cutting, from a pre-war fashion magazine, Priscilla was pictured standing on fake snow, modelling Mainbocher's green gaberdine plus-fours. The most electrifying discovery was a report from the *Chichester Observer* that was pasted on the reverse page with Bassano's photograph of me, and referred to an incident that took place in 1950, seven years before I was born.

A woman who won 50,000 francs – about £50 – by backing a 50-1 outsider at a French race meeting and who bought a crocodile-skin handbag with the winnings was fined £35 with £2 costs at Lewes today for customs offences.

Mrs Priscilla Rosemary Thompson of Church Farm, East Wittering admitted trying to smuggle the bag through Newhaven Customs and making a false declaration to Customs officers. She was said to have been formerly married to a Frenchman and to have escaped from a German concentration camp with papers provided by the Resistance movement.

Then this: *Until France was liberated she lived the life of a hunted animal.*

The handbag reminded her of Paris before the war. The inside was black-lined and smelled less of alligator than of stale Chesterfields. In it she kept her cigarettes, reading glasses, green Hermès diary and pencil ('You'll find a pencil more useful,' the shop-lady had said, 'you can rub it out'). She carried it all the time. One cutting showed Priscilla at the Goodwood Fashion Parade, in a grey flannel suit, white beanie cap; and the bag over her shoulder.

Priscilla had bought it with Raymond's winnings from a horse race in Deauville. It was a time of crippling restrictions. Exchange Control was at its most severe. On 1 September 1950, she and Raymond landed back in Newhaven when a customs inspector approached.

She felt herself perspiring. He looked like a railway policeman, one of those who stopped her outside the Métro to check her identity papers.

Raymond did not know this, but on visits to Paris she could still hear the march of synchronised boots, down the Champs Elysées, past the Traveller's Club.

Footsteps on the pavement or a dog yapping at her fur coat, and everything reassembled into the courtyard at Besançon, snow on the ground, her handbag open for inspection. On that occasion, she had gone through the contents with a German woman, keeping only her comb.

Her upswell of dread at the sight of a uniform had never diminished. Once, when her five-year-old stepson was behaving in a particularly mulish fashion, she said 'Carleton, I despair of you' – and marched him to the police station in East Wittering, very nearly getting there.

'How much further?' Carleton wanted to know, and she, despairing all the more because he was willing to go along with this, said: 'No, no, I think we'll have to go back.'

Carleton observed that though she kept schnauzers, she passionately hated Alsatians. He wondered if she had been hounded by them.

She had tried to obliterate another memory – of the bright light in her face and the SS man behind the desk who wanted details of her past four years, how she spent them, who with.

The inspector, Mr Druitt, asked to see her handbag.

Eleven days later, Priscilla stood up in the County Hall in Lewes and pleaded guilty to customs offences. But she wished to make a statement.

'I have spent a considerable part of my life in France having lived there from 1925 to 1932 and subsequently from 1937 onwards.

'I was married to a French citizen in 1938 and was living in France when the country was occupied by the Germans. In view of my original British nationality I was arrested and put in a concentration camp in December 1940, but in 1941 I was able to obtain my release on grounds of ill health and from then onwards until 1944 was living in France with false papers.

'As the result of this, I was on several occasions arrested and interrogated by the Gestapo, once for more than 24 hours, and as the result of these experiences have been afflicted with a nervous horror of any sort of interrogation by any sort of official.'

Repatriated to England in 1944, she married her present husband in 1948. She had returned to France on average twice a year. She was quite accustomed to customs formalities.

'On this particular occasion I was asked to show my handbag and asked where I had obtained it.

'I very foolishly stated that it was a present from my first husband and I did not know its value, but I gave him my first husband's correct name and address.

'On my statement not being accepted, the recollection of previous interrogations in France came back to me and in somewhat of a panic I maintained my story.'

She closed by saying how sorry she was and that the reason for subsequently making a false declaration was 'the idea gained from my previous experiences that the only thing to do was to stick to my original story and avoid any prolonged interrogation.'

As a result of her plea, reduced fines were imposed. But her appearance in court had rattled Priscilla. When she faced the magistrate, she felt that he was sitting in judgement on her years in Occupied France.

4.
TRUCK DRIVER

My father did not pretend to know what made Priscilla tick, but he was familiar with her reticence. His own father, an army doctor in the First World War, had not elaborated at any time on his three years' service in France. 'I came to realise that what he'd seen in Ypres was incommunicable. The gap was so great between him and his listeners, he didn't feel he could bridge it.'

Priscilla was like many of those my father befriended in Paris in the 1950s, who, having survived the war, protected their memories of it; her years in France fell into the category of what the French call 'les non-dits'.

I was just too young to question Priscilla's father – he died when I was eighteen – but I read what he had written about her in *Buffets and Rewards*, one of his three volumes of autobiography.

'Priscilla, born in 1916, is lovely. She contracted a disease of the leg when she was training to be a dancer in the Russian ballet in Paris.

'She married just before the war a Frenchman of whom I know little beyond the fact that he was a count and drank port in the morning.

'On 12 May 1940 she was in Amiens. So were the Germans. Apparently they treated her reasonably in her first concentration camp. Indeed, she prevailed upon the sentimental German camp doctor to release her on the grounds that she was about to have a baby. She was not, of course, about to have a baby. She was indiscreet about this. When they caught her, they put her into another concentration camp in the Vosges where life was much less pleasant. When I next saw her she had divorced her husband. She remarried, an Englishman this time who grows strawberries and tomatoes on the Sussex coast. He too had already been married and had two small children.' That was all.

I wondered what more Raymond, who died in 1988, might have added. He had worked in Air Force Intelligence before he met Priscilla, during the war bicycling every day from Bosham to Hayling Island; in his long absences, his first wife was left free to nurse, and then fall for, his best man, who had come to stay with them on being released from a POW camp. But not even Raymond was able to extract further information from Priscilla during the thirty-four years of their marriage. I know this because after Priscilla died he told his daughter-in-law that Priscilla could never discuss with him what had happened in her previous life.

Carleton and Tracey confessed to growing up with 'a total lack of curiosity' about Priscilla's past because, they said, 'she didn't build it up in any way'. And so for every one of us – sisters, husbands, brothers-in-law, stepchildren, nephews – it became easy to read nothing unusual in Priscilla's reluctance to speak about the war. Her choice to bury herself in silence seemed part of a normal *omertà*, consistent with my paternal grandfather's clamp-down.

Annette Howard, whose much-decorated father had been a POW of the Japanese at Kwai Bridge, was Priscilla's god-daughter. 'I was used to people not talking about things, so it didn't surprise me that Pris didn't want to talk.' And yet from conversations with Annette and others, an idea formed about what Priscilla had got up to – in part because of what Priscilla omitted to say, but also because of details that emerged and were given interpretations which she did not strain herself to deny.

Her god-daughter was raised on a story that Priscilla drove trucks during the war in northern France – an arena in which she had performed, apparently, 'incredibly well'.

Priscilla's neighbour, Vicky, who had designed a dress for her, told me: 'I know she'd been a pretty brave lady in the Resistance.'

A woman called Phyllis, who had worked as a mushroom picker at Church Farm, understood that Priscilla was dropped behind enemy lines – 'as a translator, that's what I was led to believe,' and recalled an injury to her leg. A wound? It seemed plausible. And perhaps explained why she hid her legs and body and never wore a bathing costume when she came to stay with us.

It was exciting to imagine that Priscilla might have worked in the French Resistance and that this was the reason she did not talk about her past; why there was always a finger to its lip. Those who behave heroically say little. The rule of the female agent Agnès Humbert was 'Admit nothing'. Women like Humbert or Odette Hallowes used code names that were difficult to trace and never appeared on any list. Most continued their normal lives, forgotten when the war ended. Could this have been the case of my truck-driving aunt?

I spoke to Annette's sister Judy, who was certain that Priscilla was an agent. 'She was in SOE in France and was tortured by the Germans. And when she came back from France she had no hair. I was told by my mother, "Priscilla brushed her hair and it all grew back again." So I've brushed my hair religiously ever since.'

5.
THE PADDED CHEST

One day – a year or so after Priscilla died – my mother revealed to me that she had been kept in the dark about Priscilla's existence, and that she had not met her sister, or known anything about her, until the last months of the war. She was in her first term at Cheltenham Ladies' College when she received a letter from her father, who, pricked into action by Priscilla's return from Occupied France, was writing to break the news that my mother and her younger sister Imogen had an older half-sister; moreover, not one half-sister but two. About the upbringing of these two girls, Priscilla and Vivien, and about the circumstances of their lives until 1944, my mother admitted that she possessed, even now, only the haziest outline.

The idea that my mother had been unaware of her father's other family until the age of thirteen was too irresistible not to follow up, and I contacted Priscilla's sister Vivien.

Vivien was four years younger than Priscilla and so totally different from her that it was hard to understand how they could be sisters. They were unalike physically – Vivien was dark, Sophia Loren to Priscilla's Grace Kelly – and they were unalike in temperament as well.

I had seen little of Vivien as a boy; her life had been marred by the death of her eldest son, as a result of which she had developed peculiar beliefs about the afterlife.

At her home in Henley, Vivien seemed relieved to have the excuse to unburden herself. In her slow and deliberate voice, she provided details of their childhood, first on the Sussex coast and then in Paris.

'Frightened of life' was how Vivien described her late sister, with whom she had, I felt, a fond but not always easy relationship, one in which Vivien was the sibling making the effort. 'When she was growing up, she was always terrified of everything, always having nightmares.' Priscilla's fear manifested itself most scarily in sleep-walking. 'She used to stand on the top of the stairs, screaming – but sound asleep.' Everyone had been relieved when she married the Vicomte.

Vivien was present at Priscilla's wedding in Paris in December 1938, but had returned to England before the German invasion and could shine no light on Priscilla's marriage or on her life during the Occupation. Nor could Vivien provide details of Priscilla's experience in the concentration camp, not even its name.

Vivien died in 2004. Another five years went by before I decided to pursue my interest into Priscilla's French past.

In the summer of 2009, I contacted her stepdaughter Tracey whom I had not seen since I was four years old and living in Paris; Tracey had for a short while been my nanny. I explained how curious I still felt about Priscilla, and asked if my aunt might have left behind any personal papers.

'It's odd that you should ring up now,' Tracey said.

She had in her possession a cardboard box filled with photographs, letters, diaries and manuscripts, including a stab at a novel, which Tracey had salvaged, soon after Priscilla's death, from the striped padded chest at the end of her bed – 'on which the telly used to sit'.

One glance at the material had convinced Tracey that it was too private to show Raymond and so, without mentioning to her father what she had found, she chucked everything into a box to be stored away, and only lately had she come across it again. She had never examined the contents in depth because, she said, they related to Priscilla's life before she met Raymond.

Tracey had been wondering what to do with the box.

* * *

In France, they are known as the Dark Years; in wanting to pull down a padded lid on them, Priscilla was not unique.

I had discovered from reading and talking to people about this period that certain sections of the French National Archives in Paris are still closed to the historian, beginning with the year 1940. The same secrecy surrounds the police archives, or what remains of them – the Wehrmacht when they retreated took back to Berlin the most important files, many of these being shipped on to Russia in 1945. Even now, you cannot discover what denunciations were made against your family seventy years ago in France. Most of the Gestapo's archives in Paris, in particular those concerning the group known as 'the French Gestapo', were destroyed in the autumn of 1944. Archives in London are hardly more helpful. MI6 keeps secret most of its papers, and the Bureau Central de Renseignements et d'Action (BCRA) for which Priscilla's best friend Gillian Sutro worked, was so afraid of Vichy infiltration that few records were kept.

Aside from the difficulty of access, there is the magnitude of the destruction: those papers burned in courtyard bonfires or dumped into the Seine or obliterated in Allied bombing raids, like the archives of Caen, the city which controlled the region in which Priscilla's Vicomte lived.

Furthermore, this was a time of restrictions. It seems inconceivable in this Internet age that someone could live no more than twenty miles away across the Channel and yet not be able to make contact with their family in Sussex, by letter or by telephone. But this describes the hermetic news black-out that existed between 1940 and 1944.

The Occupied Zone was sealed off. Carrier pigeons were forbidden, no photographs out of doors were allowed to be taken, and anyone who concealed letters on their person risked severe punishment. The Germans outlawed letters in packages, any writing on the backs of photographs, and books with passages underlined. Priscilla could not write abroad – even if she had the means; paper shortages compelled Jacques Audiberti to compose his novel *Monorail* on strips of wallpaper.

As a result, fewer people wrote things down at the time (and some of the diaries that historians have depended on turn out to have been written up long after the events). As for those who did write to each other in Occupied France, it is surprising how little correspondence has survived. Hard for us to believe, it was not a time to keep letters. And Tracey told me that she had a box of them.

My cousin Tracey's house near Goodwood dated from the 1960s. One wall was of plate glass giving a view over a long lawn. On another, I recognised Vertès's portrait of Priscilla. Tracey had laid out on the dining-room table Priscilla's blue scrapbook and two of her alligator handbags. Also on the table was a shallow cardboard vegetable box containing the papers that Tracey had transferred from the padded chest.

What could be in those photographs, letters and manuscripts which Priscilla had concealed beneath the television set, directly under Raymond's unforgiving nose? ('I remember that chest,' my mother said. 'I thought she kept rugs in it.'). I knew from researching a biography how ancient documents can disappoint.

For the rest of that morning, I read through Priscilla's scrapbook. Then after lunch I started going through the box. I picked out a black and white photograph, turned it, and found myself staring at an arrestingly beautiful woman who lay sprawled on a loose bed of hay. I had little trouble recognising Priscilla, who was naked from the waist up.

There were other photos, no less sensational. A chateau. A beach. And portraits of men. One man, in tight swimming trunks and his youthful face masked in a pair of brass goggles, smilingly held up an eel. On the back someone had written: 'Sainte-Maxime, October 1940' – that is to say, two months before Priscilla, or la Vicomtesse Doynel de la Sausserie, was arrested and interned by the Germans. But who was this swimmer?

And this other young man on a ski slope, lying back on the snow and embracing Priscilla – on this occasion wrapped in a fur coat? And the leather-helmeted racing driver gripping the wheel of a Delahaye – 'Pour toi, Pris, en souvenir de la Coupe de Paris'? And what about this older man, more educated-looking, podgier, in a double-breasted suit of pale grey worsted and wearing spats, who was photographed seated in a room beneath an Impressionist painting? Written in blue biro on the back, in English: 'Well, here it is – your beloved open fireplace.' But in what house was the brick fireplace, what city? None of the faces had addresses or names attached. The anonymity, I could not help feeling, was deliberate. The only identifiable face was a signed photograph of Robert Donat as Richard Hannay in *The 39 Steps*.

I opened a folder of letters. There were about 150, dated from 1938 to 1947, the year before Priscilla married Raymond. The ones composed in English were mostly from Donat, who wrote in green ink in the last winter of the Second World War. 'I wish I could undress you very slowly, very, very slowly indeed, and then be wonderfully sweet and kind to the wounds on your tummy, and dress you again in exquisite black-market undies, including sheer silk stockings, and send you back home safely to your mammie and grannie with a copy of Peter Quennell's latest drivel – just to show you how platonic my love for you is.' I read on. 'Darling, where were you born, when, and above all why? Is that really you and are you really real? Can that extraordinary face have been achieved by accident or design? What does it all mean?'

The majority of the letters were in French, in half a dozen different hands, written earlier to Priscilla when she was at large in wartime France. Like Donat's, these were surprisingly passionate and tender – and from a period when it was always dangerous to speak your mind. It was astonishing that they had survived at all.

Fugitives have to travel light – and yet Priscilla had kept these photographs and letters. Had she carried them with her around France? The folder contained envelopes postmarked 'Brittany', 'Paris', 'Annemasse'.

Many were from Priscilla's husband, le Vicomte Robert Doynel de la Sausserie. There were also love letters from a man who signed himself Emile, and who was cited in the divorce papers that I unfolded from a separate folder, some of which were dated 1943, some 1944, and some 1946, the year in which Priscilla's first marriage was dissolved.

In addition, there were letters from lovers named Daniel, Pierre and Otto. Without exception, they cast Priscilla in the role of Emma Bovary or Anna Karenina: a vulnerable, intelligent, sophisticated woman in need of saving. But without surnames or addresses, there was no way of tracking the lovers down, or of matching them with the faces in her collection of photographs. One thing was becoming clear, though: my aunt Priscilla appeared to be having a racy time in Occupied France.

A few letters dated from after the war. I pulled out one, written in January 1946 from an American naval officer who was impatient to marry her, and containing this tantalising remark: 'You told me all about your past, darling, and I loved you in spite of it, although if conservative Bostonians heard of it frankly they would be shocked. That was another reason why I thought we should live abroad for a bit; it would be better.'

Another correspondent, an Englishman, had typed out and sent her the verse of a popular song:

Oh, they call me Venal Vera,
I'm a lovely from Geizera
The Führer pays me well for what I do.
The order of the battle
I obtained from last night's rattle
On the golf course with a Colonel from HQ.
I often have to tarry
On the back seat of a gharry
(It's part of my profession as a spy).
Whilst his mind's on copulation
I'm extracting information
From a senior GSO from GSI.

I had suspected my aunt of working for the Resistance. Could this be a reference to the sort of espionage that she carried out for them?

Also in the cardboard box was a thick folder containing a browning bundle of typewritten pages. I leafed through them, but it was hard to concentrate on what I was reading – more or less everything that someone seeking to unravel Priscilla's enigma could hope for: diaries, fragments of autobiography, medical records, her statement at Lewes County Court, letters (including an unsent one to Tracey), some twenty short stories, as well as the draft chapters of a longer book that Priscilla had begun to write, but not completed.

I began reading the first chapter, and it became clear that the fiction was not fiction at all, and that what Priscilla had been striving to put down on paper, not merely in this novel but in her short stories, diaries and autobiographical fragments, was nothing less than an account of her years in France.

I asked Tracey if I might take the box away.

PART TWO

PART TWO

6.
STRANGE EXISTENCE

Although I could not have written this book without Tracey's box, I did find some riveting information about Priscilla's upbringing by going to the more conventional source of my grandfather's papers. These were lodged with the West Sussex Records Office in Chichester. From his diaries, correspondence and manuscripts, I formed a picture of Priscilla's early years.

She was born in the summer of 1916, nine months after a doctor explained the facts of life to her parents.

Her father, thirty-one at the time, was teaching at Sherborne. His name was Stuart Petre Brodie Mais, which he pronounced as 'Maize' – and claimed was Saxon, meaning 'sons of May'. But everyone knew him by his initials. Priscilla's mother Doris, then twenty-four, was the pampered daughter of a retired major from Bath and a four-foot-ten-inch Scot of irrepressible efficiency who called everything and everyone 'bonny' – with the exception of her son-in-law. The marriage was a catastrophe from the start.

SPB had met Doris at a tea dance four years earlier. The girl who stood before him in the Assembly Rooms was slim, with pale cheeks framed by a straight fringe of dark brown hair, a narrow oval face and pointed chin – and clustered about by young men. Up until then, at Oxford and in Tansley, where his father had the living, SPB had known only 'girls of shop assistant type'.

He became tongue-tied with sisters of fellow undergraduates. When Doris looked at him with her cat-grey eyes and pouting mouth, he strode up and demanded as many dances as she could spare. She gave him eleven.

They danced again on New Year's Eve at the Lansdown Cricket Club Ball. Doris wore a strawberry-pink frock and revealed a taste for schnauzers, biscuits, and gin. At some point, she led him to a dark corner where, without warning, she kissed him. Her kiss overwhelmed him – he forgot, as he later wrote, everything. He looked into Doris's eyes and holding her long thin hands which, he imagined, 'bespoke a wealth of character and breeding', uttered the seven words from which ensued the capital error of his life.

'Does this mean that you'll marry me?'

Doris nodded. 'If you want me.'

They were married at St Anne's Church, Oldland, in Gloucestershire, on 6 August 1913. The couple knew nothing about each other, just as they knew nothing about sex. At twenty-eight, SPB had married the first girl of his class that he had kissed. His innocence would be the driver of his torment, a fundamental blankness that remained to the end of his life and clouded his understanding of why people behaved as they did.

SPB was a schoolmaster earning £150 a year and already in debt; furthermore, he could not take Doris back to Rossall, on the Lancashire coast, since the school did not employ married teachers. Major Snow, her father, had consented to the marriage on condition that SPB insure his life for £1,000 and settle it on Doris.

His mother begged him to cancel the wedding. 'You're going to regret this all your life.' Rather in the way that Major Snow shuddered to contemplate SPB, so had she formed an 'ineradicable aversion' to her prospective daughter-in-law (and after their marriage refused to have anything to do with her). She viewed Doris as a flibbertigibbet out to snare her only child and sensed, correctly, that the pair had no common interests. The Snow family regarded reading as a waste of time ('I always think that books spoil the look of a house,' said Mrs Snow). Doris hated walking and was not demonstrative about scenery. She liked playing the pianola, billiards and bridge, otherwise basking in the glow of male attention. She did not like cricket.

Doris at least had the gumption to try and call off the engagement. A week before their marriage, SPB took his headstrong fiancée to a cricket match from which she bolted. She said she was going home, hated the sight of him, and wanted no more to do with him. It was his last chance and he should have snatched it. But SPB was by then obsessed with the thought of their soon-to-be-life-together, and threatened suicide if rejected.

The extent of his mistake was revealed on honeymoon in Porlock Bay. He dragged his new wife through thick bracken to watch the staghounds at Cloutsham, Dunkery and Exford. They paddled up Badgworthy Water to the Doone Valley, went bathing at Porlock Weir, climbed to the top of Selworthy Beacon, caught an excursion steamer to Ilfracombe to see his aunt, and watched polo in the grounds of Dunster Castle. The one thing they did not do, according to Vivien who told me this, along with other extraordinary details, was to make love.

There were two explanations. Doris had her period, which invariably caused her agonies, said Vivien. 'Ma was used to lying on the sofa and being brought cups of tea and biscuits, with much love and empathy. On the other hand SPB knew nothing of such things, never having had anything to do with young women and their monthly sufferings. So the honeymoon was a disaster, because one of these periods occurred after a week, with Ma expecting tea and sympathy in the hotel lounge, and her adoring husband – who had no sympathy for such lack of 'oomph' – going off into the countryside to walk and explore and chat with anyone he met.'

The second reason was that neither partner knew how to consummate a marriage. SPB wrote that his father had preserved his silence on the topics of money, God, and sex. Major Snow seems to have been just as non-communicative with his daughter. Vivien told me: 'Ma allegedly had no idea how babies were created, and SPB, apparently, was equally ignorant of the "how". It took three years before they finally sought advice about procreation, and on 12 July 1916 my sister Priscilla Rosemary Mais was born in Sherborne.'

SPB's novels were so autobiographical that they gave me additional information which I did not receive from Vivien. I learned that on the day of Priscilla's birth he spent the morning at school to keep his mind from brooding. 'From nine to one I taught, speaking all the time, trying to concentrate on quadratic equations and Army English. I went up at lunchtime and was told to disappear to four o'clock. I went for miles on my bicycle seeing nothing, my mind a blank, except for the ever-recurring sentence: "Oh, God! grant that it may be all right."'

He was shown Priscilla in her cot on his return. She had been born at half past one. 'She is beautifully proportioned and has large blue eyes and regular features.'

Still, his eldest child made him afraid. The first time he held her, he found it impossible to believe that this new life was part of himself, 'something which would in the future regard him as her father'. He seems to have infected Priscilla with his fear, planting in her a fundamental insecurity even before she came to consciousness.

A fortnight on: 'She has an extraordinary amount of individuality: unluckily, she is terribly frightened of any sudden noise. This must be inherited ...' He stood over Priscilla for hours, trying 'to probe into the future for what it held in store for her'.

In the summer of her birth, a local fortune teller in Sherborne supplied one of two predictions for Priscilla. I found it among her papers, written in an upright pencilled hand. 'Generally shrewd, deep thinker, critical and alert. These are her main characteristics. Very secretive, she would make a safe friend to entrust confidences to. But to these qualities must be added a too ardent love nature ... short journeys are good, especially when unexpected and require to be taken at short notice ... Her happiest time will come after marriage, which should come early in life and probably to a man older than herself who will be devoted and most kind and generous to her ... The death of father will end much disagreement.'

The second prediction took verse form.

Priscilla was three months old when a former pupil of SPB at Sherborne sat down in his room at Sandhurst and composed a poem to mark her birth. Its author was eighteen and unknown. Published two years later, 'To Your Daughter' introduced Alec Waugh's sole volume of poetry, *Resentment*. By then, Waugh, who became a sort of muse for Priscilla, was exceptionally famous.

In the Bodleian Library in Oxford, I ordered up *Resentment*. Published at 3/6d in July 1918, it was a virgin copy: the pages not yet cut. A young librarian took a table knife out of a drawer and sawed the poem open.

Dedicated to Priscilla's parents, 'To Your Daughter' is long and rather gloomy. A few lines give the flavour:

And dust's the end of every song ...
Yet happiness is not life's aim.

Unflinching you will face the truth,
And others not so nobly wise

Will lay before your feet their youth,
Their hopes, and their heart's treasuries.

So though you deem the gift of life
Better not had, those others torn
And bleeding in the throes of strife
Will thank their God that you were born.

Priscilla's first home was a new semi-detached red-brick house overlooking Sherborne Castle, called 'Coldharbour'. SPB rented it for £35 a year. He had accepted a teaching job at Sherborne after turning down an offer to be the Government Inspector of Schools in Ceylon, mainly out of pressure from his mother-in-law. The jerry-built house was crammed with ugly oak furniture ('the monstrosities of Maple') and a Persian carpet that Mrs Snow had bought as a wedding gift, and became associated in SPB's mind with a period of his life that made him flinch.

The only child of a preoccupied vicar and a reluctant mother who farmed him out to elderly relatives, SPB knew very little about how to be a husband and a father. This was his first experience of family life and he was shell-shocked. Alec Waugh spent a weekend with SPB, Doris and the four-month-old Priscilla, afterwards describing to his father Arthur the amazing difference between the Waughs' home life and the chaos of the Mais household. 'Mais rolls down to breakfast swearing and shrieking. "Your shoe is undone," says Doris. "Do it up," says Petre and puts his foot on her knee...'

It did not help that Mrs Snow visited often. A son had died young and she found it a burden to be separated from her only daughter. Her visits increased after 'bonny' Priscilla's birth. A photograph in Priscilla's album shows a tiny woman with round wire spectacles and door-knob cheeks. She has cleared any smile from her face. Her son-in-law longed for her departure, but she seemed to take root.

An admirer of Thomas Hardy, SPB was one day proud to report that he had spent the morning with the novelist's wife. Mrs Snow's acid response was: 'A most unpleasant and unhealthy-minded writer.' She accused SPB of being selfish in buying a bicycle: he was no longer a carefree bachelor. 'You must learn to save for the sake of the house.' She commented on the size of his appetite, his bad manners and untidiness, and irritated him into saying nasty things to Doris that he did not mean – until the day arrived when Doris, adopting Mrs Snow's nagging Scots accent, declared that her husband seemed to love the countryside more than he loved his wife.

Her parents' antics were Priscilla's bedtime stories. How SPB walked and biked and ignored Doris, preferring his precious Downs; how Doris had gone off with one of his pupils. Mainly, it was SPB in the wrong – selfish, obsessive, spendthrift.

'Authors as a rule are much better in their books than they are in real life,' SPB wrote in *Rebellion* – a novel that he managed to complete in the first fortnight of 1917 while staying with Priscilla at Alec Waugh's home in North London. This was also Doris's opinion.

What Doris was too naïve or inexperienced to recognise was her husband's predisposition to manic depression. The Downs were not an escape from her; he needed them in order to re-enter himself.

There are people who walk into a room and immediately hijack it. At Oxford, SPB had been a cross-country running Blue. Alec Waugh remembered him striding through the Courts at Sherborne with a pile of books under his arm, as though limbering up for a marathon. Writers who had been his pupils looked back on him as their best teacher; he fired in them a passion for plays, poems and novels, and gave them a warm and friendly shove into becoming authors themselves. But his energy was fuelled by a bipolar disorder that remained undiagnosed until 1964 and rigged his sails so as to be swelled with any gust of enthusiasm – and to be emptied just as abruptly. 'He had over-flowing enthusiasm, but very little ballast,' the Master of Sherborne wrote in 1917 after sacking him.

When SPB was skimming the waves, no one was more invigorating; anything seemed possible. 'Then everyone wanted to be near him,' said my mother. But the down periods were costly, confusing, painful and chaotic, and made him hard to live with. Then his black moods and self-generating dramas threatened to capsize his professional contacts, as well as his nearest and dearest.

Priscilla grew up listening to SPB remonstrate with her mother: 'But you loved me once.' And Doris snapping back: 'For God's sake, don't keep harking back to the past ages – I may have liked caper sauce once, but I've out-grown my love for you, and nothing can bring it back.' The quarrels were protracted and savage – the clocks never wound up, the flowers always dead, the silver unpolished. Doris frequently was left weeping on the floor.

When Priscilla was three, Doris shifted her affections from SPB to another young man who had been his pupil. Neville Brownrigg was a demobbed lieutenant from the 20th Hussars whom SPB had taught at Rossall before the war, 'an unruly angular Irish boy of no intelligence but a certain ease and charm of manner'. SPB once invited Brownrigg home to Tansley, where his mother viewed him in the same incinerating light as she did Doris. 'He's a born parasite. He'll eat all you've got and then rob you and run. You'll see.' But SPB admired Brownrigg, a good cricketer, for his wildness and courage. 'He had no brains, but he was great fun and never cared what he did.'

They had met again, in 1919, on the station platform at Tonbridge where SPB had gone from Sherborne to teach. Brownrigg was staying nearby with his uncle, out of a job after five years fighting in Egypt and France. In an impetuous move, SPB invited Brownrigg to stay in the large house that Tonbridge School had provided. He needed a secretary, while his wife and daughter, he felt, could do with the companionship.

In the High Court seventeen years later, Justice Sir Alfred Bucknill observed the outcome with bewilderment: 'I am sorry to say that the result of Mr Mais's kindness was that his wife and Mr Brownrigg fell in love and misconduct started between them.' Doris was twenty-seven. Her relationship with someone four years younger marked the start of what the Divorce Court judge described as 'this strange existence of Mr and Mrs Mais'.

A brown envelope in SPB's archives contained cuttings from *The Times*, the *News of the World* and the *Daily Mirror* – which devoted its front page to the story, under the headline 'PETITION DISMISSED IN COMMUNITY'S INTEREST'.

On 16 July 1936, in one of the most publicised cases of the year, Doris Mais had sued Priscilla's reluctant father for divorce. She wished to dissolve her broken marriage to a spouse with whom she had not lived since 1925.

Doris's case being weak, for those days, counsel advised her to cast SPB in the role of sexual pervert. In a move no modern court would condone, Doris summoned Priscilla to give evidence against her father. Priscilla's humiliating experience in the witness box forced her to relive her childhood in churning detail.

She remembered her parents as always on the move, carrying their unhappiness with them. The fraught atmosphere had helped to make Priscilla a difficult and neurotic child. Doris's mother guarded Priscilla 'like a dragon'. Redundant, her father fed on the patter of his daughter's feet, her thrice-repeated 'g-night, Daddy' after he left her to go down to supper, 'and even her cries at night'.

Her cries pursued SPB to Tonbridge, to Lincolnshire, to Hove; even to Wengen where he took Priscilla skiing, her first trip abroad. The following summer they travelled to north Devon. He wrote in his autobiography: 'One of the happiest holidays I ever spent was at Woolacombe in the society of my daughter Pris when she was about six years old. We spent a golden, unforgettable month together which passed like a dream, of which I remember very little beyond continually rolling down the steep sand-dunes, getting hot sand in our hair and clothes and then washing it off in the cool sea. I do not think I have ever been so close to her in my life before or since, and I do not mind betting that Pris has forgotten all about it.'

The only flaw in an otherwise perfect holiday was his daughter's habit of screaming aloud in dreams.

Priscilla's nightmares continued to torment her, no matter how many times she changed address. The last home that the Maises shared together as a family was a sea-front flat in Hove where Priscilla lived with her parents, Brownrigg, and Priscilla's baby sister, born in 1920 and christened Sheila Vivien. Her father had given up teaching for journalism and worked at the *Daily Express* as the film and drama critic. Dropping her off at school on his way to the station, he noticed that Priscilla did not like passing the same people. He wrote in his diary that she disliked 'all shut doors and the noise of the water running out of her bath'. He listened to his daughter tap the wall with her fingers. 'Screams at night after visit to cinema and dreams of attacks by wolves.'

Priscilla's shrieks tracked the disintegration of her parents' marriage which had been tumbling about her ears since she was born.

SPB appears to have had no inkling of his wife's affair with Brownrigg until Vivien was four years old. In May 1924 Doris confessed – telling an incredulous SPB that his secretary-cum-chauffeur had been her lover, was Sheila Vivien's father and that she had never loved anyone in the world as much. Justice Bucknill's comment: 'I cannot think of any act more blameworthy than the act of a wife who over a period of years permitted misconduct in her husband's house with a young man whom her husband has brought to the house and befriended.'

Overnight, SPB's world had collapsed. He was to be permanently injured by Doris's flagrant adultery. He wrote that he did not feel that he could visualise his wife in the arms of another man and live. In Hove, he wandered vacantly over the Downs – once or twice through the night. 'On these smooth slopes all tangles seem to come unravelled, and all problems solved.' But not even long walks on his cherished hills consoled him. Something had harassed him 'to the point of a morose insanity', observed Henry Williamson, later the author of *Tarka the Otter*, who came to know him at this time. In a novel that Williamson wrote about SPB, he recalled Priscilla's father striding at a furious rate, 'and though it almost exhausted him, he breathed, when I was near him, I noticed, almost silently through his open mouth. He seemed to be walking to escape his thoughts; a horsefly had got into his brain.'

SPB's one consolation was his daughter. He looked forward to a time when Priscilla would be able to join him on his walks. Thank God, he wrote, there was still Priscilla. 'She at any rate would provide him with a purpose in life.'

Priscilla was eight when Doris – following Brownrigg's abrupt departure – took up with another lover, a journalist on SPB's newspaper. To escape censure, the couple went to live in Paris. Vivien accompanied them on the stormy crossing: 'I can still see a big communal cabin with bunks and me lying on one, moaning.' Priscilla remained behind in Hove with SPB, and at the end of a year was to choose between coming to France or staying in Sussex. Doris now wanted a divorce. To facilitate this, SPB grudgingly agreed to remain celibate for twelve months, in order to be perceived as the innocent party.

Their time together in Hove was the most precious that Priscilla ever spent with her father. They trotted on horseback along the cliffs at Rottingdean. They went to the cinema and fed pennies into the slot-machines on Brighton Pier and bathed off Brighton beach. They explored SPB's childhood haunts in north Devon, searching for prawns in the pools that he had fallen into as a small boy, and joining a stag-hunt. A hunt meet for SPB was the symbol of a lost England. They were not father and daughter as they followed the hounds on foot through the long grass, but two companions. He read to her in bed, and after she went peacefully to sleep he wrote in his diary, relieved: 'Love of unlocking doors. Collecting cigarette cards and leaving them about. Tousled head on her pillow.'

If Priscilla did not grow up with the Darwinian instinct that would allow her to home in on a person who was right for her, then her father was largely to blame. Her only chance, with a mother like Doris, lay in SPB seeing her through her childhood years; his dependability was her one possibility of redemption. But Priscilla was severely under-parented.

It is hard to tell the exact point when she became 'the girl who gets let down'. Probably in May 1925 when, almost immediately reneging on his agreement to remain celibate, SPB brought home Winnie Doughty, a teenage Irish model not much older than his daughter. According to Priscilla, they hated each other at first sight. Priscilla resented someone taking her mother's place, and became 'rude and tiresome' to Winnie, who was jealous of Priscilla and wished her out of the way.

Less than a year later, to stop Winnie leaving him, after she threatened to go off with a young novelist, SPB offered to sacrifice the most precious thing he possessed. A dismaying entry in his diary reads: 'I sent a cable to Doris telling her she could keep Priscilla just to make Winnie happier.' Down the corridor, he heard a child howling and return to sleep. At the age of nine, Priscilla packed a small suitcase and feeling, as she put it, 'unloved and unwanted', took the train to Newhaven with her father.

It was a golden day. She remembered the game they played on the train, counting haystacks on one side of the carriage against the other. And SPB's story – invented to distract her – about a lady who could breathe under water and had discovered caves full of jewels on the ocean floor. Already, Priscilla followed her father's example and wrote down stories in a green notebook. 'Wonderful stories of princes and magic,' SPB described them in the journal that he had kept since he was thirteen. He urged Priscilla to keep a journal, too.

SPB saw her off on the boat. Both dreaded their impending separation. 'Priscilla like myself cannot eat before going away. Purposely one numbs oneself. How one clings to last moments, the dinner the night before, the promises to write, the sailing of the boats.' He was left with the harrowing image of Priscilla standing against the rails. He must have suspected the damage he was doing, because the expression in her face continued to pursue him. 'The dawn of sickness. The puzzled blue eyes.'

When he chose Winnie above Priscilla, apart from sabotaging Doris's plan for a divorce, SPB caused irreparable harm to his daughter. How he squared it in his own mind was a mystery. Priscilla went from being the purpose in his life to nothing, catapulted aged nine into redundancy. It was a rejection from which she never recovered.

An early witness to SPB's terrible legacy was an English girl living in Paris. Priscilla met her that spring, not long after she was collected off the boat at Dieppe. I must now properly introduce Gillian Sutro, who was to be a most important mine of information and a close friend of Priscilla for the rest of her life.

7.
GILLIAN

'Two gazelles,' murmured someone who observed them after they were reunited at the end of the Second World War. A dark foil to her taller blonde friend, Gillian was raised to Priscilla's height by the charisma of her deadpan looks. 'I possess,' Gillian wrote of herself, 'the capacity to hide rancour behind a mask of indifference.' Small, with long black hair, big slanting green eyes, and noticeable cheekbones, which she emphasised by sucking in her lips, Gillian could be mistaken for the actress Vivien Leigh, and sometimes was. Men found her beautiful as women found her husband ugly. In a hectic private life, Gillian's lovers included the writers Joseph Kessel and Arthur Koestler; the film directors Carol Reed and Henri-Georges Clouzot; and the Hungarian artist Marcel Vertès.

Gillian was startlingly clear what her appetites were, and honest about the fact that she was highly sexed. Priscilla was relatively monogamous by contrast. Her sensuality is frustrating to pin down. She aroused it in others, to a pitch that rendered men helpless, and as a result had many experiences, which shaped her life; but how much she needed sex or enjoyed her sexuality is harder to establish, and I repeatedly searched for clues. Beyond doubt is that the two women's tastes in men – with one possible and divisive exception – could not have disagreed more.

Priscilla was attracted to youth; to good looks, good dancers. Gillian recoiled from anyone who resembled her handsome father. 'I like tired-looking faces, odd, moody, obsessed people, loners. I dislike jaunty cocky men. My instinct is to bash their ego.' In the improbable event of their falling for the same person, they had a code of conduct drawn up by Gillian when they were teenagers. 'Never poach on a girlfriend's territory and don't inflict bastards into marriage.'

Everything else, they viewed with the same eye.

Gillian is a key figure in Priscilla's story. Their 'rackety' backgrounds, as Gillian put it, were interchangeable to a striking degree. They would grow up together in Saint-Germain-en-Laye, attending the same lycée, and sharing a governess and ballet-teacher. And both handicapped by 'impossible parents'.

Gillian's mother Daphne was the daughter of Albert Gamage, founder of a London department store that in its day rivalled Selfridges. In 1914, Albert had packed Daphne off, at the age of twenty-one, on a cruise to see the world and to sever her relationship with a rich socialite. But at a dance in Ceylon,

Daphne met Cyril Hammond, 'a wild, hard-drinking Anglo-Irish tea-planter' – twenty-five years old; Trinity, Cambridge; rowing Blue; Irish Guards. Gillian wrote: 'They were glued together by the sex urge, like stamps to an envelope.' Unlike with the Maises, congress occurred almost instantly. They married in secret, to the fury of Daphne's mother, in the local registry office.

Gillian's parents were young, good-looking, well educated, with enough money, but flawed. Their pattern was set by the time they arrived in France after the First World War – a pattern of bridge parties, alcohol and sex, into which they stitched Priscilla's mother. Prominent members of Paris's 30,000-strong English community, the Hammonds had settled in the north-west outskirts in 1921, and were to be influential figures in Priscilla's childhood. They were also responsible for Doris coming to live in France.

In 1925, her new lover Dominic Bevan Wyndham-Lewis had suggested to Doris that they emulate Gillian's father, whom he had known in the army, and cross the Channel to avoid the outcry provoked by his elopement with the wife of a fellow journalist. They rented two rooms in the Hôtel de la Bourdonnais, near the Eiffel Tower, where Doris adopted the name 'Mrs Wyndham-Lewis' and tried to forget that she had a husband in England.

The parties, the dances, the time on their hands. At a young age, Priscilla exchanged her father's literary circle in Hove for a worldly expatriate clique – promiscuous, gossipy, dependent on the lowness of the franc – in which Gillian's parents set the tone and pace.

The Hammonds and 'Mr and Mrs Wyndham-Lewis' went out a great deal. Like Doris, of whom she was strangely jealous, Gillian's mother was a bar-addict. The two women sat beside each other on high stools at the zinc counter, beautiful legs crossed seductively, as they thought, beneath their Poiret frocks. After her miserable years in Hove, Doris, in her tight-fitting emerald cloche hat, was in her element flirting with Cyril.

Back in 22a First Avenue, Hove, SPB groused that his estranged wife, to whom he continued to send a monthly allowance, had got in with the worst possible set. 'She drinks, she smokes too much, she's extravagant, she appears to be living entirely for dancing…'

Georges Carpentier's bar off the Champs-Elysées was a favourite. Another haunt was the Cintra. Afterwards, they might join friends at Scheherazade. Priscilla remembered seeing Gillian's mother dance a Black Bottom stomp with someone she fancied, her belly rubbing against her partner's groin. It was heady stuff for a young girl, and a change from the slot-machines on Brighton Pier.

Two more inconsiderate mothers would have been hard to find. Daphne, though toothy, fancied herself to be irresistible, which made her contemptuous of other women – Gillian included – and explained why she was late for drinks and dinner parties. The sole occasions on which her punctuality could be depended were bridge parties.

Daphne's weekly bridge afternoons were sacred. Her regular partner was Doris, who behaved in the same regal way – down to smelling like her (of Shalimar). Gillian was made to assist with the sandwiches, as was Priscilla when it became Doris's turn to play hostess. Towards seven, Gillian's father, ensconced in armchair, pipe in hand, would shout – one eye on the clock, thinking of dinner: 'When are those bloody women leaving?' Across the table, Mrs Hochstetter would become fidgety while Daphne, who hated losing, pretended not to hear. 'Really, partner,' she liked to scold Doris, 'you are not concentrating.'

To ease the tension, Doris would lay down her cards and wander over to the Hammonds' satinwood piano. Gillian observed how Doris's playing aggravated Daphne's jealousy. 'My mother did not take into account that children are voyeurs. Small, silent, nosy, prowling around with lethal innocence.'

Gillian's father, though more handsome, took after his friend Wyndham-Lewis. Both were members of the Savile Club, both veterans of the First World War, both pipe-smoking drinkers, with vile tempers; both randy.

Cyril Hammond had not longed for children at all: 'I don't want my wife turned into a milking cow.' His wife gave him four – Nicky, Gillian, Jacqueline and Nigel. Gillian found him opaque, impenetrable. 'My father really was a pig.' She loathed him, and he her. He would glare at Gillian: 'Always being different.'

Gillian's father had an aversion to people enjoying themselves. At their rented house in Chatou, he stalked into Gillian's bedroom and tore back the sheets, shouting: 'Get up, you slut.' One evening when Gillian was in her teens, he chased her round the table because she was wearing a trouser suit. If a boyfriend rang, he yelled out: 'Dago on the phone!' He always used that expression for a slightly dark-skinned man, and dark-skinned men accounted for most of Gillian's boyfriends.

A financially reckless philanderer, Cyril Hammond was an army man without an army. He battled to conduct his home life with the discipline of a former Guards officer. 'But he treated the family far worse than soldiers,' Gillian wrote. A creature of rigid habits, he expected his wife's inedible meals to be served on the dot – and everyone to be turned out impeccably. He wore thick wool khaki knee socks and shaved every morning, save for the neat stiff military moustache that he never discarded. On evenings when he did not don a dinner jacket, he wore a blazer with Irish Guards buttons which he took care to polish every day. Dinner over, he immersed himself in a book.

When she thought of her joyless father, Gillian visualised a skeletal figure sunk back in his armchair, twiddling his moustache and reading Evelyn Waugh, P. G. Wodehouse, Somerset Maugham – and war memoirs. He was hooked on battles. The German officer who occupied their Paris apartment in 1940 said approvingly, examining the shelves: 'The English officer is very knowledgeable about history.'

Gillian tensed to recall the hollow snapping sound of books being opened and banged shut to let the dust fly off. The *clop-clop* was like a sharp slap in the face. Nor did she forget the *glou-glou* of wine being poured from bottle to glass when no one was around.

Drunk, her father bragged about women. One of his conquests was Priscilla's mother. Gillian once overheard him boasting. 'At the drop of a hat, she'll lie on her back, hooves in the air.' Gillian wrote: 'He had sampled Doris. I remember thinking how odious he was to speak in such a way of a woman he had bedded.'

This was the society into which Priscilla first came to live in 1926, a skinny, nervy child, as Gillian recalled, tall for her age, with pale lank hair scraped back from her face. Paris would be her home for the next seven years.

* * *

Priscilla's new 'stepfather' Dominic Bevan Wyndham-Lewis was, when her mother met him, a satirical journalist on the *Daily Express*, thirty-three years old, a short, stocky, combative Welshman with a box face, receding black hair and fierce blue eyes. In the family he became known as Boo. He was a friend of Hilaire Belloc, who described Boo as the wittiest man he had ever met – this despite his pronounced stammer, a result of two bouts of shell-shock in France. At the *Daily Express,* he had shared an office with SPB – who described Boo, later, as 'a bald, irritable man who quarrelled violently with everyone in a very excitable voice that rose almost to a treble as his anger became less restrained'. Boo in his turn parodied SPB as a travel writer of such classics as *With My Wombat in the Vosges.* He wrote a humorous column which he signed 'Beachcomber' and on defecting to France bequeathed the pseudonym to J. B. Morton, who made it famous. During the eight years that Boo lived with Doris in Paris, he wrote tart biographies of three French kings, and compiled a well-received anthology of bad verse, *The Stuffed Owl.* He described himself as 'impulsive, lazy, easily imposed upon, distinctly Celt, full of strong loves and hates'. To Priscilla, he was a temperamental and difficult man, a recent Catholic convert who ultimately never forgave himself, or Doris, for the fact they were living in sin.

'I thought he was wonderful,' said Vivien, who had originally christened him 'Boo'. 'I couldn't understand for many years why Priscilla hated him more than anyone.'

But hate him she did. A photograph in Priscilla's album shows her standing on the beach at Brighton between her father and Wyndham-Lewis: SPB holds her left shoulder, Boo her right. His face has been scratched out.

* * *

At the time, Priscilla explained only to Gillian the cause of her rupture with Boo. Until war separated the two girls, they knew the backwaters of each other's lives, every painful detail. 'My most intimate girlfriend' is how Gillian described Priscilla in one of her notebooks, adding 'Pris and I were birds of a feather.' Priscilla felt the same strong pull: 'We were closer than sisters.'

But their lifelong friendship was slow to germinate. Thrown together because of their parents, and enrolled at the same lycée at 25 Rue Alexandre Dumas and in the same ballet class, they began by disliking each other enormously.

Promiscuous, and mired in her own vapours, Doris had nevertheless brought up her daughters 'fairly strictly'. She made Priscilla wear her hair in plaits and forbade her to read newspapers or visit the cinema. If she attended a concert, she needed a chaperone. And politeness at all times. Aged fifteen, Priscilla was stopped from going to the theatre after she uttered the word 'bugger'. She did not smoke, or drink anything stronger than milk and orange juice.

Gillian considered Priscilla an inexperienced ignoramus and a prig. Although one year younger, Gillian was the more mature and street-wise. Her obsession was the cinema – her ambition to be an actress. Ever since

Priscilla could remember, Gillian had adopted the habit of not smiling. Smiling, Gillian had read, would give her lines.

Indifferent to film, Priscilla had never heard of Gillian's icon, Greta Garbo, nor the stars whose photographs Gillian pinned to her bedroom walls, cut out of film magazines like *Pour Vous* and *Cinémonde*. Instead, Priscilla's brightest moments came when she was alone in the two-storey studio apartment in Rue Galvani, which Boo rented from 1930. In the sitting room, the Maples Persian rug was rolled up so that she could put on a record and invent a dance. There on the polished parquet floor, Priscilla Mais balanced on her sandalled toe and pretended to be Anna Pavlova.

Her cheerful Russian governess Nina had introduced her to Pavlova. Priscilla was mesmerised when she watched her perform 'The Dying Swan' at the Théâtre des Champs-Elysées. She moved as Priscilla had never seen anyone move. Priscilla stuck a newspaper cutting of the dancer into her first scrapbook – 'On shoe tip she had looked more like an air-borne sylph and less like an earth-bound woman' – and above the photograph wrote her own name, 'Priscilla Mais'. Pavlova was what Priscilla, still a shy and relatively passive girl, now decided that she wanted to be.

Enrolled with Gillian in Madame Nesterovsky's class, Priscilla impressed the teacher with her physical grace – unlike Gillian, who detested ballet, and was, Priscilla felt, 'about as graceful as a young elephant'. For four years, she attended lessons. 'I studied ballet-dancing very seriously as I intended to make it my career. It was a passion – I never had any doubts that that was how I wanted to spend my life.' But her passion was cut short brutally.

On 23 January 1931 Pavlova died of pleurisy at The Hague aged forty-nine. One afternoon, Priscilla raised her right leg and felt an ache. Within hours, she came down with a high fever.

Round the corner in Boulevard Berthier – where, following Cyril's bankruptcy, the Hammonds had moved to a studio a few months before – Gillian overheard her parents discussing Priscilla. A priest was by her bed, Priscilla's mother was away with Boo in London, it was all very sad.

'Is she going to die?' Gillian asked hopefully.

Priscilla's illness was a flare-up of a baffling pain in her jaw. Exacerbated by her concentration on ballet five days a week, the soreness had crept into her legs. The diagnosis: osteomyelitis, a serious bacterial infection of the bone.

Priscilla ran a temperature of 104 degrees Fahrenheit for seventeen days. 'She was at death's door,' Vivien said. 'They carved open her upper legs, scraping them down to the bone, leaving hideous open wounds three inches wide and eight inches long – and this before penicillin or painkillers.'

Doris hurried back. Priscilla told Gillian: 'She found a priest praying at my bedside and very little hope left for my survival. As soon as I saw her, I took a turn for the better and gradually got stronger, until after three months I was allowed to leave the nursing home. I couldn't walk, of course, and had to be carried everywhere.'

Gillian was ashamed of her earlier reaction and decided that if Priscilla recovered she would be 'very, very nice to her'. She visited Rue Galvani and was startled to find a plump-looking girl lying on a bed with her blonde head completely shaved, an image that Gillian remembered sixty years later.

Priscilla's high fever had caused her hair to fall out. Doris's hairdresser insisted that it would never grow again unless it was all clipped off. Doris had clicked the scissors.

Gillian was as riveted by Priscilla's bald head as by the scars on her legs. Priscilla shrugged. 'If people don't like them, they can look the other way.' Gillian sensed that the scar left at having to give up dancing was deeper. A ballet career was out of the question.

'As Priscilla couldn't go out or move off her bed, she didn't mind as much as she might have done.' Impressed by her stoicism, from now on Gillian tried to see Priscilla every day after school.

Of the four Hammond siblings, Priscilla initially had much preferred Gillian's elder brother Nicky – in September 1926, SPB had met Priscilla off the steamer at Newhaven: 'P talks of nothing but proposal of marriage (at 10) for Nicky Hammond (aged 11).' Five years on, Priscilla began to transfer her attention to his fourteen-year-old sister.

In December 1998, the upstairs neighbour in Gillian's apartment block in Monaco forgot to turn off his bathroom tap. Gillian's living room was flooded and the novel ruined which she had been writing about Priscilla. Gillian lamented in a notebook: 'Parts of my MS got soaked and caused ink to run, rendering the text illegible. I have had to dry out soaked book, weigh down swollen pages with heavy irons.'

She died a few months later, before having rewritten the text, but from her notebooks, and from Priscilla's novel which featured Gillian as a central character, it is possible to establish a detailed picture of a friendship that lasted fifty-seven years and took root during this period.

Gillian spent most of her spare hours with Priscilla. She helped Doris's Italian maid carry her from room to room and, if Marguerite was unavailable, had Priscilla lower herself on the Persian rug and dragged her around the parquet floor.

Priscilla's bedroom was their den. Gillian knelt beside her and they talked. There was not much else to do. United by a similar 'inferiority complex', as Gillian called it, they were opposites who absorbed each other, Gillian all elbows and sharp (despite her adolescent chubbiness) to Priscilla's passive roundness. This tension kept their relationship alive. Gillian saw it as her duty to distract Priscilla from the reality that she would never perform 'The Dying Swan'. Priscilla became Gillian's outlet for all that Gillian, or 'Chou-chou' as Priscilla nicknamed her, could not discuss at home. For the year that she was confined to her bed, Priscilla entered the world largely through Gillian's eyes.

To keep Priscilla's mind from gnawing on her disappointment, Gillian lent her film magazines and helped with her lessons. Priscilla's education had been neglected owing to her dance classes and then because of illness. She was unable to attend the Lycée Carnot, Gillian's new school, but as part of a joint cost-cutting exercise they now shared a stern governess, Mademoiselle Yvonne, who set them homework. Gillian sometimes finished Priscilla's homework for her while Priscilla locked herself in the lavatory with a book – a habit that Gillian adopted. All through their lives, Priscilla and Gillian were to use the lavatory as a place of escape, to read books or love letters.

A halted dancer, her limbs still 'full of lingering', Priscilla filled the sudden empty space with reading. Banned from newspapers, she escaped into the pages of Jane Austen, the Brontës, Tolstoy. Her favourite novels at fourteen were *Wuthering Heights* and *War and Peace*.

Her father chose many of the books: it was how he kept in touch – with regular parcels of novels. After her operations, too busy to get away, and not believing for an instant that she was dying, he had sent a daily postcard in his crabbed handwriting. Finally, she wrote back. She missed him desperately, but she had taken badly the news that he had started another family with Winnie. Gillian found Priscilla in tears just before her fifteenth birthday. SPB had written to her, announcing the birth of her half-sister, Lalage – my mother.

Doris was unsympathetic. She put her daughter down for resembling her father too much, and blamed Priscilla for the sacrifices that she had had to make. 'I would have left your father years before if it hadn't been for you.' That was a frequent gripe.

8.
SPB

While she convalesced, Priscilla conceived the two ambitions of her life. To have a child; and to publish a book, like her father.

She saw him in Sussex for a few days each summer, heavily chaperoned by her French governess. But in Paris, depending on favourable atmospheric conditions, she listened to him as often as possible, twiddling one of the three round knobs on Boo's wooden wireless to the National Programme – radiated from the Daventry long-wave transmitter on a wavelength of 1554.4m. Stretched out on the couch, immobile, she heard SPB's disembodied voice speaking 'with the gloves off', and immediately was pushing through the heather, breathing in smells of mud and wet tweed as she followed him on foot after the hounds, always struggling to keep up. Hunting, he used to say, was 'the purest of human pleasures'.

Priscilla had a lot of her father in her. She adored him, and went on adoring him, despite periods of separation and disappointment. But their relationship was complex because he was such a public figure, and had a life that did not involve her.

While Priscilla was living in France, her father had become famous. In 1927, his rich mellow voice attracted the attention of the BBC. He made his impact as a pioneer of radio, with a belief, compellingly expressed, that without radio '*any* man – but especially the workless man – is only half alive today'. The philosopher Bryan Magee told me: 'I grew up in a working-class home in Hoxton and even I was entirely used to hearing him mentioned.' In 1954, Magee hired SPB's youngest daughter Imogen as his secretary. 'When I said to my grandmother and two aunts, "My secretary is SPB's daughter," they were awe-struck. It was a little bit like, "My secretary is Salman Rushdie's daughter," or during an earlier generation, "My secretary is Somerset Maugham's daughter."'

SPB epitomised Englishness: most of his many books and radio talks were celebrations of England's history, geography, culture and language. He was – in a phrase he concocted – 'the golden voice of radio'. 'My voice,' he wrote with apparent absence of irony or embarrassment or false modesty, 'was held to be "a clean steady trade-wind blowing".' It was heard in corners of the Empire as far away as New Zealand, and familiar on programmes like *Time to Spare*, *The Kitchen Front* and *The Brains Trust* where his audience was not limited to the working class. In January 1933, *The Times* reported that 'the Queen listened with great interest to the broadcast talk by Mr S. P. B. Mais recently on his tour of unemployment centres in Liverpool and Birkenhead.'

He rose to prominence during the Depression when he came to be known as the 'Ambassador of the English Countryside'. In January 1932, the BBC commissioned a topographical series, *This Unknown Island*, to encourage tourism to Britain's holiday resorts. SPB travelled to seventeen regions and spent a week exploring each. A book with the same title appeared soon after, one of more than two hundred books that he published.

His message for people to go out and explore what lay on their doorsteps, preferably on foot, held a powerful appeal to those who could not afford the cost of travelling abroad, still less a car. The public responded in huge numbers. In July 1932, he was joined by 16,000 people – including Priscilla – on the Sussex Downs to watch the sun rise over the Iron Age fort at Chanctonbury Ring. Four special trains had to be laid on for this midnight excursion.

E. M. Forster praised his broadcasts, suggesting that for his next venture he might visit 'the Unknown Tyne, Mersey and Clyde', and, rather than winkle out beauty spots, examine 'the quite intolerable horror of the unemployed man's life'. SPB jumped at the challenge, persuading the BBC to let him deliver a series of eleven talks on the unemployed. The series was introduced by the Prince of Wales, and proved vivid and popular, giving a human face to the misery and hopeless condition of three million men and women. A second series was commissioned in April 1934, transmitted at peak listening time and causing a nationwide furore on the eve of the final reading of the Unemployment Bill. Angry questions were asked in Parliament, with MPs citing SPB's talks to mock the government's claims that the unemployed were better off. The BBC's prickly director-general John Reith was summoned to Downing Street and ordered by the Prime Minister, Ramsay MacDonald, to desist with the programmes. Reith replied that he would order S. P. B. Mais to report on air that the half-hour silence about to follow was owing to the Government's refusal to allow the unemployed to express their opinions. The programmes continued.

When SPB travelled to America the following winter, he was the first to transmit a series of live weekly programmes from the United States, or indeed from anywhere outside Britain. He invited Priscilla to come as his secretary, but to Priscilla's everlasting bitterness Doris refused to allow this. The groundbreaking talks, aired simultaneously on NBC, were introduced by the American ambassador, with this impressive claim: 'It is the first time in the history of broadcasting that such an effort has been made, in which a national of one country will visit another country, study its people, and try to interpret them to his own nationals.' His discursive method worked, and trail-blazed the way for, thirteen years later, Alistair Cooke's *Letter from America*. Billed as 'a modern Columbus', SPB toured fourteen states in three months, and President Roosevelt granted him an audience. 'I had been called the Ambassador of the English Countryside,' SPB wrote in the inevitable companion volume. 'I was now to be regarded as the Ambassador of the English People.' I have not been able to listen to the recordings, but the talks were incorporated into his book *A Modern Columbus*, and reading them I understand his popularity. Unsnobbish, he approached everything with excited curiosity.

SPB's correspondence fills two trolleys at the BBC's sound archives in Caversham. His producers, who included George Orwell and Graham Greene's cousin Felix, experienced the same problems with his handwriting as did Priscilla, and routinely had it typed out. 'Dear Petre, Thank you for your brief illegible letter,' is a typical complaint.

So atrocious was his handwriting that when invited to lecture at Bomber Command he sent back a letter asking if he could bring his wife. A telegram came by return: DELIGHTED BRING BITCH BUT STATE SIZE BECAUSE OF RATIONING. He answered that his wife was not a bitch, weighed 9 stone 6 pounds and stood 5 foot 7½ inches. The reply this time: SOME MISTAKE SURELY NO BITCH 9ST 6LB WE HAVE TWO MASTIFFS BETTER LEAVE BITCH BEHIND. The 'bitch' was my grandmother. Alone in being able to read what he had written, to Winnie fell the task of typing out his journals and books.

He never owned a house. As his fame grew, so did the procession of visitors to the homes he rented, in Sussex and then, after war broke out, in Oxford. My mother remembered meeting Henry Williamson ('he didn't like beds and slept on the floor'), George Bernard Shaw, H. G. Wells, John Betjeman (he gave the speech at her wedding) and A. P. Herbert.

Graham Greene told me that he, too, had made a pilgrimage to see my grandfather. A scourge of old fogies, SPB had been kind to him when he was a young writer and he felt genuine gratitude – which Greene acknowledged by using his name for a character in *Brighton Rock*: 'See that man going to the Gents'? That's Mais. The brewer. He's worth a hundred thousand nicker.'

In the real world, SPB was worth nothing of the sort. It seems unfair on him that he flourished at a time before journalists with his profile were properly paid. I grew up with the lesson that his fame had brought him no fortune at all. And yet he continued to cling to a hope – which Priscilla inherited – of writing that one book which would rescue him from penury and the bailiffs, and earn a life-changing sum greater than the £100 advances which he latterly received for *Books I Like*, its sequel *More Books I Like*, and for leisurely travel books such as *Mediterranean Cruise Holiday*, *South African Cruise Holiday*, *Continental Coach Tour Holiday*.

He wrote in his diary on 30 December 1939: 'I would give a great deal to write a really good book that would move people.' But he was too oppressed by financial worries and depression to apply to his own work the craftsmanship that he admired in his successful friends. His syntax betrayed his agitation. 'I still feel I have it in me, but I can't as yet dig down to it because I've never had enough time to write it before having to switch off to earn quickly money to live meanwhile.' In his struggle to maintain some kind of footing, he may have been unable to sit with his work longer. One of his radio producers complained: 'You seem to write books faster than I can write letters,' after receiving a copy of SPB's 'boy's book', *The Three-Coloured Pencil* – puffed by its author as 'a superb achievement in the true Buchan manner which I hope you will both approve and read *in that order*'.

SPB most aspired to write a book like *The Thirty-nine Steps*. He regarded John Buchan's spy thriller, published in 1915, as containing one of the finest descriptions of a man-hunt that he knew, and was twice spurred to emulate it. *The Thirty-nine Steps* was among the first novels that he sent to Paris for Priscilla to read in her convalescence, and which caused Doris to complain in her sharp voice: 'You always have your nose buried in a book.'

With Gillian's support, Priscilla recovered her health – until the day arrived when she could stand up. Gillian observed her walking across the bedroom and recognised how Priscilla had grown while she had been ill. The transformation was striking. The immature girl who had spent a year on a stretcher was a young woman with a figure. Her puppy fat had fallen away, her straight hair had sprouted back in thick blonde curls. Her body was riper, and she was as tall as Doris.

Her mother did not hide her resentment. 'You think you are pretty. Fair hair and blue eyes are very commonplace – your sister and I with our dark hair and grey eyes are far more interesting. We are exotic.' She made personal remarks about her daughter in front of others: 'Priscilla is developing quite nice breasts.' Priscilla would blush furiously and leave the room.

Doris insisted on dressing Priscilla in itchy black woollen stockings which French children never wore, causing Priscilla to feel self-conscious. Her only attractive clothes were a white broderie Anglaise party dress and a tweed suit which Doris had bought her – grudgingly – on Boo's persuasion.

Boo was another who appreciated how Priscilla had changed.

Doris and Boo were not getting on. Their violent rows woke Priscilla in the night. The arguments had grown more acrimonious since it became clear that SPB was most unlikely to sue Doris for divorce. Doris later explained to the divorce court judge: 'He said it would ruin him and nothing was done.'

On Boo's part, the friction caused by his Catholic guilt over their unorthodox marital state was sharpened by Doris's flirtations with Gillian's father, and by her tendency to nag Boo about his drinking habits and short temper.

On Doris's part, Boo's inability to earn a living from his writing was too reminiscent of her husband.

SPB paid them a visit, leaving Winnie in a café while he called on Doris. It was the only time he came to see Priscilla in Paris. Looking around the apartment, he recognised the oak commode, the Persian carpet. Priscilla and Vivian ran up to give a welcoming kiss. Priscilla dragged him off to inspect the books in her bedroom.

Boo said that he would not be joining them for lunch.

'He only takes his meals in liquid form,' said Doris after he left.

'I hope he never comes back at all.' Priscilla scowled.

There was a reason for Priscilla's vitriol. Years later, Vivien discovered that Boo had tried to molest her.

Boo's interest in Priscilla had started when she was back on her feet. He took her side in any argument with Doris and offered to help Priscilla with her homework or piano practice. Soon he was paying too much attention, said Vivien, 'nothing beyond attempted caresses in unmentionable places, but naturally causing anger and upset'. Priscilla told Gillian: 'Whenever I ask him to help me with my Latin he starts mauling me.'

The tariff that Boo imposed for his Latin tuition was that she should kiss him and let him shove his hand under her skirt. Priscilla found this sinister, but was not frightened until one night, while Doris was away, Boo got drunk 'and tried to rape me'. Priscilla revealed this to her mother only when, during one of his trips to London, Boo wrote to say that he would not be returning. Priscilla found it difficult to forgive her mother's reaction: 'She slapped me hard on the face. She blamed me, of course, for the break-up. Slowly, I was beginning to see her as she was: a selfish, vain, stupid woman entirely wrapped up in her own affairs.'

The family packed their belongings and left for England. Priscilla was sixteen. They would never hear from Boo again. The next time Priscilla read his name she was sitting in a London cinema watching Alfred Hitchcock's film *The Man Who Knew Too Much* – and saw Boo credited as the screenwriter, and remembered his exploring fingers.

9.
MARRIED ALIVE: 1936

When Priscilla returned to London in 1932, her father already had one daughter with Winnie. Doris finally served divorce papers on SPB because she wanted to marry again. In 1934, after being abandoned by Wyndham-Lewis, and following a series of unhappy relationships, including one with the English cricket captain Wally Hammond, Doris was introduced to an adventurous young naval surgeon, Bertie Ommaney-Davis.

Bertie was twenty-nine and had recently received a congratulatory telegram from George V for sailing a 54-foot ketch without an engine from Hong Kong to Dartmouth. Practically the first woman he met on stepping ashore after a year at sea, with only four naval officers for company, was forty-two-year-old Doris. 'He fell like a ton of bricks,' said Vivien. 'He was out of his mind with love. I couldn't think what the hell he was on about.' But Doris saw in the infatuated Bertie an anchorage, and after ten choppy years hoped to start a life with him 'and have someone she could call her lawful husband'. The problem was that in order to end her twenty-one-year marriage, either she or SPB had to agree to be the guilty party. And SPB, after initially agreeing, refused.

To read the press coverage about Doris's unsuccessful petition is to be reminded of the shame that hedged the subject of divorce. In 2011, there were 144,000 divorces in Britain. For the first time, more than half the children born in Britain were born out of wedlock. But what we now take for granted was inconceivable seventy-five years ago.

Nothing more characterised the judgemental atmosphere in which Priscilla was raised than the Matrimonial Causes Act, unaltered since 1857. To obtain a divorce in 1936, it was essential that both parties did not agree to seek one: an agreement constituted collusion. To protect the sanctity of marriage one party had to be seen to be at fault. This role fell by tradition to the husband who, even if not guilty, was advised to travel with an amenable woman to a hotel, normally in Brighton, and there arrange to be caught in flagrante by a credible witness – explaining Doris's request for Priscilla to 'give evidence and say in court that she had seen her father in bed with Winnie'.

The MP and writer A. P. Herbert who did most to change this antiquated law was a friend of my grandfather. In his 1934 novel *Holy Deadlock,* Herbert drew on details of SPB's domestic situation to lampoon the ludicrous legal pickle in which SPB had found himself – and as a result Herbert believed that he 'helped to create a more favourable attitude' to divorce law reform.

The Maises' divorce case was heard two years after Herbert published *Holy Deadlock*, and marked a watershed, mobilising public opinion, drawing attention to an unjust statute, and stimulating Parliament to reform it. After Doris appealed to 'the discretion of the court', Justice Bucknill decreed that neither party was fit for marriage, both of their records being 'too bad to allow either to be free to contaminate other partners' – and according to this twisted logic refused to grant a divorce. Until their deaths, SPB and Doris would be 'joined together in unholy matrimony' – in Herbert's phrase – or 'married alive'. In November 1936, four months after Justice Bucknill delivered his verdict in the community's interest, Herbert introduced a more humane Matrimonial Causes Act, which became law on 1 January 1938 and allowed divorce without requiring proof of adultery. Priscilla's evidence, and specifically the requirement that forced Doris to make her daughter testify against her father, had played a contributory part.

* * *

Another reason why Justice Bucknill decided against granting Doris's petition was that SPB fought it.

At the time that Doris had first requested a divorce, in 1925, SPB was not so hostile to the idea: he could cast himself as the wronged party without injuring his standing as a journalist. The arrival of Winnie and a child complicated his position. Plus the fact that he now worked for the BBC. When Doris got in touch again nine years later, after meeting Bertie, SPB agreed not to defend her action. His one condition: she would have to divorce him. He changed his mind only after Doris's lawyers demanded that he play the guilty partner.

First, SPB could not stomach the systemic hypocrisy of the conditions. It was Doris who had run off – not once, but twice. He explained in the witness box that he wished the whole truth to be brought into the open in order to preserve his reputation. One after another, he named his wife's lovers. Brownrigg. Wyndham-Lewis. A man called Frank Young (Doris denied this). He may not have known about Wally Hammond or about Gillian's father.

Second, SPB wished to keep his job. He could not, professionally speaking, risk entering the public record as a divorcé. The BBC, in which he had now forged a successful career, was an institution that refused to employ divorced people on its staff. In 1929, the director-general John Reith sacked his senior engineer merely for being cited in a divorce case; in the following year John Heygate was expelled from the BBC after eloping with Evelyn Waugh's wife. It is likely that Reith would have withdrawn his patronage even from such a well-known freelance as SPB, and evidence exists that for a time Reith did so. A confidential internal memorandum from the head of children's programmes reads: 'Mr Mais is seeking further work in *Children's Hour* ... Am I right in believing that there is a feeling militating against this speaker?'

This was the punitive situation that A. P. Herbert had dramatised in *Holy Deadlock*, converting SPB's dilemma into the character of Martin Seal, 'who was employed by the British Broadcasting Corporation and must not be so much as breathed upon by scandal'. Seal's predicament was SPB's: 'He's on the BBC and is afraid of losing his job. They're very particular. Used to run

Children's Hour. He's one of the announcers now … It would never do for the British public to hear the "Weather Report" from the lips of a co-respondent.'

Either SPB's fear that a divorce would jeopardise his career was greater than his concern to keep secret his irregular domestic life, which was about to become still more irregular since Winnie was eight months pregnant with their second child; or else he hoped that once he contested Doris's petition, she would withdraw it. Whatever his calculations, they misfired. Asked to lie, he was punished for telling the truth. He wrote in his diary: 'I am unable to regard the law of the land with anything but suspicion and contempt after that.'

The financial and social repercussions were mortifying. SPB was ordered to pay the costs of £880 (approximately £50,000 in today's money). 'I am reduced to no assets. I cannot overdraw for 18 months.' He was forbidden to take communion in his local church – 'I was excommunicated,' he wrote with bitterness in his diary; and when his youngest daughter Imogen was born one month later, *The Times* refused to let him place an announcement in the birth column.

Doris had to change her name to Mrs Ommaney-Davis, although she and SPB remained legally married. Meanwhile, Winnie, who had changed her name by deed poll to Mais, remained unmarried, with Priscilla, the legitimate daughter, a standing reproach to her two illegitimate daughters. It was something that Winnie lay awake thinking about every night. Four years later, when they moved to Oxford, she remained in a permanent panic, not only about what was going to happen if their new social circle found out, but anxious as to how SPB would earn a living. 'The ensuing scandal did nothing to enhance his repute among his public,' she wrote in an unpublished memoir – yet another instance of my extended family and their friends writing stuff down, and so enabling me to reconstruct their story. 'Lectures, broadcasting and commissioned work all suffered.'

It is not too much to say that Vivien had her life altered by the scandal. She told me that after the *News of the World* printed a double-page spread on the court case, 'I wasn't fit to know. I got an exemption from my matriculation and I had to lodge with the cleaner.' To avoid anyone suspecting her of being Sheila Mais, as she had been christened, she changed her name to Vivien Irving and went to work as an au pair in Germany.

Doris's divorce case was partly why Priscilla left London early the following year. She wanted to wait in Paris until the dust had settled. But that was not the only reason. She was also three months pregnant.

10.
MEETING ROBERT: 1937

The encounter that marked Priscilla's whole life took place after she had spent five years back in England, on a fine spring day in 1937, at a moment when she least expected kindness.

On that morning, 11 March, she had caught the train from Victoria. She bought a newspaper, then stumbled – no hat on, gripping an ochre suitcase – along the platform and into the carriage, upholstered corner seat, with a book.

Under a grey lamb coat, a gift from her mother on her twentieth birthday, she wore her one and only black suit. She had £5 in her pocket, borrowed from a friend.

The train journey – second-class, to Newhaven – was tedious. She cleared a patch on the pane and stared out in detachment at the green fields, struggling to break her connection with the past.

The fields threw her back against her will to another spring day and SPB seeing her off at Newhaven – alone again – on the French steamer. But it hurt Priscilla to think of her father. They were too similar, as her mother kept pointing out. Always remembering and regretting mistakes.

Priscilla drummed with her fingers on the window – another of her father's traits. She had wanted a child so much. She felt sick and young and very frightened. And Tom, the man who had got her pregnant, not even seeing her off.

The truth was, Priscilla did not much care what happened to her.

There is such rich detail both in her unpublished novel and in her diaries that we know to a remarkable degree what she was thinking. We even know what she replied when the passport inspector at Victoria station enquired how long she planned to be away: 'It depends on a lot of things.'

Being under twenty-one, she had needed her parents' consent for a new passport. She had sent a wire to her mother asking her to come urgently to London. Doris, self-engrossed and living in Tintagel with her besotted young naval surgeon, was irritated more than shocked to learn that her daughter was expecting a child by a feckless South African, Tom Ewage-Brown. Priscilla had met him after Doris announced that she was moving with Bertie to Cornwall and Priscilla would have to find digs and earn a living. Tom was renting the next room in Priscilla's Earl's Court hostel, thirty years old, in adver-tising, drove a Ford V8 very badly and owned an exotic uniform, from the period when he claimed to have fought in Bolivia. They had moved in to a double room in Lexham Gardens on his promise to marry as soon as he was earning enough to keep them both. But no sooner were they installed than Priscilla discovered that she was pregnant and that Tom had a Chilean girlfriend. His reaction was hysterical. She should have been more careful, they could not afford it, she had got herself into this mess, she could get herself out.

Doris offered Priscilla no sympathy and no financial help. 'I can't think how you made such a fool of yourself. I always told you that men are out for all they can get. Perhaps this will teach you a lesson,' and wrote down the address of an abortionist in Paris.

SPB, who had quite liked Priscilla's fiancé, was even less helpful. He had been separated from Doris for twelve years and was based in Shoreham with Winnie and their two girls. When Priscilla asked him for £50, saying that her life was at stake, he refused. He might be a well-known broadcaster, but he was covered in debts following her mother's divorce case, and having difficulty as it was keeping body and soul together. Plus, he did not approve of destroying life. 'Why don't you have the child?'

Priscilla replied that she did not earn enough to keep herself in her bedsit, let alone keep a child.

Winnie, whom she abominated, was the only person who tried to talk her out of it, offering to take care of Priscilla until the baby was born, and then Priscilla could have it adopted. 'But Doris had already persuaded you to have an abortion,' Winnie reminded her twenty-one years later.

A clandestine abortion cost about £50 in England (approximately £2,700 in today's money) – beyond Priscilla's means. After completing a course at the Triangle Secretarial College, she had found work as a typist in Mincing Lane, translating French correspondence and operating the switchboard for £2.10s. a week. Her only option was to go back to Paris, where abortions were affordable and where she had friends. Priscilla was confident of Gillian's support.

Priscilla's employer agreed to keep open her job for three weeks. She bought the cheapest ticket, then telephoned Gillian to say that she was in trouble and needed her assistance and would she be at the Gare Saint-Lazare at 5.38 p.m.?

Priscilla began to gather her things as the train approached Newhaven. In the corridor, she observed a man staring. Suddenly, she remembered she had been buying her newspaper at Victoria station when she'd heard a French voice – 'Oh, elle est mignonne!' – and on turning, realised that she was the object of the remark.

Later, Gillian demanded to know every detail of Priscilla's encounter with Robert. 'I love hearing how people meet. All the people who have counted in my life have met in the oddest way.' What seemed a hazard of circumstances had been written at one's birth, she believed.

Priscilla's admirer – he had been addressing a friend – was tall for a Frenchman. He had on an overlong navy-blue coat and a dark brown derby pulled down over his eyes. His gaunt face was lined and he must have been about forty. His feet splayed out as he walked, with a slight stoop.

Priscilla wondered how anyone could find her attractive in her present state. She did not feel mignonne. 'I felt like hell'.

She followed the crowd on to the boat, hoping to shake the man off. She disliked talking to people on trains – one more thing she had in common with her father. 'In the train and across the Channel,' SPB wrote in *I Return to Switzerland*, 'the Englishman regards his fellow traveller as Cain regarded Abel, and only looks for a chance to eliminate him.' Her admirer gave the impression from behind as though he might have trafficked in white slaves.

The sea was calm. She sniffed the air. Travelling the cheapest route at least enabled her to spend longer on the Channel. She found a deckchair and opened her book, looking forward to sitting for the next three hours on deck.

After a while, she grew aware of someone standing beside her. She turned towards the morning dazzle of sun and sea, and tightened her coat round her body. Trying to keep her eyes averted, she directed her attention at the gulls poised above their shadows.

And Robert, her Prince of Aquitaine, what did he see? Very blonde untidy hair, eyes of a washed-out blue. Above all, how thin and pale she was. She seemed to have something on her mind and he wished he could help. It was this paternal instinct that made him approach and gently ask, in French, if he might sit down.

She nodded; fear and rejection may have dulled the voice but without destroying politeness.

His name was Robert, introducing himself. She explained to Gillian: 'He spoke no English, so if my French had been non-existent the affair would have ended then and there.' But her French was as good as her English.

'He told me afterwards that I looked small and ill and he felt sorry for me. He said I was like a cork in a rough sea being tossed hither and thither.'

She was beautiful, he now saw, the sunlight on her face.

He asked if she was going to Paris. In her throaty voice, she replied that she was.

He was travelling with a friend and supposed to be motoring from Dieppe to Rouen. 'But having made such a charming acquaintance, he intended to take the train to Paris so as to have more time with me.'

He fell silent after that. Priscilla listened to the seagulls and wondered what was coming next. She felt shy, frightened.

For something to say, she asked if he lived in Rouen.

'No, I live part of the time in Normandy and part of the time in Paris.'

She put on her face the same encouraging smile as she wore when a man was telling a story. Slowly, it emerged. He was the youngest and favourite of eleven children. His father had died two years before, but his mother was living in the chateau in Sainteny with his elder brother Georges. The family – deeply conservative and Catholic, Priscilla gathered – was one of the noblest in the north of France and could trace their roots to William the Conqueror.

'But enough said of me. Tell me about yourself. How is it that you speak such excellent French?' Was she Russian?

She was English, but had been at school in Paris.

Her reply did not satisfy him. Why had she spent her schooldays in Paris?

She looked at him with tired helplessness, fretting her head against the deckchair. The question was innocent enough. She began to shiver.

Priscilla had flung a net of amnesia over her earliest years, but when questioned with unexpected tenderness by this gangly Frenchman, it put her back in another life. She could feel herself breathing with the tensions of the household in which she had been brought up. Her decision to confide lay behind this future remark of Gillian's: 'Through life, I have noticed that on train journeys people often tell one the story of their lives. Things kept to themselves.'

Three years later, in a blacked-out train during wartime, while on his way to record a talk to British troops in France, SPB also reflected with characteristic inconsistency on our readiness to relinquish our innermost secrets to people we do not know. 'It is only when notices are put up in every railway carriage warning us not to talk to strangers that we feel the strongest temptation to talk.' On the boat to Dieppe and on the train from Dieppe to Paris, Priscilla spoke to Robert with the seriousness of someone telling it for the first time.

Robert confessed a few weeks later that when she had finished talking he looked at Priscilla's pale face and felt that he wanted to protect her against the world.

'Are you all right?'

She admitted to not feeling well, but would love a glass of milk. They made their way to the dining car. Robert ordered a quarter bottle of champagne for himself, a glass of milk for Priscilla. She did not enjoy it much because it was boiled, but sipped politely.

'Don't you ever drink anything stronger?'

She smiled that she did not drink or smoke – and was constantly being teased at parties. But it made her cheap to entertain.

He asked where in Paris he could reach her – 'I said I had no idea which seemed to shatter him slightly.' He produced his card and made her promise to ring him once she knew.

Shortly before 6 p.m. the train drew in to Gare Saint-Lazare.

11.
THE ABORTIONIST

A young woman stood in a haze of ascending steam. At the sight of Priscilla, she ran forward.

It astounded Priscilla to see Gillian, a plump schoolgirl when they last met. Dressed in black, slender, with dark wavy hair, she had grown beautiful.

They embraced. Priscilla introduced Robert, but he left at once. Gillian had not caught his name. 'Who was that?' Her voice was lower-pitched than Priscilla remembered and she spoke English with an accent.

'A Frenchman I met on the boat.'

'He's very good-looking' – which surprised Priscilla. Robert had been an attentive listener, but old enough to be her father.

Gillian grabbed Priscilla's suitcase and they descended into the Métro. A whirl of hot air rushed up to meet them. Compounded in its suffocating gust were the smells of a Paris she had not seen for five years.

'You haven't told your parents about me, have you?'

'Of course not.'

Gillian had booked Priscilla into a ten-franc hotel on the Boulevard Raspail. In a bare top-floor room reeking of drains, she watched Priscilla unpack her few belongings.

'What is going on?'

Priscilla looked at her with grave eyes and out it came. How Doris had given up the mews house in Kensington – how Priscilla had moved in with Tom Ewage-Brown, who seemed surrounded with glamour to her inexperienced eye – 'I was so lonely and I hated not having a home' – how he wanted to marry her – 'he made me think he loved me' – how he had not believed in using a sheath – 'having a toffee with the paper on' – how she was pregnant.

Priscilla was calm, but Gillian knew what she must be feeling. 'What are you going to do?'

Priscilla stared to one side. 'I'm going to have an abortion.'

'But I thought you wanted children.'

'I did. But not this one.' Then her composure cracked. 'Chou-chou, I am so sorry to bother you with all my worries.'

The following afternoon, Gillian accompanied Priscilla to the address that Doris had written down. She promised to wait in a café opposite.

Her long legs moving in her tweed skirt, Priscilla climbed a staircase to a door on the third floor and pressed the bell and when a voice called out she entered. Smoke rose in a grey spiral in a minute vestibule. There was a divan, a table with a jug of water on it, two white chairs. In one of them sat a small owl of a man, fortyish.

He wanted to know who had given his name. Her mother. He washed his hands and asked her to lie down on the divan and open her legs. He examined Priscilla, still holding his cigarette. When was her last period? Why didn't she keep the child? She was very pretty. How old was she? Twenty. He examined her at length.

She re-dressed. He mentioned the price. Gillian had advised Priscilla to say that she was a dancer from the Folies Bergère and that her lover had disappeared and that she had very little money.

He lit a new Gauloise. So a dancer. He would operate if necessary, but he preferred to try another method first, which would be cheaper for her. He asked her to exercise and dance a lot – 'to shake it down'. She was to come back in two weeks. He repeated how attractive she was. If she had no money, he hoped that she would be his petite amie.

Priscilla rejoined Gillian in the café. 'I think I could use a cognac.' Before it arrived, she went to the lavatory and vomited.

Both for the woman and for the person carrying it out, abortion was a crime punishable in France by five years in prison. The only way for a girl in Priscilla's position to deal with her problem was dangerous and clandestine. When Gillian had helped to make her parents' double-bed four years before, Victorine, the girl who cleaned for the Hammonds, whispered how she had spent the night trying to bring on a fausse couche with a metal knitting-needle.

Posters for maladies vénériennes covered the walls of the Métro couloirs; quick relief, discrétion absolute, prix modestes. No telephone numbers, only the names of train stations in sleazy quarters. Priscilla had never lingered before these posters, passing on quickly to the sweet machines that offered Pastilles Vichy. She had no false illusion about what she was planning. 'One couldn't have such an operation without one's health being impaired.'

Once more, Gillian saw it as her duty to distract Priscilla. They walked in the Jardin de Luxembourg; fed pigeons; sat in the Café Dôme, where the waiters knew Gillian and let both girls stay for ages in front of a glass of lemonade. They walked and talked.

Gillian was now an art student. In the autumn of 1932, after Priscilla left for London, she had enrolled at Atelier Dupuis off Place Saint-Sulpice. Still determined to be an actress, until that day arrived she was scraping a living by selling her drawings to fashion magazines. The trouble was that magazines paid per sketch – not enough to fund the independence she craved.

At home, nothing had changed. Her mother continued to shove her father's bankruptcy in his face. Gillian could not wait to leave their orbit and marry.

Unburdened, Priscilla longed to hear about Gillian's love life. 'I wonder if our tastes are still as different? Do you still dislike dancing and good-looking young men?'

First love for Gillian had been a disaster, too. She had lost her virginity, aged sixteen, to a French aristocrat in September 1933. At a party given by the editor of *Le Matin*, she met Yves de Constantin, baron, writer, member of the

Cour des Comptes. Unmarried, forty years old, with his first novel just out, he had seemed a judicious choice.

He had spotted Gillian from across the room and made a beeline. How lovely to meet a true jeune fille, he said, exhaling a black gold-tipped Muratti.

She looked him in the eye. 'This jeune fille is sick of being one.'

'How very interesting,' and wrote down her name in a leather agenda. They must get together.

He invited her to dine at his apartment in Avenue de Tourville, a tiny room crammed with filing cabinets and a sofa-bed. He showed her his first editions on rag paper of Pierre Frondaie, all signed by the maître, and served veal. Halfway through dinner, he knelt while Gillian was chewing on a piece of gristle. 'Do you want to do it tonight?'

She stared at him, thinking how idiotic he looked. For one awful moment his clipped moustache reminded Gillian of her father. But she knew how hard it was for a pretty, unconventional girl in the early 1930s 'to find someone suitable for the deflowering task'. She nodded.

Gillian followed the Baron to the sofa-bed. He wore carpet slippers and his trousers, she noticed, hung in a pouch. Moments after what she called 'his excavation efforts', Gillian stood in the bathroom doorway and observed him on all fours scouring the bed. 'No blood,' he said. 'None at all.'

'At least you've still got nice clean sheets.'

After her session with the Baron – 'my aristocrate dépuceleur' – Gillian felt sore for a few days. 'Suffering from piles?' her father enquired.

Since then Gillian had had other boyfriends. The most serious was a married Hungarian artist who was twenty-two years older, but he saw her only when it suited him. Determined to bring him to heel, she had loftily declared that she would break off their affair unless his behaviour changed. At the time of Priscilla's return to Paris, Gillian remained in limbo, waiting for her married lover to get back in touch, while enjoying a passade with a young financial adviser she had met on holiday in Houlgate. But her love life would always be complicated. 'My mother was highly sexed,' she reminded Priscilla. 'I inherited her genes.'

As for the tall, thin man that Gillian had seen alighting at the Gare Saint-Lazare – who, before the week was out, had telephoned the Hammonds to ask for Priscilla's number – Priscilla had nothing to worry about there. Robert, even if old enough for her taste, looked too distinguished, too charming, too much an arch-Catholic of la vieille France.

And hadn't they sworn never to let a man come between them? 'Pris and I had a code of conduct which entailed no poaching on each other's premises.' The two friends had made this promise five years earlier, on the eve of Priscilla's departure from Paris. Gillian would stick to their pact. It is less clear whether Priscilla did so.

Priscilla's new friend Robert ought to have been pleased to be back in Paris. He disliked his absences from the Bourse. His habit was to spend two hours each afternoon at the stock exchange, preserving the modest fortune that he had inherited from his late father. But he felt restless since returning from England.

He did not have a camera or he would have taken a photograph of Priscilla as she embraced her girlfriend on the platform. He began to ask himself if he was in love. He told himself not, but why had she not contacted him? How could he get hold of her? What was her English friend called? Ham – or some such name. He looked through the telephone book and found it. Gillian's father angrily passed the receiver over to Gillian, who provided the number of Priscilla's hotel. That evening Robert invited Priscilla to dinner.

Priscilla felt a surge of relief to hear his voice. Wanting to dress well for him, she put on her stylish green frock with pockets – her only other item of clothing. At 7.30 p.m. a taxi appeared outside the hotel, Robert inside.

He lived on the other side of the Seine behind the Gare Saint-Lazare, in a modern block like a barracks at the bottom of Rue Nollet. They took a lift to the sixth floor. He had forgotten his keys and a little old woman opened the door and looked at Priscilla with curiosity.

Robert ushered Priscilla into his bed-sitting room; small, with brown velvet curtains, brown carpet, a bureau. He explained that he shared the apartment with the elder of his two surviving brothers, Guy. His fingers were very long and white as he poured Priscilla an orange juice – he had not forgotten her aversion to alcohol. He worried that she might have telephoned while he was visiting his mother in Sainteny. 'I thought I might have lost you for good!'

Priscilla had done all the talking on the boat-train and had not assessed Robert clearly before. Without his hat and coat on, he no longer resembled a slaver. He had jet black hair, amber eyes and a dignified face, like a clean-shaven George V. His grey flannel suit, tailored in London, was cut immaculately. His best features were his hands. Priscilla sipped her orange juice, examining them. She had never seen nicer ones. They were slender and well cared for, like a Byzantine saint's. She began to feel less shy and afraid.

Guy, four years older, bustled in with his long-standing girlfriend, Georgette Graeff. She was a dressmaker, originally from Alsace, in her mid-thirties. Her hair was dyed blonde and she had kind, large brown eyes. Georgette and Guy had been together fifteen years, despite his family's disapproval. Priscilla learned that Robert's widowed mother was opposed to the idea of their marrying, but Guy refused to give Georgette up: instead, he had taken the dramatic move of rejecting his birthright in favour of his middle brother Georges, the only son with children. Georges had assumed the position as head of the family and inherited the family's main chateau in Sainteny.

The old woman announced dinner. They went into a dining room full of heavy marble-topped furniture. Over a reasonably good meal, Priscilla's confidence grew and her voice relaxed. Guy had been at the races with Georgette – who groaned that he spent as much time gambling on the horses as Robert spent at the Bourse. Priscilla liked her. She did not like Guy. He was cross and rude to Georgette, and fussed over Robert as if he was his mother.

Coffee was taken in Guy's room, which was furnished identically to Robert's, except that the carpet and curtains were green. Georgette questioned Priscilla about England. Was the food in England so appalling? Priscilla defended dishes like porridge, suet pudding and mint sauce. Robert grimaced. Mint sauce was the limit.

The brothers' talk was about war. There was an atmosphere of unease in Paris that March; in England, it had been less noticeable. Robert had volunteered in 1916, when he was seventeen. He feared another European conflagration, in which France and England were certain to be beaten. Priscilla could tell that his experience in the trenches had marked him.

To change the topic, she asked Robert if he travelled much. That set him off on his favourite subject: every summer he and his other brother Georges visited Hungary where they had friends who owned estates teeming with pheasants and wild boar. His greatest pleasure was hunting, he said.

At the end of the evening, Robert took Priscilla back to her hotel in a taxi. She found him soothing and different from the juvenile South African she had left behind in London. He promised to telephone the next day. He left without trying to kiss her.

Robert invited Priscilla to see the Bluebell Girls at the Folies Bergère. The dance troupe comprised twenty girls who looked just like Priscilla, all blonde, British and over five foot nine. They were choreographed by an Irish woman, Margaret Kelly, whose title on the programme – 'Maîtresse de Ballet' – brought back memories of Madame Nesterovsky.

Another evening, they sat in a boîte in Rue Marbeuf and listened to a violinist play a Hungarian romance.

A fortnight passed.

Robert took her dancing. He was an indifferent dancer. He had no idea that Priscilla was following the orders of an abortionist.

It was obvious to Gillian, joining the couple under the Coupole, that Robert was falling for Priscilla. Also, that Priscilla was no longer concerned about their age difference. 'I have never met anyone so gentle and sweet.'

One night at Jimmy's, among the couples dancing was a tall, wafer-thin woman. She wore a beaded, Chinese style copper-coloured dress and a matching skull-cap on her cropped hair. Priscilla asked the waiter who she was. The Georgian princess Roussy Mdivani. The sight of her on the dance floor, bare feet in flat gold sandals, provoked Priscilla to jump up and lead

Robert, who did not seem to mind how foolish he looked as his pigeon feet struggled to follow the tango. The scene was unbearable to Gillian: her young friend who had wanted to be a dancer, who had wanted a baby, dancing away her child. 'Pris danced non-stop hoping to bring a miscarriage. We left the nightclub at five in the morning feeling exhausted.'

Priscilla's employer wrote from Mincing Lane. Owing to her prolonged absence, she was sacked. She had still not told Robert that she was pregnant.

On her way to Professor Laurens' drawing class one hot morning, Gillian called at Priscilla's hotel. She was informed that a doctor had taken Priscilla away. Priscilla had left an address for Gillian, not to be given to anyone else.

The address was a woman's prison near Montparnasse cemetery. Frantic, Gillian headed to La Santé. She walked fast along the warm tarmac, the length of the prison's huge wall, until she reached a small building.

'On the door was a copper plate with the words Maison de Santé. I rang. A fat woman half-opened the door. I told her I wanted to see Mademoiselle Mais. She let me in without a word and disappeared. Beyond the entrance was a rectangular room on each side of which were a number of curtained-off cubicles, about six each side. I heard groans and howls and sniffed the odd smell of disinfectant, sweat and tobacco. A man appeared in a blood-stained apron, the sort butchers wear. He looked worried. He led me into one of the cubicles where Pris lay looking very flushed and ill. "You must remove her at once," the man said. "She has a very high temperature. I don't want any trouble. Je ne veux pas d'histoires. And not a word about this place or she will be in trouble too." I asked if I could telephone for a taxi. "Not from here," the man said. "There's a telephone in the café opposite the prison." Off I went to the café, where I made two calls, one for a taxi and the other to Robert to say I would be arriving shortly at Rue Nollet with Pris. I could not say more as the telephone was near the zinc counter and people were listening.'

Bit by painful bit, Gillian extracted from Priscilla what had happened. The dancing had triggered heavy bleeding. In agony, she had telephoned the abortionist who decided to take her to La Santé and operate.

Priscilla was bundled into a dirty room where a radio played at full volume. There was a table covered with a cotton sheet, flooded with a brutal light from a low hanging bulb. On a stove, chrome instruments were being boiled. Handkerchief in hand, she lay back on the couch.

A knock on the door and he entered. She recognised his owlish features. He wore rubber gloves and held a syringe. 'I'm going to give you an injection.'

Naked, she touched her stomach to see if the injection was taking effect. Nothing yet. And remembered Tom lying on her. His blond moustache against her cheek and his puffy face without much expression.

If she could have retraced her steps a year. She never forgot the next moments.

The man opened the window to let out a fly. She saw his profile in the glass and felt a narrow instrument penetrating the deepest part of her body. After the third dilation, the pain in her uterus was horrible.

'This is atrocious, stop it, I can't go on, I can't.'

A hand covered her mouth.

Handkerchief between teeth, she shook her head from side to side.

'I beg you,' the abortionist murmured, 'don't move.'

The radio played 'Le Petit Coeur de Ninon', punctuating the metallic click of an instrument that made the same noise as the inspector in the Métro when he punched her ticket.

'For heaven's sake, keep still.'

Another raucous cry through the handkerchief. Once again, the nurse's hand clamped her mouth. Her nails gripped into the arm of the woman, who flinched. 'You're scratching me.'

'Courage. Almost there,' said the abortionist.

She felt a warm liquid inside her, the sensation of a death.

Covered in blood, she cried out.

The nurse ordered her in a harsh voice to shut up. In the corridor someone was going to the toilets. Minutes later she dragged her wounded body to the cubicle where a shape appeared in the room and developed into Gillian.

'She was already out of bed and looked pretty feeble to me,' Gillian wrote.

'However, she put on some clothes and we crept out of the place like a couple of thieves. Many women died from botched abortions. Priscilla had a narrow escape.'

To the end of her life, Priscilla suspected that dirty instruments had been used. The days afterwards were not very coherent. What did its face look like, what would its features have become, its smile? She had never seen its face.

'I remember Pris being butchered and going septic and nearly dying in Paris.' In Robert's apartment in Rue Nollet, Gillian sat through the night beside her.

Robert had been unfazed by the appearance of two distressed young Englishwomen on his doorstep. Next morning, to Gillian's relief, he took charge. Priscilla was to move into a cleaner hotel nearby as soon as she was well enough, and look for a job; she could eat her meals with him.

Priscilla had run through her £5. Confused, feeble and without funds to pay the motherly hotel owner in Boulevard Raspail, she was packing her suitcase when a young man stumbled into her room, tall, well-built, platinum blond hair and a moustache: Tom Ewage-Brown, begging her to marry him. 'Men are mad,' she reflected to Gillian of the man who had probably been her only previous lover. 'He said that he hadn't realised how much he loved me and that he couldn't live without me.' She told him to go to hell.

She settled into the hotel which Robert had found for her in Montmartre, and through a contact of Doris's accepted a job as a secretary in a translating bureau, run by an erratic Irishman who was a member of the anarchist movement.

It was a beautiful spring. Robert swept her under his wing. They sat out of doors, Gillian bringing a sheet of paper, a paintbrush and bottle of ink, in case there was anyone to draw. A Swedish magazine had commissioned her to take notes 'on what the tout-Paris women were wearing'.

Priscilla's memories of this time are full of gaps, but her itinerary is possible to follow because Gillian made lists of the cafés and what they ordered. A tournedos at the Café de Paris, a chocolate cake at Rumpelmayer, dinner at Drouant in Place Gaillon. And who they saw. The artist Christian Bérard waddling out of the Café de la Paix, beard, hair, clothes spattered with paint. And one afternoon outside the Café Flore, Picasso, sprawled in the back seat of a chauffeur-driven Hispano Suiza with a pile of canvases, and dressed in a black bowler hat and striped crimson sweater. His car was trapped behind a lorry. 'So we had leisure to stare.' And in the evenings a play at L'Atelier or a film at the Apollo in Rue de Clichy.

Cinemas, cracking cacahuètes, fumes of High Life, which Priscilla had taken up smoking in packets of ten. From Gillian, too, she learned the trick of putting her odds and ends into a handkerchief which she dropped the whole time, so that Robert was finally moved to whisper to Gillian: 'Don't you think she could do with a handbag?' Off the two of them went to Hermès where Robert chose for Priscilla a beautiful leather bag, her first.

For a dernier coup, Robert took them for drinks to the Panier Fleuri, a small brothel behind Boulevard Sébastopol, where a madam sat beside a pile of fresh towels, in front of a board of lights indicating which room was free. Gillian recalled: 'None of us went upstairs. We just sipped a cognac or an anisette. The girls wore open cotton gowns, knee length, and between clients touted for easy money. Robert would place a coin on the corner of the table and the woman would suck it up with her pussy.' Another girl smoked Guy's cigar through her vagina. On these evenings, Gillian said, 'It was as natural for Robert and his brother to go to the Panier Fleuri as to stroll down the Champs Elysées and have a drink at the Café du Rond Point.' Priscilla speculated with Gillian about what went on in the rooms overhead.

The abortionist had warned that it would be many months before Priscilla could resume a normal sex life, but after what she had been through Priscilla did not mind. She told Gillian: 'I am finished with the physical side of life for ever.' It was almost a relief to discover that Robert did not seem to mind either. When she went away with Gillian to Sainte-Maxime, he wrote notes to Priscilla in a neat minuscule hand, addressing her as 'mon tout petit bouchon' and ending each note with the sentence 'Je t'aime et je t'embrasse comme je t'aime.' And still not even a kiss.

'No one had ever been kind to me before, and he filled a sort of need in me. It was almost as if he were father, brother and sweetheart all in one. He never made love to me, but he was gentle and sweet and quite good company.' Something sad in Robert's character touched Priscilla. 'I felt very sorry for him because he was an unhappy person – neurotic, I suppose. He had been brought up in luxury with his ten brothers and sisters and now they had very little money and had lost all their splendour.' If she had wanted to put his character in a nutshell, she would have said that it was a curious mixture of frivolity and hauntedness.

'Passer à la casserole' was Gillian's phrase for ending up in bed with someone. Back from a family summer holiday on the Côte des Basques, she rekindled her affair with the married Hungarian artist. Afraid of bumping into anyone who knew his wife, he took Gillian to obscure cafés and they made love in semi-brothels. Priscilla, not having met him, believed that Gillian was wasting her time: Marcel Vertès would never leave Mrs Vertès.

Gillian flashed back: 'What about you? Has Robert proposed yet?' He was taking his time.

Even though handsome and charming, Robert struck Gillian as 'a very limp, boneless character'. By mid-autumn, Gillian decided that he was the caricature of the idle aristocrat and too old for Priscilla. He had a good brain, why didn't he get a job? Robert and Guy were a pair of vampires. 'They feed on your youth.'

It was not lost on Gillian that Robert kept Priscilla away from the family chateau in Normandy. Had Robert invited Priscilla to Boisgrimot to meet his mother? Gillian had the impression of a crowd of stuffy and elderly relations presided over by a widowed matriarch who would find plenty of reasons to disapprove of Priscilla, as she had of Georgette. The Doynels were keen for Robert to marry, so Gillian understood from his brother Guy, but they were overly conscious of their lineage. A penniless English girl from a broken family, who had aborted her illegitimate child – this was not what fourteen generations of in-breeding, and not one divorce, had taught them to look forward to.

Priscilla defended Robert to Gillian. 'He is worried about his mother. She won't approve of a foreigner as a daughter-in-law. Besides there is the question of religion.' The Doynels were strong Catholics. Priscilla believed that 'his family would be very upset because I was a foreigner and I was not a Catholic.'

'After a year in Paris, I decided that it was time to take a decision of some sort.' Still uncertain of Robert's intentions, Priscilla resigned from the translation bureau and travelled to England to 'see if that would shake him'. She left her return date open.

In London, she had tea with her father at Bendicks, where he had previously taken her with Alec Waugh. A year had passed since their dreadful last meeting. SPB found Priscilla highly strung, generous-hearted, sensitive. 'I'm so terribly afraid that she may run into trouble, by marrying without thinking,' he wrote in his diary. 'She's tremendously attractive. It's odd having a daughter almost marriageable. And it's hard for me to talk to her.' Doris had for too long indoctrinated Priscilla with bitterness towards him.

In April 1938, SPB was writing and broadcasting at full tilt to pay off 'the ruinous costs' of his wife's unsuccessful divorce case. Radio was his mainstay, but in order to earn the £700 that he owed his lawyers, he had begun working for the BBC's fledgling television service. When he met Priscilla, he was finishing a television play, and in the middle of presenting a television series on *Craftsmen*. With the idea of securing Priscilla a job in this exciting new medium, he introduced her to a producer, Andrew Miller-Jones, writing to him afterwards: 'It was awfully nice of you to see Priscilla, who fell heavily for you!'

Miller-Jones, who later co-founded *Panorama*, responded: 'In meeting your daughter the pleasure was mine, I only hope we shall be able to do something' – which suggests that Priscilla was open to the possibility, although there was no further mention of a job.

Priscilla had not lost her ability to bewitch. In May, a tall, good-looking captain in the Irish Guards wrote to her from Gloucester Gardens: 'You are the loveliest thing that ever happened and I adore you with every fibre of my being. Please be kind to me and forgive me. We were meant for each other – no matter how long we have to wait – our end will be together. Even if you marry Robert, eventually you will come to me and I to you. I know that is so, I can see nothing else.'

But would Robert marry her?

At his chateau in Lower Normandy, Robert could not decide.

He knew that Priscilla wanted a child. Was his health up to it? He had been fragile and frail since boyhood. No one could work out what was wrong with him; whether it was an accident, as with his brother René, who had tumbled to his death from a horse; or illness, like another brother, who had died of meningitis; or the fact that he was the product of so many cousins inter-marrying; or that his mother was forty-three when he was born.

And memories of the First World War continued to wake him.

Some of Robert's behaviour was a consequence of his months in the trenches. He had been wounded in the German counter-attack in 1918. Not physically, like one his friends, also nineteen, who had his jaw blasted away and whose screams he heard his whole life long, but in his core. Nothing else had affected his character so much, not even his Catholicism. Anything that reminded Robert of the mud and the lice had the power to make him retch.

On 25 January 1938 Robert had witnessed an exceptional aurora borealis which many locals in Sainteny seized upon as an augury that predicted another conflict. Towards 6 p.m. the clouds dispersed and in the north sky Robert saw a brilliant display of emerald and rose-hued lights, 'taking on the aspect of a flag agitated by the wind'. One old lady declared that this was not a good sign – she remembered the same pulsing red and green lights in her childhood, immediately before the German invasion of 1870. Many looked on it as a premonition. Zizi Carer, the daughter of Robert's 'intendant' or steward, was nine at the time. 'We thought it meant the end of the world,' she said.

If that was the case, would it be wiser to have no children?

I imagine Robert at Boisgrimot, pacing the lawn in his hacking jacket and trilby, his awkward walk, tall when he remembers to stand upright, devout to a deity who was not always there, his nights interrupted by the gurgles of disappearing comrades weighed down by 20-kilo packs, images of men on barbed wire, the flooded shell craters, smells of gas, mud. Robert could not confide to Priscilla about his dreams. So often he became emotional – here he was, with her, a wonderful meal and wine … and his friends were trapped in mud, and he might have been there with them, and he would start to shake, unable to hold his cup of coffee, let alone a young woman. The doctors put it down to 'nerves'. He no longer had fainting fits, but every day he woke up exhausted, and went to bed in the same state.

'Mon tout petit bouchon,' he wrote to Priscilla in England, 'I feel fractured every time I leave you. Je t'embrasse avec tout mon amour.' And a few days later: 'This is the third time I've written to you since you left and only God knows how much it has cost me to be separated from you. I'm still hesitating about making you come back to France …'

Why Priscilla and not any of the others? He had had girlfriends before. Swedish, Hungarian, Austrian, French. Probably he would never be able to work it out, this fatal impulse to want to rescue someone. To believe that he could.

His mother would need persuading, of course, but he had his eldest brother's support. Guy would vouch for her social credentials. And if he could get Priscilla to become a Catholic – that might facilitate matters tremendously.

'I love you more and more,' he wrote. 'I, too, am very concerned about events and would much prefer it if right now you were in France. I have made a very surprising decision and out of prudence I am going to send a telegram to ask you perhaps to return.'

By 'events' he meant Munich.

The noise of an aeroplane died down. Cars ceased to hum. In Shoreham with Winnie and their two daughters, SPB turned on the wireless, a new Ecko radiogram for which he had paid 39 guineas. 'Waiting for the 9.40 news was like waiting to hear the news of an operation. How strangely knit are men's fortunes that we should be dependent on this one man's voice.' At 9.45 p.m., SPB wrote down in his journal: 'Hitler has made his speech. He warned London and Paris and we heard the high excited pitch of voice of the madman and the wild cheers of his young Nazis.'

Three days later, Chamberlain's decision to fly to Germany to speak with Hitler was 'the most surprising news of a wild week. It has been a dreadful time of tension.' SPB recorded the sight of men and women hand in hand with drawn faces, 'the total absence of laughter and whistling'.

His anxiety intensified after the two leaders met on 22 September.

'24 Sept Saturday. The worst day of year. Chamberlain flies home. All quiet in Westminster. No flags. Business at usual. Though in a few hours we might be wiped from the air.'

On the Sussex coast, SPB's mind was 'in a shambles' after he had a gas mask fitted and saw visions of his gasping daughters. He had converted the dining room in case of an attack. 'We look for cellophane to do our windows. There are gas-proof devices for babies, and gas-proof devices for animals. Is any war worth the sight of a child being killed by poison gas? I have got £70 in £1 notes sitting in a drawer waiting to be used for racing the children to a junk-hole if the worst comes.' On 30 September, hours after the signing of the Munich Agreement: 'Every train westward out of London is crammed in triplicate.' SPB did not dare to play tennis, listen to the radio, read the news. 'Walked over downs and it seemed that perhaps they too would take on an immortal scar.'

Across the Channel in Paris and Caen and Sainteny, mobilised soldiers had been commandeering buses and painting the glass shades of the street lamps blue. Robert sent a telegram to Horsham, where Priscilla was staying with her grandmother. PLEASE RETURN IMMEDIATELY STOP WAR IMMINENT STOP WISH TO INTRODUCE YOU TO MOTHER.

12.
BOISGRIMOT

In Paris, a Doynel told me with pride: 'We are related to the Montmorencys who came over to Hastings with William the Conqueror.'

The first written mention of the name Doynel does not occur, in fact, until 1391 – although the family's unofficial genealogist, Jean Durand de Saint-Front, wrote tantalisingly that 'in a fragment in my possession' there was a 'Doisnel living in 1280'. Saint-Front at least allowed that the origins of the Doynels' elevation to the aristocracy were obscure.

Before they were Vicomtes, the Doynels were caretakers-cum-milliners. They held the keys to the windmill of Hautonnière in Fougerolles – so that clothes and bows and arrows could be kept safe: fourteenth-century hat-check girls, in other words.

Saint-Front was tireless in his pursuit of every Doynel who ever breathed, to nab and to name them. In the Saint-Lô archives – not very extensive, following the flattening of the city in 1944 – I combed quite quickly through his 1200-page family history, hunting for Priscilla's name.

A Jean Douesnel was condemned to death in 1391 for violence in the town of Teilleul; a Doynel cousin, Robert de la Sausserie, was Eleanor of Aquitaine's caretaker. In 1637, François Doynel galloped into a wood with 100 cavalrymen under his command – slap into an ambush: 600 men on horseback and 120 musketeers. 'In the presence of such a danger, there was but one thing to do – flee.' In 1800, the Doynels spread their shoots into the German aristocracy when Vicomte René Doynel married the Westphalian heiress Caroline Giessen. But not until December 1895 was the name expanded – after Robert's grandfather René insisted on changing his surname from Doynel to the more noble-sounding Doynel de la Sausserie. Like many Doynels, René became strong only when he looked backwards.

Saint-Front terminated his lifetime's project with a caveat: 'To sum up, a great family, brilliant, who contracted the best alliances, but who are not as ancient as they have tried to make one believe, and some of whose claims – their presence at Hastings, for example – do not seem entirely justified.'

One has to leaf through a thousand of Saint-Front's pages before arriving at the family trees of Robert's parents. I followed the branches of their eleven children – all with the names of their spouses and offspring – until I came to the last, Robert René Francois Henri-Joseph.

The entry was simple and chilling: 'Married an Englishwoman, no children (divorce).' No dates. Not even a name. Six hundred years of Doynel alliances scrupulously recorded, and yet her identity was not considered worth mentioning. Her excision fitted with the legend told to me by the present Vicomtesse, who had the clear and firm impression that Priscilla had died 'very young, near the start of the war'.

'Priscilla? A mystery. The enigma of the family,' said a local historian.

But in the village of Sainteny they remembered her.

The farmhouse looked run-down and empty. I was turning to leave when the door shuddered open and an old man stepped out. He carried a stick and had a fresh scab on his bald dome.

I did not say her name. I told him only that my English aunt had been married to Robert Doynel.

'Priscilla Mais!' peering at me through his spectacles, stunned, and clapped a hand to his head.

Joseph Carer had been the son of the family steward. This was a powerful staff member, who, unlike an English estate manager, controlled the whole staff as well as the property itself. To talk to Joseph was to be plunged into the pre-war feudal relationship that existed between the peasants and the nobility.

The Carers – Breton-speakers – arrived from Brittany in 1937. Joseph's father looked after the Doynels' three farms: Le Chalet des Pins, La Paysanterie, Le Pavillon. Another of his duties was to collect the family from the station at Carentan in a horse and buggy.

One summer – he was eight – Joseph watched his father trotting down the oak avenue with Robert and a young woman seated beside him in a wonderful fur coat. Robert's fiancée.

Joseph invited me inside. He was shaking as he sat down at the table. The kitchen was bare. The only decorations: two cracked blue plates wired to a beam above the stove.

'Your aunt was a beautiful woman, everyone spoke of her beauty, that was what they talked about.' Her name – uttered unprompted and pronounced as 'Ma-ease' – was bringing everything back. 'Priscilla Mais...'

Joseph recalled what Robert's oldest brother Guy loyally said about her: 'Priscilla is from an English noble family.'

He remembered seeing Priscilla with Robert up at the chateau. 'On Thursdays, I would carry milk from the farm to Boisgrimot. I would open the bedroom door to Robert's mother, followed by Robert, or if he was not there, Georges, and a maid carrying a tray.' He remembered the day when Robert gave him the two blue plates on the beam – he had rescued them from an attic in Le Chalet des Pins after the Americans destroyed the house with grenades. 'If those plates could talk...' He looked at me. 'Priscilla Mais!' shaking his head, his face reddening. And taking off his spectacles, he started to weep.

The Doynel chateau of Boisgrimot lay on the edge of the village of Sainteny. Before visiting the house, I walked to the main square. Old postcards show that before the Second World War the square was smaller and had an area of flattened earth scattered with gravel. Place Saint-Pierre was now tarmacked over, the cast-iron pump no longer there. Outside the reconstructed church of Saint-Pierre, glinting in the weak sun like malachite, a traditional layering of broken green glass covered Robert's plain grave.

Jacqueline Hodey was witness to these changes: she grew up in the café opposite when it was a grocery run by her parents. She could recall the three Doynel wives riding their horses through the square. She was at Robert's funeral in 1978, as she had attended his mother's funeral in 1943, and his father's before that, in 1935.

Jacqueline's father had been gassed in the First War. 'He couldn't stand people who didn't do anything, but he had great respect for Robert's father, the chatelain.' Jacqueline's memory reached back to Joseph Carer's father pushing the old Vicomte in a wheelchair around the estate. 'He was called Le Père-Grand and I thought he was God.'

And his children? 'As they did no serious work, they were not respected so much.' In particular Robert's brother Georges, the heir, was regarded warily because of his over-familiar manner with the villagers, always tutoying them.

Jacqueline was fourteen when she walked for the first time up the oak avenue to the chateau, to collect funds for the parish. The avenue was reserved for God's car – a black three-door limousine with a chauffeur. Peasants made sure to keep to the side. 'If you decided, to hell with this, I'm going up the avenue, and you didn't have the right, you were thrown out.'

Only the children who attended catechism at the local school were allowed to walk up the middle of the avenue on the heels of the priest. Plus the family. On Sundays for Mass, and for Vespers, the Doynels trooped into Sainteny. Jacqueline remembered Priscilla strolling on Robert's arm to church, and watching my aunt genuflect in the Doynel chapel.

'I was very small, but I saw Madame Robert. It was a big attraction to see people of the chateau. Because I was from another world than them.'

The chateau was the scene of some of the fiercest fighting in Normandy. By the time the shelling stopped, Boisgrimot, Saint-Pierre church and the Doynel tombs had been obliterated, and hardly a house in Sainteny remained standing.

Sainteny's mayor told me: 'The community was literally destroyed.'

The destruction included the archives, said Jean-Paul Pitou, who was the local historian. He had spent two decades researching into Sainteny's past. Such was the resistance to talking about this period at all, not to mention the mistrust in the neighbourhood towards those who might have collaborated with the Germans, that even when documents did turn up, they were destroyed. And in a morose voice from which he could not keep his regret, Pitou recalled the secretary of the association that looked after war victims, a woman whose responsibility was to assess the refugees, and who removed their papers and photographs from their houses for safekeeping. 'When she died in the 1960s, her children made a bonfire and burned all the files, for two days and two nights.'

A photograph in Comte Paul Doynel de la Sausserie's privately printed *Genealogical History of the House of Chivré* was one of the few images to survive of the chateau of Boisgrimot as it looked in 1944. The windows blown out, the shutters gone, the brickwork torched as if a bush fire had swept through. The trunk of a solitary oak twists up over the damaged roof, charred and spindly.

The black and white ruin bore no resemblance to the magnolia-painted building that I approached on a mild September afternoon. I walked over a narrow moat filled with water, over a lawn planted with pampas grass and pressed my face to a window. 'Now it's a bourgeois house, excuse me,' the local historian had cautioned.

Destroyed by bombs in July 1944, and sold with panic-stricken haste by Robert's brother Georges, Boisgrimot had endured a sterile renovation, and was now available for rent. Visible through a windowpane was the sole link to the former proprietors, a stone fireplace engraved with three mallards – the Doynel crest.

There was no one around – the present owner lived in Cherbourg – and I made a circuit of the buildings, poking into the conical dovecote. In a corner of the stables, covered with hay, was a dilapidated wood carriage, streaked with blue paint.

The only image of Boisgrimot as it was in Priscilla's time was a tinted postcard of the chateau, owned by Jacqueline Hodey. Pitou told me that it took eighteen months to persuade her to show it to him. When I explained to Jacqueline that I was here to find out what had happened to my aunt, she said: 'On fera sortir les fantômes' – It'll bring out the ghosts.

On this, her first visit, it was a warm day without sun; not a good hunting day, what the French call a jour des dames. The steward, Monsieur Carer, collected Robert and Priscilla from Carentan station in the blue pony trap. The French government had issued Priscilla with a gas mask, a grey oblong box which hung at her side.

The stout horse lumbered them though a flat landscape bordered by thick hedges into Sainteny and down a gravel drive overarched by oaks. These ancient trees were the joy of Robert's father, who had forbidden his children to saw off a single branch. His dying words: 'Leave my trees alone.' Robert felt a peace whenever he saw them.

The chateau that emerged from beneath this natural arch was a long two-storied manor house, painted oatmeal and rather plain on the outside. The building dated back to the tenth century, but more recently someone had added on a pigeonnier – a sign of aristocracy.

Stables in sight, the horse quickened pace, throwing them together on the buggy seat.

Small dogs pressed their noses into her skirt as Priscilla stepped down. Robert's mother Adelaide stood on the steps, a small, very old, alert-faced woman dressed in a black jacket edged with embroidery. She kissed Priscilla with some affection and led the way, through a hall that smelled of gun oil and expensive leather tackle, into a large square drawing room, with windows on both sides.

About twenty Doynels stood waiting – Adelaide's seven surviving children and their families. Priscilla's overriding impression was how ancient they were. Two of Robert's four sisters seemed old enough to be her grandmother. An unmarried woman, Priscilla shyly kissed their hands.

Forty-three-year-old Guy, Priscilla already knew. She was now introduced to the brother who had somersaulted over Guy to become head of the family.

Georges, who was forty-one, was the wealthiest and cleverest of Adelaide's three sons. He had married a rich woman and made money dealing in antiques and paintings. In looks and in temperament he was quite unlike Robert: astute and energetic, but with a dreadful temper, generally sparked by the most trivial incident. The family tip-toed around him.

His twenty-nine-year-old wife, Yolande de la Sayette, was a crashing snob who believed in living 'selon son rang' – according to one's rank – and mingling with exclusive people only. But an eccentric dress code sabotaged her bids to appear stylish. 'She had no taste in clothes and when she was well dressed it was generally a fluke,' wrote Priscilla. Their character was conveyed by an advertisement placed recently in *The Times*. 'Young French Married Couple, best society, would take well-educated young people desiring to learn French in their comfortable villa near Dinard, July–September.'

Yolande greeted Priscilla, and smiled as far as her narrow mouth would let her. She sported a strange bird's feather in her hat. 'She took an immediate dislike to me,' Priscilla wrote, 'when I told her in answer to a question that I had not been presented at Court.'

English girls were rare at Boisgrimot. Yolande was automatically suspicious of the young woman whom Robert had invited to stay. Priscilla's white complexion challenged Yolande – those lazy blue eyes that could suddenly become very concentrated, those rounded arms and shoulders, those firm breasts, that tall and slender figure, that hair, and smoothing a dress so obviously purchased for her. Yolande saw une arriviste, a provincial interloper from the old enemy. In this part of France, she would warn Priscilla, they did not much care for the English – they knew the history. But she could not deny that Priscilla held herself well. She had radiance, she had presence. And Robert loved her.

Robert had told his family about Priscilla; how splendid she looked, standing on deck in a warm wind. Her provenance, Sherborne, the town of Roger of Caen; her ancestry, one of aristocrats and eminent authors.

Catholic? No. But that was being seen to.

What did her father do? A famous writer. On the wireless. The Prince of Wales had introduced one of his programmes. The Queen listened to him.

He had met President Roosevelt. They nodded.

He did not tell them about the situation of her parents. Divorce for the Doynels was an insupportable disgrace.

And no word of Priscilla's circumstances when he met her.

The room subsided back into its dark sensible proportions. A niece ran forward to give Priscilla a flower she had picked, and showed her upstairs to change. Robert led her down to dinner.

A woman from the village served the meal. Priscilla's gaze faltered over the main course, a slim slice of goose breast like the sole of a ballet shoe. The gloomy panelled room made Yolande's powdered face look whiter as she watched for Priscilla to do the wrong thing.

Priscilla glanced down the long table. There were no napkins. And the manners of the family surprised her. 'They all wiped up their sauce with a bit of bread between finger and thumb. When eating eggs or drinking tea or coffee they always dipped bread into the mixture. Also, they ate several different courses with the same knife and fork and never changed the plates.'

Dinner over, everyone retired to the drawing room. They sat in scrolled couches overlooked by cracked ancestral portraits of men decorated with the Order of the Holy Ghost. On the black and white wallpaper, a still life of a dead deer on a wooden table, a couple of antique hunting horns ('Mes fils adorent la chasse'); and a bookcase containing the works of Claude-Joseph Durat bound in red leather. During a visit lasting several days, Priscilla did not remember anyone opening a book. Some knitted, some played cards, some talked. Conversation hovered over the situation in Czechoslovakia and moved on, but every eye in the room was paying attention to Priscilla.

Princes and magic. Was this what Priscilla had envisaged as a child? Did she creep into Robert's room? Bounce on the bed, draw the heavy curtains, fearing to whisper in case she woke his old mother in the next room. Or disturb Georges, gassed in the First War. Or Guy, who had done such sterling work to uphold the façade that Priscilla was from the English nobility. Guy understood perfectly – he had had to endure Yolande's smug censure of

Georgette. Yolande, her prejudice fixed like the pigeonnier at the corner of the chateau, had declared Georgette 'socially unacceptable'.

The chateau slept. From her window, Priscilla could see fields and a hard tennis court overrun by weeds. She looked down the sacrosanct avenue of oaks. Out there was fear and the sound of boots, the sense of six hundred years and a way of living – feudal, religious and embodied in the small black shape of Robert's mother – about to totter to an end. The house was so imposing and grand, at the same time it looked ready to crumble into the tennis court.

My mother told me that when, after the war, Priscilla discovered Giuseppe di Lampedusa's novel *The Leopard*, the portrait of an ancient family in full disintegration, it became her favourite book.

The shadow of Robert's father Georges continued to fall over Boisgrimot like the branches of his precious oaks. His funeral in January 1935 had attracted one of the largest gatherings of the regional nobility in the Doynels' history. The archpriest of Chivré had headed the cortège which carried the body from the chateau to the cemetery in Sainteny. Robert and his two brothers were chief mourners. During a sung mass attended by the district's priests, the eighty-four-year old Vicomte was lowered into the family sepulchre beside his two dead sons.

Invitations to his funeral listed the Vicomte's five addresses. He owned a further ninety-four properties, and by leading a careful life had contrived to leave his children ten each – plus, according to Priscilla, 'enough money to allow them to live at leisure, without working'. Robert had never done a stroke of work in his life, she told Gillian.

The archpriest in his oration described Robert's father as a 'fervent traditionalist' who had embraced his civic duties with passionate seriousness. He had twice served as mayor of Sainteny and had founded a free school for the local children. An equally fervent Catholic, he paid for the schoolchildren's education so long as the boys became priests and the girls nuns.

Not one of the Vicomte's own children had grown up to take Holy Orders. In a worn anecdote which summarised for Priscilla their profligacy, the

Vicomte invited his three sons to a restaurant. He chose a sardine and a veal cutlet and passed the menu to Georges, who found it depressing to scan a menu without selecting the priciest item. 'I think I will have oysters.' Guy then ordered caviar, and Robert lobster. After stroking his beard for a long moment, their father threw up his hands: 'Why not? I will have oysters, caviar and lobster too.'

The Vicomte had greater luck in passing down his love of hunting. The archpriest alluded to it in his prayers, how the forests echoed with the old man's horn. 'The great distraction of the late lamented was la chasse; in every part of the region he had a reputation as an excellent shot. He continued to shoot from his wheelchair, even when an unfortunate accident rendered him immobile.'

In the morning, Priscilla went riding with Robert along a sun-speckled bridle track. It was a hotter day and she had wanted to put on shorts, but he asked her not to: it might shock the villagers.

Hooves clopped furiously on being led on to earth. The breath of honey-suckle sweetened the air; pigeons circled overhead.

Robert showed her over the estates, pointing out the milking cows, the buckwheat fields, and introduced her to the farm workers. Monsieur Bezard descended from his tractor, followed by his dog. He discussed the changes Robert would like to make. Priscilla had difficulty in understanding the Breton dialect. On poles on top of the haystacks, someone had tied live crows to scare off the birds.

They rode back through the village, between cottages built of pressed earth and clay. Priscilla found them primitive compared with houses in Sussex or Devon – and recalled her father nearly cancelling a tour through Normandy after his first day in France, he had never slept in such a filthy hotel. In SPB's opinion, the roads were straight and monotonous, the countryside dull, the villages smelly. 'The country people, all dressed in black, looked as unhappy as the houses they lived in.' Sainteny was like this, a feudal backwater where nobility and clergy dominated unchallenged.

Robert's late father had appeared in frock coat and hat, gloves in hand, for 6 p.m. prayers in the drawing room. This pious tradition continued under Georges, the new head of the family. 'One always had to be at Mass and Communion at least once a week, not to mention Vespers.'

To demonstrate her religious credentials, Priscilla joined Robert and his family in their processions to the village church. 'They were very drab – they looked like crows all in black – one could hardly distinguish them from the peasants, which was odd as both parents had great distinction.' Robert seemed to be the only one who had inherited this distinction. The rest of his family were decrepit, expiring. Priscilla, surveying these gruesome Doynel aunts and uncles 'always going and coming from church', wondered 'what sins they could have committed to go to confession so often'.

Increased acquaintance with Yolande only served to make her more unpleasant. Georges's glacial and exalted wife did not alter one jot her opinion of Robert's long-legged and shy English fiancée. 'Elle ne dit jamais un mot!' her voice rising in a determined effort to maintain her top-dog position. She bent her playing card and waited for it to snap back. Her complaints were various: Priscilla never played belote, never joined in the conversation, never offered an opinion about Art or Music, never…

But Yolande's conversations were about people whom Priscilla did not know, about politics, which she did not understand. Just looking at Yolande made Priscilla cough.

Their battles formalised over what Priscilla called 'the bath question'. There were only two baths at Boisgrimot, zinc tubs with swan's neck taps, installed by Robert's father. Adelaide, the reigning queen, had access to one of them; Yolande to the other. Everyone else was supposed to wash out of buckets. Priscilla's gentle insistence on using Yolande's bathroom – reached by walking through her bedroom – ratcheted up the hostilities.

Strangely for one so timid, Priscilla was not at all in awe of Yolande's husband Georges. When, on the second evening, Georges had another of his grand explosions, Priscilla was comforted by a sense of déjà-vu. Instead of shrinking with everyone else behind the uncomfortable Louis Quatorze settees, she took strength from one of SPB's bedtime stories, about his grand-father in Georgeham, a man of extraordinary irascibility who once whipped the village blacksmith and left a scar on his back. Priscilla's father had been the one family member not afraid of him.

On the other hand, Priscilla got on famously with Robert's traditional Catholic mother, Adelaide. Priscilla wrote: 'She was very agile for her age. She walked up and down stairs several times a day and she still had quite good eyesight and could hear everything one said in spite of her 85 years.' A portrait in the drawing room showed the young Adelaide to have been attractive – 'more so than any of her daughters'. But she had exhausted herself giving birth to eleven children and now looked forward to joining her husband in the family crypt. Her single outstanding desire – having given up on Guy – was to see her youngest son Robert married. She had heard glowing reports of Priscilla from Guy and Georgette.

Priscilla became very fond of the old lady. It helped that Adelaide had a tricky relationship with Yolande, who, to Adelaide's impotent fury, had taken control of the kitchen and housekeeping. Adelaide viewed Priscilla as an ally who was likely to be more amenable. 'She could not have been nicer to me.'

Adelaide leaned on her arm in walks around the garden. They sat on a bench side by side. Once, they were chatting with Robert when he was called away to see Monsieur Bezard. Priscilla looked out over the tennis court, the cooing pigeons, someone riding through the trees, the sweet-smelling bonfire, the gap in the hedge where the late Vicomte liked to blast away at hares from his wheelchair. She would come to recognise that rarely a day went by without Robert thinking of Boisgrimot.

Bells were ringing across the field. In the declining light, Priscilla led the old woman, the ferrule of her stick crunching on the gravel, slowly down the avenue to Vespers. Talk was of Robert. He had told his mother. 'She was overjoyed at the idea of his settling down at last.' He had not yet asked Priscilla, but in the morning he was taking her into Caen to propose formally. The city – forty-five miles away – had an excellent jeweller's.

Adelaide, getting ahead of herself, held her hand and patted her while giving Priscilla advice on her future life. Where she would live, what she would do, and about children. Priscilla would have children, not so many as Adelaide perhaps – but lots of them.

Priscilla's blushing face studied the dovecote. Dimples appeared with reluctance in her cheeks as she pretended to have no idea what Adelaide was talking about. But her heart pounded.

13.
LETTER FROM AN UNKNOWN MAN

At twenty-two, Priscilla's vulnerability was part of her appeal. Most men flatter themselves that certain women want looking after. She brought that sense out in a lot of them. She had the careless allure of Grace Kelly which Alfred Hitchock sought (but failed) to put on screen in *Marnie*. Interviewed by the *Daily Express* in Bodega Bay, the director remarked that people had the wrong idea about Grace. 'They think she is a cold fish. Remote, like Alcatraz out there. But she has sex appeal, believe me. She has the subtle sex appeal of the English woman and this is the finest in the world. It is ice that will burn in your hands.'

This was Priscilla's impact on a young French aristocrat in Caen only a few days after her visit to Boisgrimot. She had not exchanged a word with him. It was one of plenty of instances of men being electrically attracted to her across a bar, a room, a street.

On the night of Sunday 2 October 1938, feeling lovestruck, the Marquis de T. walked back along the deserted Boulevard des Alliés to the restaurant where he had spied Priscilla earlier in the week, and handed a letter to the patron, asking him to give it to that lovely girl, which he did. Air raids were feared and de T., recently mobilised, had spent the previous days painting the streetlamps. But his mind was not seething over the political crisis. In the dim blue light, there would have been something ghost-like about him.

'Mademoiselle,

'I am the officer whom you saw at the Brasserie Chandivert. I don't know what you think of me or if you think of me, or even if you noticed me. Myself, I think about you constantly. I have managed to find out your name and address, and this morning I commit the folly of writing to you.

'I hope that my letter moves you and that you won't be annoyed at my audacity. As for me, I fear nothing except that you will be angry with me or that someone intercepts my letter.

'That night, when you went out to the kiosk on Boulevard des Alliés to buy a newspaper, I desperately wanted to talk to you, but I did not have time because you walked back into the restaurant. I don't know if you will be returning. Meanwhile, I can't imagine life without you. The last time I saw you, as you entered the restaurant, it seemed to me that you looked at me and I can't forget that look.

'Since I saw you, I have not stopped thinking about you. I can't go into the Chandivert without looking at the place where you were sitting. I can't walk past the hotel in the Place Royale without imagining you in the reading room, your back to the window, your legs stretched out on a chair, your head turned to a book of which I regret not being able to read the title. Time and again, I have asked myself what could explain your presence in Caen. I rather presumed that the gentleman who tracked you like a shadow had to be your brother or that a marriage proposal must have been the reason for your visit. I am very unhappy because I refuse to believe that a young woman as beautiful as you isn't engaged, or at least loved by some young man. At any rate, I try to convince myself that you don't love him back.

'You will consider me completely mad for writing these things to a young woman whom I have hardly glimpsed. You mustn't, because I mean everything I have just written. I hesitated before doing so, then I realised that this is my only chance of seeing you again, which is why I have decided to risk everything. I know nothing about you and yet I have to see you again, whoever you are, wherever you are.

'I wait anxiously for your reply.

'Lieutenant de T., Pax-Hôtel, Rue Vanquelm, Caen, Calvados.'

She had kept the letter, but then most would. You would sense at once the character of the person who wrote it, a romantic who has given everything, exposed himself totally. But Priscilla never saw him again, not as far as I know.

And she had a further reason for saving his letter. The Marquis de T. was a reminder, the last before she committed herself irrecoverably, of the life she might have led. Only a day or two before, another upper-class Frenchman, 'the gentleman who tracked you like a shadow', had asked her to marry him.

In the Hôtel Place Royale, in the room where she had been reading, Robert reached out for her hand. Priscilla was not an obvious catch, as can readily be seen by a bleak inventory of her life to this climactic moment. Her childhood was a fragile amalgam of the betrayals, deceits and self-deceptions of those people she depended on to offer her protection and example. If you are rejected by both parents, you would go into another world. You would build a shell, first possibly with books and then by seeking love through men. She was beautiful and so she attracted them, but not one of them was willing to commit himself, at least not convincingly, not until Robert. When finally he proposed in the febrile last days of September 1938, at a time of unprecedented public apprehension – when, as her father wrote in his diary, 'we couldn't believe that there could be no war' – she accepted.

The date was set for 15 December 1938, the wedding to take place in Paris, at Saint-Honoré d'Eylau, the Doynel parish church in Place Victor Hugo – once Priscilla had completed her instruction.

Religion was not the impediment that Robert had feared. Vivien said: 'Pris had positively wanted to become a Roman Catholic like him.' Priscilla informed the priest in Paris that her grandfather was a Derbyshire vicar, and her father a lifelong and devout member of the Church of England, who prayed daily and had 'a good working relationship' with God: 'Nous sommes Catholiques-Anglais,' SPB would inform a French priest in the late 1940s.

Immediately on his proposal being accepted, Robert travelled to England, not to request SPB's permission for Priscilla's hand, but rather to ask Doris in Cornwall. The pair hit it off, Robert later joking that if he had met Doris before meeting her daughter 'he would have made love to her'. But in a letter to Priscilla at the time, Robert vented his exasperation at the English, their grating pace. The train down to Exeter was 'a real wheelbarrow'; in the restaurant car, an Englishman with round blue eyes had described as 'slow' the waiter who ended up not serving Robert's meal; on the train from Dieppe, another Englishman offered to teach Robert to speak English 'very *slowly*'. He exempted his little cork: 'I love everything that surrounds you, everything that you can see with your eyes, everything that you love. Je te quitte, mon petit bouchon.'

So began Priscilla's three-month engagement, a sundial that marked only the bright hours.

They broke the news to Gillian over tea at the Café du Rond Point. On 22 October, Gillian wrote to her mother in New York: 'She is marrying Robert in December and is busy getting her "trousseau" together. She's going to London on Wednesday till the wedding. After, she will live in Paris.' Gillian suspended her reservations. 'I'm so glad she is getting married and has found someone to look after her as she never had a very happy time up to now.'

On her arrival in London, Priscilla was surprised to see the guards no longer wearing bearskins but tin hats. There were anti-aircraft batteries along Horse Guards Parade and the traffic lights were protected by black metal shields with crusader crosses cut out. Four weeks after the signing of the Munich Agreement on 30 September, the euphoria that SPB had recorded was less evident. Then, he had written in his diary: 'The scene of joy is so great that I can't even bawl a prayer of thanksgiving to God. It seems quite impossible to believe. Yet the *Daily Express* says Peace. I dare not write it in capital letters lest it should be false news.'

Priscilla's request for money to buy a wedding dress brought her father down to earth and up against his own shortcomings. On 31 October, SPB wrote: 'I saw Priscilla today for longer than I have for years. It is queer for a father to see his twenty-two-year old daughter only in taxis and a few minutes at a time. She is happy about her forthcoming marriage – and curiously sympathetic about my own great unhappiness in being deprived of her when she was small. It is even more curious how detached I have become. It seems strange to me that I should ever have been so unhappy as I undoubtedly was, and I should never have told her. She found out and wept, so she says, on finding out in *These I Have Loved*. Apparently both she and Vivien were taught, deliberately taught, to hate me.' But he enjoyed seeing her. 'So long as she is happy, I don't mind. She's had a poor deal all through life.'

On 16 November, 'a memorable day', SPB escorted his daughter to the station where Robert had first noticed her. 'At tea I met Priscilla, and Priscilla and I sitting outside the Ladies lavatory at Victoria station had a heart-to-heart talk about her failure as a daughter. I gave her £60 as a wedding present [approximately £3,200 in today's money] and felt mean. It is I who have failed as a father. We were getting nearer than we have ever been when the train was due to go. Robert apparently knows about her abortion and about my separation from Doris.'

Why SPB did not then attend Priscilla's wedding in Paris is a mystery. Perhaps he could not stomach the prospect of seeing Doris, whose legal case against him still smarted. Perhaps Winnie put her foot down. Or maybe he was too involved in his work. In January he wrote to his producer: 'My own daughter was married on the 16th Dec, but from that day to this I have had my nose well down into my children's thriller and written to no one about anything.' It may have been more important for him to finish his Buchanesque novel than to witness Priscilla's marriage.

But he followed the news of it. '*The Times* which refused to print the announcement of Imogen's birth two years ago now prints my other daughter's engagement top of its list.' He glued the *Daily Telegraph*'s report into his journal. 'I console myself with this sort of press cutting. The world may be in a very dangerous state, but it is still ridiculous.'

FAMOUS BROADCASTER'S DAUGHTER TO MARRY.
Among the most interesting of the marriage announcements this week is that of Priscilla Rosemary Mais eldest daughter of Mr and Mrs SPB Mais, who has

become engaged to Vicomte Robert Doynel de la Sausserie, Chateau de Boisgry-mont, St Eny.

Miss Mais has spent most of her life in France, where she went to school, so that when she goes to her new home in Normandy, she will find nothing unfamiliar in the life which differs in so many essentials from that of England. Neither she nor her youngest sister who has just left school share their father's gift for writing: Miss Mais said to me the other day that they felt that one in the family was quite enough!

Priscilla's fiancé had not been sufficiently alarmed to cancel his annual trip to Hungary. With no input from the Maises, Robert, back from shooting what Priscilla thought was 'pheasant or something', took charge of the marriage preparations. He organised the wedding according to Doynel traditions – Priscilla to wear white; and a family procession behind the couple as they left the church.

In Paris, there was snow on the ground. On 14 December, Gillian wrote to her mother: 'Tomorrow I am being "witness" to Priscilla and Robert's civil marriage at the Mairie du 16. Then we are going to have lunch to celebrate. We will be four, as only Robert's brother Guy is coming to be his witness. And on Friday is the wedding at the Church! It's a scream. Dad will be in the 'cortège'…!! It will be so funny to see him walk up behind Priscilla leading a member of Robert's family!…Doris and Vivien and the grandmother and the uncle are coming for the wedding.'

With her mother and sister away in New York, Gillian invited Doris, Mrs Snow and Vivien to stay in Rue de Clichy, the cold fifth-floor apartment with no lift where the Hammonds had moved in October. Priscilla slept the night before her wedding in Gillian's room. Doris, who had been nicer to Priscilla since her engagement, brought them breakfast. Photographers were arriving at 10.30 a.m.

Among SPB's papers is a black and white portrait taken on that morning. 'Pris sent a photo of herself laughing in her wedding dress which made her look about 15!' Priscilla, jubilant, stands on the carpet in the Hammonds' drawing room clasping a bouquet of white flowers, a long veil draped over her shoulder-length hair.

The wedding was at noon, in the church where Yeats's muse Maud Gonne had married John MacBride. In the absence of SPB, Doris had conjured up a distant uncle, a Mr Tapscott of whom no one knew much, to give Priscilla away. There were no bridesmaids. Two little pages, Arlette Doynel de la Saus-serie and Jean de Tonquédec, followed Priscilla up the six steps to the threshold.

All but five of the hundred guests who swivelled to look at her were from Robert's family. Priscilla's wedding was the last occasion when the Doynels convened in such numbers. Marquises, barons, counts – they represented some of the grand branches of French aristocracy: de Bonvouloir, de Chervariat, de Chèvre, du Fay, de Fredy, de Montécot, de Parigny, du Quengo, de Tonquédec, de Thieulloy, de Traissan. The coming war would rip them apart.

Priscilla walked down the aisle on Tapscott's arm. In the sea of faces, she recognised hardly one – until she arrived at the row reserved for the bride's family. The five people who stood there were her mother, sister and grand-mother; and Gillian and her father.

She took her place beside Robert in a large armchair. He was dressed in morning coat and tails. He smiled at her, his expression tender. He did not seem nervous. A priest stepped forward.

It was over quickly. Gillian made notes: trousseau from Paquin, white lace wedding dress, church organs, flowers everywhere, the Ave Maria, three priests in ceremonial robes, Mendelssohn's Wedding March. And then that cortège, relatives walking two by two behind the bride and groom, like Noah's Ark.

Soon she was outside again. A married woman with a strange name, posing for more photographs. Her new sister-in-law Yolande appeared in one, with the expression of a defanged cobra. Priscilla wrote in her diary: 'On this particular occasion she had gone completely haywire – she had on a low-cut black silk frock and red trimmings, black shoes with red heels, and a black hat with a red veil.' Priscilla caught sight of Robert's mother. With some satisfaction she noted Adelaide 'looking in horror at this apparition'.

There was a reception in Georges and Yolande's flat nearby in Avenue Victor Hugo. No tears, everyone in good spirits. Outside, the sun shone forever on the snow, as in a picture. Towards the end of the afternoon they slipped away to a hotel.

Two clouds marred an otherwise perfect day. Priscilla had hoped for a honeymoon in Spain or Morocco, but Robert protested that it was too cold to go anywhere. 'He had decided that one week in a hotel in the centre of

Paris was sufficient.' Priscilla's other concern sprang from a conversation which had taken place two days earlier and touched on a topic that she had brought up before. 'I mentioned that I wanted children badly.' Robert replied that right at this moment he was physically out of sorts, but he hoped to recover and to have children eventually. Priscilla wrote: 'We had still never made love and I was slightly worried about his ability to do so.'

On their wedding night, Robert went calmly to sleep in her arms. Priscilla was tired herself after the day's excitement and did not mind. Like a date that is always pushed back, it could wait. It would happen. 'I refused to think about it.'

Not until the last night of their honeymoon did Robert try to make love. Priscilla was terrified. 'He became a different person. He was no longer gentle and tender, but brutal – his features changed and became distorted – his breath came in gasps.' Sex to her was 'a natural, normal thing – nothing to make a fuss about – it could even be beautiful,' but there was something 'horrible and unhealthy' about Robert's attempt to possess her. After what she called his 'one infructuous essay', Robert would not attempt to make love to her again.

Priscilla had taken on the role of a daughter to a man seventeen years her senior. On his part, their marriage was an extravagant mésalliance, a flutter on the Bourse, or a ring he had slipped on his finger, hoping for his flesh to grow inside her; on her part, a desperate berth, coloured by childhood stories of princes. His impotence was disastrous for the marriage and for her.

14.
VERTÈS

In those few months left before the war, the only victory was to live well. Gillian asked the newly-weds to Christmas dinner. She wrote to her mother in New York. 'It's egg stuffed with mousse de foie gras and truffle, and around it there's jelly and lettuce.' She had ordered the first dish from Prunier's. 'After, we will have turkey stuffed with chestnuts, new potatoes and salad. Then the Xmas pudding and fruit. I shall buy a pineapple as it looks rich, also some dates and some chocolates. There will be coffee. I think it will be a very good dinner.'

Priscilla had supplied the nuts and champagne, but at the last minute had to cancel 'as she was ill again with her leg. It was a pity.'

Robert took his wife of two weeks to convalesce at Boisgrimot for the New Year. His family were present in substantial numbers. Priscilla had become 'tante Priscilla' to a confusing crowd of individuals of all ages, from three months to forty years. She attended church; she learned to play belote – which she considered an inferior form of bridge; she walked on her husband's arm through the icy flat countryside. She adored him, and only occasionally had misgivings when she remembered that terrible night.

Even so, her stay at Boisgrimot was 'not very exciting' – the high point was catching her father's voice on Adelaide's Bakelite wireless, talking about the heroine of *The Secret Garden*. She breathed out when Monsieur Carer rode them to the station.

Her new name had a curious potency: Vicomtesse Priscilla Doynel de la Sausserie. The whole programme, as the French say. But she did not feel very different. She had spent many similar days.

Honeymoon over, she had moved into the apartment in 103 Rue Nollet, which Robert still shared with his brother. Guy showed no sign of shifting. Priscilla could not be mistress of her own home. It was a ghastly set-up.

When he was not gambling at the race track, Guy ordered the food or did the shopping. Georgette came by most evenings for a meal, returning to her own apartment nearby. On Sunday after Mass, dressed in their Sunday best, the four of them solemnly went out to lunch having first worked up an appetite by going for a walk.

Early on, Priscilla had been touched by the way Guy protected his little brother. But Guy's reluctance to relinquish his mothering role started to chafe. Guy's eating habits, his early morning cough, his inevitable arguments about where they should go for Sunday lunch and deciding anyway, soon got on Priscilla's nerves. 'His views and mine were diametrically opposed.'

She could not ask Robert to evict him. Robert was much older than Priscilla. She dared not scratch the precious surface by criticising his actions, few as these were – the effort requiring him to marry having further sapped his energy. Robert never asked Priscilla what she thought about anything, never consulted her, and made conversations over her head. She was 'treated as a child'. Her marriage was not living up to the engagement.

To give his young wife something to do, Robert paid for Priscilla to attend a cordon bleu course at the Académie d'Art Culinaire. Robert did not own a car, so she caught a green platform bus to the cookery school in Rue Léon Delhomme. There, she studied hard 'to try and learn all the things I should have known already'.

Robert's habit was to stay in bed until noon, rise for an early lunch and rush off to the Bourse. 'I would fetch him at 2 p.m. Then we would wander through the streets of Paris and occasionally go to a cinema or have tea in a café. Then we would go home for an early supper and so to bed. I would sleep as soon as my head touched the pillow, but Robert would read far into the night.' It was no recipe for having children.

Why live in Paris at all, she wondered. The same life could have been led in the wilds of Africa. Her new name was her only compensation.

To enliven her day, Priscilla bicycled to the Bois de Boulogne and went swimming at the 'Racing Club'. Since she had no allowance and Robert rarely gave her money, she started to take a few francs out of his pocket for bus fares. One day, he noticed that silver was missing and accused her of stealing. 'So we had our first row.'

Robert still maintained that he wanted children: 'he just thought that there was going to be a war and things might get difficult.' But it was two years since their encounter on the boat-train to Dieppe and they had not made love. It also upset Priscilla that Robert had taken to talking about his ex-mistresses and showing her their photographs. 'They were very beautiful, but had he really slept with them? If so there was something wrong with me, as I couldn't get any result.' She admitted: 'I was very worried about the situation.'

On a visit to England in February, SPB gave Priscilla 'a lot of books' as a wedding present. He found her 'radiantly pretty'. At the same time, 'she looked restless and unhappy'.

Séverine is a beautiful but bored Paris housewife. The heroine of Joseph Kessel's 1928 novel *Belle de Jour* (played by Catherine Deneuve in the 1967 film adaptation) is, like Priscilla, locked in an unphysical marriage with a decent man whose interests exclude her. Séverine breaks the montony by spending her weekdays, anonymously, in a brothel. My aunt took her relief more vicariously – at least to begin with.

Robert had never learnt English, and Priscilla lacked the patience to teach him. But she could speak in her own language to Gillian. With Robert at the Bourse or in bed, Priscilla turned for colour and excitement to her best friend. Gillian was 'the only bright spot in my life at that time. We used to spend afternoons together and gossip by the hour.'

Gillian was surviving – just – on her fashion drawings. She had commissions from *Harper's Bazaar*, *Femina*, *Britannia*, *Eve*, *Rester Jeune*, and, her favourite, *Bonnier's*, a Swedish equivalent of *Harper's* whose readers wanted '5% information, 15% opinion, 85% dreams'. Nothing in Gillian's career rivalled the moment when *Bonnier's* published her first cover. She sat for an hour outside the Café de Paris, looking at the copy on display in the kiosk, waiting for someone to buy it. The cover showed two girls, one dark-haired, one blonde. The blonde was modelled on Priscilla.

Readers enticed by the image of a woman advertising 'Madame Schiaparelli for the blue hour' had no idea that this figure was the twenty-three-year-old Vicomtesse Doynel de la Sausserie. Priscilla modelled for Gillian throughout 1939: in hat and veil; wearing gloves; in a violet evening dress with puffed shoulders.

Priscilla had been chaste two years; Gillian anything but. During those afternoons when Priscilla posed for her, they came clean about their private lives.

Gillian was leading the kind of existence – free, adventurous, with no taboos – which in less than a year the Vichy government would condemn for having caused the fall of France. In the summer after Priscilla's abortion, she had contracted gonorrhoea from a British lieutenant-commander whom she had met on holiday in Saint-Jean-de-Luz. He had come up to her when they were having coffee: 'I feel you don't like me.'

'You're too classy,' she said clumsily. Anyway, she was in love with her married Hungarian artist. But Gillian was also her mother's daughter. She never stopped believing that 'un homme et une femme qui couchent pour la première fois, ça peut-être de la dynamite.'

For months afterwards, her mother questioned Gillian. Had she heard from that charming naval officer?

'No, nor do I wish to.'

'She only likes dagoes,' her father said.

Gillian laughed. She longed to answer: 'Dagoes haven't given me the clap.' Instead, she said: 'That's right. Only dagoes.'

Her nightmare, Gillian told Priscilla, was to be caught by her father behind the curtain, straddling the bidet while sluicing herself with permanganated water. This needed to be done twice a day and the bidet scrubbed with disinfectant. The treatment went on for three months and to pay for it Gillian had to persuade her Aunt Muriel to give her the post office money that Muriel was saving for Gillian's twenty-first birthday.

But she had infected her married lover, Marcel Vertès. In a Paris museum, he slapped her twice to relieve his feelings.

Vertès had been in Budapest when he started 'peeing razorblades'. He sent Gillian a furious letter, the first he had ever written her, ordering her to go to a reputable doctor for treatment. Gillian destroyed it. She did, though, keep 600 of his subsequent letters. 'From the day I met him in 1933 until his death in 1961 we loved each other, we hurt each other, we lost each other and found each other again, each of us living different adventurous lives, but never stopping thinking about each other. That sort of passion does not go with marriage.' In its humid sexual nature and pathological jealousy, Gillian's twenty-eight-year affair with Vertès was everything that Priscilla's virginal marriage with Robert was not. But in their own ways, both relationships were as important, as enduring.

Whether Vertès went to bed with Priscilla, as only much later Gillian decided he may have done, is impossible to say with certainty. The question is crucial because it led to so much more knowledge about Priscilla than would otherwise have been available. What is undeniable is that Vertès was a pivotal presence in both of their lives in the months up to the Occupation. It was during this period that he painted the portrait of Priscilla which hung at the bottom of the stairs at Church Farm.

If ever a man was likely to come between them, it was Marcel Vertès. Unknown in Britain, he is famous if at all for the Oscar he won in 1952 as costume designer for the film *Moulin Rouge*, about the artist Toulouse-Lautrec.

Vertès's work was frequently mistaken for Lautrec's. His talent was to remember a woman's body, still or in movement. Sinuous, sensual, executed at speed, his drawings were erotic without being sordid. In 1948, Vertès had dinner in Paris with Lucian Freud and Christian Bérard at La Méditerranée and he drew 'on some bits of paper tablecloth little girls sucking erected penises, very erotic and somehow not disgusting'. Gillian later tried to buy them, but was outbid.

Vertès was born in Budapest. His older sister advised him when he was fourteen: 'Be a painter and you can have a studio filled with big couches covered with furs and naked ladies.' Aged seventeen, he worked for *Fidibus*, an erotic magazine, and for *Le Courier de Budapest*, drawing the faces of murderers and their victims. He went to the morgue to sketch their heads, and his friend Alexander Korda wrote the text. In 1919, in Vienna, he won a prize given by the Red Cross for his drawings of starving Austrian children, and met a Polish girl, Dora. In 1920, they left for Paris. They married in 1926; he was thirty-one, she twenty-four.

In Paris, he earned his living from drawings, paintings, magazine covers, book illustrations. In 1928, he illustrated Joseph Kessel's scandalous novel, *Belle de Jour*. Most of all, Vertès loved to draw Gillian, etching her outline on a piece of copper using an old-fashioned gramophone needle. There are numerous drawings of her in his letters. Gillian as naked centaur. Gillian sprawled across a hotel bed. Gillian sketching in an open book propped up by a man's penis, presumably the artist's. 'Vertès's letters acted on me as an aphrodisiac, not well written but erotic and full of sperm juice.' The last time she saw him was at lunch at La Méditerranée in June 1961. After the meal, he wrote to her: 'Gill, qui a été inspiratrice de presque la totalité des dessins … ton ami qui t'aime, Marcel.'

Like SPB, Marcel Vertès was a loner who belonged to no movement – fragile, stubborn, moody, impatient. He had a springy walk, and when rattled one eyelid would twitch. If he loathed what he was looking at, he would say in an accented voice, 'Interesting. Très intéressant.' He had said this to Gillian at their first meeting five years earlier.

In London at the time, Priscilla learned the details of Gillian's romance only on her return to Paris. The relationship had begun inauspiciously. Gillian wrote of that wintry afternoon in 1933: 'Strange that encounters which are going to shape one's life don't seem so very important at the time.'

Oscar Kokoschka, the famous painter, had told Gillian to try her hand at fashion drawing; failing that, theatre decors or costumes – 'but stop your *ghastly* nude drawings.' A composer friend of her parents agreed to write a letter to Vertès who had designed costumes for his operettas. Armed with this letter, Gillian had turned up at 5 p.m. at Vertès's studio in 78 Rue de la Faisanderie. She was sixteen. Vertès was thirty-eight and still married to Dora.

Gillian found herself standing before a brusque man, large glasses on his nose, shaving cream around his ears and on his head a bizarre round hat. There was a table covered with China inks. The telephone was hidden by copies of *Vogue*.

His green eyes examined her. They were pale, flecked with orange, and one eye was greener than the other. A small dog yapped at his feet.

She admired his drawings, she blurted; she needed advice.

'I heard the sound of footsteps. Mrs Vertès appeared. A handsome middle-aged thick-set woman, a bit on the heavy side. Vertès did not bother to introduce us – anyway he had forgotten my name.'

Gillian sat stiffly staring at her shoes and the dog while a heated conversation took place in Hungarian. 'We eyed each other for a few seconds, unaware that afternoon that the three of us were going to be involved in a long tug of war which only death would end. After a glance at the girl in the shabby clothes, Mrs Vertès walked out. Nothing to fear from that shy little figure.'

After his wife had gone, Gillian showed Vertès her drawings. 'I'm experimenting, trying to find my style.'

He flicked through them. 'Interesting.' But her nudes were like firemen. Why had she picked on him to learn about fashion drawings? She had chosen the wrong man. In a gruff voice he said, 'Come back when you have found your style,' and returned to his work.

She gathered up her portfolio, said goodbye and left. Kokoschka had been nicer.

Gillian was drawing in her room three days later when she heard 'Dago on the phone!' and ran downstairs, wondering who it could be. Vertès. He apologised for having been so unpleasant and invited her to dinner next evening.

'But I haven't found my style,' she said, taken aback by his volte-face.

'Vous le trouvez. Come without it at eight o'clock, chez moi,' and rang off.

He had given her a meal in his studio. Dora was not present, only his dog. After dinner he said: 'You're not a virgin, are you?'

She looked at him, shocked. 'No.'

'Anyone at the moment?'

She shrugged. 'One makes do.'

'How old are you?'

'Sixteen, nearly seventeen.'

Another evening, he took her to a café, his vile dog Billy pulling at the leash.

On the way home, they stopped before her building. To his surprise, she stayed rooted to the pavement, looking at him: 'I would like ...'

'What?'

'I would like you to embrace me,' she murmured.

He hugged her to him, kissing her on the nose in an extraordinarily innocent way.

She pressed the bell, ran upstairs.

'What's funny?' he asked many months later.

She laughed, throwing a pillow at him.

'Well, I went to see you to be my maître and I ended up being your maîtresse.'

Their affair was now in its sixth year.

Vertès had a Buick, black with tan leather seats. Hood down in the summer, he drove Gillian to an auberge in Ville d'Avray. 'I was called Madame instead of the inevitable Mademoiselle which made us laugh. I always looked like a schoolgirl, une jeune fille bien élevée, Koestler called me.' Vertès said that Gillian was too young to smoke – her cigarettes had to be bought for her. But as Gillian crisply observed to Priscilla, she was not too young to bed.

The majority of their rendezvous were in maisons de passe. Paris was full of discreet places of assignation for couples without suitcases, the addresses passed around by word of mouth. Nothing from the façade indicated that the building was anything other than a respectable hôtel particulier.

Vertès's favourite maison de passe was in Rue Cambacérès. Gillian described to Priscilla her first visit. Her outfit: a tartan skirt, but no petit culotte underneath, exactly as Vertès had instructed. Her perfume: 'Shocking', from a bust-shaped bottle that he had given her. A pretty blonde soubrette with white collar and cuffs ushered her into the lift. The small stylish room was furnished all in black. Headlights from passing cars lit up rose-coloured paper pompons, brushes filled with strands of hair, and two night tables, each with a napkin carrying the words: 'Bless the love you owe your life'.

Gillian also went with Vertès to the notorious One-Two-Two in Rue de Provence. When his finances were low, they ended up in less grand establishments, smelling of cheap powder, where the madam asked, 'C'est pour un moment ou pour l'après-midi?' There was a wash basin, a collapsible bidet hidden behind a ramshackle screen, thin walls. 'We listened once to a couple next door making love. The woman said, "Fort, fort, trésor."'

The madam always banged on the door if they overstayed their 'moment'. Vertès used these places to gather material for his lithographs. Gillian said:

'I would suggest other quarters that I had heard about. So we explored crummy rooms frequented by whores.'

One rainy night Gillian suggested the Panier Fleuri, the brothel where Robert had taken her and Priscilla. Both girls had longed to know what went on upstairs. Gillian was now able to report back. While she sketched Priscilla wearing a pair of Schiaparelli beach pantaloons, she revealed what she had seen.

Vertès escorted Gillian through a metal door and paid the fee, 30 francs for men, 20 for women. They climbed to the first floor. Lined along the corridor were eight portable bidets filled with water. Two women stepped out of a door, in long white cotton shirts and wearing black velvet masks, and quickly washed, wiping themselves with a serviette, and left as fast as they came.

'This looks promising,' said Vertès, pushing Gillian after them.

They entered a crowded room smelling of tobacco 'and wet dog'. A heavy-jowled man in a leather jacket sprawled across a couch, two women in his arms. On Gillian's right, a soldier, belt still on, made love standing up to a woman whose feet did not touch the ground. On the carpet, a man in a taxi driver's cap was spread on his back, a woman's mouth in his black pants. Gillian watched a blonde girl allow, 'with an expression of tragic indifference', a couple to mount her from behind. Was she drugged?

Gillian felt ashamed, but also disturbingly excited. She leaned against Vertès, who put his arm on her shoulder. He slipped his hand under her bodice and cupped her breast with his palm. A warm flush burned through her. Soft, moist, every nerve taut, there on the couch right away, she could ... But he removed his hand. Unappeased, humiliated, she turned on her heels. She tried to leave, but Vertès held her, whispering reassurances, and she stayed.

'Let's go next door.'

There the crowd was less dense. A fat middle-aged woman reclined on a couch, smoking and chatting to two men. Suddenly, the door opened, letting in one of the masked girls, who ran over to the couch and seized the woman's hand, kissing it. 'You're not still angry?' The woman deliberately paid no attention, until the girl stopped her kisses and lifted the woman's skirt.

Gillian saw that she had nothing on underneath. Light from a garnet cloth shade fell on a very white belly and a dark triangle. The girl spread the woman's legs, long and fleshy, with rolls of fat above the knees, and buried her face between them. The woman crushed out her cigarette, lay back.

Vertès and Gillian joined the silent circle that formed around the couch. Ten minutes at least passed before the woman, writhing under the girl's kisses, abruptly raised her arms, fists beating against the wooden sides of the couch, back arching, head shaking in every direction, and collapsed, panting, folded in half, still squeezing the girl's masked face between her thighs.

Some images from that night remained so vivid and shameful, that for months afterwards Gillian blushed when she thought of them; and yet she could not stop thinking about them.

It pained Priscilla to have to listen to what a sensational sex life her best friend was enjoying. It was not just that her married life lacked this erotic dimension. Robert and Guy had few friends. 'They were all forty or over and I found them very old and dull.' Untouched by Robert's fastidious hands at night, posing by day in Schiaparelli's latest outfits, which showed off a figure crying out to be caressed, she feasted on Gillian's stories. The question is, did it stop there?

On 12 July 1977, Priscilla wrote to Gillian in Monaco: 'It is my birthday today and I'm thinking of you and of our friendship which has lasted 50 odd years of undiluted pleasure and happiness for me and as far as I can recall only one serious disagreement which was my fault anyway!' Was the disagreement over Vertès?

Once Gillian had brought Vertès out of the shadows to meet Priscilla, the artist was in touch with my aunt until his death. But the door is shut on their relationship. Something did happen between Vertès and Priscilla, although it is hard to say exactly what this was.

Priscilla ran down Vertès in her novel. The Priscilla-character Crystal 'hated him'. She and the character based on Gillian, Chantal, 'hardly ever discussed him for that reason'.

Was this hatred the source of her later conflict with Gillian? Or could there have been another reason?

The answer lies locked in the portrait that Vertès painted of Priscilla in 1939. While Priscilla was modelling for Gillian, she had also been posing for Gillian's lover.

Their friend Zoë Temblaire was the origin of the story behind the portrait. Gillian heard about it first only after the war. Zoë confessed: 'At the time, we thought you would be too upset had we told you.'

One year older than Priscilla, curly dark-haired and plainer, Zoë was the third member of their trio, the daughter of Gillian's elephant-faced landlord when the Hammonds lived in Boulevard Berthier. Zoë's mother was a strange, furtive creature; Priscilla would see her hurrying along, hat down to her eyebrows, cheeks rouged, on her way to watch a film.

The three girls had known each other since 1930, but because of a mutual dislike between Zoë and Robert, Zoë had not been invited to Priscilla's wedding.

Zoë told Gillian during a telephone conversation fifty-three years later: 'I have rarely detested a man so much,' and thought it odd that with her beauty Priscilla should have married him. Gillian explained that Priscilla, recovering from her abortion and penniless, had little choice. 'She was in very bad shape. Aged twenty-two, marriage to Robert seemed the best solution.' But Zoë's omission from Priscilla's wedding list sparked a grievance that found a destructive outlet.

Gillian wrote: 'What I most disliked in her after the war was her desire to wound, to hurt one.' The story that Zoë told Gillian about Priscilla and Vertès was an example of Zoë's deviousness.

Zoë's first version was as mixed up as her character, which preferred to live at second-hand through her girlfriends' adventures. This is how Gillian initially came to understand what had happened: 'Through me, Vertès had met Pris and had asked her to model a hat for the cover of *Vogue*. (The gouache was not used and he gave it to Pris as a present.) I knew that Pris was sitting for him, but she did not tell me that he asked to meet her at the café on the corner of the Rue Cambacérès, the idea being to end up in our usual haunt.'

Priscilla, according to Zoë, met Vertès at the café, but had second thoughts about accompanying him to the maison de passe. Zoë said waspishly, 'I wasn't astonished at Vertès's behaviour, but what did surprise me was Pris not going to the Cambacérès.' Then: 'She's such a weak character. She floats along like a leaf.'

Gillian had previously understood that an editor from *Vogue* was present at the sittings. She also knew, by now, Zoë's habit of stirring up trouble between Gillian and Priscilla, 'always running down one to the other and vice versa, a proper Iago'. Gillian admitted to Zoë, 'I'd rather have known at the time' – but repeated: 'Pris and I have never cheated on each other.' She held fast to this conviction for most of her life.

Only the portrait can say what really went on. I look at my aunt's face, inscrutably beautiful, to find a key. Something in the smile that is half formed, as she fastens the straps of her hat, reminds me of Kessel's Séverine. One day a man whom Séverine finds odious makes a pass at her. She rejects him, but feels an indefinable voluptuousness which she does not know how to slake.

* * *

For the moment, neither Gillian nor Robert had grounds for suspicion. Priscilla was the outwardly passive young wife of a scion of the French upper classes. Anyone meeting her on the 'Boule Miche' arm-in-arm with Gillian would have taken them for two well-brought up women bent on having an innocent time, while this was still possible.

Gillian associated certain phrases with Priscilla at this time.

'Message reçu,' in her laconic voice.

'Not fit for human consumption.'

'Chum' – a word that Gillian never used.

Right hand on hip: 'I must push off.'

When not modelling for Gillian, Priscilla still attended cordon bleu classes. With Zoë, she accompanied Gillian on rounds of magazine offices to give moral support. On chilly afternoons the three women sat in a cinema with their coats buttoned to the neck. In sunny weather, they sunbathed naked on Gillian's fifth-floor balcony in Rue de Clichy. Or went shopping in Rue Bonaparte for slips to wear under their frocks. Gillian passed on to Priscilla her taste for uncluttered couturier clothes.

One afternoon, late spring, they were walking in the Carousel Gardens when Gillian bumped into her deflowerer. The Baron wore his bowler hat and a small, plump, round-faced young woman hung on his arm. 'My wife Suzanne,' he said with pride.

'I bet there's been blood with Suzanne,' Gillian remarked after the couple strolled off. Meanwhile, she wrote to her mother that a young man had proposed. 'I suppose it is flattering, but when I marry, he has got to be *the cat's whiskers.*' She mentioned Vertès only as someone who could further her career. 'I see a lot of Vertès, we have large teas at the Dôme. He's most cheerful and goes on drawing as if nothing was happening, or ever going to happen.'

Still wanting to be a film star, and feeling depressed about her drawing, Gillian decided to join an acting class. 'Vertès thinks it an excellent idea. He says that after I've had some training he can surely help me as he knows so many cinema people.'

Priscilla was present when Gillian had her studio photograph taken, and for Gillian's debut performance as Agnès in Molière's *School For Wives*. Gillian's elation was contagious. 'I felt like I was throwing myself into space . . . I realised that mastering my fear, my painful shyness, gave me a kick. That's when I understood what made me tick.' Priscilla had felt this exhilaration on the ballet floor.

Dressed in her customary black, Gillian chose the part of Sonia in *Crime and Punishment* for a performance to be attended by important agents. Priscilla and Zoë agreed that she looked like a crow among all the gaudily dressed girls. 'Crow or not, I was the only drama student top impresario André Trives picked out.'

Trives told Gillian to come and see him. She had the physique everyone was looking for, a cross between Michèle Morgan and Simone Simon. 'At last!'

The snag was the year.

15.
WAR OF NERVES

After the mobilisation scare in the autumn, the streets were no longer dark or empty; there were buses again and Britain's Prime Minister was a hero, as Pétain was to become. Even Robert bought a Chamberlain umbrella, shielding Priscilla with 'mon chamberlain' from the snow that fell. But the peace was short-lived. 'In our time' had been the time of her engagement. On her way home from cookery school, she halted before the *Figaro* building and read the newspapers pinned up in glass cases. Fares and stamps were going up. And the price of telephone calls. Vertès did not think there would be a war. Robert was convinced there would.

They were staying at Dinard with Georges and Yolande in August 1939 when the explosive news came that Germany had signed a pact with Russia. Priscilla remembered the last seashore walk, the smell of seaweed and salt. She filled her lungs with the wind blowing from across the Channel.

War was declared a week later. From her hotel room on the Polish border, the *Daily Telegraph*'s reporter Clare Hollingworth telephoned the British Embassy in Warsaw. 'Listen!' and held the telephone out of the window to catch the roar of the invading German tanks. 'Can you hear it?'

Priscilla and Robert rushed back through torrential rain to Boisgrimot. Robert was mobilised and ordered to a unit near Rouen: to prevent German agents from working out the size of the French army, a soldier had delivered his call-up papers in person.

He donned a uniform of sorts, a pair of requisitioned dungarees, but had to provide his own boots and a torch. On a moonless night, Monsieur Carer drove them to Carentan. The station name had vanished. Priscilla watched her husband of nine months step on to the train, two haversacks slung across his shoulder, shaking out a handkerchief to wave, and felt like one of the trees stripped of its iron railings in the now anonymous town square. They still loved each other.

Paris was militarised – you needed a pass to enter the city. She was to stay at Boisgrimot, in the care of his mother. Robert had seen too many separations in the last war, people not finding each other again. She wrote: 'It didn't occur to me not to obey orders. I was used to being treated like a child.'

The chateau overspilled with evacuated Doynels. Yolande and her children; Marie-Thérèse and her children; de Thieulloy children. It had to be explained to them why their fathers had gone away. Georges and Guy had joined their units believing that a trembling Hitler would not attack before the spring. Robert was more pessimistic – the French were gearing up to fight the last war, pushed into this one by the British. With censorship of troop movements, it was hard to know what was going on.

At night in the drawing room, where Yolande with a pained expression stood in for Georges, they prayed for peace. Protected by the priest, the thick-boughed canopy of oak trees and the pigeons in the dovecote, the chateau closed its eyes. Monsieur Carer walked around the house checking the shutters for cracks of light. Priscilla remembered September and October chiefly as a period of religious silence, no bells; and a landscape without signposts. Only the searchlights groping above Caen.

Battle recommenced over the bathroom. Priscilla still insisted on going through Yolande's bedroom, past her sister-in-law's new clothes, sent on approval and laid out on the bed. Priscilla, recognising one dress, did not reveal that she had modelled it. She hated Yolande's deformed elegance, her polite insolence, her virtuous bristle. Yolande, who had not believed for one second in Priscilla's alleged origins, had started to air gentle doubts about Priscilla's ability to provide Robert with an heir.

On their walks through the garden, Adelaide was asking questions. Yolande, hair frilled out from under another absurd hat, nodded, her powdered nostrils growing wide. Yes, why not? Nine months. She should be pregnant by now. The cries of small boys racing each other along the untrimmed hedges rammed it home. It was one reason why Robert had been called up: he had no children.

Adelaide patted her arm. She had not had her first son René until two years after marrying.

With no maternal responsibilities, Priscilla milked the cows, helped Monsieur Carer to paste brown paper strips on the windows, stitched curtains for the blackout. Talk after dinner was of the Maginot Line, and of the German side of the family. What would happen to them? The room smelled of worn chintz and black felt.

It was lonely to be left with all the people you cannot stand. Cooped up at Boisgrimot with her sisters-in-law and their young families, Priscilla read by lamplight and yawned incessantly. The dead deer on the wall kept her company. Behind her eyelids she listened to the rustle of dresses. The fire continued to crackle until it was time for dinner.

And then one day the children and their mothers were gone. Off to another chateau.

Inevitably, they were spun together, the old Vicomtesse and her young English daughter-in-law. They saw a lot more of the priest, Henri Yon. They walked unprompted to Mass, to Vespers. Shrunk back into her tapestry chair, Adelaide could not believe how the past was repeating itself. The sunlight of 1914 was filtering through the window. She looked through it at the tennis court laid by her late husband, the muddle of weeds, and remembered the last time her three sons had gone to war with Germany, the tearing-to-pieces. When Georges had left for the Front, she had said: 'Georges, be careful you don't catch a cold.' Gassed, he had lost half his lungs. She reached out her hand. Priscilla was the future.

From the only telephone, Priscilla dialled Trinité 4319 and spoke to Gillian. There had been sirens in Paris for three nights in a row. Waiters in cafés asked Gillian to pay up front 'in case of having to rush off'. Her family was living on tinned food. The best place to be was the country, she reassured Priscilla. 'Mother wonders whether I should go to London. I'm appalled at the idea of leaving Vertès.' But Daphne had decided, and on 22 September the Hammonds boarded the Golden Arrow for England.

The chateau was freezing. Priscilla stuffed more wood into the round iron stove in her bedroom. She listened to the morning ritual of Joseph Carer bringing the milk to Adelaide next door. And always Monsier Bezard in the field on his tractor, and his lame black dog hopping after seagulls, and the squawk of pheasants.

On 2 October 1939, SPB wrote: 'I heard from Priscilla who says she will go mad if she stays alone in the big chateau in Normandy much longer. Quiet does not bring all people peace.'

If she stood Adelaide's Bakelite wireless on edge and swivelled it in various directions, she could get a good reception. Tuning in one morning, she had caught her father talking about edible fungi – evacuated townees were on no account to eat mushrooms that they found in the fields.

SPB was speaking from the BBC's secret new headquarters: a country house like Boisgrimot, in a wood bounded by an electric fence. The recording vans had branches of trees on them as camouflage against aerial reconnaissance. He had arrived at Wood Norton, outside Evesham, not knowing he needed a password and was arrested when he asked a constable for directions to the BBC. The superintendent had laughed, telling the constable: 'If you don't recognise that voice, you damned well ought to. It's the best-known voice in England.'

That autumn, Priscilla listened to it give talks on caterpillars, fields, and the art of diary and letter writing. Conversational, solid, at arm's reach, her father's voice crackled out of the mesh: 'We have talked about the newsy letter, writing letters to your parents and your friends, even people you don't know, but I wonder if you ever think of the news in your letters which you don't know you've sent e.g. the way you write it, pencil or ink, etc. and what you tell about yourself by the things you write.'

At last, a letter from Robert. He had found a primitive billet on a farm, a house with manure piled up outside. His room was freezing. To heat his hands so that he could write to her, he brewed coffee on an alcohol stove. Overtaken by everything that he had feared, he was working in an office in the industrial quarter of Grand-Quevilly as a corporal – the same rank that he held in the First World War, as if he had been on extended leave for twenty years. He was part of the third Section de Commis et Ouvriers Militaires Administration, a 'rice-bread-salt unit' based at the chateau of Montmorency, an ugly nineteenth-century building set in a denuded park near the oil refineries. Every morning in the icy winter fog he took the tram along an endless avenue bordered by low workmen's houses and deserted gardens. He had to arrive by 7 a.m. and sat at a desk in a large whitewashed room on the second floor, listening to the constant chatter of a socialist photographer, a croupier, a stammerer who had fought in the First World War. In the evenings he drank calvados and played ping-pong.

'Here, life is terrible' he wrote to Priscilla, 'there's nothing, and to top it off it's glacially cold. I'm told that restaurants are closing, but that a few people are still going to bars, theatres and cinemas, hoping to find some animal warmth.' A friend had left for the Front. 'Poor kid, he was a little excited, but tried not to show it. At exactly his age 23 years ago I also left for the Front. How quickly life has gone by and how old I've become. This terrible war has destroyed everything around me, burying even my most precious memories.' He imagined with winter coming on that 'poor Boisgrimot' would collapse a little more each day. 'What will happen to us after these dreadful times? Every day, I beg God to protect you. I have only one wish – to see you happy.'

Towards the end of October, Priscilla was called to the telephone. On the other end, Gillian – back in Rue de Clichy! Fed up with shoving shillings into a gas fire, fed up with drinking tea, and the excitement of Heinz tomato soup having waned, the Hammonds had returned to Paris. The war was unreal, Gillian said. The most dramatic incident had been the sinking of HMS *Royal*

Oak with the loss of all 785 men, including the naval officer who had infected her with gonorrhoea. Otherwise, not a thing, except that her chilblains had restarted. 'But the bliss of seeing Vertès again.'

In November, Priscilla snapped. With money saved from modelling, she bought a second-hand grey Simca for £5 and announced to Adelaide that she intended to motor to Rouen to join Robert. She had her passport, to which she was determined to cling – she had discovered that the British were the only foreigners in France who could travel without a laissez-passer. 'It was the first time I had shown any independence or initiative, and everyone was most surprised, including myself.' Adelaide was reluctant to let her go. But how else could Priscilla get pregnant?

Robert was pleased to see his wife. Her appearance galvanised him to take a room in a large hotel in the centre of Rouen. Each morning at 6 a.m., Priscilla chauffeured him past the storage tanks of the oil refinery to the chateau where he continued to work in an 'executive position of no importance'. Outside, the coldest winter since 1889 was icing the flag-poles and cobbles.

Back in her hotel, Priscilla spent the rest of the day beneath the bedclothes with one of the novels that her father had given her. Saint-Exupéry's *Wind, Sand and Stars* promised more clarity and warmth than what was going on beneath her window: the roll calls, the drill inspection, the guard duties, the non-stop trundle of vehicles. She kept the wireless on all day, tuned to the BBC.

In England, SPB was adapting his favourite novel for transmission. 'I'm trying to read *The Thirty-nine Steps* for broadcasting,' he wrote to his producer, 'and all the time consumed with fury because my *Raven Among the Rooks* hasn't sold like that.' On 9 December, he worked on Buchan's thriller to the sound of dance music being broadcast to the British Expeditionary Force in France. 'It's an odd feeling to be sitting in cosy comfort and know that they're listening just behind the line to the same dances and longing for their girls and England.' Starting in March, he gave a weekly talk to the troops on poetry and prose.

* * *

In France, the days passed monotonously. The English troops had little to do. They listened to SPB on the radio. They organised races on carthorses. Dug ditches. Played ping-pong and soccer (the BEF had donated 2,000 footballs). The 'bore war' they were calling it. Some of Robert's French officers requisitioned cars to fetch hairdressers for their girlfriends.

Anxious to keep alive her pilot flame of independence, Priscilla put on a prickly uniform and joined the YMCA, transporting canteens to the Belgian border and dispensing tea, cold drinks and bully beef to English troops. When Robert raised an objection, she said that she was only putting to use what she had learned at cooking school. She made friends of her own age, other girls in the YMCA and in the ambulance units, like Elisabeth Haden-Guest, who drove a Ford lorry. This was the period when Priscilla learned to drive trucks. 'It was fun,' she wrote.

But she was disturbed about her husband.

In November 1939 General Alan Brooke inspected a regiment of troops from Normandy and was appalled. 'Seldom have I seen anything more slovenly ...

men unshaven, horses ungroomed … complete lack of pride in themselves or their units.' He could have been describing Robert.

Numbed with apathy and cold, demoralised by the guerre des nerfs, or 'war of nerves' as the French called the Phoney War, Robert's spirits failed to rise, not even when the Paris stock market reached a new high. 'He had taken to wearing long woollen undergarments and was full of morbid thoughts and prognostics.' The woollen pants reminded Priscilla of the stockings that her mother made her wear, 'although I must admit that he needed them as his uniform was not very warm'. Still, it worried Priscilla that Robert did not remove them when he came to bed. His hands, long-fingered, the nails no longer trimmed, rested inert by his side. 'I was amazed at the change only a few weeks had made in him. He had always been fastidious and something of a dandy, but now he was unwashed and refused to shave. He had also completely lost his sense of humour. In fact, he had gone to pieces. When I remonstrated with him he merely shrugged his shoulders: "You are just a child," he told me. "You don't understand. I was in the 1914–18 war and I know what wars are like. This is the end. We have nothing to look forward to."'

Buoyed by her youth, Priscilla refused to be gloomy. The trams in the evenings were packed with English soldiers in khaki, young, brilliantined, laughing. She had known several of the officers in London, 'mostly fairly high rank'. Pleased to meet up again with Priscilla, they invited her to cocktail parties and out dancing. Robert was asked to come too, but declined: he did not speak English, he had an inglorious job and he was embarrassed to be seen in his rough serge corporal's tunic. She started going to parties without him.

English soldiers filled two smart cafés in Rouen, a female jazz band playing in each. The largest was Café Victor, with a band dressed as pierrots. Café de la Bourse was the other, where a jolly tubercular woman conducted a less eccentric orchestra composed of younger girls. Priscilla was taken to both, to her husband's displeasure.

On 23 December 1939, SPB recorded in his journal: 'Priscilla writes from Rouen that her brothers-in-law are getting sick because she sees so much of British officers.' It alarmed Georges and Guy, visiting Robert on leave, to observe how fully she appeared to be enjoying herself. Priscilla denied that she was behaving badly, and insisted that she remained loyal and faithful to Robert. 'Various people tried to make love to me, but apart from mild flirtations I behaved myself.' Untouched by her husband since their honeymoon, Priscilla was, even now, leaving a space for physical love to move in. But after her experience of driving a YMCA tea-van she was no longer willing to be treated like a child who did not understand.

Priscilla had two persistent admirers during her months based in Rouen. One, a blast from her English past; the other, a harbinger of the life that she was to lead during the Occupation.

Ted was the tall Irish Guards captain who had courted her in London when she was waiting for Robert to make up his mind. Over a meal in a brasserie in Rue Grand-Pont, he told her how upset he had been when Doris told him of Priscilla's marriage.

'Why did you do it?'

'I don't know,' she said. 'It just happened.' And when pressed: 'He was so kind to me. He replaced the father that I never had.'

'Have you ever regretted it?'

'No ...'

On 27 January, the temperature sank to minus 36 degrees Fahrenheit. Roads were icebound, horses could not move. With Robert stuck in his office trying to drum up extra blankets and socks, Ted pursued Priscilla. 'You used to be pretty, now you are beautiful.' He had not got over his infatuation. He wanted to go to bed with her. 'Life is short, darling. We must live from day to day.' But Priscilla batted him off. She did love her husband, even if he was old enough to be her father and never touched her. 'He taught me all I know. He had a good influence on me.' Furthermore, he was a Catholic. 'He doesn't believe in divorce.'

Her second suitor was more tenacious. Priscilla nicknamed him 'The Scarlet Pimpernel'.

Daniel was thirty-five, a sprightly Paris businessman, with a wife and four children whom he had sent to the south of France upon being mobilised. Priscilla did not find him attractive. He was short, compact, with dark eyebrows that almost joined, and a way of crinkling his eyes when he gazed at her. But he was different from anyone that Priscilla had met in Robert's circle. 'To begin with he was rich and knew a lot about food and wine. He enjoyed life to the full and had been happily married for ten years. He had never been unfaithful to his wife (which was rare in France).'

She had been aware of him in the Café Victor, his keyed-up face weaving through the crowd on the dance floor. From the moment he introduced himself, Daniel laid siege – inviting her to dance, to play poker, to dinner, to a chateau near Rouen that belonged to his in-laws. He teased her. They talked nonsense and ate chocolates named after Joan of Arc's tears. She loved it. But she did not love Daniel, energetic and attentive though he was, and repulsed him gently but firmly. When in the New Year, owing to the fact that he had a young family, Daniel was demobilised, he begged Priscilla to call on him should she ever come to Paris.

Nevertheless, Gillian was the person Priscilla most wanted to see. In one of the long uncertain days of late spring, Priscilla secured a forty-eight-hour permission of leave, and made an excursion to Paris without Robert, standing all the way in a packed train.

Sandbags were heaped up around the fountains. In the pitch dark, it was hard to recognise her favourite restaurants behind the careful drapes. When she knocked at Prunier's, she was whisked through the revolving door before an officer from the défense passive had time to bellow 'Lumière!'

At dinner were Gillian's sister Jacqueline, and her fiancé Max Ruppé, an exquisitely mannered Egyptian Jew in a teddy-bear coat, who was Maurice Chevalier's manager. The couple had met at the Casino de Paris, where Chevalier was performing; Jacqueline had been dancing an acrobatic rumba. When Ruppé proposed, Jacqueline, seventeen, as eager to leave home as her sister, accepted.

Jacqueline admitted to Gillian, 'I never thought I'd be marrying before you.'

'I don't think marriage is for me,' Gillian said.

Vertès arrived late, in an ill-fitting uniform and wearing a hideous khaki rice-stitch scarf which Gillian had knitted for him in London. He held the same low corporal's rank as Robert, but his experience of the war was upbeat. Vertès had been put to work painting murals in the Officers' Mess at General Gamelin's HQ. The General – commander-in-chief of the French army – was a gourmet who had bagged the best chefs for his Mess. According to Vertès, Gamelin had a weakness for 'elaborate confections of meringue, crème Chantilly and spun sugar of various hues'.

Vertès was confident of victory, despite the bad news from Denmark and Norway. The Germans would be 'pushed into the sea'. Gillian wanted to believe him. She was the happiest that Priscilla had seen her. She had done a film test for Marc Allegret and been given a part in *Parade en Sept Nuits*. Max Ophuls had also offered her a small part in *Sans Lendemain*. Jacqueline's fiancé knew all the film producers – he would speak to them about Gillian. 'One believed what one wished,' Gillian said. Priscilla and Robert might even have their baby.

The following Friday, 10 May 1940, German troops invaded Holland and Belgium, and the Luftwaffe bombed Brussels and Lille and airfields across northern France to Le Bourget.

'I have noticed the sun shines at its most perfect on the most ghastly occasions.' On a beautiful spring day from her balcony in Rue de Clichy, Gillian watched the refugees from Belgium. Everyone was streaming south. Cars with red and white number plates, mattresses strapped to their roofs as protection against bombs, suitcases tied with rope, horse carts laden with boxes, peasants seated on top, bicycles, families on foot mopping sweat from blackened faces.

At the Café de Paris, a policeman checked Gillian's documents. Fifth columnists were about. 'We were obsessed by rumours of phoney nuns dropped by parachute. If we spotted a nun we looked at her feet in case of boots.' If the Germans really were floating down as nuns or ballerinas – another rumour – they shouldn't be surprised if Allied troops ravished them, someone joked.

Walking home down Rue Royale, Gillian heard a man's voice behind her. 'Look, they're burning the archives!'

Smoke rose from the Quai d'Orsay. She came closer and saw ashes flying about.

'That's dreadful,' said a girl's voice, 'what are we going to do?'

'At least we're not Jewish.'

But Vertès was. On 18 May, disregarding the petrol shortage, he drove Gillian to Ville d'Avray where they ate a meal of melon, filet de boeuf and fraises des bois, and made love. She saw Vertès one last time, on 7 June, to say goodbye. 'You'll see,' he assured her, 'the Germans will be definitely stopped and your mother will regret her departure.'

On Sunday 9 June, Max Ruppé crammed his fiancée into a car, along with Daphne and Gillian, and drove them to the Gare Montparnassse to catch the train to Saint-Malo. They carried food and water for forty-eight hours and one overloaded suitcase each. 'The train was the last one, it turned out.'

At Saint-Malo in blazing sun they queued until dark for an exit visa. Gillian could hear the distant sound of guns. Her ankles swelling in the heat, she sat on her suitcase in which she had packed her film test. The French authorities took their time, intent on examining all documents. 'Nothing would hurry them, in fact they seemed to grudge us the chance of escaping out of France.'

Around midnight, the Hammonds boarded a battered cargo ship. Gillian pushed through a crowd of passive Italians to the rail. She looked back at Saint-Malo and thought of Vertès fleeing south in his Buick with his wife and yapping dog. 'I wondered when I would see that coast again, if ever. And Pris, left behind in Paris.'

In fact, Priscilla was not in Paris, but at Boisgrimot where the German invasion meant little bits of lampblack floating from the sky.

One of General Weygand's first acts on replacing General Gamelin had been to order women away from the front. That was on 19 May. Priscilla was one of the refugees Marshal Pétain later spoke of as clogging the roads.

In Rouen, Priscilla said a hurried goodbye to her husband – Robert had been ordered from his desk to carry sacks of earth to barricade the bridges over the Seine. The English held responsibility for the left bank, but all those troops who were camping there had vanished.

She drove west in her Simca. There was no traffic on her side of the road. 'But hundreds of cars were going the other way, piled high with luggage and mattresses and all the personal belongings of the owners who were trying to get as far south as possible. It was a pathetic sight.'

The road to Caen was dangerous, covered in broken glass, pitted with steaming craters. Summer had been early and dry, and her eyes were red from the dust. Anguished faces peered at her through dirty or cracked windscreens, many of the hands that gripped the steering wheels belonging to boys or girls. The traffic juddered along at a cow's amble, and a warm breeze blew the smell of phosphorus into her face. She was forced to drive in first gear. Progress was painfully slow.

What she recalled was the noise: the non-stop, ear-splitting honk of car horns, the groan and rattle of engines of all sizes accelerating and slowing, the lorries that thundered past taking with them lines of grey paint from the side of her Simca. The stream of oncoming vehicles extended bumper to bumper to the horizon. In the absence of directions or reassurance, the nation was in flight.

In the sky, sunlight on metal. German planes in tight little groups with black crosses on their wings flew over with a roar. She heard piercing sirens, hellish explosions, horses neighing, children shrieking. The effect of this din on her nerves, the girl who used to wake screaming from dreams, was something that she would battle with for the rest of her life. When she heard the first bombs, she was so nervous that she wanted to laugh.

The invasion had been inconceivably rapid, the German army advancing not at the walking pace of Robert in 1916, but at the speed of their tanks, spurting flames, ploughing up land, crushing into corrugated mats the carts piled up across the country lanes. Every hour another thirty miles of French territory was added to the Reich. Birds let out of their cages flapped about, and horses roamed ownerless in the fields.

Priscilla had read *War and Peace*. It was like a scene from that, she later told Gillian. Exhausted men slept on the grass. She kept thinking that she saw Robert's face among them. The countryside was littered with the debris left by the British army as it ran over itself to reach Dunkirk and Saint-Malo: abandoned jeeps and lorries, packets of Woodbines, cans of bully beef, blankets, even brand-new motorbikes thrown aside in the stampede to reach the coast. He was out there somewhere.

She reached Caen at nightfall. A sentry waving a red light stopped her, checked her papers. Looking back, she saw orange flashes in the darkness.

The clock on a bell tower tolled ten, but over a world where time no longer had relevance.

At Carentan next morning, the level-crossing gates were shut. On the platform where Priscilla had seen off Robert nine months before, women in light cotton dresses stood in tense silence, their eyes fixed to the end of the tracks. Priscilla drove on for a further two miles, then her car gave a sputter and stopped. The strain of driving it in first gear had burned out a piston. She had to be rescued by Yolande, 'whom I still disliked as much as ever'.

The Doynels were back at Boisgrimot in force, but their genius for surviving cataclysms was deserting them. On their faces, pandemonium and fear. Little attention was paid, just then, to Priscilla. Ted, her Irish Guards officer, managed to telephone from Cherbourg: leave right now and he could squeeze her on to a boat. But she refused. 'I have to stay to learn Robert's fate,' she told him.

At Boisgrimot, the country lanes belonged to an earlier world. The birds appeared to be singing more. Then, on 7 June, Priscilla sat in her room, windows open, listening to gunshots. The sounds came from the direction of the pigeonnier. Monsieur Carer, in obedience to a government missive to destroy all domestic pigeons, was shooting the birds.

Two days later, black snow started falling, the sky went dark. The chateau lay under a greasy canopy of smoke which rolled west from the burning refineries at Rouen. Four British officers were responsible for the conflagration: Robert had watched them pass by his window from the ugly chateau where he worked – their mission to set fire to the petrol dumps in Quevilly to prevent the Germans from using the fuel.

The smell was terrible and there was something terrifying about the darkness. 'At midday, we had to light candles,' said Joseph Carer's sister Zizi, the steward's daughter. She remembered the aurora borealis of two years before, the premonitions. 'We thought the misery had arrived.'

Adelaide sat in her wheelchair behind the closed windows. No news of her three sons. In the distance, muffled detonations. Incomprehensibly to those congregated in the room, General Weygand had announced on the radio, which had become the focus of their prayers, that the enemy had suffered considerable losses. Victory was in sight. 'This is the last quarter of an hour.'

On 10 June, the smoke dispersed. Priscilla no longer needed candles to see her soup. In the evening there was a great thunderstorm. She could not work out which were lightning flashes and which explosions from German artillery.

Her relationship with her in-laws became more intense. At 7.30 p.m. the family stopped eating and listened in silence to another bulletin, holding their breath to catch the sounds which would tell them how the war was going. Rouen had been taken. Nothing about Paris, the whereabouts of the French army, the British. Her father probably knew more, but the only means of communicating with England was to wire via New York at 8d a word – and she had no money left. On 12 June, the Germans crossed the Seine. A pirate edition of *Paris-Soir* had put it about that the English would fight to the last Frenchman. Priscilla felt that Yolande held her responsible for the sounds in the distance.

A report on 16 June that the British Government had offered to join France and England together in a Franco-British Union was the last mention of the subject. On 17 June, Priscilla heard the dry coughing voice of an eighty-four-year-old man saying that he had asked the enemy to put an end to hostilities and that he would remain with them in the dark days as the new head of the government. 'Nous, Philippe Pétain …' The plural was majestic, comforting. A narcissistic and doddery philanderer who fell asleep at cabinet meetings had woken with a jerk to find himself king.

Pétain made no mention of England's position, merely hinted that the Old Enemy had failed France. 'In June 1918 we had 85 English Divisions with us … in June 1940 we had ten English Divisions.' Priscilla was aware that she had straightened in her chair. 'The attitude taken by Mr Churchill is inexcusable.' When she heard Pétain say that France owed its disasters to the 'people's love of pleasure' and to 'too few babies' her eyes met Yolande's and Priscilla knew that her time was running out.

On 25 June, the Armistice came into force. Its terms were not divulged, but Yolande and Georgette took for granted that it would bring about their men's release and that the invasion of England was imminent. Weygand's opinion: 'Britain won't wait a week before negotiating with the Reich.' The navy's head, Admiral Darlan, was certain that England would be completely conquered by Germany within five weeks.

Yolande was in the hall, moving forward the hands of the clock. As Priscilla stepped outside into the unmowed grass, she saw grey feathers and black ash. The chateau was no longer languorous, but stifling. She walked down the avenue to the village, now occupied by a German parachute division.

Sainteny had sent 200 men to fight in the First World War. Sixty did not come back and their houses had remained empty. The majority of those who did return were invalids; or, like Robert, they remained traumatised by their experience. One veteran who watched German troops enter Sainteny that summer fell on his face with the shock.

Jacqueline Hodey remembered the morning when the Germans arrived. 'On 17 June, at 11a.m. they made a tour of the place and they came into our grocer's shop. They were wearing helmets and machine guns. One took his bayonet off and we thought we'd be killed. But he was looking for butter.'

No one could get over the amount of French butter Les Fritz ate. They wolfed it straight off the slab like ice cream.

Vehicles surged night and day through the narrow streets. Dark green tanks with black-goggled faces taking in the tower of Saint-Pierre from the open turrets; troop-carriers; motorbikes with sidecars, canvas-covered wagons with branches on them. Robert's general in Rouen had possessed not one detailed map of the region under his command. These men knew every lane.

And how strong and handsome and young they looked. It had needed only half a million of them to rout a French army ten times the size.

French newspapers had trumpeted that German soldiers had nothing to dress in but rags. They survived on a diet of 'fishless fish paste'. Their tanks were made out of cardboard. But the men who marched in neat grey-green uniforms past Sainteny's graveyard, singing their songs, past the Mairie draped with a swastika, looked like film stars: proud, healthy, tanned. 'They must really have been chosen,' a woman told me who had watched them. 'They looked straight ahead like effigies, like something abstract, like symbols. And as the day went on, more people came into the street – and more smiling people. "But look, they behave correctly."'

The villagers had heard of their brutal behaviour in Poland, but Jacqueline Hodey recalled only one instance of violence in those early days, when the Germans requisitioned the teacher's car and manhandled two lady teachers who objected. Otherwise, the men who occupied the vacant houses were very polite as they emptied your petrol tanks, very disciplined. Two of them, simple NCOs – after seventy-one years she could remember their names, Hans Schumann and Albert Jung – were billeted upstairs, in rooms next to her. Jacqueline's mother forbade her to talk to them.

German soldiers stripped outside the grocery to wash their naked torsos from the water pump. It troubled the priest, Henri Yon, the way the young women of his parish lingered to watch these blond barbarians shave or perform their gymnastics. 'They are sons of the devil, you'll catch a disease.' But it was hard to tear your eyes away.

'It was like being fascinated by a snake,' a woman wrote. These men doing their outdoor exercises in short red swimming trunks were so unlike the pitiable shambles of the French army – the columns of defeated poilus whom the Germans marched through the village to an unknown destination, heads lowered, spattered in mud and blood, uniforms ripped, falling down with fatigue. So unlike Robert – wherever he was.

At the entrance to the oak avenue, a German soldier stopped Priscilla. 'I was asked to show a proof of my identity so I showed my driving licence. This had British written on it, but I kept my thumb over the dreaded word and was allowed to pass.'

German planes flew continually over, heading north. After France, England.

Priscilla had become an alien with the signing of the Armistice. It was forbidden to speak English. Forbidden to listen to the English wireless. 'The English tell us only lies.' But if she reversed the positions of the aerial and earth leads, closed the doors and windows and kept the volume turned low, she could hear her father's voice talking about tinned food.

* * *

Tyres on the gravel. A German officer in a scarlet-lined cloak. He strode into the house, down the corridor, past the smoke-cracked portraits, saluted Adelaide in her wheelchair. He was requisitioning the chateau.

Most officers found billets in Sainteny. 'But the Grand Capitaine lodged at Boisgrimot,' Jacqueline Hodey said.

The Captain left it to the Doynels to decide which rooms they required for themselves; he promised to treat these as out of bounds. His men would live in farm buildings or in tents.

In the summer heat, the Captain's men lay on the grass with their shirts off, studying maps of England and plotting the inevitable invasion. The crossing of the Channel was a formality. See that moat, it was no wider than that. President Roosevelt shared General Weygand's view: 'The show is over. I don't think Great Britain can hold out.' The Germans planned to put ashore 90,000 men in the first wave in a simultaneous landing from Folke-stone to Brighton. In a few weeks' time, the Captain would march into SPB's favourite pub in Shoreham and, after shooting dead the publican, tell his men to help themselves. England was doomed. England was everyone's enemy. England stood in the way of the new order which every day brought a fresh decree.

There were so many decrees, it was hard to catch up. Robert's shotguns were to be handed in at the Mairie. The Tricolore was banned, the word Boche forbidden. Clocks had to be moved forward an hour to Berlin time. You could not go outside between 9 p.m. and 5 a.m.

In their bewilderment, the Doynel women were like every wife, daughter and mother of an estimated 1.8 million French prisoners of war. All they cared about was for their captured husbands to be freed. Three empty chairs kept the men's places at dinner.

The days passed. Still no news of Georges, Guy, Robert. At the belote table, the women laid out their cards and waited as they used to wait for the sound of male voices bringing back pheasants and rabbits. The Captain thought their husbands would be home soon. If they were alive. He told Yolande that British soldiers in France had been paid twenty times more than French soldiers. And in surprisingly good French reminded her that it was England who had got France into this war, England who had deserted her.

A chill went through the room in the first week of July. To prevent the ships from falling into German hands, the English had opened fire on the French fleet at Mers-el-Kebir, killing 1,297 French sailors. The Maréchal sounded incandescent.

On 4 July, France broke off diplomatic relations. Pierre Laval, the man appointed by Pétain to lead his government, spoke from Vichy: 'France has never had and never will have a more inveterate enemy than Great Britain. Our whole history bears witness to that ... I see only one way to restore France to the position to which she is entitled: namely, to ally ourselves resolutely with Germany and to confront England together.'

The family mood had shifted. When Priscilla looked at Adelaide's face, it seemed familiar but unrecognisable, like the street in Carentan that had been renamed after Pétain.

In a stream of bulletins, the Maréchal promoted his new order of Family, Work, Fatherland; in each area, Priscilla was made to feel by her in-laws as if his decrees were a direct response to her shortcomings. On 4 August, Pétain ordained it compulsory for beach-goers to wear knee-length two-piece bathing costumes. 'No more shorts, no more French women disguised as men – La Révolution Nationale marche.'

Furtively upstairs, Priscilla struggled to tune in to the BBC. The Home Service transmitted on medium wave in three wavelengths and on short wave in two, including, since February 1940, a new *Programme for Forces*. But it was harder to pick up than before. A radio station was a beacon to anyone flying towards it; to avoid giving help to the Germans, the BBC had established a system 'which confused the transmission from the navigational point of view'. Reception was apt to be good during daylight hours, but poor after sunset and liable to deteriorate during air raids.

Priscilla was only twisting a knob. Even so, it was dangerous what she was doing. The act of listening to her father constituted 'wireless crime', punishable by up to two years in prison – and in extreme cases, later on in the Occupation, death.

One evening, Yolande surprised Priscilla adjusting the angle of the wireless on the window sill, desperate to hear a matter-of-fact English voice. Priscilla waited for her to say, 'Isn't it time you made up your mind?'

The French radio to which they listened downstairs was predicting that the invasion was days away. Very soon the English would be sharing in this defeat. And then Georges would come back and the Germans would leave, perhaps.

Some whole days they managed not to talk of their missing husbands, the war. Georgette, who had hurriedly married Guy in May, scissored up an old grey bed sheet and showed them how to sew it into blouses. Priscilla collected the dogs' clippings to make a sweater. Yolande, doing something with a tablecloth, had learned that the children of the Belgian king were living on the other side of Carentan with their gym teacher.

Convinced that 'Il faut s'arranger avec eux', Yolande could be overheard making nervous boasts to the Captain about her German connections, the Westphalian cousins, Georges' chalet in Kitzbühel. Her small mouth was laughing. She dropped Georgette's name, now that Alsace was part of the Reich. She watched Priscilla take a candle to bed, as if she was going to signal the enemy.

12 July. Her twenty-fourth birthday. Priscilla celebrated it with a walk through the fields. Monsieur Carer, the steward, in a black jacket and a streak of mud on his shoe, took her aside and warned her to be careful of denunciations. And to avoid a certain woman from the village, Yvonne Finel. One word to the Kommandantur about a 'sale Anglaise' living in the chateau . . . Madame Robert must do nothing to alert anyone's suspicion.

She learned to accept the news from Monsieur Virette, the town carpenter, as though she was hearing it for the first time. Ex-Prime Minister Blum's arrival in Argentina with a sackful of jewels. De Gaulle's death sentence. The destruction of London. She betrayed none of her worries to Monsieur Philippe when he insisted on giving her a punnet of his gooseberries, wanting to know who was going to bring in the harvest.

The champing of the German horses kept her awake at night. She thought of Rottingdean and felt a pang for rolling downs and white cliffs. Seagulls flew in front of her windows, mimicking the planes still passing overhead. Monsieur Carer said the birds had come in from the ports looking for waste food. She watched them settle greedily in the furrows behind the tractor that Monsieur Bezard was driving up and down, sowing 'only products decreed by the German authority'. The buggy which had collected her from Carentan now lumbered with wooden boxes to the station, packed with meat and butter for the Reich. Another decree banned shooting. Priscilla had never seen so many hares in the fields, so many pheasants strutting along the hedgerows. How envious Robert would be, she thought.

Had he survived? If so, was he wounded? Was he getting proper medical attention? The Captain had confiscated the Doynel limousine and her Simca, but she persuaded Monsieur Carer to ride her to Carentan so that she could scour the list of prisoners and casualties outside the train station. In the middle of August one afternoon, she watched a woman younger than herself stagger back.

And still they waited. During the last war, someone remembered, many German soldiers were not repatriated until 1921.

On 23 August, a new decree: Englishwomen had to go daily to their local police station to sign a book. Priscilla heard the news before her sister-in-law hastened to bring it to her. She had decided not to notice Yolande, but turned at once to the window when she walked into the room. 'What are you going to do?' She realised Yolande was speaking to her. Confronted with her own deliberately unseeing reflection, Priscilla was frozen by a vision of Winnie with her father and their two daughters in Shoreham. Ignore it, Priscilla replied. 'I reckoned that I could pass as a Frenchwoman any time.'

Across the room a white nose flaunted its hostility. Georgette, too, had a doubting smile. The problem of Priscilla continued to absorb them until, in a flurry of news, all three sisters-in-law learned that their husbands were alive.

Georges had been 'lucky as usual and was in the Free Zone'. He had reached the south of France after evading capture at Evreux; he was expected at Boisgrimot shortly.

Guy had been captured and sent to a POW camp in Germany.

The Red Cross communicated Robert's fate in a salmon pink postcard pre-printed with phrases, all crossed out with a pencil except for the seventh: 'I am a prisoner and in good health.' He was in a camp near Chartres.

'I immediately decided to go and see him.'

Not waiting to welcome Georges home, Priscilla took a train to Chartres. She passed through a landscape littered with derelict cars and prams. She saw no men working in the fields, only women.

The street signs of Chartres were in German, in unfamiliar Gothic letters. A soldier at the Kommandantur issued her with the wrong pass – to a POW camp outside the city. When she reached it, Priscilla was told that her husband was on a farm a few miles away. She started walking. A German truck stopped and picked her up and dropped her in a village that she identifies only as 'C.'

In a field on the far side of C she recognised a dreadfully thin figure leaning over a wooden gate. Robert. She had been impatient to see him, but the badly shaven man who looked at her was in total shock. His hands began to shake. He was in such a state that she did not know if she should kiss him. Tears fell down his face, the only sign that he knew who she was. He fumbled to wipe them away and his eyes stared at her and he smiled.

She walked with him to a café in C where, over a lukewarm chicory coffee, he told her what had happened since they last saw each other three months ago. He had fled Rouen on foot – his battalion reduced from 1,200 to a few sergeants and corporals. No orders. No officers – they had taken off in staff cars. Not even a bicycle. A lorry had come loaded with bicycles from Belgium, but the prices rocketed from 25 francs at the time of Priscilla's departure to 1,000 francs. Robert had stuffed a serviette into the barrel of his rifle as a sign of surrender, and walked and walked towards the south, walking until his shoes flapped apart. He had stolen chickens and lived off half-eaten meals in houses that had been hastily abandoned. Eventually, he arrived in

Tours – France's capital for two days – only to find that the bridge had been blown up. Robert stood on the riverbank, looking at the dead fish in the water and wondering how to cross the Loire, when the Germans arrested him. His rifle was taken away and crushed under a tank. The tears started to fall again.

In Chartres, a group of women had famously smeared themselves with mustard to sting the Germans if they raped them. But the women were left alone, and French soldiers once taken prisoner were not harmed; in the case of Robert, they were not even guarded.

Robert spoke reasonable German and mentioned to his captors that he knew about agriculture. After a few weeks in a camp, he was put to work on a farm, digging up potatoes. The work was hard, he was not treated well. He did not know when he would be freed.

Priscilla tried to sound upbeat. 'But you have no guards, why don't you escape? I'll come again and bring you civilian clothes and we will both get down to the Unoccupied Zone.'

Dejected, Robert looked at her. She did not understand. If he escaped, the Germans would retaliate and seize his lands or imprison his mother.

Her husband's defeatist attitude touched a rebellious nerve in Priscilla. 'Damn his mother and his lands. This was an opportunity too good to miss. From the south of France we could get to Spain and perhaps even to England.'

She asked: 'What am I supposed to do?'

But Robert had frozen up. He told her, staring at his hands: 'I can't make any decisions.'

They spent the night together on the farm. She brought him up to date with the situation at Boisgrimot, the fate of Guy in Germany, Georges' imminent return. In the morning, he told her to go back to Normandy and ask Georges for advice. His brother was head of the family. He would know what to do.

Priscilla had no suspicion of the murky discussions which had been taking place at the Doynel stronghold.

A civilised new officer had come to the chateau, a German doctor with the parachute division. 'For him, uniforms meant nothing,' said Joseph Carer, the steward's son. The doctor was a morphologist, interested in the shape of people's skulls. He announced to Joseph one day, after inspecting the boy's mouse-coloured hair: 'You're not from Brittany. You are from southern east Europe.' It chimed with a story that Joseph's parents had told him about his first ancestors. How knights on the First Crusade, on their way home from Jerusalem, found an orphan by the side of the road, shoved him up on to their saddle and brought him back to Brittany.

The story alarmed the Doynels. If a German doctor, by the mere act of glancing at little Joseph's head, could tell where his family came from 700 years before, how soon before he recognised Priscilla's origins? He had no suspicion – yet – when he greeted Priscilla in the hall that he was saluting an English national, possibly because he had not measured her skull. Like the Captain, he assumed the young Vicomtesse to be French. But the local historian believed that Priscilla made 'a monumental error' when she insisted on holding on to her English passport, which had enabled her to travel unchallenged through the French streets only three months before. 'She believed her British identity would protect her. In July, August 1940, perhaps – but after that …'

Priscilla refused when Yolande bustled her into the bathroom and hissed that she had to flush her passport down the lavatory. Like France, she was physically occupied, but some part of Priscilla's mental space must have felt free through keeping her British papers – her last link to England and to her father. 'The fact that I had retained my British nationality didn't strike me as being important.' That was until the Captain 'put up notices to the effect that any inhabitant hiding a British subject would be shot'.

On 15 October, the Kommandantur in Paris published a decree to come into force on 20 October. 'As of this moment any citizen sheltering or housing a British citizen must immediately declare the name of this person and their whereabouts, and consequently any person found negligent of this act will be condemned to death.' This notice 'produced a big impression upon my mother-in-law'.

The catastrophe that awaited her had been smouldering since the Armistice. She had taken it for granted that the family would protect her, but Yolande was right: Priscilla was not one of them. Word had got back about her behaviour in the jazz cafés of Rouen. Priscilla's close relationship with her mother-in-law was over.

On his arrival home, Georges held an urgent family conference about Robert's English wife. Beside the carved stone fireplace? In the drawing room? Outside, in the oak avenue where the Germans exercised their horses? Details of this crucial moment are not entered into any diary. I can only speculate where it took place and who was present. Yolande? Tante Priscilla's nephews and nieces? Georgette, who had become known to locals as 'l'Autrichienne' – the Austrian? Gillian Sutro was always doubtful about Georgette's attitude to Priscilla, suspecting that she may have intended to denounce her. Did Adelaide attend? Or did the old lady prefer to leave it to her son, and remain in bed, sipping Joseph's milk, her thin hair gathered in a knot behind her head, while Georges made his way upstairs to tell a stunned Priscilla of the Doynels' plan for her?

At Vichy, France's former Prime Minister Leon Blum had watched 'all the courage and integrity one knew certain men possessed disappear before my eyes, corroded and dissolved in a human swamp'. There is no doubt that Priscilla came to feel that this was how the Doynels had behaved. But although she could be forgiven for feeling betrayed, it does not fairly describe their treatment of her.

Robert's family was, in a sense, powerless; the old belle-mère, the daughters-in-law, the brother and heir. Germany had won the war in six weeks; England was about to fall. No one could imagine how long the Germans would stay – the writer Vercors believed that the Occupation might last another hundred years. And Georges, as head of the family, was the sort of local worthy whom the Nazis took hostage to ensure that the local population behaved themselves. The presence among them of a twenty-four-year-old potential Fifth Columnist was a threat to a dynasty which was supple in defending its interests, and limited in its choices. Perhaps it would have been different had Priscilla given Robert a child, but Georges was the only Doynel brother on the spot. If Priscilla was so pig-headed that she would not give up her British passport, why should the Doynels risk death to protect her? Every single person in the village would have known that she was English.

What she remembered was how rigid Georges looked. 'You can't stay here.' The voice was emphatic. His polished round spectacles enhanced his ragged expression. 'My mother is too old to run the risk of hiding you. Go back to your flat in Paris and go to the police.'

'As usual I did what I was told.' Terrified, she caught a train to Paris and registered with the Préfecture as an enemy alien. The German military authorities ordered the young Vicomtesse to sign a book daily at her local police station. She was not to leave her apartment in Rue Nollet after sunset, the city at any time, and Robert's wireless was taken away, although not her telephone. 'Life in Paris,' she wrote about the next two months, 'was far from gay.' She lived through these weeks in a haze.

The waiter in her usual café glanced at Priscilla curiously. The tables were grey with Germans taking advantage of the official policy: 'Jeder Einmal nach Paris' – everyone must visit Paris once. She no longer fitted. Everywhere she looked there were Germans. Speeding past in sleek open cars; on the balconies of the Hôtel Meurice, reading and smoking and, except for small bathing slips, naked beneath their peaked hats.

She soon went through the money that Georges had thrust into her hand. Pinned to the bolted door of the British Embassy, now being used as a furniture depository, a note advised her to seek help at the US embassy, where she was eligible for a relief payment of £10 a month. The deputy British Consul had reported to London in July that the distress of British subjects was growing more acute every day. There was concern that with not enough men to gather or sow the crops 'something like famine conditions' would soon prevail. 'Maybe the BBC would authorise a week's good cause appeal to such cases.' But the British government had priorities closer to home.

At Boisgrimot early in September, Priscilla had heard on Paris Radio that a bomb had hit Victoria Station. 'Bombs fall all over the place, and the fires flame up. Thick clouds of smoke spread over the roofs of the greatest city in the world.' The Luftwaffe strafed the city again the following night, and for fifty-five consecutive nights.

Rumour in France was that 250,000 troops were about to land on the south coast of England. A mysterious gas used to capture the fort at Liège was to be released over Britain to send the population to sleep. Priscilla pictured Piccadilly with German soldiers goose-stepping up it towards Eros, Nazi officers in Bendicks, a red and black flag draped over the upper floors of the Ritz.

Dancing was forbidden while the Germans made their final preparations to cross the Channel. The silence at night was that of the countryside around Boisgrimot, a bark, a car accelerating, the stammer of a telephone, the hollow tap of a wood-soled shoe hurrying to beat the curfew. The Eiffel Tower blinked with red warning lights. From her bedroom, Priscilla watched the searchlights go up, pale and white like Robert's fingers.

Out on Rue Nollet, strange boiler-shaped cylinders appeared, bolted to the backs of buses and certain cars, called gasogenes. Fed by wood and charcoal – some of it coming, she later discovered, from the oaks at Boisgrimot – the gasogenes did not travel fast. The smoke that they belched out gave her a headache.

Lonely, hungry, cold, she found the telephone number of the Scarlet Pimpernel – her married and chaste admirer from Rouen – who was delighted to hear Priscilla's voice. Daniel's wife and children were still living in the south, and he was temporarily on his own in a grand apartment in Rue Beaujon. They arranged to meet. 'He paid enthusiastic court to me,' Priscilla wrote. He invited her to restaurants, exhibitions, bought her clothes, 'taught me to take more care of my appearance, to see my stockings were on straight etc.' However, she refused to let him take her stockings off.

Priscilla liked Daniel and was grateful to him, but 'I must confess that I had no difficulties in keeping him at arm's length.' This was fortunate, because at the end of November the telephone rang. Robert had been released. A crop-producing landowner, he was suddenly vital to the German war effort.

Her husband spent a distressing night with Priscilla on his way to Boisgrimot. Fearing a famine, the Germans had set him free 'on condition that he should cultivate his land in Normandy'. But he would not be able to live with Priscilla whose status as an enemy alien prevented her from joining him in the countryside. He planned to spend the weekdays at Boisgrimot, the weekends with his wife in Paris. Yet what a life it was going to be. How could he farm with enthusiasm, knowing that he was growing his crops for the Reich? Guy was still in Germany. Robert realised the situation would not change. He felt guilt over his capture. He was miserable and difficult to talk to.

Priscilla tried in vain to cheer him up. It was better than digging potatoes in Chartres. Or being in a prison camp. At least he was free.

She remembered his fingers whitening around the knife handle; his bloodshot eyes bulbous and shiny. 'You still haven't grown up. You don't realise what war means. There will be nothing to smile about until this war ends.' There were cuts on his cheeks where he had shaved with cold water. It was one of their worst evenings – made more fraught by the news from Boisgrimot. A tempest had torn through the avenue which the Doynels held so sacred.

Monsieur Carer believed that the wind-broken oaks which fell crashing to earth would have obliterated the division of Rommel's troops that, until the day before, was camped beneath them. The gale came at night and was strong enough 'to take the horns off a cow'.

'I remember that tempest,' said Zizi Carer. 'It was like a tornado. Almost all the trees blew down.'

It was snowing when Robert departed. Left on her own in the freezing apartment, Priscilla renewed contact with an English friend.

Jacqueline Grant – fair-haired, slim, the same age – had arrived in Paris with her mother Ruth. British passport-holders like Priscilla, the Grants had been ordered to leave their home on the north coast. Priscilla visited them in their hotel on the Ile de la Cité.

Jacqueline's father was a professional at the Golf Club in Le Touquet and a friend of P. G. Wodehouse, who was writing the last chapters of *Money in the Bank* when the Germans arrived. Jacqueline had worked as secretary to Wodehouse's wife Ethel, helping out with parties and driving Ethel to Paris to do her shopping – on these excursions meeting up with Priscilla.

She told Priscilla about the May invasion. How she had built a bonfire on Wodehouse's terrace and burned his 'anti-German' articles. How her family and the Wodehouses had fled Le Touquet together, 'Plum' leading the small convoy in his blue Lancia, followed by Jacqueline driving a Red Cross van and her father behind in his Simca. But after two miles Jacqueline's van broke down, its carburettor clogged with sand. Wodehouse reappeared to say that the confusion on the road ahead was too awful and they had returned home, going to sleep with pillows over their heads to drown out the sound of bombs. They were trapped in Le Touquet when the Germans rolled through the pine forest – first the motorcycles, 'noisy, brutal and fast', in Ruth Grant's words, then car after car in which grey-green officers sat in tiers, all facing ahead. 'Nobody seemed to be watching them but the trees.'

Jacqueline's father had since been interned with P. G. Wodehouse in a former mental asylum in Upper Silesia. Ordered with her mother to Paris, Jacqueline retaliated in small ways. One day, a Mercedes drove up with four officers who asked her the road to somewhere, 'and I told them very politely to go in the opposite direction'.

Warmly wrapped – Priscilla in a ski jacket and thick wool socks that Daniel had bought her, Jacqueline in a beaver fur coat purchased in Harvey Nichols a year before ('I'm sure that comes from Austria,' said a German soldier, stroking it) – the two young women walked past their pre-war haunts: W. H. Smith's on Rue de Rivoli, which had once displayed SPB's books – now called 'Frontbuchhandlung'. Maxim's – taken over by Göring's favourite chef. The Champs Elysées – 'Man spricht deutsch' signs in Valrose where, encouraged by Gillian ('That's for you!'), Priscilla had bought a navy off-the-peg frock. This time Priscilla saw nothing in the window – the dresses, hats, stockings all snapped up by Wehrmacht soldiers for their Gretchens.

One day, Priscilla visited Gillian's building in Rue de Clichy where she learned from the concierge that the Gestapo had turned up on 15 June, the morning after the Germans entered Paris. Cyril Hammond's name was on their list. 'We are too late,' muttered the Gestapo agent, when informed that the Hammonds had departed six days earlier. A Wehrmacht officer now occupied the apartment.

Back in the street, Priscilla flicked her eyes to the fifth-floor balcony where she and Gillian used to sunbathe. She was overcome by thoughts of Gillian. 'I missed her badly.'

16.
FRENCH RESISTANCE

In England, Gillian had not forgotten Priscilla. She had arrived in London with her family on 10 June, occupying the lower part of a house in Moore Street. 'Vertès was very much on my mind that day in June. Also Pris.'

Knowing no one in London, Gillian posted Vertès's letter of introduction to the art director Vincent Korda, who invited her to Prunier's for lunch, and in the afternoon showed her around Denham Studios. Korda was about to fly to New York, but he urged Gillian to contact the producer John Sutro. When Sutro came to see Korda off at Waterloo, Korda slipped him a piece of paper with Gillian's telephone number on it. 'She's a refugee from France. She knows Marc Allegret, she's an actress, please help her.' Sutro telephoned Gillian on returning to his office.

At 7.30 p.m. the following evening, 24 June, Gillian observed a large, dishevelled man heaving himself out of a chauffeur-driven Armstrong Siddeley. Her father also was watching from the window.

'"Who is that negroid-looking man ringing the bell?" he asked me, true to form in his usual ghastly way, not realising he was seeing for the first time his future son-in-law.

'"That man is a film producer who is taking me out to dinner."

'I went to open the door to John and said, "Let's go off at once." I saw no point in introducing him to my parents.'

Gillian plonked herself in the back of the car, followed by her dinner-date whose name had vanished from her head. 'For me, John was a film producer who I hoped would help my career.'

John Sutro was thirty-seven. Today, the grass has grown over his name, but at Oxford, where he had founded *Cherwell*, he was at the centre of a circle that included Harold Acton and Evelyn Waugh. He wrote in an unpublished memoir: 'Harold became, I suppose, with Evelyn my closest friend.'

After Oxford, Sutro pursued a career in films, but his character was too vulnerable and trusting. His involvement with ruthless impresarios like Vincent Korda's brother Alexander ended up ruining him; that and what Gillian called 'his fatal weakness' for putting pleasure first. His production company was named Ortus: Sutro spelled backwards.

Gillian was clutching her studio photographs from Paris to show him. But he neither asked to look at them, nor invited her to audition for the film about which he talked with great excitement over dinner at the Dorchester. This was *49th Parallel*, starring Laurence Olivier. The money had at last been found: Sutro had come directly from signing the contract to Gillian's door.

John Sutro's failure to give Gillian a screen test became a grievance that she nursed in bruised silence for forty-five years, not bringing it up until June 1985 when he lay dying in a hospital room in Monte Carlo. 'When John could still make sense and speak, we came out with things which had been left unsaid for many years.' One of her complaints dated back to June 1940. 'I always thought I should have been tested for the part. I could have done it. I was the right age. Even my accent would have been right.' John looked up at Gillian, stunned. 'If only you had spoken at the time.' It had never occurred to him. Of course, Gillian should have been tested. Of course, he should have looked at her photographs. 'Instead, I fell in love with you.'

Their evening ended at the 400 Club in Leicester Square. A waiter fetched John's individual bottle of whisky with his name on it, and they danced in the dim light. 'He swung around, light as a gazelle in spite of his bulk,' Gillian remembered. The sirens went off while he held her. They stayed on, dancing, until the all-clear sounded at 4.30 a.m. When John dropped her home, they found Gillian's mother on the doorstep in her pyjamas, 'worried to death about being out so late with a total stranger in an air raid'.

Gillian tried to put John off when he broached the subject of marriage. 'I told him I was not marriage material, wild, undisciplined, and that the idea of being caged in by wedlock appalled me. I needed, because of my childhood, my freedom.' Plus she could not cook. She omitted to tell him about Vertès.

But Gillian's Hungarian lover had not been in touch. And John was persistent. Towards the end of summer – after learning that Vertès was living in the Waldorf Astoria with his wife – Gillian consented to marry him. 'I had to punish Vertès for choosing New York instead of London.'

She liked John Sutro a lot. His lethal send-ups made her laugh. His father was a rubber merchant, and Sutro's mobile face seemed composed of the same material. With his crunched-up nose, generous mouth and musical voice, he reminded her of Erwin Blumenthal, a photographer she had known in Paris – so ugly that he was attractive.

John's absence of vanity appealed to Gillian. She approved of the fact he was Jewish – he told her that his name in Hebrew meant 'small in the eyes of the Lord'. His self-deprecation touched her. 'Unfortunately, I am a Jew born without the characteristics which make a Jew successful.' In Harold Acton's opinion, John was too sensitive to flattery; but he was also a man of great intelligence and innocence, easily hurt and fragile, and she could picture herself with him. 'Beauty and the beast,' one friend inevitably called them. His pet name for himself to Gillian was 'Boro'. She always called him John.

She was proud that she had never lied to him. 'I told him whom I was lunching or dining with, as it seemed to me far simpler, if someone saw me in a restaurant and then told John, that he knew it already. Of course, I never went into details about what may or may not have occurred later. He didn't ask, I didn't say.'

Their relationship would be open and rocky, but it calmed with the years. 'I was very unfaithful, but at the same time very faithful,' she decided at the end of her life. 'Faithfulness belongs to the heart, not to the body.'

Analysing why the marriage had endured, she thought it was because of an essential tenderness between them. He wrote to her once: 'Darling, I love you so wonderfully, so strongly, so wistfully that there is nothing I would not do to make you feel happier.' And once on a hotel message pad after an argument: 'I love you, I love you, I love you, you are my life, you are my life, you are my life, fortunate, fortunate, fortunate Boro.'

Gillian did not want children – 'I never wanted them even when I was young.' Nor did he. She was his child, as Priscilla was to Robert, and for all her unfaithfulness Sutro trusted her. He continued to regard her, she said, with the eyes of a love that refused to spot the flaws. 'I was like a picture he had chosen because he admired it. If the picture was loaned out at times to various galleries, this did not disturb him. It was always returned undamaged, even if now and then the frame was chipped.'

She repaid his trust. 'I've had lots of adventures, but only one true love.' Whoever Gillian's lover of the moment, her husband remained her priority: 'John always came first. All the men who have loved me have hit on that hurdle.'

Despite its oddities, the marriage made sense. 'In some ways he could not have married more suitably. I possessed all the qualities he lacked: resilience, resourcefulness, courage and total fearlessness. In other ways, he married someone who hated "society" and was a loner who functioned like a man and was highly sexed. John was probably highly sexed in his head, but the body did not follow.' This did not worry Gillian. 'John offered me something I valued far more, marriage with freedom.'

Strangely, sex was the one subject that remained taboo on his death bed. 'That was the most dodgy part of our marriage. And the cause of many disasters.'

Like Priscilla, Gillian had married a much older father figure with whom she had no physical relationship.

On the night before the wedding, Gillian's mother tried to give her 'virgin daughter' the facts of life. 'Darling, tomorrow is your wedding day. There are certain things I feel you should know.'

'Mother, please.'

Daphne looked relieved. For one moment, Gillian felt like telling her about the Baron and Vertès 'and the Rue de Provence and the clap and the brothels and that yesterday I'd been to a gynaecologist whose verdict was "clean as a whistle".'

Meanwhile, Harold Acton, whom John had asked to be best man, was visiting the groom in the Royal Court Hotel – 'so as to see him for the last time as a bachelor'. It is a bit of a mystery whether John was bisexual; Gillian does not say so, but the implication is there. She recalled Acton's 'shrewd eyes examining the girl one of his closest friends had chosen to marry'. Prepared for a disagreeable surprise, Acton was seduced. 'Behold a slim shy girl more French than English, who looked as if she had just been let out of a convent,' he wrote in his memoirs. 'Her voice evoked Colette's Claudine and she moved with the natural grace of a Persian cat.' Acton had quickly become resigned to the marriage, writing to the couple after it: 'You two doves … warmed the old dry cockles of my heart. So that they are now … alive alive oh.'

Gillian described her wedding day, 19 October 1940, as 'a brute of a day'. She wore a black dress, out of memory for her past and out of anxious solidarity with Priscilla. 'John never thought it odd that I got married in black from top to toe. I don't think he even noticed I felt in mourning for France, for the smashed love affair, my childhood girlfriend stuck in Paris and probably in peril.' Gillian had been the witness at Priscilla's white wedding. She bemoaned that not one of her friends in Paris knew of her marriage. Gillian's desolate mood, exacerbated by the extraction of a wisdom tooth, which had left her with a swollen face, set the scene for what happened next.

After a reception in Moore Street and a dinner at the Carlton Grill, the couple were driven twenty miles to Nonsense House, a small rented property near Slough, not far from Denham Studios, which was to be their base for the next three months. As the chauffeur carried in the same battered suitcase which Gillian had lugged from Rue de Clichy, John said with a satisfaction that infuriated Gillian: 'Well, we're spliced.'

The word snapped something. 'Spliced,' she said, tugging off the ring and throwing it out of the bedroom window. 'John looked stunned. I realised I had hurt him. And said "Why do you use that word?" I rushed outside to search for the ring, John lumbering behind. I needed a torch as it was dark.'

The chauffeur appeared, alerted by the commotion. He wondered what they were doing rootling through the bushes – 'instead of being in bed as newly-weds'. It took forty-five minutes on all fours to find the ring, 'by which time we were too exhausted for anything but sleep'.

'Let's go to bed,' Gillian said. 'Tomorrow is another day. It can't be worse.'

She took possession of the master bedroom and installed John in the second front bedroom. 'After all, it was the agreement.' Her wedding night turned out to be even more chaste than Priscilla's.

Night after night German bombers thrummed over Nonsense House. The rooftops of Slough were jaggedly black against the copper glow. A single bomber could start up to 150 fires in a three-mile radius. The raging flames kept Gillian in 'a state of permanent tiredness, living on one's nerves, smoking too much, going out most nights'. She wrote in her notebooks of the long months that followed: 'I was very unhinged during those war years,' and cited as contributing factors her strange marriage and her brutal separation from

Vertès. But another reason for her frenetic behaviour was 'my worry over Priscilla – no news at all from her'.

She shared her worries with Vertès, who had got in touch, sending a hurt note from the Waldorf Astoria after learning that she was to be married. 'You're starting a new life. You must try and distance yourself from me. I've already taken enough years of your life.' Gillian's reply is lost, like all her letters to him, but in it she appears to have offered up the example of Priscilla's fidelity to Robert as a model to which she could aspire, from now on, in her relationship with Vertès: she could be faithful to Vertès despite her marriage.

Vertès, for whatever reason, was doubtful. He wrote back on Christmas day: 'It's so touching, it's so good and kind of you to assure me of your fidelity … but do not compare yourself to Priscilla, mon amour chérie, because Priscilla does not like physical love. But you, you cannot change your temperament.'

49th Parallel kept John away at the studios during the day. For three months, Gillian sat in sullen silence at Nonsense House, glaring with loathing at her smouldering surrounds. She was back in her own country, but it did not seem so to her. Stranded at the end of a long lane in this 'aptly named' house with a pond, and looked after by a dour couple with eyes like black olives, Gillian felt herself to be 'this Brit-Frog', a foreigner with an accent. 'Through my marriage I had gone back to square one again. I was a phantom wife.' What pained her most was the total disregard for France of the people she met. 'I suppose they felt that France had let England down and now they were left alone to face the Nazis.'

Determined to maintain a connection to France, Gillian visited the Labour Exchange after she and John moved to London in the New Year. 'I said I wanted to work for the Free French. The woman said in the bossy way of civil servants, "Mrs Sutro, you can't pick and choose. You'll be put where you're most use."' Somehow Gillian landed up in censorship and was given an exciting 'black list' of people to report on. The outgoing French mail was dumped on her desk, any mention of bomb damage to be censored in case the enemy gained possession of the mailbags. The letters were mainly from the wives and sweethearts of soldiers and sailors posted abroad. 'They all reflected sadness, fear, loneliness.'

Their sentiments reinforced Gillian's sense of isolation. 'As well as missing my friends, I longed to speak and hear French.' In her lunch breaks, she tore back on the number 25 bus to the two-room, first-floor flat which John had rented in Avery Row. 'I yearned to sit again at the Dôme, Deux Magots, Café de la Paix.' She made herself a Nescafé and put an old French record on her portable gramophone, which had to be wound up like a clock. Chewing a biscuit and sipping her instant coffee on the sofa, she listened to Josephine Baker in her childish voice sing 'J'ai deux amours, mon pays et Paris'; or Maurice Chevalier, 'Paris, reine du monde'. Turning back the hours.

And in the evenings haunted the bars and lower ground floor restaurants of the expatriate French: Le Petit Club Français, Prunier's, the York Minster, Le Coq d'Or, Les Ambassadeurs in Hanover Square. 'I was avid for news of Paris. At the Petit Club Français one heard snippets of information.' The worst problem was said to be the heating. People wore wood-soled shoes. The black market flourished. Everyone bicycled, except the Germans; and the 'collabos' who had cars.

The owner of the French pub in Soho, hearing Gillian speak French, once passed her a slice of contraband beef hidden under pommes frites (Graham Greene told her it must have been horse-meat: 'Didn't it taste a bit sweet?'). With butter and margarine rationed, oranges and bananas never seen, and her weekends spent picking nettles in the ditches near Denham ('thickened with powdered milk they made quite a good soup'), Gillian chewed the steak in silence, savouring the images that it released, of tournedos in the Café de Paris, hot chocolate and warm brioches at the Café Weber. 'They brought back recollections of Priscilla and Vertès.'

Still with no news of Priscilla, Gillian resigned from the censorship department in October 1941 and went to work for the Free French secret service, or BCRA. She was employed as a bilingual steno-typist for £17 a month. The first premises were at no. 10 Duke Street. She had to be there at 9 a.m. to take down words phonetically on a small machine. She never learned shorthand and had trouble deciphering what she had written. 'A man hearing I could draw said I would be far more useful in their cartographic section.'

At her art school in Paris, Gillian had learned the elementary rules of poster-drawing – invaluable for stencilling names – and was an old pro with tire-ligne, ruler and compasses. 'The BCRA work required exactitude and preciseness.' Day after day, she stood over a map of the country the Germans had compelled her to leave, selecting and marking up targets for the RAF to bomb.

'Bombing expeditions were based on exact locations of German munitions, hideouts, trains carrying food to Germany or loaded with stolen works of art, hangars where Stukas lay camouflaged, ready to tackle their next bombing of England. I would have cold sweats wondering if I had located the right target.'

Her target was at times no more than a rough plan originally drawn on lavatory paper or a ripped-off corner of restaurant table-paper. One night, from a crumpled sketch 'brought back from France by a Free French parachutist who had found German munitions stocked there', Gillian had to stencil in 'Aubagne' as a bombing target. The name was new to her. She perused the maps in the map-room, where the gloomy Madame Passy was in charge, and calculated the kilometres. There was a sense of fear and secrecy about these bits of paper.

Through her work for BCRA, Gillian came to know agents who parachuted into France, like Vertès's friend, the novelist Joseph Kessel. 'In London,' Kessel wrote, 'all the surviving leaders of the Resistance turn up sooner or later. Framed by the great bay windows of a Chelsea drawing-room, I talked with three men who had been sentenced to death, who smiled as they looked out on the trees in the garden, and who were going back to France to resume command of their group and turn into shadows once more.' In addition to Kessel, there was Gillian's boss, Colonel 'Passy' ('a tall, balding top-booted man'); Wing-Commander Edward Yeo-Thomas ('The White Rabbit'); Pierre Brossolette ('Brumaire'); the actor Claude Dauphin; the aviator Edouard

Corniglion-Molinier; the Hungarian writer Arthur Koestler (who worked at the Ministry of Information and whom Gillian met through Vincent Korda). Chief of operations was Colonel Roulier, who became 'Rémy'. 'Kessel m'a beaucoup parlé de vous,' he told her.

Gillian took advantage of her position. She was attractive, a Francophile, available. 'While John was working on a film in Denham, I was carousing at night.' Several agents became lovers. 'Corniglion loved me, so did Kessel; for the others, I was a beautiful girl of whom they were determined to obtain the favours. Some lovers overlapped when we moved from Avery Row to Lees Place. The prospect of death at any moment increased the sexual urge. One lived in a state of fatigue mingled with a sense of urgency.'

It was natural that Gillian should ask her lovers, when on their missions to France, to find out what had happened to Priscilla.

Of the French agents whom she charged with this task, none amused Gillian more than a pre-war friend of her husband's, Edouard Corniglion-Molinier. 'He was a colonel serving in the Free French Airforce. Later, he became a general. A skilled pilot, a friend of de Gaulle and a shameless womaniser.' Gillian had met him at Wood Cottage, a weekend retreat near Denham which John rented after giving up the lease on Nonsense House. 'My colonel was living in the next cottage with a French woman, Madame Roque-maire, who had been torpedoed and had her buttocks bitten by a shark.' A Rabelaisian character who considered himself irresistible, Corniglion-Molinier possessed what Gillian called 'l'oeil rigolard' – the grinning eye. Witty, with a humorous face, he knew how to make a woman laugh, and how to seduce. 'I don't think he failed when he set himself a goal.' He succeeded with Gillian.

He invited her to Claridge's. The hotel – a convenient short walk back to Avery Row – offered quite a cheap three-course meal. The head waiter was a sturdy Frenchman, and doted on Gillian, who always sat at the same table and treated the place as her bistro du coin.

Life was never dull with the Colonel, who talked non-stop. 'He told me that he had a weakness for English girls, and that virgins smelled of shrimp as they never used or possessed a bidet.' He was proud of his penis which, he proclaimed, had served him well. 'It was a quite memorable one because of its slight curve and perfect size. "Très rare, et très apprécié" – these revelations delivered during meals at Claridge's.'

Even more than to seduce women, the Colonel loved to fly. Gillian knew of his operations to France. She called in a favour.

'As I was worried about her, I told him about Priscilla who had married a Frenchman but who had kept her British nationality. As far as I knew, she was still in Paris, although her husband had some chateau in Normandy. Edouard thought my friend was in a bad position as the Nazis had brought in a decree stating that hospitality given to Britishers, military or civilian, had to be declared at the Kommandantur before 20 October 1940. After that date, anyone harbouring a Britisher without informing them would be shot. I told Edouard about the weedy husband and the brother and sister-in-law. I felt sure they would denounce my friend! "In that case," Edouard said, "she'll have been interned in the Besançon camp for Britishers."

'"Are you sure?"

'"Quite sure," he said. "Hope she's not Jewish."

'"No, she's the sort of girl Germans go for – blue eyes, fair hair, tall, with a marvellous figure."

'"Why didn't she come to England?"

'"She loved Paris and has many friends there."

'"She's made her choice," Edouard said, "and can only blame herself for whatever happens. So stop worrying about her." He gave me a sexy look. "Worry about me instead."'

Gillian wrote in her notebook: 'Although I was not to know the facts, I was right to be worried about her fate.'

PART THREE

17.
BESANÇON

Priscilla was woken by the bell ringing. Bleary-eyed, she opened the door of her apartment and saw a gendarme standing in the freezing darkness. He asked her to pack a suitcase.

'What have I done?'

'We have orders to pick up all British subjects.'

He had received his instructions at 5 a.m. All over France that morning, without warning and with military efficiency, the same procedure was taking place – wherever a woman with a British passport had registered with the Kommandantur.

The gendarme allowed Priscilla to dress in private. From her bedroom, she quickly telephoned her sister-in-law, Guy's wife Georgette, who was back in Paris. As Priscilla replaced the receiver, she could not help regretting that had she stayed the night with the Scarlet Pimpernel, as he had pressed her to do, she might have avoided this trouble. 'The news would be all over Paris in a few hours and I could surely have got down to the south and perhaps to England, given sufficient warning.' She packed into her suitcase the book she was reading, culottes, a pullover, ski gloves – it was bitingly cold; on the way out she grabbed her fur coat and handbag.

The blackout was still in force and she followed the beam of the gendarme's torch down the stairs to a waiting car. She could make out people watching in silence from windows and balconies. The gendarme said nothing and neither did Priscilla as they drove to a building which she recognised: the police station where she walked each day to sign her name.

Inside, chaos. 'Women of all sorts and sizes, of all colours and of all nationalities were gathered there. They had only one thing in common: a British passport.' She presented hers to a policeman, who took down the details. Priscilla was one of 1,965 British women recorded by the Germans as living in the Paris area and arrested on 5 December 1940. Approximately only a quarter had been born in England.

Georgette arrived on foot. Seeing that Priscilla was nearly in tears, she approached a kind-looking elderly lady and asked her to look after Priscilla. This was Miss Norah Beresford, a retired Indian Army nurse. Over the next weeks, the fifty-five-year-old Beresford or 'Berry' became a mentor for Priscilla and for Priscilla's young English friend Jacqueline Grant, who left this description of her. 'She had white hair parted in the middle and dressed over her ears in macaroons, and she mothered us. And she was dressed for the event, as she had very thick woollies and jodhpurs and she looked capable of tackling anything.'

After waiting for several hours with nothing to eat, Priscilla and Berry were packed into a police van and transported to the Gare de l'Est.

Still arriving from all over France, hundreds of panic-stricken figures milled about on the platforms. Women of every class and age, with young children and babies, some pregnant, some middle-aged with dogs. A handful of bewildered old men stood out, mostly poor, who had avoided the round-up of Englishmen in August.

Shula Troman was a seventeen-year old art student arrested that morning. She described for me the pitiful scene, the German soldiers yelling orders in terrible French. 'They were always counting. "Put yourselves in groups of four!" "Young people with young people there, mothers with children there!" We didn't know where we were going.'

Coal-fired locomotives hissed out jets of black steam. Rumours rippled along the platforms. Their arrest was a reaction to Hitler's thwarted invasion, now delayed to the spring. It was a reprisal for the British government's internment of German civilians on the Isle of Man. Their destination was a concentration camp in Frankfurt. Troman said, 'We all thought, because it was Gare de l'Est, we were going to Germany.'

Towards evening, Priscilla and Berry were crammed shivering into an unheated carriage. Through windows on the platform side, stony-faced German Red Cross nurses passed cups of pea soup made from powder, even as soldiers wrapped barbed wire around the door handles to seal the compartment. A shriek of whistles and the train shuddered and began to grind out of the station.

Sixty-one years later, I was in Paris on the winter day when the chief executive of the French national railway delivered a public apology: 'In the name of the SNCF, I bow down before the victims, the survivors, the children of those deported, and before the suffering that still lives.' He made his landmark contrition in the suburb of Bobigny, from where 20,000 Jews were taken to Nazi camps. France was the first European country to give full rights to Jews, and yet between 1941 and 1944, the SNCF carried 76,000 European Jews in cattle cars to the French–German border, and thence to extermination camps in Poland.

Less well known is the SNCF's part in transporting upwards of 4,000 British female passport-holders, not to an extermination camp but to an internment camp in Besançon near the Swiss border.

Who were these women? Incredible to relate, no complete record exists. Priscilla's name does not appear in Besançon's archives, nor in documents relating to English internees in the French National Archives. Priscilla's father never knew where the Germans had interned her. Why was her experience not accurately reported, more widely discussed?

Two explanations seem likely. First, hers was but one of millions of similar stories; a civilian narrative of dispossession, degradation and deportation that no one wanted to listen to by the time it became possible to tell. Secondly, the internment camp was German-run and involved non-French detainees, and so the French were not that interested. Rita Harding arrived at the camp at the same time as Priscilla. 'I still have French schoolfriends who whenever

I mention Besançon look blank,' she said. 'No French person knows. I don't know if they're ashamed. It's never, never mentioned. But now I think about Besançon all the time since I met Jimmy.'

I managed to find Jimmy Fox in Paris. He suggested a drink at the Hôtel Lutétia, 45 Boulevard Raspail. 'This used to be the HQ of the Gestapo,' he said, sipping his tomato juice. It was in this room of looking-glasses, black marble and chandeliers that the Gestapo plotted Priscilla's arrest and transportation.

Fox, a former editor-in-chief of the Magnum photographic agency, had spent his retirement investigating the history of the British internees. He knew more about what happened at Besançon than anyone alive – more, it was possible to believe, than many of those who were imprisoned there. Rocking forward in his red velvet chair, he talked of crucial documents locked in an archive near Paris, of files going missing – the interrogation reports from the SS offices in Rue Lauriston, for example. 'Someone wanted to make a film, but they had a big problem with the Prefect of Police, Maurice Papon. Oh no, it still smells.'

My aunt's name rang no immediate bell, but Fox promised to look through his papers.

Priscilla's first piece of writing after returning to England in October 1944 was an account of her months in Besançon. Her experience of internment dictated the way that she lived for the remainder of the Occupation, and it was so vital for her to get down on paper that she interrupted her love affair with Robert Donat. With the help of this memoir, I tracked Priscilla's journey to the camp.

I also went to see three women who were imprisoned with her:

Shula Troman lived surrounded by books and paintings in a cottage on the Brittany coast. An artist born in Palestine, she showed me her drawings of other inmates, plus a photo of the doctor who had saved Priscilla. Our conversation lasted eleven hours.

Rita Harding lived in Rue Paul Doumer in Paris, in a period apartment of gilt mirrors and cornices. I sought her out because it was possible that she had shared Priscilla's room in the camp.

Yvette Goodden, aged ninety-three, lived outside Sherborne, Priscilla's birthplace in Dorset.

These three women, all widows living on their own, were among the last articulate witnesses who could help me to comprehend Priscilla's experience.

Her fellow passengers were a diverse group, from jockeys' wives to the daughter of an Indian maharajah, who had boarded the train dressed in a veil and a sable coat. Many did not speak English and had never been to England, but had married an Englishman. Some were trapped in France like Priscilla's companion Berry, on her way to Nice to fetch home a friend who was invalid, or on holiday when the Germans invaded. They numbered aristocrats, governesses, nannies, nurses, couturiers, prostitutes, professors, students, bar owners, clairvoyants, dancers, Palestinians, Canadians, Australians, South Africans, plus 487 nuns from eighty-nine orders – including a nun who had remained in the same cloister for thirty-five years and of the outside world had only ever seen 'the planes that flew over my head'.

Priscilla shared her compartment with eleven women, sitting face to face on slatted wooden seats and standing up in turns so others could stretch out. There were no corridors. One woman defecated into her sponge bag.

'You've never seen a third-class French train carriage in 1940 ...' said Yvette Goodden, who was picked up that morning in Bordeaux. She had not forgotten the spectacle of her fellow passengers, some still in their dressing gowns, and of being shunted back and forth during a journey that in her case lasted two days. Goodden, then twenty-three, was married to an English naval commander and had a two-year-old son, Michael, whom she was forced to leave behind in Bordeaux. Like Priscilla and Shula Troman, she feared that the train was taking her to Germany.

Jacqueline Grant, who later worked for British Intelligence, believed 'that Intelligence had informed Churchill and he warned Hitler that if we crossed the border into Germany he would retaliate against German women interned on the Isle of Man.' This might explain why the precision of the round-up contrasted with the disorganised reception. The secrecy surrounding the initial arrests had been well kept, even from the German soldiers who were supposed to guard them. They were unprepared utterly for the arrival of an estimated 3,900 British-passport holders, mostly women, some with screaming babies and dogs, some old and ill, all hungry and anxious and cold.

The train jolted to a halt in Besançon, in the Jura. 'We arrived like a flock,' said Shula Troman, 'in a kind of dream.' Yvette Goodden recalled a funny little station with German troops lining the platform. It was snowing hard. A convoy of vehicles, hastily arranged, waited to bundle the older passengers to the camp. The youngest had to walk. Priscilla's legs were swollen from hours on the hard-slatted seats. She trudged up the hill, passing under a stone bridge and the gaze of French women and children who leaned over the parapet, staring down in silence: they had been told that these women were spies. 'Oh, it was ghastly,' said Rita Harding.

Priscilla was herded through the thick snow and between the tall iron gates of a disused barracks. Just inside on the left was a manège, a covered yard of beaten earth used for exercising horses. Numb and dirty, she was ordered to wait until a cart rolled up spilling suitcases. She dug hers out and opened it for inspection to a German woman who also riffled though her handbag, searching for flashlights, sharp objects, mirrors, books proscribed by the Otto List. The novel that she had been reading was confiscated for a censor to examine. Her name was written down and her passport removed.

Besançon, birthplace of Victor Hugo, means House of Light. The internment camp that looked down on the town – situated in the Forbidden Zone on the Swiss border – was Caserne Vauban or Frontstalag 142. More than half a century later, Gillian was incensed to read that my aunt had called it a concentration camp. But the Germans did designate the penitentiary at Besançon a *Konzentrationslager*, and the term was common at this period, used by Gillian's friend Arthur Koestler, himself a prisoner in France, as well as by Yvette Goodden: 'I call Besançon a concentration camp. My son picks me up every time. Always, it was referred to as concentration camp. We didn't know how bad a real concentration camp was. We just thought it was a place where one was imprisoned.'

Priscilla's father was another to use the term. In his book *Continental Coach Tour Holiday* (1960), SPB wrote in the copy that he gave her: 'We started off again at 2.50 p.m. to face the climb over the Vosges where my eldest daughter Priscilla was imprisoned in a German concentration camp during the war.' Priscilla, responding to all the errors, had marked '!!!!' in the margin.

> There were several German pointers in the town but I saw no sign of an Alsatian dog anywhere.
> Dolores told me of a restaurant in Paris near the Gare St. Lazare where they give you the choice of 150 different cheeses for 100 francs.
> It was not until we were leaving that Dolores told us that Colmar was the birthplace of Albert Schweitzer.
> We started off again at 2.50 p.m. to face the climb over the Vosges where my eldest daughter Priscilla was imprisoned in a German concentration camp duing the war. She was captured in Amiens on 6th May 1940 at the age of twenty-four, and we heard no more of her until 1945.
> At the entrance to the foothills we passed through the quite enchanting medieval Alsatian village of Kaysersberg which con-
>
> 147

SPB never made it to Besançon on his 1959 coach trip with Winnie. The closest he came was Saint-Dié-des-Vosges, a hundred miles north. 'At one place we passed an inn bearing the sign "À la Bonne Truite" just beyond which we caught up with a girl with long flaxen hair of the same colour as Priscilla's and about the age that Priscilla was when the Germans captured her. It was odd and made me feel a little frightened.' SPB and Winnie stopped for a drink at the Nouvel Hotel. 'I was very much moved when Winnie suddenly said, "We will dedicate our book to Priscilla."' The dedication would read, with geographical inaccuracy: 'For PRISCILLA who has good reason to remember the Vosges'. It was the only book that her father dedicated to her.

Priscilla never went back to Besançon. On the sole occasion that Shula Troman attempted to look around the barracks, many years after the war, a French sentry barred the way. Troman laughed. 'I told him: "For five months, the Germans would not let me out."'

To gain access is hard even today. Caserne Vauban has been closed since 2006, but Brigadier Fouquet in command of the 19th Régiment du Génie – which is stationed in Besançon and formerly occupied the premises – organised for one of his men to unchain the gates and accompany me. Excessively polite and equipped with a camera, the officer had instructions to photograph our visit. The internment of British women in what used to be the regimental headquarters had come as news to his Brigadier: he wanted a record. Also in our group was a local journalist, Eric Daviatte.

The officer re-padlocked the cast-iron gates behind us. The cold air smelled of dead leaves. We stood facing a potholed tarmac quadrangle surrounded by buildings dating back to the eighteenth century.

Bâtiment B lay on the far side. I knew where to go, thanks to Jimmy Fox, who had emailed: 'With a magnifier on faded paper and written in pencil, I suddenly found the name DOYNEL and the number of her room.'

A chipped tiled staircase led us to the fourth floor. The rooms no longer had numbers, but B. 71 would have been among the largest.

I walked down a high-ceilinged corridor, darting my eyes into room after empty room. A poster of a beach in Tahiti. Graffiti of a skull. A row of smashed urinals. You could tell that the place had been occupied by soldiers.

The Vauban barracks, built in the Napoleonic Wars, was arranged about a huge cinder courtyard planted with small trees. It comprised three dour buildings, four storeys high, with architraved windows and grey mansard roofs. The Germans labelled them Bâtiments A, B and C. Each building was divided into nine blocks and each block contained 33 sections. Loudspeakers affixed to the side of the Kommandantur, an elegant building near the gates, played German classical music. It was impossible for Priscilla to lose herself in the music since this was continually being interrupted by announcements.

The barracks until a few days before her arrival had housed 10,000 French and British POWs captured in the Maginot Line. These men had been hurriedly moved out to a stalag in Germany, leaving their mess. Jimmy Fox said: 'The Red Cross didn't have time to come and spruce it up.' Instead, two English 'Tommies' in shabby battledress, acting as interpreters, and 150 French soldiers, many of them black Senegalese, stayed behind to receive the new detainees. Priscilla wrote: 'They looked rather astonished when they saw all these bedraggled females arriving.' In the mistaken belief that they were preparing the camp for the Wehrmacht, the POWs had flung buckets of water into the rooms, tossed mattresses out of the windows and stamped on the cutlery. Not for another four days was Priscilla given a tin plate.

A timid French sergeant dressed in leather gaiters led her up four flights of cement steps that were swimming in mud, to room 71. A black stove stood in the centre. Scattered about on the soaking wet concrete floor were thin decaying straw mattresses, old shoes, helmets; urine and excrement were everywhere.

Priscilla looked around. Stacked close together against the walls were simple wooden double-decker bunk-beds. Priscilla let Berry because of Berry's age have a bottom bunk, and took the top one.

Shula Troman in Bâtiment C managed to get hold of two brown blankets. 'I put them over my coat, but a French soldier who was helping everyone said, "Never put them together. Put one underneath and one on top, because it's warmer." Till now, I always do.'

At 9.30 p.m. a bugle sounded and the dismal lights blinked; five minutes later the lights were switched off. Priscilla lay in the dark with her fur coat on. She slept badly, kept awake by sounds of coughing and sobbing. A woman moaned in her sleep, 'I'm cold, I'm so cold.' Further away, Priscilla heard the noise of convoys leaving Besançon, of trains hooting. Rita Harding said, 'I get gooseflesh today if I hear trains tooting.'

The most horrible sound was a tiny *plop* that came not from the direction of the station but from above Priscilla's head. The bugs dropped on to her face as soon as the lights went out. Yvette Goodden said: 'They crawled out of the holes left by pin-ups on the walls and bit your arms and neck, leaving red lumps. Small flat brown things, the size of the top of my little finger. You could smell them coming towards you, a putrid, disgusting smell.' When Shula Troman squashed them with her shoe, they emitted a smell even more revolting.

Priscilla's education at the lycée in Saint-Germain-en-Laye had prepared her. She could cope with the punaises de lit by pouring boiling water onto the wall behind her bed. What she could not cope with was the lack of sanitation.

Hygiene was non-existent in the camp, the lavatories a single hole-in-the-ground privy on each floor, doorless, with ridged footprints on either side of the hole, and covered by a grating. Jacqueline Grant said: 'We called these places "Stand and Deliver".' The latrines were for hardened troops, not suitable for women and children. They were not sanctuaries where you could lock yourself away with a book. They quickly blocked and were closed off, forcing long queues to form outside in the snow for an 'awful hut' known as a 'tinette'.

There were five of these hazardous sheds, built by French POWS and mucked out by a retired English jockey from Chantilly called W. C. Bottom. He was paid for his labours – 80 francs a week – and called out 'Bottom' before he entered, blowing on a whistle. He joked that he had never seen so many bottoms before and that his job might be dirty 'but the money I earn is clean'. The women knew him as Fred.

P. G. Wodehouse wrote of his shifts in an internment camp lavatory: 'until you have helped to clean out a Belgian soldiers' latrine "you ain't see nuttin.'"'

Besançon – les "lavabos"

The women perched on planks with holes in them, placed above a deep trench. The draught coming up through the hole was always icy. Another of Fred Bottom's duties was to retrieve watches and rings that had slipped out of pockets into the trenches. The stench was appalling and the ditches alive with rats 'as large as rabbits'. With one latrine for every 200 inmates, the excrement overflowed on to the ice and mud. It was impossible for Priscilla to keep her clothes clean.

'Most of the older people couldn't cope with the straddling,' she wrote, 'so they performed on the side and everything got frozen up and one sometimes slipped and fell in.' In the local cemetery, a row of white crosses marked the graves of a mere nine out of a much greater number of elderly prisoners who, in temperatures below zero, failed to scramble back out and in the morning were found dead in the snow.

Not until 20 May 1942, sixteen months later, did Sir William Davison, MP for Kensington South, stand up in the House of Commons and challenge Anthony Eden. 'Why was no information given to the public of the indescribable sufferings of these 3,000 or 4,000 British women and children who were locked in trains at the Gare de L'Est for many hours before their 18-hour journey?' Was the Foreign Secretary aware that owing to the conditions which existed at Besançon 'over 700 British women and children died'? Replying, Anthony Eden stated his belief that only twenty-four deaths had occurred.

Bâtiment C.

The nauseating cesspits below the tinettes were hurriedly filled in just before a visit by the Geneva Red Cross, and the number who had fallen into them is unknown. But Davison's figure was close to the estimate of one of the few male prisoners, Samuel Hales, a seventy-two-year-old New Zealander: 'During the three and a half months we were there about 600 died!' Most of the women who perished at Besançon – of frostbite, pneumonia, diarrhoea, food poisoning or the dysentery that spread through the camp in the New Year – were 'buried like a dog' in an anonymous grave.

Priscilla was interned at Besançon during its very worst months. That winter of 1940 was even colder than the year before. Arctic winds blasted up the stairs, slamming shut the door which had to be opened with a penknife. Snow slanted into Shula Troman's room through a hole in the roof, and icicles formed on the inside of the windows. In Priscilla's building, the water pipes burst. She developed chilblains, for which the only remedy was an ineffectual green ointment dispensed by one of the nuns who visited the room each morning in the company of a German nurse.

She was shivering all over. The whole day she was shivering. In Jacqueline Grant's building in January, a mother discovered her four-year-old boy dead on the top bunk.

So cold was the camp – and so under-dressed the inmates – that the Commandant, a stocky former PE teacher called Otto Landhäuser, issued sleeping bags: cotton bed-sacks, crudely dyed in a blue and white check which rubbed off on Priscilla's skin. From a stash discovered in the north tower, Landhäuser also distributed a hundred pale blue military cloaks, their brass buttons still on. 'Alas! They were mostly blood-stained,' wrote a Scottish nun. Children of five and six ran about the yard swamped in these cloaks, which were leftovers from the First World War, belonging to French soldiers who had died. The visit on 28 January 1941 by the International Red Cross – a group said to include Göring's wife – was followed by an official report which noted that Landhäuser had additionally handed out 'heavy boots in leather with wood soles'. These oversized hobnailed army boots were far too large for Priscilla and she continued to walk around wearing her Paris shoes inside them. Many things would fade from her memory, but not the double echo of her cumbersome footwear clattering up the draughty cement staircase.

A young French prisoner in an earlier war had scratched these lines on the wall of his cell.

Only when crows are white
And snow falls black
Will the memories of Vauban
Fade from my mind.

Rita Harding said: 'It's all fresh in my mind as though yesterday, though seventy years have passed.'

The black stove provided the only heat. Priscilla and a room mate collected the firewood in a two-handled box, dragging it back across the snow with a rope. The firewood was damp and green, producing a bitter thick smoke that stung her eyes and made her cough.

'In the room I was in there were 48 other women,' she wrote. Like each of her room mates, Priscilla was assigned further voluntary chores. Stella Gumuchian, who organised the 'tasks' of various detainees, mentioned – in a document unearthed by Jimmy Fox – 'DOYNEL, PRISCILLA' in group 'C'. The functions assigned to Priscilla were: 'waitress/canteen, library, housework'.

The canteen was open two days a week, 9 a.m. to noon, and 4 p.m. to 6 p.m., the items paid for with a prisoner's monthly allowance of 300 francs. Shula Troman remembered buying a tube of toothpaste with money earned from her sketches of other inmates. Priscilla bought ginger beer and cheese. Prices were high, but the canteen was so popular that internees wearing armbands had to be dragooned to stop women pulling off each other's coats as they fought for places in the line-up. Serving behind the counter as a waitress, Priscilla was fortunate to work indoors. Her duties at the camp library also kept her out of the cold and the quarrels for the silent hour between 1.30 p.m. and 2.30 p.m.

The prisoners' library was in the former French officers' library and consisted mainly of 'musty old military history'. The bookworm daughter of a prolific author, Priscilla was a natural choice to spice up the selection. She requested donations from the YMCA, the American Library in Paris, and art books from the Red Cross. The German censor checked the titles against the Otto List, ensuring that none were anti-German or written by Jewish authors. Once lessons started up in February, Priscilla arranged for maths, French, German and Latin texts to be sent up from the town. She used her imprisonment to read Chateaubriand's memoirs and *Candide*.

Her third chore – 'housework' – involved everyone in B.71, and explained why she never did housework at Church Farm.

Older women like Berry were known as the Vestals. They kept the stove going and swept the floor. It fell to the younger women to carry back buckets of water from the horse troughs in the ground-level washroom; to go out into the courtyard and collect the meals and firewood; most of all, to queue.

'We had to queue up all day long in the snow,' Priscilla wrote. 'We had to queue up for letters, for parcels, for our midday "soup", for the canteen, for a wash and for the "lavatories".'

Jacqueline Grant said: 'Our lives became obsessed by queuing.'

The dark liquid that Priscilla ferried back to her building was groaningly called 'cuvée de café'. Another inmate wrote in an unpublished memoir: 'We drank it until one day we found a mass of tousled hair at the bottom of the can.'

At midday Priscilla was out queuing again, for lunch – a monotonous broth called 'Eintopfgerichte', a sweetish brown mixture of animal lungs and barley and stirred with a long wood pole. She wrote, 'Our food consisted of one soup a day which tasted like dish-water with a few rotten potatoes thrown in.'

The meat was generally horse, scraped from one of the pack animals that had been tethered in the manège, and tossed into the aluminium vat by a prisoner with fingers bandaged in dirty rags. Once, a German guard shouted at two girls who had a dog, 'That dog will have to go!' and pointed at the vat; but they sobbed in such a frantic way that their pet was left alone. Nettles were ladled out when there were no potatoes; or mangel-wurzels, a yellowish root used before the war without much success to feed cattle.

The diet gave Priscilla stomach pains. Jacqueline Grant fainted from hunger. 'We just weren't getting enough to eat.'

Priscilla was back outside at 6 p.m. to collect the evening meal. 'We had one tea-spoonful of synthetic grease or jam in the evening' – a dollop of beetroot jelly or tasteless ersatz cheese ('made from the bark of some tree', suspected Jacqueline), and which Priscilla squeezed from a tube on to a finger of black bread.

The German bread was the most horrible aspect of Priscilla's diet. She queued for it every two or three days in the perpetually falling snow, with another inmate holding out a blanket to catch the round loaves that were dropped from a window in a long low building behind Bâtiment C. The ration was two kilos per person per week and the bread, baked from rye and bran, was hard-crusted and green with mould. A date was stamped on the outside, almost always days old. Priscilla toasted her portion on the side of the stove, or else rolled the rancid-smelling uncooked dough into pellets to plug holes in the wall.

She concocted fantasy menus. Her memories of studying cordon bleu relatively fresh, she invited Berry to fictitious banquets. She selected the dishes from her meals with Robert and Gillian in pre-war Paris.

* * *

I tried in Besançon to find anyone who remembered the English internees. At Le Coucou restaurant down the hill, the patron Patrick Langlade greeted my questions with a dubious smile. 'No one ever told me – and I arrived here in 1960.' In 1972, as a nineteen-year-old parachutist, Langlade spent four weeks' military service at Caserne Vauban. 'Perhaps I slept in her bed!' But he looked unconvinced. I was finishing my meal when I heard a shout. 'Come over here!' He had googled it. 'Look! Margaret Kelly. She was at Besançon. The Bluebell Girls were prisoners!'

Until the camp's Christmas Eve party, Priscilla had not realised that the dance troupe and their Irish founder were inmates. Their show at the Folies Bergère was the first that Robert had taken Priscilla to see, three years before. Moreover, she had pretended to the abortionist that she was one of the dancers. Now, in the large shed that doubled as a projection room, lit by candles which the nuns had provided, and wearing dresses stitched from bedsacks, the Bluebell Girls performed what Yvette Goodden remembers as 'a good dance routine – there was an enormous amount of double meaning and the Germans didn't see it and laughed their heads off.' Laughing and sobbing, Priscilla watched comic sketches which mocked the long queues. She listened in silence to the choir that followed. And at the top of her voice with a thousand others sang 'J'attendrai', in a version which included new lines about escaping, and – once the Commandant and his staff had tactfully stood up and left – 'Rule Britannia', 'Land of Hope and Glory' plus two emotional renditions of the national anthem.

It was the largest assembly that Priscilla had attended since her arrival. Several tear-stained faces calling for encores were familiar. Jacqueline Grant and her mother. The wife of a British trainer whom Priscilla had met at Chantilly with Guy and Georgette. A gigantic black man in an apple green turban who made the coffee at Maxim's, one of the small group of men caught in the round-up. A broad black hat also seemed familiar – worn by the sixty-eight-year-old theatre designer Edward Gordon Craig. Priscilla recalled Craig visiting Gillian's parents in Boulevard Berthier. Suddenly vivid in her memory was the inlaid wooden box that Craig, son of the Victorian actress Ellen Terry, had given to Gillian's mother.

At other times Priscilla bumped into women she had known in Paris. An English friend married to a Frenchman and torn away from her two babies. 'She was feeding the youngest still, but was not allowed to take it with her as it was born in France and therefore French. She nearly went mad.' She also met a contact from her modelling days who had worked as a designer for Norman Hartnell and was adept at converting army greatcoats into skirts and bonnets. Then there was Elisabeth Haden-Guest, the daughter-in-law of an English MP, who had been interned with her three-year-old son Anthony (later the inspiration for a character in another favourite novel of Priscilla's, Tom Wolfe's *The Bonfire of the Vanities*). Like Priscilla, Elisabeth had lived in a chateau in Brittany and was passionate about ballet. She had been a regular at the downstairs café of the brothel Panier Fleuri and had watched the same naked girl hoover up coins from the corner of a table ('She tried to teach me how to do it ... '). Elisabeth had been driving ambulances in Rouen the last time Priscilla saw her.

Priscilla left no glimmering wake at Besançon. None of the three women I spoke to recall hearing anything about her or recognised Priscilla from photographs that I showed them; not even Shula Troman, who used to draw portraits of the internees with charcoal from her stove.

Unremarked, she was anonymous, like the nameless in the Cimetière Saint-Claude. In this respect, she did not stand out from anyone else in the camp. Though alive, they were, all of them, effectively dead to the world.

Jimmy Fox had also put me in touch with the journalist on Besançon's main newspaper who had accompanied me around the barracks. Eric Daviatte was yet one more person to register surprise when he learned the story of British internees. He sympathised with my frustration that no one in his town, or in France generally, seemed to have been aware of their incarceration. And told me of his aunt in Pas de Calais. In the Resistance, pregnant, captured, taken to a camp in Germany, baby born – 'then a German soldier kicked it with his boot and killed it.' The aunt survived, but lived the rest of her life outside the village, mad, a taboo. 'I don't even know her name.'

After our tour of Caserne Vauban, Daviatte agreed to run an interview in his newspaper *L'Est Républicain*. His article was given a prominent display. In it, I appealed to readers who might have any recollection of several thousand British women imprisoned in Besançon during 1940–41, and my email address was supplied. The readership of his newspaper was over 300,000. Not one reader replied.

The camp's only full-length mirror was at the entrance, for the German guards to dress properly when they walked into town. On the whole, it was just as well that Priscilla could not see herself.

Her gums turned black from the diet. She lost 30 pounds and stopped menstruating. Her grim face, thin and dirt-streaked, was covered in blue marks from her bedsack and bug-bites. Until the arrival of Red Cross parcels, she had no access to proper soap, make-up or shampoo. Other women's heads became piebald as their dyed hair faded. Priscilla's thick blonde curls falling uncombed over her collar were the chief indication of her sex and youth. A young inmate wrote: 'Jokes were made as often as possible, but in repose these faces were mostly stamped with a melancholy that I shall never forget.' Dressed in the scratchy blue capot of a dead soldier, with a pair of old underpants around her neck as a scarf, and her shoes slopping around inside overlarge boots, Priscilla resembled no one more closely than Robert when he was a POW.

At the police station in Batignolles on the morning of her arrest, Priscilla had asked Georgette to contact Robert. Priscilla was confident that once Robert found out where the Germans had taken her he would not rest until he had secured her release. But the German authorities allowed no post for the first weeks. Almost a month passed before Robert discovered Priscilla's whereabouts.

In January, detainees were permitted to send and receive two letters per month via the Red Cross – typed messages of less than 25 words. Yvette Goodden showed me a communication that she wrote to her husband in Sherborne on 23 January 1941. 'Am well, hope to join Michael soon, inform Swansea, don't trouble.' A censored message like this was not appropriate for what Priscilla had in mind. 'I decided that it was no fun at all. I must escape. I wrote several letters to Robert telling him how awful everything was and I managed to get them smuggled out of the camp.'

Priscilla had befriended a French soldier, Sergeant Lune, who, since he was local, was able to bribe the guard at the gate, and thus went home every night. At tremendous risk to himself, since a pot-bellied Gestapo official nicknamed 'Bouboule' was liable to frisk him, Lune agreed to post Priscilla's letters in a box at the Café Lapostale on Place de la Révolution – and, using the café as a poste-restante, to bring any letters to her.

December passed and then January while she waited for Robert to communicate. On 8 January, workmen started to install indoor lavatories following an outbreak of dysentery. Word in the corridor gave the credit to Winston Churchill: via the Red Cross, he had apparently let it be known that unless sanitary conditions improved significantly he would shift all German civilians in Britain to the frozen tundra of northern Canada.

In the makeshift chapel in Bâtiment C, Priscilla knelt before her new Catholic God and prayed that Robert was following Churchill's example, putting pressure on the German authorities to let her out. Whenever the music stopped on the Commandant's wall, she broke off what she was doing and moved to the window.

From December to early February, the loudspeakers rasped out the names of more than a thousand women who were being freed under certain conditions, either because of ill-health or old age or having left young children at home.

Among the first to be released was Edward Gordon Craig, the man with the black hat, following the intercession of a German thespian who wanted to buy his theatre archive. Early in the New Year, it was the turn of Elisabeth Haden-Guest and her son, the result of an appeal to Fernand Brinon, the Vichy government's representative in Paris. Elisabeth, considered a 'prominent' hostage, was taken to Paris by armed guards to be kept under house arrest. On 4 February, Priscilla's English friend who had been separated from her two children was let go, 'as were all women with children under 16 and all women over 65. This didn't include me or my elderly friend Berry. Then the

Commandant decided to set free all the Australians in the camp. It appeared that Australia had not interned German women, so this seemed reasonable.' The large black man from Maxim's was also liberated: the German clientele had complained about the decline of the coffee since his arrest.

And still from Robert, nothing.

Listeners that winter to *The Brains Trust*, a BBC programme on which Priscilla's father sometimes appeared, heard the panel respond to a question from the fiancée of a wounded POW in hospital in enemy-occupied territory.

What in the opinion of the panel was the best way for a prisoner to pass time?

All that Priscilla's second husband Raymond had to report about her life as a prisoner was that she spent most of it asleep. With no radio and no newspapers, she was blind to the world outside and forced in upon herself.

'We were like children,' said Jacqueline Grant. 'I suppose that being confined to one room with the same companions for most of the twenty-four hours of every day, seven days a week, week after week, brought us back to our schooldays.'

On her bunk in B.71, Priscilla remembered the lycée that she attended with Gillian in Saint-Germain-en-Laye, her only formal education. Like Besançon, the lycée had its own rules and uniform. She remembered lessons starting at 8.30 a.m., and entering class wearing a pink pinafore and carrying a heavy satchel loaded with books. She sat at a desk fixed to the floor. The teacher had walked up and down, slowly reading out dictée – each phrase twice, with punctuation. Priscilla, knowing hardly any French, felt bewildered. She remembered the sound of sergeant-major nibs scratching on lined paper and the purple ink in its little porcelain container on the right of her desk – she recognised the same purple ink in the police station at Batignolles and in the parcel office at Caserne Vauban.

If nature called, Priscilla put up her hand and said: 'Madame, je peux sortir?' She remembered the scratchy rolls of paper in the lavatory, the smell of dust. And the skulls of two girls who had been shaved for lice.

Lunch took place in the school refectory. Priscilla ate at one of the long wooden tables with nine other girls; on her table, a carafe of vin ordinaire and a wicker basket of sliced bread. She began the meal with beetroot salad, potatoes, and a triangle of La Vache qui rit. Then: navarin de veau on Monday, sausages and white beans on Tuesday, parmentier potatoes on Wednesday, cassoulet on Thursday and fish, generally cod, on Friday. Dessert was an apple or orange. At 4 p.m., she was entitled to a petit pain, grabbed from a woman distributing them at the open window of the refectoire. In her room at Besançon, she remembered with a pang of hunger those petits pains passed through the window.

For the first time, Priscilla wished she had gone back to England. She wished the cold outside was winter from her childhood in Hove – a log fire in the main room and her father singing 'Widecombe Fair'. She remembered walking with him through the snow-covered Grampians, the whole length of Loch Rannoch below. And his broadcasts on the unemployed. The family in Birmingham who had 11s. 4d. a week to spend on food. The slag heaps in Glasgow, men lying on the still-smouldering embers in an attempt to keep warm, leaving one side of their body frozen, one side scorched. She remembered him saying how dangerous it was to be left on your own with nothing to do. 'Few things are harder than the capacity to put yourself in the place of someone who is suffering if you are not suffering. If you have never been out of work you can no more realise the horror of unemployment than you can realise the horror of leprosy.'

Sitting in her coat before the stove, which smoked so thickly that the windows had to be opened, Priscilla thought of London fog.

In London, SPB was broadcasting *The Kitchen Front* to an audience of five million. 'In many ways this was my finest hour.' At fifty-four, he was too old to don goggles and fight, but after a stint as an air raid warden on the South Downs, he soared on the airwaves. The war allowed him to expand his repertoire. Following his series on the countryside and on the unemployed, and after his years of broadcasting on English literature to schools and the troops and the Empire, he had found a new role: 'to play the part of low comedian'.

He had received the telegram in early June: CAN YOU COME BROADCASTING HOUSE TOMORROW MIDDAY TO DISCUSS URGENT BROADCASTING PROPOSAL.

SPB was asked to join a panel for a series of early morning discussions based on information supplied by the Ministry of Food. The five-minute talks would go out at 8.15–8.20 a.m. and SPB would be paid a fee of £6. The series was to be called *The Kitchen Front*. Largely because of it, SPB would become 'most unexpectedly, one of the most famous men in England'.

The first series kicked off on a glorious summer morning as the Germans advanced on the French capital. 'Friday 14 June 1940 Germans take Paris. I broadcast food at 8.15 a.m.' He cast himself as a Socratic gadfly, irritating his listeners into sitting up and concentrating on the cheap and easy recipes that he offered. 'But the most needful recipe is the general one of cheerfulness.' He promoted Potato Pete and issued warnings against the 'Squander Bug' – slogans which gave one of his producers, George Orwell, whose wife Eileen worked on the programme, good copy for the Prolefeed dispensed by the Ministry of Truth in his novel *Nineteen Eighty-Four*.

SPB wrote in his diary that the programmes created a 'quite extraordinary interest', and told with relish the reaction of a porter on Taunton station who, spying the letters SPBM embossed on his attaché case, exclaimed: 'The one and only.' Letters from listeners poured in at the rate of about 500 a day, to tell Priscilla's father that he was their early morning cup of tea, their daily tonic, and causing even Winston Churchill to say of him, 'That man Mais makes me feel tired.' SPB's producers congratulated him. '"The Mais Tonic" … seems to have been exhilarating a lot of people recently …'

'I am desperately keen on the series,' SPB replied. 'After all, it was my child.'

He had not heard from Priscilla since 6 May. On 20 June, halfway through the series, wearing the red tie that she had given him for his fiftieth birthday, he lunched with Alec Waugh at the Gargoyle Club, anxious to learn at first hand what was happening in France. Waugh had been evacuated from Boulogne on 23 May. He had no news of Priscilla.

On 22 January 1941, a van drove through the gates. Loudspeakers announced the arrival of food parcels from England. Within seconds, women were running out to snatch packages. In each was a tin: 18 inches by 9, containing dried milk, blackcurrant purée, steak and kidney pudding, Cooper's marmalade, Lyon's tea and Woodbine cigarettes. And a greeting card from the Queen.

Priscilla wove the string into table mats and used the tins for cooking. Nothing was wasted. Whatever she could live without, she bartered. She swapped cigarettes for soap, and gave three Woodbines to Sergeant Lune in exchange for posting another letter to Robert.

She had not lost faith that her husband was agitating on her behalf. Ruth Grant, after being released in February, hammered on door after influential door in a bid to extract her daughter. Jacqueline said: 'Mother did everything she could think of to get me out of the camp and plodded from one Kommandantur to another, saying her daughter was skin and bone and telling them they were inhuman, unmenschlich.' Her persistence seems to have worked: the Germans finally freed Jacqueline in July.

Classes started up in the projection room. Miss Owen taught Babylonian history. Professor Eccles, an Oxford don, gave lessons in French literature. Out in the courtyard, Miss Stanley, a lesbian with wonderful legs, organised open-air gymnastics. Yvette Goodden joined a Welsh choir. 'I made a note in my will that I want "Bread of heaven" sung at my funeral.' She belted out her descants in the shed where Priscilla peeled frost-blackened mangel-wurzels.

Rita Harding said: 'I don't know how the days passed. We just meandered.'

Some did go mad. They remained in bed weeping or reciting Shakespeare. Or reverted to childhood, speaking in a baby voice. An Indian mother with three children attempted to burn herself to death.

Fortune-telling flourished in this febrile atmosphere, where no one could imagine the future. Among Priscilla's papers is the result of a palm-reading: 'In your life you have had some difficult passages. Very soon you will receive news from a person who is dear to you and with whom a little later you will make a happy journey.'

A happy journey . . . Around her, Priscilla was conscious of people trying to get out of the camp to reach the Swiss mountains. Jacqueline Grant said: 'We all used to stand up and look out of the window and see lovely hills and we'd protest, "If only we could escape."' She remembered 'a dear little roly-poly woman, very plump, beautiful white sweater, I'm afraid we called her United Dairies,' who jumped off a high wall in her tight sweater and high heels, only to land on a group of German sentries. Not all attempts were so ill-planned. 'Several people did escape,' Priscilla wrote. 'Some dressed in German nurses' uniforms and some in Red Cross uniforms.' A nurse, appropriating a patient's X-rays, managed to reach home on medical grounds. Two Senegalese POWs carried out a young woman curled up inside a dustbin. From Paris came news that Elisabeth Haden-Guest had escaped with her son through the station buffet immediately on arriving at the Gare de Lyon. These reports intensified Priscilla's despair – what Jacqueline Grant called that 'awful feeling of not being able to get out, being trapped and very young. One was afraid of going round the bend.' Jaqueline was thinking of Priscilla in particular – and was not the only person alarmed by her mental state. 'Berry was very worried about Pris and she said, "We must get you out of here," and Pris said, "I don't see how you can because I'm perfectly healthy."'

Sergeant Lune had pinned the letter inside his narrow khaki trousers. Priscilla recognised her husband's minute handwriting. But her excitement evaporated even as she read it. 'Robert answered solemnly that I was not to do anything rash because of his lands and his mother etc.' He had not lifted a finger. 'I was beginning to get very fed up with this line of argument.'

It had taken six months for Priscilla to appreciate the extent to which Robert and his family had failed to support her. She never forgave them. 'After all, I was going through this catastrophe entirely because of him.'

Now that he knew where she was, Robert did at least organise food parcels to be sent from Boisgrimot. In Normandy, there was no shortage of fresh dairy products. Maurice Bezard, working on Robert's farm, recollected, 'As part of our lease, we needed to supply butter, chickens, cream and milk. The family would come to Boisgrimot to eat – and they would eat well, above all during the war.' The steward's daughter packed up the meat and butter and sent a weekly food packet to Paris, from where it was forwarded to the parcel office in Besançon.

Thanks to the neatness of her handwriting, Yvette Goodden secured a position in the parcel office, a job that required her to write out a list of the recipients and pin it on the door by lunchtime. In the presence of a German soldier, Goodden or another volunteer opened Priscilla's packets in front of her, to check whether they contained books or written material; or forbidden products – like white 'meta' tablets used to heat up food. 'The Germans were afraid that if you chewed them, you would commit suicide.'

Priscilla was one of few internees to receive fresh food parcels. 'Most people had to wait for things to come from England, and of course that took months.' She shared the Doynels' chicken, cheese and butter with her room mates, which meant that her diet did not radically improve. Quite often she bartered her portion to post yet more uncensored letters, not all of them to Robert.

'I even had a visit while I was there.'

In early February, Sergeant Lune sidled into her room. A man had smuggled himself into the camp, desperate to see Priscilla. He refused to give his name, saying only that she would know him as 'The Scarlet Pimpernel'. He was downstairs.

Tears sprang into Daniel's eyes when he saw how she looked. The last occasion they had seen each other was the night before her arrest, when Daniel invited her to dinner in Rue Beaujon. Priscilla had found the scene set for seduction: flowers everywhere, champagne – which she had primly refused to drink. Daniel cooked her a meal and afterwards, ignoring his warm invitation to stay, she put on her coat. When he repeated his request ponderously, staring out in front of him, she said: 'I had better go home in case Robert rings up early.' It was 11 p.m. by the time she returned to her empty apartment. 'Because of my virtuous behaviour I spent the next three months in a concentration camp.'

Besançon had changed her. She was touched by Daniel's unequivocal response to her appeal for help. He 'moved heaven and earth to get me out of the camp' – whereas Robert, she wrote scathingly, 'did nothing at all'. She did not reveal how the Scarlet Pimpernel planned to extract her, but his willingness to put himself in danger for Priscilla's sake – and endanger his wife and children who might have been punished had she escaped – had a transforming effect. Daniel was not in her terms handsome, but 'he showed such devotion and friendship that I felt I had treated him very badly by not giving him what he wanted so much. I resolved to become his mistress as soon as I was free to do so, as I was fed up with Robert and the whole of his family. However, before I could escape I had an opportunity which I seized and which enabled me to get out miraculously.'

The five doctors in the camp, French POWs under the charge of an incompetent young Prussian, met once a week to discuss which prisoners might be eligible for release.

Priscilla was in her third month at Caserne Vauban when the list of those entitled to leave was expanded to include anyone expecting a child. One morning loudspeakers summoned the Bluebell Girls' founder to the Kommandantur: Margaret Kelly was several months' pregnant. Another beneficiary was Priscilla. After dreaming all her life of having a child, she was to be saved by the 'miracle' of a phantom pregnancy.

'One day our German nurse came round and asked if any of us had any children. When she came to me, without thinking I answered "Not yet" (meaning I hoped to have one some day).

'She looked at me straight in the eye and said, "You can have a medical examination tomorrow."

'When she had gone, I was very worried about it.'

But everyone else in B.71 expressed delight. 'You're pregnant!' said Berry. Priscilla's pregnancy would ensure her release.

More than forty years later, Jacqueline Grant recalled Priscilla's droll reply: 'She said, "Well, that's rather sad and rather funny. But I can't be. My husband, although he's a perfect dear and comes from a very good family, is impotent."'

Her pregnancy was a physical impossibility, Priscilla explained. Married for two years, she had not made love since her honeymoon.

'The Germans don't know that,' said Berry, and told Priscilla what to tell the doctors, that she was being sick every morning. 'After all, you did see your husband recently – it is feasible.' And hadn't her periods stopped?

The others agreed. Priscilla must pretend to be pregnant. 'My companions told me I had better try and bring it off,' she wrote. 'So the next day I presented myself trembling to a French doctor who was also a prisoner.'

The French doctor who examined her was Jean Lévy.

Shula Troman exclaimed when I mentioned his name. Of course she remembered Dr Lévy! He became a lifelong friend as well as Troman's doctor in Paris, where he had ended his career as professor of gynaecology at the Hôpital Foch. 'He delivered both my children, and when I had breast cancer he operated.' She hunted around for a black and white photograph, taken at the camp in 1941 and showing a clean-shaven man in French army uniform, smiling. 'He was lovely, with a formidable sense of humour and an extraordinary silhouette, a little bit hunched, like a faun.'

A French Jew from Colmar who had joined the army as a doctor and was captured by the Germans, Lévy was in constant danger. His mother and sister lived in Paris, but his wife and small daughter – who died soon afterwards of scarlet fever – were in hiding. The potential that existed for reprisals against Lévy's family was considerable and underscores his courage. 'I owed so much to him,' wrote Drue Tartière, another inmate of the camp, after Lévy convinced the Germans that Tartière had ovarian cancer and needed treatment in Paris. Priscilla, too, had reasons to be indebted.

Dr Lévy examined my aunt 'in front a lot of nuns and old bodies'. In Priscilla's account, he looked at her carefully and then winked.

'Yes, madame,' he said. 'You are pregnant, but I am afraid that you will have to see a German doctor to confirm my verdict.' He added in her ear. 'He is very young and probably won't know whether you are pregnant or not. It is difficult to tell at three months. Good luck.'

Priscilla returned to her room and told Berry that Dr Lévy had agreed to provide a medical certificate stating that she was expecting. But she was nervous.

'What do I do if they keep a check on me after I get out? Walk around with a pillow under my dress?'

'You can always say that you have had a miscarriage. Anyway the next thing to do is convince the German doctor.'

When the summons came, Priscilla did not have time to worry. She was shown into a small room and a young fair German in uniform greeted her curtly.

'I am told that you are expecting a child.' He stared at her. 'Are you quite certain of it?'

'Oh yes,' in a feeble voice. 'Absolutely certain.'

'Very well. That being so, you will be free to go soon.'

Her legs could hardly carry her from the room.

Early in February, the loudspeakers interrupted a Schubert piano sonata and called out Priscilla's name: she was to report to the Kommandantur.

On the day of Priscilla's departure in spring 1941, she was searched. Her British passport was returned, plus her compact mirror and flashlight. She was handed two typed documents in German. The first entitled her to free transport by bus or train, and asked the authorities to allow her to travel unhindered. The second demanded that she present herself each day to the Mairie of her Paris neighbourhood – she was not allowed to take up residence in any 'coastal region' – and listed six further orders.

Her husband did not know that she was coming home. But she no longer worried about the possibility of retribution on Robert or his family. Her thoughts were of Daniel, the Scarlet Pimpernel, who cared so much for her that he had risked his wife and children. A strange starved determination to start living spread through her. 'I was hungry for pleasure.'

PART FOUR

18.
LONDON: OCTOBER 1944

An autumn evening, three years later – after the Nazis had left Paris. Gillian Sutro heard a taxi draw up outside her home in Mayfair. She pushed back the curtain and observed Priscilla step out.

'She was carrying a suitcase, wearing a navy polka-dot frock. She was suntanned and looked beautiful. I rushed out and we fell into each other's arms. I still remember her first words, "Oh, it's good to see you. I got out just in time." In the euphoria of our retrouvailles, I hadn't time to ponder her words.'

Jubilant, Gillian bustled Priscilla into the house, 'a shoulder-bag swinging as she walked through our front door'. Priscilla begged for a cup of tea and collapsed on the sofa while Gillian boiled the kettle.

'I asked Pris about her journey to England. Being British, she managed to get on to a military freighter. No seats. She sat on the floor, relieved to get away as the witch hunt had started.'

Priscilla could share her bedroom, Gillian said. 'I told her that John had his own room,' and gave a summary of their marital situation as she helped Priscilla upstairs with her suitcase – 'which I couldn't wait to open. It was packed with French couture clothes, Schiaparelli, Patou, metres of pure silk … which made my British clothes look all of a sudden rather dreary.' An ivory dress prompted Gillian to recount her excitement at discovering that this house,

5 Lees Place, had sheltered Elsa Schiaparelli before the war: 'It was near her couture shop on Grosvenor Street.' And hanging up the frilly dress in the built-in cupboard, Gillian was carried back to those afternoons in Paris when she had sketched Priscilla modelling Schiaparelli's very latest designs for *Britannia* and *Eve*.

The war dissolved. They were two single girls, sharing secrets. 'The bliss of seeing Pris again. She slept in my room – there were two beds. We talked and talked about our lives. It took us days, weeks to catch up on our mutual friends, news.'

Priscilla's arrival at 5 Lees Place had a tonic effect on Gillian's husband. Gillian's ugly beast stood looking at her and his thick lips grinned. Gillian noticed how Priscilla hugged him 'as though she had known him all her life'. The two sat on the sofa while Gillian served drinks. 'Pris had a sort of cat-like behaviour with men. She stroked John's hand as they talked. John was almost purring as Pris ran her hand over his hair in an absent-minded way. I had not seen her for five years. I had forgotten the caressing act which was second nature to her and which enchanted her admirers … I was delighted that John and my closest friend got on so well, as she was to be our guest while she sorted out her life. She stayed for quite a few months.'

I got out just in time. Only much later did Priscilla's words keep coming back to Gillian. 'This seemed to me at the time an odd thing to say. Why the hurry after the Nazi departure?' Gillian had used the same phrase in June 1940, when telling John about her exodus from France. 'But what was Pris fleeing from? I didn't know exactly what was going on in France, except that there were a great many réglements de compte at the Libération. It was called the Epuration and sounded horrid. Women who had slept with Germans had their heads shaved and were paraded in the streets for all to see.' Sure enough, Gillian noticed a 'roaring trade' in wigs on her return to Paris a few months later. 'On a windy day I saw a woman clutching her mop of hair as though it were a hat. Une tondue.'

Even so, for the next forty-eight years Gillian chose to ignore Priscilla's words. 'I loved Pris. We were childhood friends. Anyway, who am I to pass judgement?' She thrust what Priscilla had said to the back of her mind. 'I was so excited to see her after so long that her words did not penetrate me until later. But I never forgot them.'

Priscilla was evasive about her activities after her release from Besançon. On 3 December 1963, she stood up at an Alcoholics Anonymous meeting in London and, in an exercise intended to lay her life bare, condensed into a few lines the three and a half years following her internment. Normally such gatherings are confidential, but – extraordinarily – Priscilla wrote out her speech.

'I went back to my flat in Paris and tried to make a go of my marriage on the rare occasions when I could see my husband but, in 1942, I decided I couldn't go on. I left home on my bicycle, leaving everything I possessed, and went to stay with friends. From then on until the end of the war I led a precarious existence with no money and false papers, unable to get a job or get a divorce. In 1943, I had a serious internal operation and again in 1944 I had another. When Paris was liberated I was repatriated.'

No mention of any Daniel, Emile, Pierre, Otto.

Nor do her father's diaries fill in the blank. SPB did not hear from Priscilla between May 1940 and October 1944. From what he wrote about her in his autobiography, he seems to have assumed that his daughter had remained interned all this while, either in Besançon or in Vittel; or perhaps she allowed him to go on believing this so that she would not have to account for her actions. Her sister Vivien told me, 'She couldn't get away till the end of the war. I don't know what went on. There was absolutely no communication at all. No, that's not true. There was one call. I was staying with my grandma in Horsham. Her telephone number was Horsham 87 and I picked it up and said "Horsham 87", and a man spoke a whole conversation in French. I said: "How did you know I spoke French?" He said: "Your voice is exactly like your sister's," and he told me the news. She was living in the country, more or less all right.'

And yet she was not living with Robert at Boisgrimot, according to Jacqueline Hodey, the grocer's daughter: 'After 1940, one never saw her again.'

As far as Hodey and the Carers and the Bezards were concerned, Madame Robert had been uprooted from the landscape as emphatically as the oak trees in the Doynels' avenue.

19.
BRAZEN LIES

So what was Priscilla doing between the spring of 1941 and the autumn of 1944 when she came through Gillian's door in Mayfair?

I had hoped the contents of her padded chest would tell me. I was mistaken. All that the letters made clear was that Priscilla had had a relationship with a Frenchman called Daniel soon after her release from Besançon, and then, or at the same time, with men called Emile, Pierre, Otto. But as to who they were, and in particular Otto, who sounded suspiciously German, I had no answer. And while I had learned more about Priscilla from her incomplete manuscripts, large parts of her puzzle were missing. She remained a passive enigma, drifting in and out of view; a cork on a troubled sea.

There she might have stayed. Without knowing the identities of her lovers, I could not make Priscilla's story with all its ambiguities and blanks come whole. Although I am a novelist, it seemed to me that to resurrect Priscilla in the guise of fiction would not be true to her life, however falsely she might have lived it. And I was troubled by the manner in which the Doynel family had denied her – not mentioning her name in their 1200-page genealogy and killing her off forty years early, at the start of the war.

Then, in the Special Collections Room of the Bodleian Library, less than a ten-minute walk from where I lived in Oxford, I made an elating discovery.

I was in the final stage of putting to bed an edition of Bruce Chatwin's letters, a project which had occupied me intermittently since 1991, when I noticed a reference to a Sutro Collection, recently catalogued and stored in the same building. In no real spirit of expectation, I pulled out the catalogue and saw that the Sutro archive had been bequeathed by Gillian; further, three specific boxes related to my aunt.

I ordered them up. The first box contained letters from Priscilla to Gillian. There were photographs of the two of them in France before the war, on holiday soon after it in Sainte-Maxime, of Gillian's wedding in London, of Priscilla's second wedding to Raymond, and of the Sutros at Church Farm. Interesting, I thought, but nothing more, and opened the second box, which was full of red and yellow notebooks.

Then I read my name.

This was the line: 'She was never in a concentration camp like Nicholas Shakespeare writes in his piece in *Telegraph* magazine 14 November 1992.' Besançon, Gillian wrote angrily, was an internment camp; but the mistake – which was my mistake, since Priscilla had never spoken to me about it – had a combustive effect, uncorking a lifetime of deliberately suppressed information and of secrets and suspicions about my aunt which Gillian had bottled up, until now. 'Since reading the brazen lies she told her journalist-writer nephew, I have no scruples over telling the truth about her life and war record in Occupied France. Had she not lied I had intended to keep to myself what I knew.'

A phrase can be a clap of thunder. *Brazen lies? The truth about her life? War record in Occupied France?* In a minor but vital way I was suddenly now part of this story, the reason why Gillian was motivated to fill notebook after notebook with explicit memories of my aunt.

In 1992, Gillian Sutro had been struggling with a memoir. It was her second attempt. She had abandoned an earlier memoir, about her marriage to John Sutro, in favour of an account of her upbringing in France during the 1920s and 1930s. Graham Greene, who lived nearby in Antibes, had encouraged her: 'Your life as a girl in pre-war Paris was most unusual. You would be a goose not to make use of it.'

But once again Gillian had become stuck. She groused to Harold Acton: 'Through following GG's advice and enlarging my canvas, it has meant a great deal more work.' Then one November morning, on her terrace in Monte Carlo where she had moved from London in 1974, she read my interview with Janina David, about growing up in the Warsaw Ghetto – and everything that Gillian had stifled for half a century poured out.

In that interview, I had written: *My aunt, captured in France by the Germans, spent time in two concentration camps. She was tortured and unable to bear children.*

Priscilla had been dead for ten years. All their lives they had been the best of friends, with not the slightest dent apparent in their relationship. But this mention of what our family believed had happened to Priscilla in the war was the back-breaking straw. It galvanised Gillian to recalibrate her past history with Priscilla and to put the record straight – 'mettre les pendules à l'heure' was her phrase. And in the act of correcting the pendulum she found herself once more pushed back down the years to their Paris childhood: the cafés and cinemas they frequented, the botched abortion, the lavish wedding to the Vicomte at which Gillian had acted as 'witness', the Hungarian lover they may or may not have shared, up to the moment when German tanks rolled into France, and Gillian fled to England on the last train from Gare Saint-Lazare, distraught at having to leave Priscilla behind.

But Gillian's recollections of Priscilla in pre-war Paris were the least of it. Her project assumed an urgency which the sifting of fifty-year-old memories did nothing to lessen. 'I was determined to find out more.'

Small details, Gillian believed, can destroy relationships quicker than big knocks. Her husband's brother Edward Sutro had left his wife because of the way she slurped her soup. The two lines that I had written about my aunt became the spark to ignite a pyre that Gillian had unconsciously been assembling under her childhood friend since the moment in 1944 when Priscilla walked through her front door in London. Now, ten years after Priscilla's death, Gillian made a retrospective decision: Priscilla, apart from lying about the concentration camp, had not told the truth in other areas and had betrayed Gillian by going to bed with Vertès. What consumed Gillian, and stirred her to confront the suspicions and misgivings that she had suppressed, were Priscilla's activities during the Occupation.

'The Occupation period has always been my obsession,' Gillian wrote in her apartment in Monaco, where she lived alone with her dog. 'Morbid I agree, but riveting in its horror and humiliation. The way it brought out the best and worst in people. The struggle for survival. How would I have coped with being clamped in a prison camp in Besançon where the Brits were herded by the Germans (this happened to my most intimate girlfriend)?' The question had preoccupied Gillian since her husband's death in 1985 and it dominated her life after she read my article. 'I have done a great deal of research in those years. Priscilla was far from helpful. She did not wish to talk about the Occupation, later pretended to have forgotten. With persistence I managed to drag some facts from her.' These, coupled with facts provided by Zoë Temblaire, 'who lived through the Occupation and saw a great deal of Priscilla, plus a book on the Occupation giving certain names, helped me to find out what Priscilla did not want me to know.'

The implication took a moment to absorb. All the time I was pestering my family about Priscilla, Gillian had been approaching other witnesses, telephoning Zoë in Paris, sending questionnaires to Harold Acton in Florence, her sister Jacqueline in Lieurey – asking the same things.

'Where did she live when she left Besançon?'

'Did she ever see Robert after Besançon?'

'"Otto" was a code name. How did she meet him?'

'What was his profession supposed to be?'

And Gillian, apparently, had discovered the answers. 'I think her experiences are worth recounting,' she wrote.

Listed in a small red Century notebook entitled 'PRIS' were intimate details of my aunt's life and loves, beginning with Robert Donat ('who met her at a party we gave'). Each lover was supplied with his surname, plus everything that Gillian could recall Priscilla having said about him. The Scarlet Pimpernel was Daniel Vernier, a married and well-connected industrialist who, after visiting Priscilla in Besançon, supplied her with identity papers. Emile was the figure at the wheel of the Delahaye, Emile Cornet, a Belgian black-marketeer and Bugatti racing driver who won the Belgian Grand Prix and finished his career as the press secretary of Princess Grace of Monaco. Pierre was Pierre Duboyon, Vernier's brother-in-law, who owned a textile factory in Annemasse fabricating nylon stockings. Gillian had even discovered the identity of the mysterious Otto. 'Over him Pris was clam-like. Nevertheless, bit by bit, I found out certain facts.'

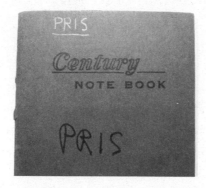

Gillian's change of mind about her best friend was painful. Priscilla had put everyone on the spot and forced those who had known her to reappraise not only their image of Priscilla, but their view of themselves.

For three months, I read and transcribed Gillian's notebooks. Again and again, I had the freakish impression of being taken by the wrist and led down, through a procession of unlocking doors, into the cellars beneath one of the most fascinating and yet, in spite of all the literature on it, incompletely explored moments of the twentieth century – a period over which France continues to draw firm bolts: 'Four years to strike from our history,' is how the French still refer to it. Because what Gillian had written down was the other half of the key.

20.
PARIS: FEBRUARY 1941

André Gide wrote in his diary near the start of the war: 'What is the best thing the rat can do when caught in a trap? Eat the bacon.'

Robert was not at their apartment in Rue Nollet, which had a musty smell after remaining unheated all winter. Priscilla did not tell her husband that she was free for another day or two. Instead, she started an affair with Daniel.

'When I came out I was hungry for pleasure and I started to enjoy myself, or so I thought.' From her fictional memoir it is clear that they first made love in Daniel's apartment in 12 Rue Beaujon where he had begged her to spend the night on the eve of her arrest. Daniel helped Priscilla off with her coat and took her in his arms. He loved her, he could not bear to see her so thin, so unhappy. 'He must have been very sure of me,' she thought, watching him pour her a strong martini. But she accepted the cocktail.

They did not say much at dinner, just sat and looked at each other and held hands, and his face was not unattractive after all. When it became time to leave, she put on her coat. Daniel watched her, frightened of making a false move. 'Please, stay longer.' With a smile formed by three months of internment, she remained standing. Taking advantage of the silence, he removed her coat.

Priscilla had not been touched by a man since her honeymoon. The last time that she had made love was four years before, with the father of her aborted child. In the draft of Priscilla's speech for her 1963 AA meeting, she left a telling note that reveals the turmoil she was in: 'Age 25, couldn't remember a thing about night with Daniel – which should have been a warning.' The effect of his lovemaking, combined with his lethal martini, not to ignore Priscilla's weakened and emotional state, was to make her black out.

She had been expelled from Besançon into a France – a Europe – where an exhilarated Germany looked triumphant. The crime novelist Georges Simenon wrote to his mother in March 1941: 'I hope the English will not hold out much longer.' Simenon – a friend of Gillian, Vertès and Kessel (who had commissioned his first Inspector Maigret story) – was in the majority. By early summer, Greece, Yugoslavia and Libya were in Axis hands; Crete would follow soon; and in June, in the largest military operation in history, German troops advanced into Russia. A huge 'V' hung on the Eiffel Tower and a banner proclaimed 'Deutschland Siegt An Allen Fronten' – Germany victorious on all fronts. In London, two parachute mines killed thirty-four people in the Café de Paris, touted as the safest restaurant in town; 33,118 civilians had died in raids by the end of March. Between March and May, 412 Allied ships were sunk in the Battle of the Atlantic. The pro-German broadcaster Jacques Doriot assured listeners on Radio Paris: 'England is defeated, her fleet is at the bottom of the sea.' In the running tide, where to turn?

In the spring of 1941, to resurface as an Englishwoman in a Paris full of Germans was not easy. Priscilla's first days were particularly traumatic. The omnipotent slam of a car door, a footstep on the stairs, a key turning in a lock, and she was ready to leap to the door. If she went to a restaurant, it unnerved her to see so many people. It was hard to eat. She felt tired, her vitality gone. It had stayed behind in Besançon, rising with the bugle at seven and lying down at six.

If anything, Caserne Vauban had fostered Priscilla's natural passivity. Released, she behaved in the same way as her fellow internee Rita Harding, who, repatriated to London, lived with her aunt. 'If my aunt said, "What would you like to do – go on Epsom Downs or to the cinema?" I'd look at her blankly and say, "I don't know." At Besançon, we didn't make a decision about anything.'

When Priscilla had put down her suitcase on returning to her apartment, bedbugs streamed out of it. Occupied France was Besançon mapped large. If she ventured into Rue Nollet, she noticed that her lassitude was something that she shared with other Parisians. It was impossible to know what anyone was thinking.

After Jacqueline Grant was released in July she went to stay in a convent in Neuilly, where Priscilla visited her. They had trouble recognising one another. Jacqueline was 'thin as a nail'. Plus, she had agoraphobia. 'I was frightened of walking down a street by myself. If I had someone to talk to, I was reasonably all right.' Indoors, she and Priscilla could talk. But when Jacqueline left the convent with Priscilla to visit wounded English POWs at the Hôpital Communal, she was assailed by a terrible feeling which stayed with her for years afterwards. 'I wanted to hug the walls.'

On top of everything, Priscilla remained an enemy alien, reminded of it at every turn. She itemised her restrictions at that inaugural AA meeting:

'I was allowed to return to Paris and live with my husband on condition that I signed at the nearest police station every day.' This was at 16 Place Charles Fillion, a ten-minute walk from her apartment. 'I couldn't move out of Paris. I was not allowed to have a wireless or telephone. I was not allowed to ride in a car or on a bicycle – only communal transport, and I had to be in just before dark.' In addition, she had 'no right to exercise a profession which involves walking' although she was allowed to ride a horse.

The Germans enforced most of these rules. Yvette Goodden was barely a month back in Paris when one morning at 5 a.m. the Gestapo knocked on her door to check that she did not have a wireless or telephone and also that she had her young son Michael with her – the reason for Goodden having been freed. Every morning she repeated to her son, 'Allons, viens, on va signer,' and they walked to the police station. If she wanted to go away for the weekend, the policeman, whom Michael knew as 'Monsieur Signer', allowed her to sign in large letters across two days. Out of doors, mother and son talked in French. Goodden said: 'I stopped speaking English with Michael in the street so as not to draw attention.'

Not to speak English was one of the deprivations that caused Priscilla most grief. That and her childlessness, her false position reinforced by the priority ration cards to which, as an expectant mother, she was entitled. She did risk riding a bicycle, though.

On Saturday, Robert arrived from Boisgrimot. 'He could still muster no enthusiasm.' They did not say much; Priscilla did not like to ask him or even to ask herself his thoughts. Every subject was a bed of nettles; they skirted, spoke of nothing, except on the subject of his farming produce – how most of it went to feed the occupying forces, with the rest flowing out to Germany at rock-bottom prices. They lay with their arms around each other for warmth. She was supposed to be pregnant, but she felt like one of the prams in the exodus which had not contained any baby. His impotence was France's. 'He soon went back to Normandy and to his gloom.' She was almost relieved that the conditions of her release prevented her from following.

'I love you,' Robert wrote, in letters adjuring her to be happy.

'I love you,' she wrote back. But they were saying 'I love you' to plug the gaps, forestall discussion, and signal, against all evidence to the contrary, that everything was going to be fine.

It was not. 'His letters became more and more neurotic and depressed.' Boisgrimot had suffered a plague of rats. Then an infestation of beetles. The pupils had been taken out of school for three days to help hunt down the beetles and destroy them.

Now when they were together, hardly a day passed in which Priscilla was not exasperated by Robert's morose inertia. It was not simply that she blamed him for Besançon and for not giving her children. He had no flavour for her. And after so long a drought, she wanted flavour. As Priscilla wrote of her alter ego, Crystal de Brie, in the novel that I found in her stepdaughter's box: 'Most of her friends were having affairs and how could anyone be expected to live in chastity for years on end?'

Priscilla's most revealing portrait of herself at this time is contained not in her novel, but in a story that she wrote from the perspective of an Austrian-Jewish writer, Hans, who bumped into her and Robert after she was freed from Besançon.

Hans was lunching in his usual cheap restaurant – 'when in walked a couple who caught my eye at once. The man must have been about five years younger than me, which made him 40 or thereabouts. He was tall and distinguished-looking. His wife was my idea of perfection. She was much younger than her husband – not more than 23 or 4. Tall, blonde and Aryan. I judged them to be married because the man read his paper throughout the meal and the girl was obviously deep in her own thoughts – they hardly exchanged a word. I couldn't take my eyes off her.'

Priscilla wrote elsewhere of meeting a Hans Mayer during the Occupation, but gave no details. It is tempting to assume that this was the Viennese-Jewish writer Hans Mayer, who may have been in Paris in August 1941, and was later transported to Auschwitz – the fate of the Austrian-Jewish writer in Priscilla's story.

Mid-forties, ungainly, with no money 'and nothing much to offer', Priscilla's Hans is a poor kinsman of the Lieutenant from Caen. One glimpse and he is bewitched.

'When they paid their bill and left the restaurant I got up to go too and I was in time to see the girl get on her bicycle and ride away leaving her husband to go wherever he was going on foot. I watched her until she was out of sight and thought that I had never seen anyone so graceful with her long legs pedalling and her fair hair streaming behind her.

'After that day, she was never out of my thoughts. I was obsessed by her. I saw her several times more in the same restaurant and my method of staring at her seemed to amuse her. She mentioned it to her husband one day. He gave me a cursory glance and went back to his newspaper.'

Hans came to recognise which café Priscilla was in by her bicycle parked outside. He judged her to be American or English, as she always carried an English book under her arm.

'I tried to think of a way to get to know her and one day I bought a bouquet of red roses and put them on her bicycle with a card saying how beautiful she was and how much I admired her.

'When I next saw her a day or two later she was cycling down the Champs Elysées and she nearly ran over me. She stopped.

'"Thank you for the flowers," she said in English.'

Hans invited her for a drink at a nearby café.

'She told me about her life before the war in England and then I made her talk of her marriage – she wanted children badly but her husband was impotent. "He was so kind to me. He replaced the father that I never had. If we had had children my happiness would have been complete."' But now, though she was very fond of him, he irritated her more and more. He lacked any sense of humour or gaiety, she told Hans.

'Why did you marry him?'

'Oh, he was different before the war – we used to have fun – but he has gone to pieces. He is so old for his age and nothing amuses him any more. He is crushed.'

Hans decided to write a book about her; in return he would teach her German. 'I lived for the short time that she spared me every day.' But his book soon ran into difficulty. 'I tried to understand her, but the more I tried the less I understood. She was desperately homesick and I think that was one of the reasons she liked me. There were few people she could talk English to. Her husband had no knowledge of her language. They led a strange life those two. He treated her like a child. They never had any meals at home because he didn't want her to be bothered with housekeeping. As a result she was bored. She had nothing to do except to get into mischief. He was often away and when he was in Paris he spent most of the time at the Bourse. She was plagued by in-laws as he was the youngest of a large family and they all seemed to be very Germanophile.' She was heartily sick of the lot of them. 'I owe my months of concentration camp to them.'

Her pleasures during those months sprang from her winter's grief as a prisoner in a camp in the Jura. 'She had been released shortly before I saw her first and she was unbalanced and out to enjoy herself at any cost. Underneath her cynical behaviour I sensed her to be good. She consoled herself by leading a wild life of her own … Often she lied to me, telling me that she was spending the day with a girlfriend, when really she was with some man … and as her husband was not jealous and gave her plenty of freedom, she satisfied her every whim.'

21.
DANIEL VERNIER

Priscilla had given herself to Daniel in the way that she jumped into the sea, eyes closed. 'I felt myself needed physically and I had no conscience as I was taking nothing away from Robert.'

From the spring of 1941, Priscilla led 'a very strange life.' Robert came down from Normandy and spent half the week with her. Despite the attrition of his physical indifference, she still wanted to be his wife. Divorce was not in her husband's religion, which was hers now; in the armistice of their marriage, it remained the demarcation line – not to be crossed.

The other half of the week she spent with Daniel. 'I was never at any time in love with him. He was a sweet person at that time – very fresh and untouched by life's disappointments and disillusions. He spoiled me as I had never been spoiled before and I was happy.'

Graham Greene told Gillian Sutro: 'What two lovers do in bed is no one's business but their own. One may have a fairly shrewd idea of what does go on, but I would not dream of putting it on paper. People have a right to privacy in that domain.' Gillian would not always be so respectful of Priscilla, but over the Scarlet Pimpernel she was discreet. The important thing that Gillian exposed about him in her 'PRIS' notebook was his surname.

Daniel Vernier had married into a wealthy textile family from Tourcoing, in the north of France. 'He was charming,' wrote Gillian, who later received from him the gift of a Hermès desk diary. 'After the war, Daniel made a pass at me on the night ferry to London. I said, "No. Pris is my dearest friend."'

According to what Priscilla told Gillian, 'Daniel was the man who helped her the most.'

The Occupation had its own morality. Priscilla's on-again, off-again relationship with Vernier reflected the ambiguity of the times. Wanting to behave well, she decided to end her 'double life' with him shortly after his wife dropped the explosive news that she was coming to Paris.

Vernier had parked Simone at the beginning of the war in a chateau in the Dordogne owned by her father. But towards the end of 1941, Simone announced that she was bringing their four children to live with him.

In panic at the prospect of his family's arrival from Siorac, Vernier asked Priscilla to leave Robert. 'Let's go away. You have no children, nothing to lose.'

'I just can't walk out on him and that is that.'

Vernier persisted. 'I will tell my wife that I can't live with her again and we will start life again somewhere else.' His proposal threw Priscilla. She was considering what to do when Vernier committed the surprising error of introducing the two women.

The meeting of Priscilla and Simone changed everything. Tall and blonde, the thirty-one-year-old Simone was a dead-ringer for my aunt. Their resemblance may explain Daniel Vernier's initial attraction; it is not too much to say that it later on saved Priscilla's life.

'We liked each other immediately,' Priscilla admitted, 'and it was then that my conscience started to worry me. I decided that I must stop the affair as I didn't want to break up their marriage.'

Her solution was radical. She informed both Vernier and Robert that she was going to escape back to England through Spain. 'I can't wait to get home,' she told them. 'I have been so homesick! You have no idea.'

On the morning of 20 May 1942, leaving behind all her possessions, Priscilla climbed on to her bicycle and disappeared.

Why, then, was Priscilla still in Paris in October 1944? It perplexed Gillian. 'I certainly never understood why she did not come to England after Besançon.'

Priscilla's insistence on staying also puzzled W. H. Aston, a wounded English soldier at the Centre Maxillo-Facial at Neuilly. Before he slipped out of the hospital in April 1942 and headed for the Spanish border, Priscilla had gone to see him with her English friend Jacqueline Grant. They sat unsupervised on Aston's bed and played board games, while he rehearsed his escape plans. Aston, who had met Priscilla in Rouen during the Phoney War, thought both young women 'incredibly pretty'. At the same time, they seemed to have lost their roots in life. 'They had broken their ties with England while resisting assimilation into the life of France.' Aston could not help thinking that they would have done better to have left Paris before the Germans entered, rather than let themselves fall into enemy hands. The one thing Aston was determined at all cost to avoid was being sent to Germany. He and another officer were 'going to hop it' – he encouraged Priscilla and Jacqueline to do the same. But how easy was it for a young Englishwoman to escape France?

Since September 1940, General Haase's forces operating out of Tourcoing monitored the northern route across the Channel. A fisherman warned: 'We are watched all the time and the waters are rigidly controlled.' One route was to travel east, across the Swiss border from Annemasse, where professional passeurs charged upwards of 5,000 francs a head. Most fugitives headed south to Marseilles, from there crossing the border into neutral Spain and then to Portugal. And yet the route over the Pyrenees, as with Annemasse, was not only formally opposed by the French government, and expensive, but downright dangerous.

Files in the National Archives in Kew show just how hazardous it could be to 'hop it'. First, there was the arms-length attitude of the British government towards women like Priscilla, whom the war had isolated on the Continent. Priscilla needed money to bribe the passeurs and to pay for travel and false documents – 100,000 francs, Aston calculated, 'for a complete set of papers and the cost of the journey to Lisbon'. But there was no question of the British government helping her out financially. One claimant, a Mrs Mainwaring, wrote to the Home Office requesting assistance for her niece who was married to a Frenchman and was destitute. The reply she received came from the highest level: 'Mr Churchill regrets that under existing regulations it is not possible for payments to be made to the British-born wives of Frenchmen in unoccupied France.'

A document dated 10 February 1941 reflected the official position: 'As regards the British women in Occupied France, while their plight is a most unfortunate one, there are other British civilians who have been much longer in captivity.' Of more concern was the repatriation of 1,200 British servicemen estimated to be stranded in France. Britain's ambassador in Madrid, Sir Samuel Hoare, remarked 'of a strange want of interest in this question in London. We have been given few, if any instructions as to the financing of this large undertaking.' It was left to individuals like Aston to make their own arrangements.

The Kew archives offer several disastrous examples of those who tried to escape. A British soldier from the 5th Battalion of the Buffs walked 180 miles south in the autumn of 1940, only to be betrayed. 'On Sept 7 met a real swine of a French captain (one of the "French German" officers) who put us under armed guard and had us marched back to the frontier to the German post – the sod!' Up until 5 May 1941, British POWs were placed under a regime of liberté surveillée which made it fairly easy for them to get away, but following strong German pressure a Vichy order imposed a stricter watch. An English soldier imprisoned in Vichy in June wrote to his parents: 'Day and night we are guarded by armed French soldiers who do not hesitate to shoot if anybody attempts to escape.'

If Priscilla did make it to Marseilles without being stopped or shot by the French, she would next have to contend with a notoriously unhelpful British consul, Major Hugh Dodds, who worked for the British Interests Section of the American consulate in Marseilles. Dodds, a Yorkshireman, was generally rumoured to be obstructive towards those whom, in a private letter, he called 'these idiots who insist on staying'.

Based in Marseilles, two British soldiers, Captain Charles Murchie and Sergeant Harry Clayton, had managed to help up to 150 servicemen escape across the Pyrenees. But the attitude of General Franco's authorities posed a threat. On 11 June 1941, the British Consul General in Barcelona wrote to Sir Samuel Hoare of his concern that nearly all the British who escaped France believed that once they reached Spain their troubles were at an end, 'whereas in many cases they have only just started, and their condition and treatment is sometimes worse than that to which they were subjected in France'. The American Consul General in Marseilles, on hearing that prisoners had been shot whilst crossing the frontier, emphasised to Hoare that it was not wise to encourage anyone who was British to escape.

In his hospital bed in Neuilly, W. H. Aston was aware of these dangers. But they would not dissuade him. Nor did they deter Jacqueline Grant and other Besançon internees like Elisabeth Haden-Guest and Rosemary Say, all of whom succeeded, like Aston, in getting back to England. 'We could not help feeling that they had been spurred on by the example of our escape,' Aston wrote, 'but we could never understand why they had not done it many months earlier ...'

The situation was obviously pretty strange and dangerous. Priscilla was an enemy alien, in a place where she was increasingly liable to be taken out and shot if caught listening to her father on the radio. What made her stay?

Priscilla had absorbed the fatalistic public mood, which, as Sir Samuel Hoare gauged it, 'assumed that we could not win and that the war would come to an end in some way or another'. If she did find the courage and luck to make it back to London, what was waiting for her? Rosemary Say wrote to her parents one year earlier, before she was taken to Besançon: 'I am busy and individual here, which suits me better than to be thrown into the melting pot of National Service anyway for a bit – perhaps I am wrong – anyway I am happy.' Was Priscilla content to glide along like this? Gillian believed that the atmosphere of wait-and-see fitted her character. 'Had she come to England, she would have been called up and made to work.' But Priscilla's ostensible inertia was more complicated than that.

She had stayed initially because of her marriage in a country which had become more of a home than England. Priscilla felt a whole tangle of loyalties and congested emotions about England as epitomised by her father, whom she both loved and hated. Despite his unorthodox private life, SPB represented wholesomeness and Englishness – at least in his broadcasting and books – and Priscilla was none of these things at this particular time. Her life – seedy by many people's standards, sordid, dodgy – was the antithesis of the uncomplicated world that SPB promoted so ardently. But what could she do? All moral values had broken down. The signposts about how to behave had been removed and she did not know where she was, what would happen.

In this muddled and futureless present, more important than any division between cowardly and heroic was the pressure imposed on her to construct a new moral system.

Priscilla never found a world into which she fitted except in Paris, and for a while, ghastly as it was, she became part of it. She would not have suspected this at the time, because it was so terrifying; but in a curious way the Occupation was when her life came to fruition. The war gave her a new identity. It taught her to live in the moment and to throw off the burden of her father and the past.

But the likeliest reason that Priscilla remained in France is also the simplest: she was – unexpectedly and infatuatedly – in love.

22.
EMILE CORNET

She remembered the cigarette burn of his look. He touched the inside of her arm and she felt the current jitter through her. I do not know how she met Emile Cornet, and there is no one left to ask. But he unsettled Priscilla from the start, and though their rapport was for the most part physical, it marked her life. Her relationship with Robert had been all about surface; with Cornet, everything flared from within, from what remained hidden.

'He was rather an ugly little man with a sort of twisted face, but he was full of vitality and personality and he swept me off my feet.'

His full name was Emile-Hubert Cornet du Fonteny. He was born in 1905 near Charleroi, the son of a minor Belgian aristocrat whose title he used when it suited him. Known on the Grand Prix circuit as 'le baron Belge', Cornet took over management of the family enamelworks, selling them in 1937 to concentrate on motor racing. He was planning to compete in the São Paulo Grand Prix when German tanks smashed over the Belgian border.

He was reckless, with a short man's large appetites. His impetuous, over-decisive nature often landed him in hot water. Months before he embarked on his 'impossible amour' with Priscilla, Cornet had attempted to flee into Spain, but according to an Intelligence report in Kew he was arrested by the Spanish police and delivered back to the Nazis in Hendaye – 'by whom he has apparently been third-degreed and has given away practically everything viz the Murchie & Clayton case, he having been in contact with these in France.' Cornet's testimony resulted in Murchie and Clayton – organisers of the chief British escape network – spending prolonged periods in various Spanish prisons. His unpleasant experience discouraged Priscilla from attempting to cross the border. Any plan to leave France was shelved after they met.

'He attracts me and makes me laugh.' For the first time, Priscilla's companion was an available man who satisfied her physically and with whom she imagined herself in love. Invincible in the strength of her infatuation, she forgot her married lover, her husband, the police. When her Jewish friend Hans expressed his concern, she shrugged. 'I don't care. Let them search for me. I shall just disappear.'

'For the first few weeks everything was perfect,' she wrote.

Cornet invited her skiing to Megève. An extension of Maxim's and Fouquet's, Megève had a reputation as 'the white capital of the black market'. The pair stayed in a hotel on the outskirts and saw no one who knew them. Cornet was an expert skier. Priscilla had difficulty in following him down the pistes, but he was patient. His winter sports clothes set off his dark looks.

He told her: 'Without looking at you, I know every movement you make and every person you talk to.'

'It's the same with me.'

She was out of her head. She felt no guilt. She had never been happier, she thought. Before she knew it, she was living with him – 'and long was I to regret my folly'.

Robert and Vernier believed that Priscilla had escaped to Spain. In fact, between May and July, she was staying with Cornet in a large house near Paris, coming in once a week to sign at the police station in Batignolles.

Jealousy can be slow to show its fangs. 'I will never let you go,' he said rather too often. 'I don't care what happens. You cannot escape from me.' She mistook his possessiveness for strength.

The couple moved about 'fairly freely'. Priscilla did not ask herself what he lived on. Cornet never appeared to work. She supposed that it was difficult for him to find a job, being Belgian. He could not motor-race, which was all he cared about. Even so, he seemed to have plenty of money, although how he made it was a mystery. Because of petrol rationing, cars were forbidden to most of the population; only 7,000 private vehicles were licensed in Paris. But Cornet enjoyed unexplained access to a car – and sometimes to a lorry – in which he chauffeured Priscilla at full throttle.

Her love of speed dates from this period. Cornet later reported to Priscilla how he had driven with the wife of the motor-ace René Dreyfus: 'She is very sporty and drives like a man. *Almost as well as you*. Which is a compliment.' She continued to drive like the clappers in post-war England. 'I am not a lover of motoring,' SPB wrote, after a hair-raising car journey with Priscilla through the Highlands. 'Usually we go too fast. Pris likes touching the hundred and reminds me of Mr Toad.' Like Mr Toad, she was heedless of the dangers that she raced towards.

'I still intend to marry you if one day you ever make the mistake of accepting me.' Cornet's obsession with Priscilla outlived the war. His letters confirm their mutual attraction. 'Since you left, it's been impossible to envisage having a love affair, still less a liaison. And everything is empty, empty, empty.' He addressed her as 'femme fatale', 'mon ping-pong', 'mon future better-half'. He longed to settle down with her. 'You were, and will always remain for me, the woman I loved most. And I do not regret our "impossible amour". Oh no!!' One letter ends: 'Write me when you feel like it, and if once you want to come back let me know and don't go straight back to Robert! Bye! Your best friend. Emile.'

Cornet hated the thought of Robert touching her. 'I can't bear the way he looks at you and speaks to you,' Cornet said, following a charged encounter with her husband, after Robert discovered that she had not escaped to England. She had known Cornet barely a month and already he was pressing Priscilla to divorce Robert and marry him. She was never free when Cornet wanted her; only when her sclerotic nitwit of a husband deigned it. Worn down by his demands, Priscilla finally petitioned Robert for an annulment of their marriage on the grounds that no child had issued from their union nor ever could, and 'offered to give proof of a certain number of facts'.

A burning Robert instructed his lawyer to take advantage of a recent law which encouraged the judge to seek delays and promote reconciliation. Important correspondence in Robert's possession proved that during their four years of 'unclouded union' the couple had never ceased to show one another feelings of the tenderest attachment. For instance, a few days after 'brusquely abandoning the marital home, to go and live with a certain Emile', Priscilla had written Robert a letter which concluded: 'I kiss you tenderly.' Another letter from Priscilla contained the following passage, the few sad lines being all that remain of her letters to Robert: 'I hope that everything is going to get better with E ... Thank you again for everything you did. I relax and try to think as little as possible. Until now I have managed to avoid the blues. I'm thinking of coming back just after Pentecost, but I won't stay longer than 48 hours in Paris before going to Le Touquet ... I leave you with a strong hug.'

Robert's lawyer succeeded in arguing that such documents invalidated her allegations. The judge dismissed Priscilla's application. She tried again the following year – with the same result.

* * *

Why was Robert adamant in blocking Priscilla's request for an annulment? An obvious explanation is that his family did not get divorced. It was forbidden; in 600 years, it had not happened once.

At Boisgrimot, news of Priscilla's elopement fell on his mother with the unwelcome impact of the German invasion. Adelaide's faith made it irrelevant that Priscilla might have grounds for wishing to separate from her youngest son because he had not slept with her. Until the First World War, Adelaide had refused to allow divorcees into the house. Soon after Priscilla's petition, probably broken by it, her mother-in-law died.

Priscilla's behaviour also upset Yolande and Georges – to whom had fallen the role of guardians of the Doynel family honour. More dangerous still, it set her on a collision course with the French government and with the nation's father-protector: the white-haired octogenarian whose ubiquitous features had begun to appear on ashtrays above the logo 'A new France is born'.

Marshal Pétain's regime marched to the beat of a gymnastic Christianity, but was perched on precarious legal foundations. One day in February 1942, getting out at the wrong floor of his hotel in Vichy, Pétain opened a door and found a young woman typing away on a portable table, before realising that she was sitting on the bidet. He asked what she was typing. 'The Constitution.'

It was not only the Consitution that was changing. A key act of Pétain's National Revolution was a reform of the divorce law, prohibiting divorce in the first three years of marriage, and then only in exceptional cases of physical cruelty. Adultery – to which the Maréchal was no stranger – was not considered grounds for divorce, but was to be treated as a punishable crime. A wife's infidelity was considered a graver fault than her husband's. In December 1942, the Vichy government allowed wives of POWs caught having an affair to be fined or imprisoned. This was in addition to the 23 July Law, which made a married woman found guilty of 'abandoning the hearth' liable to a year in prison and a 20,000-franc fine. With 1.8 million Frenchmen absent in German prison camps, including Robert's brother Guy, it was important not to feed their anxieties.

Ever since the Armistice, Pétain had worked to fortify the family unit as the 'essential cell' of social order, cemented by the promotion of the woman as a faithful wife and child-bearing mother who worked tirelessly and did not budge from the hearth. A woman's offspring were more cherished still. Patrick Buisson, the best recent historian of Vichy France, argues that it was better to be a single young mother with an illegitimate child than to be sexually sterile with no children at all. In February 1942, abortion became a crime that carried the death penalty – and two people were guillotined. And yet with all their men away, it was not so easy for French women to fulfil the Maréchal's expectations.

Desperate to conserve a freedom she had not enjoyed until now, Priscilla, who had had an abortion in France and sought a divorce – and who, in addition, was 'sans issue' and 'sans profession' – risked placing herself outside the protection of Church and State.

Her husband was a Catholic loyal to the French government, but more than that Robert still loved Priscilla, still regarded her as his wife, and desired to win her back. And he had a further reason for his intransigence. Robert did not believe for a moment, having met him, that Emile-Hubert Cornet du Fonteny was the man to make Priscilla happy. He was not alone in his reservations. Among Priscilla's letters is one from Berry, her former room mate in Besançon: 'I used to worry about the Belgian with whom you lived in Paris, just because, although he made money off and on, both he and you spent what he made recklessly so that there were bad times.'

Priscilla's new lover was a figure out of some black comic strip. I was reminded of Hitchcock, and also of the French director Louis Malle, as I followed my unsuspecting aunt down into the underworld to which Emile Cornet now introduced her, and in particular *Lacombe, Lucien* (1974). All because of a flat tyre, Malle's young protagonist, rejected by the Resistance, wheels his bicycle into a provincial French town, sees large cars, hears music and, before he knows it, is swept up into working for the German police. From early 1942, Priscilla drifted in the same milieu which inspired Malle's most controversial character. And the more I uncovered, the deeper I understood why its French audience had found Lacombe's amoral story hard to accept and impossible to talk about. 'Forget suicide and incest,' said Malle's brother Vincent. The subject touched on a taboo more potent and raw and shaming than either. 'It shows how easy it is to be on the wrong side and not realise it.'

Priscilla and Cornet moved back to Paris at the beginning of July. Cornet had found them 'a very nice flat' in a short cobbled street near the Etoile. The address – 11 bis Rue Lord Byron – was in the heart of Nazi Paris and less than a hundred yards from the Champs-Elysées.

But three months into Priscilla's new relationship, cracks appeared. 'I was not at all happy as too many things worried me.'

Priscilla's immediate concern was the French police: she had heard that the commissioner of Batignolles was looking for her.

It was always going to be a long shot that the Paris police had preserved a file on Priscilla. In a shabby room inside the Préfecture de Police in Rue de la Montagne Sainte-Geneviève, the archivist shook his head. My best bet was the Bundesarchiv in Koblenz. His reaction was disappointing, though hardly surprising. Most dossiers on foreigners were hurriedly removed as the Germans entered Paris, and scuttled in the Seine.

Half a dozen researchers sat reading old crime reports in silence. The archivist was walking towards the door when I went through the motion of trying out Emile Cornet's name. Heads lifted as I explained in schoolboy French that he was 'un amant de ma tante'.

But Cornet drew the same negative response as had Priscilla.

At the risk of disturbing everyone, I mentioned Max Stocklin, a name that I had read in one of Cornet's letters. Almost all I knew about Max Stocklin was that he was sentenced for espionage and collaboration in January 1946. Might a record exist of his trial?

'Non,' said the archivist, and left the room.

But the name Stocklin registered with his young assistant. Seated behind an ancient computer, she called it up. Nothing. She persisted, entering a different code, slowly accessing a separate stack in the labyrinth – and on the third attempt there he was, Max Stocklin, with his file number.

'What was your aunt's name again?'

I told her. She typed it in, pressed enter. And up on screen it came: 'Doynel de la Sausserie, Priscilla.' Through Max Stocklin, I had found her. But what was Priscilla doing in the same database as such a dubious figure?

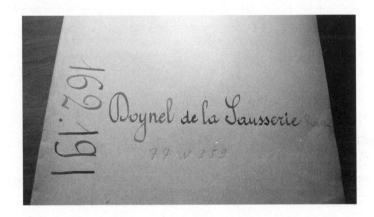

The survival of Priscilla's police dossier no. 162.191 was, everyone agreed, a piece of luck. Her name was written in Gothic script on the beige folder. Inside, documents covered her activities in Paris from July 1942 – two months after she told Robert that she was returning to England – to October 1942. They comprised six letters from the French police, one from the SS, and an interview conducted by a senior French policeman, Roger Le Meur.

On 7 February 1942, the Germans had relaxed their order for Priscilla to sign every day in a book reserved for British nationals. From now on, she was required to register once a week at her local police station. Five months passed before Le Meur reported to his German superior: 'She has not always executed this measure very regularly.'

Interest in Priscilla was aroused first on 8 July. The police commissioner of Batignolles, in charge of the book, was livid to discover that Priscilla had signed for four weeks '*in advance*'. He acted without delay to arrest her, but was too late, he wrote to Le Meur. 'Ordered immediately to the commissariat to be interrogated over this fraud, the undersigned did not present herself and it was her husband Doynel de la Sausserie, 43, grazier of French nationality, who responded yesterday. He explained that his wife had abandoned their home at the end of May, probably to follow a lover, and that from this moment he didn't know her address or what had happened to her.' The commissioner understood from Robert that 'she has changed domicile without authorisation since the end of May 1942, letting us believe that she was still at 103 rue Nollet. Her actual address has not been discovered.'

A fortnight later, perhaps alerted by Robert, Priscilla showed up at the police station in Place Charles Fillion and explained that she was now living in Rue Lord Byron. She changed address again the following week, an indication of Cornet's concern not to have the French authorities on his tail. On 30 July, she moved into a hotel in Place des Augustins and was staying there when, on 12 August, the commissioner summoned her to his office and took down her statement. He passed it on to Le Meur, chief of the Section des Britanniques, who was to decide whether to prosecute her.

Given the widespread practice among the French of incriminating each other during the Occupation, it was natural to expect Roger Le Meur, when investigating Priscilla's case, to be deluged by reports of her adultery. An Abwehr Major estimated that there were thirty million anonymous denunciations made in France between 1940 and 1945.

A fear of being denounced governed the action of *The Raven*, the classic film of this period. After the war, Priscilla met its rancorous director Henri-Georges Clouzot with Gillian, who promptly became his lover. 'No man has ever made me walk so much,' Gillian complained. All that walking, Clouzot told her, was a habit acquired during the Occupation. Clouzot was still chafing from the fall-out of having made *The Raven* with a German-financed company. Gillian wrote: 'For Clouzot, I was a girl who had been loved by men who had loathed and despised him for having collaborated by working for the Germans.

It was a bone he never stopped chewing. Out of the blue he would say, "Your friend Kessel won't shake my hand, for him I'm a collabo.'" What embittered Clouzot was that *The Raven*, shot in 1943 for Continental Productions, was an exposé of denunciation.

People in a village start receiving anonymous letters. The letters accuse the recipient of adultery. Before long, the community is at each other's throats, each person suspicious of the other – which is what happened that summer in Sainteny, after Monsieur Virette, the village carpenter, was denounced for possessing a revolver.

Priscilla heard the distressing details from Robert, how Virette was taken to prison in Saint-Lô and then shot. Jacqueline Hodey, the grocer's daughter, told me that it was the worst moment of her life. 'I saw Monsieur Virette leave. I had his young son Daniel with me. I used to look after Daniel, aged eleven, while he was doing his catechism. I was walking along the street with a crocodile of fifteen kids when the curé said, "Quickly, take the children back," because he had seen a lorry go up to the house. The lorry then passed us and I could see Monsieur Virette in the back between two armed soldiers, and Daniel said, "They're taking Daddy away." I led the children into church and that was the last time Daniel saw his father.'

Similar denunciations took place in Paris. During my fruitless search for Priscilla in the French National Archives, in a box of papers ostensibly relating to British internees I came across a chilling letter addressed to the German Commandant, Place Opéra, dated 13 June 1941. The anonymous author was '100% in agreement' with the German position on collaboration and the Jewish question – 'and this is why I hope you will permit me, Monsieur, to alert you to what is happening at the Restaurant Beulemans in Boulevard Saint-Germain.' Two Greek Jews, sisters, both of them mistresses of the owner, were leading a wicked life with German officers. Writing in an educated hand in turquoise ink on thick cream paper, the author provided further details about these Jews, 'who have done us so much harm', and hoped that by joining forces with good Frenchmen, the two nations, Germany and France, would be able to work towards universal peace.

Priscilla was not Jewish. And yet her British passport made her an enemy. Like the Greek sisters, she was a despicable example of everything a French woman should not be: a childless and unemployed adulteress who had deserted an adoring husband and former POW, to live with a highly suspect lover. In other words, a prime candidate for denunciation.

So why did the senior French official in charge of investigating Priscilla go out of his way not to prosecute her?

Roger Le Meur's interview with my aunt was handwritten over four pages. She did not hold back except to conceal the identity of her father, in case she risked being detained as the daughter of a 'personnage célèbre'. Compliantly, Le Meur recorded the names of her parents as 'Stuart and Snow, Noris [*sic*]'. Stuart, her father's first name, was not likely to excite German suspicions.

Otherwise, Priscilla told Le Meur everything: her childhood in England, her upbringing in Paris, her internment, the rocky state of her marriage, her sex life. His report betrayed his sympathies. 'Mme Doynel de la Sausserie exercises no profession and after leaving her husband, because he did not give her children, she received from him subsidies and continues to see him from time to time. He, son of a wealthy family of agriculturalists, is owner of several farms in Normandy which guarantee him a substantial income. Today aged 43, Doynel de la Sausserie is a jaded man who can hardly give great satisfaction to his young wife ["un blasé qui ne pouvait guère donner de grandes satisfactions à sa jeune femme"] and this is the main reason why she has left the marital home.' Her impotent husband personified to Le Meur the argument about national decadence that had led to the collapse of France. Up until recently her marriage had seemed 'very united', and there was general surprise in Priscilla's circle when she took her leave. 'Enquiries have revealed nothing unfavourable about this stranger, especially from a political point of view, and although her sympathies remain with the English cause, she abstains from all commentary and from all activity which could attract enemies.' Glowingly, he concluded that 'Madame Doynel de la Sausserie enjoys the esteem of all, and one cannot see in this stranger any element of eventual trouble to the interior of our country.'

Instead of locking up Priscilla for failing to sign in at the police station, or charging her for adultery and desertion as the state empowered him, and as many might have demanded, Le Meur took no further action. Why? Had he joined that line of men who instinctively were moved to shield Priscilla? Or was he acting under orders? Something did not add up. It looked as if Priscilla had a protector – if not Roger Le Meur, then someone higher in the French or German administration.

All these interrogations rattled Priscilla. One morning in the street, looking pale and ill, she bumped into Daniel Vernier. It amazed him to find her still in France.

Her eyes made the worst fault of all – looked away. Then out it came: about Emile Cornet, how Priscilla had decided to get a divorce and marry him, her difficulties with the police. She blurted out: 'I am worried about my papers.' Her French identity card was valid only until 29 October 1942.

Vernier's feelings for Priscilla had not cooled. He took it 'very badly' that she had fallen head-over-heels for an unemployed Belgian racing driver, the source of whose wealth was so murky. Even so, Vernier suppressed his hurt and agreed to help. But he 'made me promise not to lose touch with Simone or himself as he foresaw difficulties with the Gestapo'.

The French police may have shown lenience, but the German authorities were becoming more vigilant. Two years on and the reality of the Occupation was starker. The atmosphere in the streets around the Champs-Elysées – treacly with Viennese walzes when Priscilla returned from Besançon – carried a new note; tense, edgier. The Germans were no longer trying to charm the French with correct behaviour. The handsome blond youths who had first entered Paris, marching behind horses with bleached tails, had vanished to the Russian front. Their replacements were paunchy veterans who, from behind white hoardings, out of range of grenade throwers, eyed Priscilla with suspicion. Black-bordered posters carried the names of those shot for an act of violence against the German Armed Forces. Many of the condemned were Communists who had supported Vichy until June 1941. From August, there was a steady stream of assassination attempts on German officials, for which Hitler person-ally demanded 'the most severe measures' in retaliation. In February 1942, against the backdrop of a worsening war in the East, Hitler ordered the Military Commander in Paris to execute up to 100 French for every German murdered; more than 550 hostages were killed by the end of the year. The numbers joining the Resistance rose further after Pierre Laval announced the Relève in June 1942, pressing for three French workers to 'volunteer' in German factories to secure the release of every French POW. The Nazis targeted Communists, but also foreigners. Americans were as vulnerable as the British, following America's entry into the war in December 1941. Most vulnerable were Jews like Hans Mayer in Priscilla's short story. Further anti-Jewish measures were introduced in May, demanding the wearing of a yellow star and forbidding Jews from crossing the Champs-Elysées. Priscilla was aware that people all over Paris were being arrested by the French police and, increasingly, by the Gestapo.

What Priscilla feared as 'the Gestapo' was in fact a confusing maze of German intelligence and counter-intelligence networks often tangling with each other. Until now, responsibility for security had been the jealously guarded domaine of the Military Commander in France who placed control of all intelligence operations under one organisation, the Army's counter-intelligence service, the Abwehr. The SS – the Nazi party's paramilitary wing – had kept a low profile in the shadows of the German Army, with a small staff of forty restricted to information gathering. But their numbers had stealthily grown, causing resentment for their 'not always useful dealings'. The arrival in May 1942 of Himmler's personal representative in Paris, General Carl-Albrecht Oberg, signalled the moment at which the SS started to steal power away from the Abwehr. To the anger and mistrust of the Military Commander, General Carl-Heinrich Von Stülpnagel, Oberg was appointed 'Supreme SS and Police Leader'. One of the buildings that his men took over was the Ministry of the Interior near the Elysée palace, 11 Rue des Saussaies. Almost immediately, Oberg placed the French police in the Occupied Zone, who until then had functioned semi-independently, under the tighter grip of the German police, and expanded to two units the number of Frenchmen working directly with the Gestapo.

Vernier understood the dangers that Priscilla faced as a British-passport holder whose French documents were not in order. He was in touch with a 'specialist' who might sort out some new identity papers. But first, he needed to find Priscilla a less exposed address than a hotel. The best place was a nursing home. He knew a doctor who would provide her with a medical certificate.

Priscilla presented this to the French police, who forwarded it to the German authorities. On 13 October 1942, SS Untersturmführer Heise signed a dispensation order: 'In view of the medical certificate that has been presented to me, she is free from having to sign in until 30 November 1942.' For the remainder of her time in Paris, Priscilla's address was Dr Devaux's clinic, 23 Rue Paradier, Ville d'Avray, in Paris's western suburbs.

She used the nursing home as a screen. 'I had to go there once a week and always leave them my telephone number in case the Germans became curious and wanted to see me. This made Emile furious, as he hated me being away from him and he hated the thought that I owed so much to Daniel.'

Cornet punched Priscilla when he found out what Daniel Vernier had done for her. 'That was how I learnt one side of his character, which had been kept hidden till then. This insane jealousy.' Cornet could no longer camouflage his feelings; Priscilla had believed they were about love, but they were about possession. Whenever Vernier's name was mentioned, there was a violent scene. Priscilla hoped that a meeting would solve matters, but the two men met 'and hated each other'.

Her ongoing affair with Cornet had a desolating impact on Vernier. He refused to eat. He looked ill. 'There was no doubt that I made him suffer cruelly.'

Priscilla had never felt prettier or more carefree than in her first months with Cornet. She had got into bed with a man who appeared to love her and whose sensuality was appreciated. She felt like a woman for the first time. But her best days with Cornet were over. 'Being in love suited me. But not Emile. He became more difficult and demanding, and tormented me with questions about my movements, thoughts, actions, secret desires.'

What had she done this afternoon? She had taken tea with Zoë. How was he to know it was with a woman and not a man?

He told her: 'You attract too many people and you show them you are not unmoved by their attentions.'

He asked: 'How much do you love me?'

'I haven't got a tape-measure kind of mind. I love you as much as I am capable of loving.'

Whoever she spoke to made him jealous: Robert, Zoë, Daniel, Simone, even her divorce lawyer. He said: 'I want to push them away and say: she is mine, leave her alone.'

His possessiveness infuriated her almost more than Robert's passivity. 'Sometimes I lost my temper with him and stormed out of the café, but he used brute strength to stop me when he caught up; sometimes I wept and then he would be full of remorse and gentle for a while.'

Vernier begged her to leave Cornet. She refused. 'However unhappy I was, I felt more alive than I had done before his appearance.'

But the scenes wore Priscilla out. She could not bear what she called his 'Gestapo act'. And something else troubled her: Cornet's means of earning a living.

'One day he would have plenty of money and splash it around. The next day there would be nothing to eat at all. Where did all the money come from when it was there?' Priscilla in love had been 'un peu dans la lune' – head in the clouds. Only when they came back from the countryside to live in the centre of Paris did she realise that her Belgian lover was involved in the black market. 'I was slightly startled as I had never known any shady characters before and there now appeared in my life quite a number of them.'

23.
L'AFFAIRE STOCKLIN

Who were these shady characters who popped up in Priscilla's life to protect her from the French and German authorities?

So much of research involves combing for wayward threads. Most of the time you pluck and what comes away is fluff. Just occasionally, as in fishing, the line goes taut and you feel a tug like a submerged handshake.

Embedded in one of Cornet's letters was a reference to a figure whom I failed to invest with significance when I first read it. But Max Stocklin was the one loose strand poking up, from which unravelled the protected and sulphurous underworld of the French Gestapo. From what I discovered about him in his file in the Préfecture de Police, he became my initial suspect for the influential figure who could have persuaded the French police to let Priscilla go.

Six months after the war, on 21 January 1946, Emile Cornet wrote to Priscilla: 'I've been two days in a row at the Court of Assizes where they are trying Max Stocklin. I was summoned as a witness and did my best for him. He has been condemned to hard labour in perpetuity. The important thing was to save his head.' Cornet implied that Stocklin was a friend of Priscilla's, but did not mention what he might have done to deserve the guillotine.

I had already begun hunting Stocklin down; in German and French history books, in archives in London, Washington and Koblenz. But he was a fugitive footnote, appearing fleetingly, each time spelled differently and in a different guise – Swiss businessman, art dealer, Abwehr spy – and vanishing after the war. In the National Archives in Kew, I read in a report marked 'Secret': 'Max Stoecklin deceased Swiss national, recently executed by the French Government as a German agent.' And yet Stocklin had been killed off before his time. Not until I opened file No. 305315 in the Préfecture did he stir.

The person who looked up at me from his mug-shot was clean-shaven, darkly handsome, aged about forty-five. Underneath was printed: STOCK-ELYNCK. But it was Stocklin all right.

The name which had led to my aunt's dossier trailed behind it threads which, once tugged, unspooled from an address in central Paris to Hermann Göring's estate outside Berlin. From his headquarters at 1 Rue Lord Byron, Max Stocklin ran a hugely profitable Europe-wide operation into which he enticed Cornet, and by extension Priscilla. It was Stocklin who enabled the couple to live well and who provided them with a requisitioned apartment only a few yards from his office. The relationship was intimate enough for Stocklin to summon Cornet to provide the character reference at his prosecution.

The important document in Stocklin's police folder was headed 'l'affaire Stockling'. This was the handwritten transcription of Stocklin's trial in January 1946. It contained details which had eluded the published record and brought Priscilla out of the clouds.

Twice married, twice divorced, Max Stocklin was born in 1901, in Basel, to a family who owned a porcelain business. After a childhood on the Rhine, he lived in Marseilles, then moved to Brussels where he shed his first wife and sold, without success, portable microphones and gasogene boilers. But through gasogenes Stocklin met, in 1934, a bon-vivant who rescued him from bankruptcy and upturned his life.

Hermann Brandl was a mysterious thirty-five-year old Bavarian engineer who worked for a Belgian boiler manufacturer, specialising in a heating-system known as 'système Otto'. It was a cover. Brandl was an officer of the Cologne section of the Abwehr. He was reasonably close to Admiral Canaris, the Abwehr's head, and also to Göring, the ultimate controller. Like many unlikely people in Priscilla's story, Brandl will appear again.

In 1936, Brandl recruited Stocklin as an agent, ostensibly to sell his 'Otto' heaters, but paying him 2,000 francs a month to gather information on Belgian military bases.

Two years later, purporting to work for a wine company, Max Stocklin was sent to Paris. He rented a house in Saint-Cloud where he installed a clandestine radio transmitter. From the atelier of 11 Avenue de Nancy, Stocklin signalled to Brandl on the outbreak of hostilities, giving information about French aircraft numbers and the location of the military headquarters at La Ferté-sous-Jouarre.

French security police discovered Stocklin's transmissions and arrested him on 15 May 1940, two days after the German army crossed the Meuse. His crime carried the death penalty. He was incarcerated in a camp in Cépoy 70 miles south of Paris while awaiting execution.

The German invasion saved him. The camp was evacuated and the guards were marching the prisoners south when Stukas attacked. Stocklin seized the chance to escape across the fields with his French cell mate: a falsetto-voiced petty criminal, tall and strong with tiny, dark, cunning eyes, who offered to guide Stocklin back to Paris. Three days later, they stood and watched a German military band marching down the Champs-Elysées.

Stocklin bid farewell to his cell mate and made a beeline for the Hôtel Lutétia, taken over by the Abwehr. In the black marbled hall, surrounded by boxes and papers, he was reunited with the men he had spied for in Brussels. Among the most important was the intelligence officer who had first employed him, Hermann Brandl.

Stocklin's meeting with Brandl could not have been more opportune for either party. Acting under the code name 'Otto' – derived from Brandl's middle name or from his domestic boilers – Brandl was charged by Admiral Canaris with an order that Göring announced at Maxim's a fortnight after the Occupation: to strip France of everything that Germany's war effort required. Göring couched his instructions in terms of La Chasse. 'You must turn yourself into hunting dogs, be on the trail of anything which might be useful to the German people . . .' The French were expected to meet not only the food and maintenance needs of the occupying army but to satisfy the requirements of Germany's population at home. Göring's plan, admitted one German general, was to make France part kitchen garden and part brothel.

Alongside the official procurement services of the German military, there now sprang up a clandestine system organised by Brandl. He urgently needed trusted agents with a knowledge of France. On the spot he promoted Stocklin to help him.

Hermann 'Otto' Brandl and the massive looting organisation he created with Stocklin's assistance, known as 'Bureau Otto', became an obsession of Gillian Sutro during her research into Priscilla's activities. 'He was never in uniform. He spoke very good French. He was very close to Göring for whom he worked with great zeal buying up for a pittance works of art for Göring's and Hitler's art collections (Hitler had first choice) or seizing paintings from requisitioned apartments deserted by Jews who had fled. Otto operated in Paris where he had installed the Bureau Otto to which people could bring things for sale. He had agents scavenging for him in the provinces ... buying up brewers in huge quantities: 50,000 bottles at a time, leather goods, cement, copper, nickel, lead, foie gras by the ton, meat, crates of caviar, turkeys, cattle. Money was no problem, as the vanquished French had to cough up 400 million francs per day for the upkeep of the German Army in occupation; the Germans also had the right to requisition food "à discrétion du vainqueur". One can imagine what abuses went on.'

A leading architect of this abusive system was the man who sat across the Paris courtoom from Priscilla's lover: Cornet's employer and the funder of Priscilla's lifestyle.

'Brown hair, very elegant,' the police clerk wrote. Under a grey overcoat and multi-coloured scarf, Max Stocklin wore an 'impeccable' white shirt and red tie. His voice did not rise once in two days of cross-examination.

Cornet must have known a lot of what he heard in court. It was why he was there: to defend his friend's character. Stocklin needed Cornet to save his life.

The charges read out by the liberated French prosecutor against Max Stocklin for his wartime activities in France were serious:

He was head of counter-espionage in the Haute-Savoie region.

He had been sentenced to death *in absentia* for attempting to set up a clandestine radio post near Algiers.

He had tried to bribe a policeman for information about General Weygand and the French fleet in Toulon.

All false, Stocklin insisted. 'I spied before the war, it's true, but I decided to give it up and concentrate on business. After the armistice, I was just a black market collaborator.'

But his black market dealings constituted Stocklin's gravest crime. This 'dangerous enemy agent' was none other than 'the principal agent of "Otto" Brandl'.

Rules prevented the Germans from dealing directly with their French suppliers. Brandl appointed intermediaries like Stocklin to open secret purchasing offices, all answerable to Bureau Otto. Stocklin camouflaged his as a French industrial research body.

Why did the Germans set up such offices? Why not grab what they wanted? German policy was based on cynicism and deception. While Germany was still trying to win the rest of the war, it needed a docile France on side. To give the impression that Vichy was in charge of France's affairs, everything had to appear above board, and prices were kept fixed to maintain the propaganda of Pétain's programme of 'German–French economic collaboration'. But this collaboration was a fantasy. The reason that so much food was rationed, eventually making the French among the worst fed in Europe, was because most of France's wheat, fruit, vegetables, butter and meat was syphoned back to Germany. Not only that, the French were financing the operation from the Vichy treasury.

It is impossible to overestimate the spread of Bureau Otto's tentacles. Brandl did not limit his purchases to the needs of the German troops, but was interested in buying 'absolutely anything the French offered', according to Fabienne Jamet – owner of the lavish brothel One-Two-Two, the windowless seven-storey building in Rue de Provence where many of Brandl's transactions took place. Here, and in the Traveller's Club on the Champs-Elysées, Brandl bought soap, leather, metal, carpets, playing cards: all by the ton. 'The list of things he required was endless and he paid cash on the nail.'

Near the top of the list were works of art. Brandl's principal agent Stocklin was charged with stealing Matisse's *The Open Window* from the Paul Rosenberg collection, and for selling to Hitler, for 350,000 francs, Matisse's *Female Nude in a Yellow Chair*. And yet looted paintings were not the cornerstone of Stocklin's trafficking. His main concern was to snap up French textiles, alcohol and telegraph wire, and ship these on to Germany, for which he required reliable, fast drivers. This was Cornet's attraction: in his last major race before the war, driving an Alfa Romeo 1.8, Cornet had finished seventh in the 1938 Antwerp Grand Prix.

In October 1940, Stocklin opened a purchasing office at 1 Rue Lord Byron. The Bureau d'Etudes Minières Industrielles et Commerciales (BEMIC) took over suites 425–427 on the fourth floor and purported to be a company investigating the feasibility of manufacturing electric cars.

Stocklin's car passed Priscilla's entrance, on his way to Brandl's office in Rue Adolphe-Yvon. Between 2 p.m. and 5 p.m. every afternoon, representatives of the purchasing offices turned up with samples to be rejected or accepted. Reports speak of about fifty representatives, the majority of them women. They took care not to give their full identities; a pronoun sufficed. There were penalties for revealing names or addresses. Stocklin, calling himself 'Guy Max', visited often.

His sample accepted, Stocklin received an order form for delivery to a warehouse in the Saint-Ouen docks north of Paris. There was no other paper trail involved, no tax. Payment was made in new-minted French francs.

Bureau Otto's principal cashier has left a picture of how the purchase worked. A trusted agent like Stocklin – or one of his nominees like Cornet – pulled up in a car carrying four men armed with machine guns who guarded the vehicle while Stocklin loaded sacks containing the bank notes. One afternoon in October 1941, the cashier issued 322 million francs, remitted from the daily amount of 400 million francs that Article 18 of the Armstice required the Vichy government to hand over to the occupying forces. This money was used to buy and ferry goods. To any French policeman who stopped his car or lorry, Cornet flashed a special yellow and red striped Ausweis which authorised him to circulate at any time, to carry a gun and to count on the assistance of German police, who could do what they liked. An instruction printed in French and German stated: 'The French authorities have no jurisdiction over the bearer', and declared that the lorry's contents could not be stopped or inspected by French police. These were the goods, the cars and the lorries, but most of all the money, delivered in one million franc bricks, which passed through Cornet's hands. Priscilla's Belgian lover and former motor-ace was merely pursuing his wartime trade when he wrote to her after Paris was liberated: 'I've got a job that suits me perfectly. I drive a lot for the Interallied Mission, I drive at least a thousand miles a week, and I'm quite satisfied.'

Brandl's system was failsafe. The French provided the funds for the Germans to pillage their country. That is why the Germans were not worried, initially, when the situation created both a French and a German black market competing for the same items. The price was driven up, but the French were paying anyway. The daily turnover of the offices under Brandl's control made 'Doctor Otto' the uncontested Godfather of this combined black market. Few benefited more from Brandl's patronage than Cornet and Priscilla's friend Max Stocklin.

Soon, Stocklin had opened offices in Switzerland, Belgium, Spain and Portugal. His lorries transported textiles from all over Europe to the docks in Saint-Ouen. He sold on his textiles at mark-ups of five times the original price and pocketed the commission. Between 1940 and 1943, BEMIC/'Bureau Guy Max' generated 200 million francs, 'making important profits for the SS, the Todt organisation and the German navy' – and personally earning Stocklin an estimated 20 million francs.

In 1941, Stocklin expanded his operation into silk stockings and perfumes. He controlled a multitude of companies, including 'Bas Marny' stockings and 'Parfums Marny' – bought for a derisory sum off a Jewish owner who had fled Paris. The prosecution maintained that an office opened by Stocklin in Monaco to sell these perfumes was a cover for money-laundering (Cornet's decision to move to Monaco after the war may be explained by his familiarity with the Principality when working for this office). Stocklin's partner Jacques Horteur was one witness who might have corroborated the charge, but he had been murdered in front of 74 Champs-Elysées on the night of 17 August 1945 'in circumstances we have not not been able to elucidate'. If you knew about Stocklin's operations, you did not tell. But did Priscilla know?

Priscilla in a fur coat on the slopes of Megève. Priscilla dining at the cabaret restaurant Le Baccara. Priscilla speeding up Rue Lord Byron. According to the journalist Alfred Fabre-Luce: 'Anyone with a car is under suspicion of having dealings with the enemy ...'

It is not possible from existing sources to get hold of a detailed idea of Priscilla's knowledge or involvement. The only way to gauge this is to see who she mixed with. The prosecution asserted that leading a similar elite lifestyle, while the rest of the population queued in the cold streets for ten ounces of bread, was another associate of Stocklin, a haughty young Moscow-born aristocrat called Marie. 'Stocklin had in his service for some time la Comtesse Marie Tchernycheff-Bezobrazoff who installed a purchasing agency in the next two rooms, mainly of rubber products that were transported in German lorries driven by a member of the Gestapo.'

Marie had moved in the same pre-war circles as Priscilla and Gillian. A former mistress of the young Philippe de Rothschild, she had modelled for Chanel and worked as a vendeuse for Schiaparelli, before turning to film, acting an unremarkable part in Marc Allegret's *Zouzou*, as a music-hall singer who takes a Brazilian lover. By the end of 1941, she was a divorcee living in Rio. Fact had imitated the dowdy cinematic fiction.

Boredom returned her to France. She was intelligent. She was attractive. Nostalgic for her days as a future film star, she pined to be at the centre of things. In December 1941, this was Nazi-occupied Paris. That winter at the Hôtel Lutétia, she met an agent working for Brandl. When she asked who was this Max Stocklin everyone was talking about, he led her up four flights of stairs to the BEMIC office and introduced her to its dandyish chairman, whom she found elegant 'in the gangster mode'.

Stocklin rented Marie a room next door to set up her own purchasing agency. Alternately known as 'the Red Princess' or 'Mara', and often to be observed tugging behind her a poodle that answered to the name of Dingo, she proved to be a more talented businesswoman than actress. She was extending her reach into alcohol and textiles when Stocklin took her to a reception at 93 Rue Lauriston hosted by his former cell mate from Cépoy, the tall cunning man with the startling girlish voice.

Henri Chamberlin was the French criminal who had guided Stocklin safely to Paris. A mere draft-dodger and thief when he befriended Stocklin, he had become, thanks to Stocklin, the undisputed chief of the French Gestapo – and for the French Resistance, Public Enemy Number One. Aged thirty-eight, the multi-aliased Chamberlin was the person on whom the film director Louis Malle later based the character of Lucien Lacombe.

Chamberlin, or 'Monsieur Henri' as he was respectfully addressed, has a place in Priscilla's story because he embodied the milieu into which she was swept up – first by Cornet and then by her important friend Max Stocklin and his blonde sidekick Marie. It is only surmise, but due to the small size of this community, both geographically, encompassing no more than a few streets near the Etoile, and in the number of individuals involved, it is inconceivable that Priscilla and Chamberlin did not know each other. One of Chamberlin's mistresses lived directly below Priscilla in 11 bis Rue Lord Byron. Chamberlin's right-hand man lived in the same building as Daniel Vernier, to which Priscilla was a regular visitor. Gillian Sutro had little doubt that Priscilla met Chamberlin.

If not Stocklin, Chamberlin was the second of three likely candidates with the clout to strong-arm the French and German authorities to leave Priscilla alone.

'Is there anything more horrible than the French Gestapo?' asked Raymond Aron in his four-volume *Histoire de L'Epuration*. Who they were and how they fitted into the power ladder was encapsulated by the chief of the 'Gestapistes français' or 'Lauristondienst'.

On arriving with Stocklin in Paris, Chamberlin had initially recoiled from working for the enemy. He tried to get back his old job as manager at the Préfecture canteen, but an inspector there – Albert Priolet, who in 1917 had arrested the German spy Mata Hari – threatened to charge him for desertion. 'He threw me out like something dirty,' Chamberlin complained at his trial in December 1944. If in that moment the Resistance had made Chamberlin an offer, he would have seized it. 'But in the summer of 1940, the Resistance, there wasn't any. The word didn't exist!' In that moment, 'I simply had the desire not to die, to live.' He had to survive as he could. 'There was the Hôtel Lutétia, where I had made friends, thanks to my Swiss chum, Max Stocklin. I paid him a visit and he said: "Let's see, we'll find something for you."'

Chamberlin had even more reasons than Cornet to be grateful to Stocklin. Without Max Stocklin, there would have been no Henri Lafont, as Chamberlin now became known in what was his most lethal incarnation. After Chamberlin boasted that he could track down goods not available on the open market, Stocklin installed him with his new alias in a shop in Rue Tiquetonne to buy food, clothes and furniture for the Abwehr.

The instinctive revulsion of the French towards anything associated with Germany made it hard for German outsiders to procure goods and negotiate with suppliers. They depended on native informers with local knowledge, and Chamberlin became one of these quintessential French middle-men, protected by the Gestapo and doing the dodgy work.

As Henri Lafont, Chamberlin prospered. To nourish the Reich, he bought wheat in Normandy, butter by the lorry-load, furs, cattle. But he lacked henchmen, and so, with the Abwehr's connivance, he released from the cells of Fresnes prison 27 convicted felons to act as extortioners. Chamberlin's gang soon exceeded a hundred in number. Stealing, intimidating, making unauthorised house-searches of the wealthy, and buying only when necessary, his 'auxiliary police' chivvied out merchandise which the French population had attempted to conceal, and stored it in shops, garages, abandoned apartments. His Abwehr bosses were impressed. He flaunted a gun and a German police identity card, and eventually forty-four uniformed German officers were detailed to assist him. Six months on, he was indispensable to the Abwehr and exercised more power than Max Stocklin – it would be Chamberlin, on Brandl's orders, who sent Stocklin to Algeria with a radio transmitter. He had grown ruthless, rich.

Chamberlin's HQ was a three-storeyed hôtel particulier in Rue Lauriston, a short walk from Cornet and Priscilla's apartment. A clutch of receipts rescued from the premises during the Liberation showed that between April and December 1941, Chamberlin's gang amassed goods worth 142 million francs. Among the valuables were nine necklaces, seventeen gold bars and 159 kilos of children's clothes.

The boy who had left his Paris slum at eleven and subsisted out of dustbins now drove a white Bentley. White flowers were another obsession, orchids and dahlias especially. Chamberlin endowed 100,000 francs for a dahlia prize. 'Send me flowers' – his reply when those he had helped enquired how they might repay him. He could not bear to see a flower die.

When Göring outlawed the black market in March 1943, Chamberlin, now in the Gestapo, exchanged hunting down goods for hunting down Jews, Allied airmen, members of the Resistance. His men visited the One-Two-Two following a mission against maquisards in Haute-Savoie. Fabienne Jamet, the brothel owner, described in her memoirs seeing Frenchmen dressed in German uniforms sitting downstairs with a magnum and a few girls, boasting 'Did you see how I hit him? He'll be pissing blood for a week, that poor bugger ...' She said of Chamberlin's gang: 'They'd beaten people up, tortured people, and there they were, laughing about it ... We saw them all at one time or another. Horrible creatures.'

At his requisitioned home in 93 Rue Lauriston – which was equipped with cells and 'where torture was a daily practice', wrote Gillian Sutro – Chamberlin entertained journalists, industrialists, actresses, politicians, German leaders. He knew personally Hitler's Ambassador to Paris, Otto Abetz. He was on tutoyer terms with Vichy Prime Minister Pierre Laval. He was 'untouchable' said one police inspector after being locked up in a cell on the second floor. Chamberlin boasted to Fabienne Jamet's husband: 'If you have any mates inside you'd like sprung, you've only got to ask. I can fix it.' If anyone could have authorised Priscilla's freedom, it was Chamberlin.

Chamberlin's toxic influence over the Paris police is reflected in a Police Judiciaire report of 30 August 1944. 'Chamberlin-Lafont dictates his wishes to the office of the prefect of police and his demands are met, contrary to state security.' An Inspector Metra verified that Chamberlin's gang had taken him from his house to the Quai des Orfèvres, where Chamberlin ordered Metra to release a group of criminals. Four other inspectors and the police commissioner in Neuilly registered similar abuses: Monsieur Henri did what he wanted. In one hearing at the Court of Appeal, 'he freed an arrested woman he knew, drawing his pistol and threatening anyone who opposed him.'

The police report failed to reveal the identity of the woman he rescued, but Chamberlin's taste, which is what convinces me that he knew Priscilla, was for semi-aristocratic women married to useless husbands. The post-Liberation press titled them the 'countesses of the Gestapo'. Blonde, often bisexual, the countesses found the irascible Chamberlin hard to resist and queued up to debase themselves: the Marquise de Wiet, a former hairdresser who lived below Priscilla and Cornet; Annie de Saint-Jaymes, the separated wife of a gay antiquarian, who furnished 93 Rue Lauriston with antiques provided by her husband; Vicomtesse Marga d'Andurain, a former mistress of Mussolini; Evanne, the opium-addicted Princess Mourousi; Sylviane, the soi-disante Marquise d'Abrantès. Then there was the authentic Marquise d'Austerlitz, who taught Chamberlin to ride. In his interrogation, he described this ginger-headed equestrian as 'a crazy woman and a bitch', with absolutely no restraint in her choice of lovers.

Chamberlin's most representative mistress – the woman who had first unleashed in him his appetite for attractive titled blondes – was Max Stocklin's protégée: Comtesse Marie Tchernycheff-Bezobrazoff. When Stocklin introduced them at Chamberlin's reception it sparked an improbable coup de foudre.

The hothouse flowers. The foie gras. The tasteful gilt furniture – courtesy of Monsieur de Saint-Jaymes. And muffling any scream from the library, the laughter of guests, the fluting voice of her host. How could a bad actress have responded other than she did when Monsieur Henri gave Marie a tea-service that had once belonged to the Empress Eugénie – part of a carve-up of the American's ambassador's silverware collection; not to mention a laissez-passer which allowed her to circulate in Paris after the curfew, to visit him.

Marie moved into Henri Chamberlin's bedroom in Rue Lauriston, and in December 1942 set up, under his protection, her own purchasing emporium. When Marie was imprisoned in Fresnes in March 1943, during the sudden round-up of black-marketeers, Chamberlin went to see both Helmut Knochen, chief of Gestapo operations in Avenue Foch, and Karl Boemelburg, director of the Gestapo in Rue des Saussaies. Marie was let out after fifteen days.

Could Henri Chamberlin have done the same for Priscilla and stopped Roger Le Meur from prosecuting her?

All that Priscilla was prepared to admit to Gillian about Emile Cornet's racketeering was that his jacket was lined with expensive gold watches smuggled out of Switzerland. Her ignorance was almost plausible, but it begs some pretty tantalising questions. Was 'Monsieur Henri' himself one of Cornet's 'very odd friends' – and, if so, how much did the knowledge that Cornet might be engaged in something illicit and violent appal or even excite her? In *Belle de Jour*, Joseph Kessel writes about Séverine: 'In order to stimulate her desire for Marcel she had increasingly frequent recourse to imagining the dangerous and mysterious circles in which his young life moved … She hoped to watch him in the underworld and revive in herself, if only for a while, the sense of fear which was at the core of her sensuality.'

Moody, with a long thin nose and the piercing black eyes of a goshawk, Chamberlin was not a person whom Priscilla would forget; and Chamberlin, with his taste for young comtesses, would not have overlooked my blonde twenty-five-year old aunt.

Chamberlin liquidated all records of his gang, as did his contacts in the Préfecture. When it came to investigating what had gone on during these years, anything to do with the French Gestapo was sensitive. According to the book on the Occupation which Gillian used for her research, the officers charged with the inquiry discovered the rottenness to be so far-reaching that they were under orders to close the files on the grounds that the nation's morale, already severely weakened, 'would not support the shock of such devastating revelations'.

In December 1944, Chamberlin was hastily executed to ensure that he took with him to his grave as many embarrassing secrets as possible. He was sanguine about the death sentence, telling his lawyer that he had lived two lives and could afford to lose one. 'For four years I had what l love most in the world, orchids and Bentleys. So I don't regret anything.'

Max Stocklin was tried thirteen months after Chamberlin was shot. The court reconvened on 19 January 1946, to hear the verdict. There is no record of what Emile Cornet said in defence of his friend, only his reaction. Stocklin was sentenced to 'forced labour in perpetuity for espionage and commerce with the enemy' – a penalty which included 'degradation and national indignity' and the confiscation of his goods, valued at 20 million francs, once these could be located.

Cornet wrote immediately to Priscilla: 'Some time or another Max will be let out and he can go to Switzerland.' He predicted accurately. The last document in Stocklin's police file was a clipping to say that Max Stocklin had been amnestied on 23 June 1952.

24.
RESORTISSANTE BRITANNIQUE

One July morning in 1942, early on in their relationship, Priscilla ran away from Emile Cornet after he tried to rape her.

She telephoned Daniel Vernier as soon as Cornet left the apartment. 'I had to lock myself in the lavatory all night, I was so frightened.' Vernier dropped everything, picked her up at 10 a.m. and, stopping briefly at the police station in Place Charles Fillion – this is the occasion when she signed for a month in advance – drove her to a small hotel in the Dordogne. At some moment on the road to La Roque Gageac, she revealed the reason behind Cornet's assault: she had admitted to her jealous lover her previous romance with Vernier.

They arrived at the hotel at nightfall. Several actors were also staying there, shooting a film. 'The leading lady turned out to be a friend of Emile's and an acquaintance of mine. I had to explain to her that I had left Emile and did not want him to know where I was.'

The days passed. The weather was warm and Priscilla bathed in the river. Vernier stayed a few miles away in his father-in-law's chateau, Domaine de Mirabel. He came over for lunch. Gradually, Priscilla recovered.

'Then one day I received a letter from a friend in Paris telling me to expect Emile's visit as he had found out where I was.' The actress had betrayed her. 'I determined to hide, so I stayed in my room for a few days having briefed everyone carefully. Emile turned up and lunched in the hotel. He asked if I was known there and they all said "No", so he went away puzzled.'

Cornet had threatened Priscilla, saying 'You cannot escape from me.' In La Roque Gageac, his words preyed on her. She wrote a note to Vernier and took a train to Paris, lodging with Zoë Temblaire at 31 Boulevard Berthier. Then Zoë betrayed her, contriving a meeting at which Cornet turned up. 'As soon as I saw him, I couldn't help myself. I was still in love and however awful life was with him it would be worse without him. So I went back.'

In our century, Priscilla would have recognised in Cornet's blazing jealousy, punctuated by outbreaks of physical violence, the symptoms of domestic abuse. But he was a violent and dangerous man with violent and dangerous friends who offered her protection. For the next eight months, the couple resumed what she called 'their cat and dog existence' – to the despair of Daniel Vernier.

If Priscilla felt powerless to break her Belgian lover's stranglehold, Vernier most certainly did not. Outraged by Cornet's brutal attack on Priscilla and by the obsessive manner in which he kept her captive, Vernier vowed not to rest 'until he had got Emile banned from France and sent back to his own country'.

An anonymous letter to the Gestapo in Rue des Saussaies, reporting that Cornet continued to work in the now banned black market? A word in the wrong ear? Priscilla never did find out how Vernier achieved it. But an entry in Gillian Sutro's notebooks salutes his success. 'Germans came twice to search the flat. The second time Emile was seized and sent back to Belgium. Pris fled by back door.'

The Gestapo had come for Cornet early on a cold day in March 1943. Priscilla heard their footsteps on the stairs, grabbed her coat and left by the porte de service on the first floor, which was close to the kitchen. Many years later, I stood opposite the side doorway out of which she slipped, and followed her route.

Beret down over her forehead, not daring to look anyone in the face or to appear in any way conspicuous, Priscilla set off. Her reaction on her release from Besançon, two years before, had verged on the insouciant. 'One soon got used to seeing German uniforms about the place and one ignored them.' But the Paris of March 1943 was not the triumphant Paris of March 1941. The Germans had surrendered at Stalingrad in February, with 200,000 dead; the Allies had defeated Rommel at El Alamein; and the Germans had marched into Vichy. The whole of France lay under Nazi rule, with Gestapo numbers in Paris increased to 32,000. In their repressive measures, it was possible to read signs of nervousness.

Priscilla turned the corner into Rue Lord Byron and kept on walking. A gendarme glanced back at her twice, his eyes drifting down her front as if looking for a yellow star.

Cornet had prevented her from appreciating the danger she was in. She was an 'espèce sans carte' in a city where notices on every corner demanded to know: 'Etes-vous en règle?' But her documents were not in order. Her British passport was a liability. Her French carte d'identité had expired four months earlier. And Cornet's possessiveness, combined with his fierce antipathy towards Daniel Vernier, had prevented Priscilla from letting Vernier supply her with fresh papers.

With Cornet not there to protect her, the gravity of Priscilla's situation was exposed. She could not go to the Mairie without a valid identity card to claim her monthly coupons for food and clothes. But more dangerous for a 'resortissante britannique' like Priscilla was to be caught without papers or with the wrong papers. She risked being bundled into a police van and sent to Libenau, a women's internment camp in Germany, as had happened to an English gymnast she had known in Besançon.

Priscilla crossed Avenue de Friedland. A policeman stopped the traffic to let three German lorries go by. She continued walking towards Rue Beaujon, merging into the early morning crowds. Her fear was to run into a police checkpoint. Sudden curfews and round-ups were a permanent feature following the introduction of the Service du Travail Obligatoire (STO), compelling French men over eighteen and French women over twenty-one to go and work in Germany. Since February, Gestapo officers in plain clothes watched for signs of anyone going backwards at the sight of barriers being put up outside the Métro or cinemas. The Gestapo were looking for STO defaulters, but also Jews, saboteurs, spies, and – after murderous attacks on Germans – random hostages.

'The only time I was afraid was coming out of the Métro,' Yvette Goodden said. 'They would take unwitting victims at the sortie and put them against the wall in the Place des Ternes at the end of our street. I used to hear the shots early in the morning.'

All of this was against the backdrop of a much darker process that had begun in July 1942 and which took place out of sight. A young Jewish woman wrote in her diary: 'The terrible thing in all this is that you see very few people actually doing it.' A rare glimpse was afforded to Goodden. It was still dark on the July morning when she heard a commotion in the building opposite. 'My son used to play in the Bois de Boulogne with a little Jewish girl who lived there, a sweet pretty thing with dark curls and a big red bow in her hair.

When I looked outside they were picking up mother and daughter, putting the mother in one truck, the girl in another. They were taken to the Vél d'Hiver, then to Drancy. We knew they had camps. We didn't know they had death camps.'

Shula Troman, one of the Besançon three, was at Vittel when French police arrested her father. 'He was trying to get me out of the camp by proving that I was not English. He was hiding in Le Vésinet when he came back to fetch something from our apartment, and the concierge, Madame Le Brun, denounced him for being Jewish. He was asked to come to la Préfecture de Police and he thought that since he'd been asked so politely it was maybe something to do with me, so he went with my mother and little sister, and they were waiting for him and that was that. The concierge received 5,000 francs. He was sent to Drancy for nine months and in July 1942 sent to Auschwitz.'

The telephone that rings without answer, the door that remains closed, the concierge who looks away. Was this to be Priscilla's fate?

25.
'SIMONE VERNIER'

There is a simple explanation for why Gillian failed to contact my aunt during the Occupation, and why Gillian's French lovers drew repeated blanks when they enquired after Priscilla Doynel on their secret missions into France: in the spring of 1943, Priscilla went underground with a changed name.

The figure who 'stepped into the breach' after the Gestapo expelled Cornet to Belgium was the person who had put the Germans on to his tail, Priscilla's former lover Daniel Vernier.

A bruised 'I told you so' – arms folded, his face wanting to show surprise – was Vernier's reaction on that morning when Priscilla arrived breathless outside 12 Rue Beaujon and jabbed the bell. Vernier let her in, but rejection had hardened Priscilla's carefree beau of 1940 and 1941. He was thinner, pricklier, more cynical, and with a hurt glaze in his crinkly eyes. 'By now his love for me, although still strong, was bitter and he found it hard to forgive the Emile episode. He realised that I had felt a stronger emotion with Emile than I ever had with him and he resented it.'

At the height of their affair eighteen months earlier, Vernier had introduced Priscilla to his wife's brother Alain, then on the run from the Germans. Captured near Rheims, he had been put to work on a potato farm in Austria. Unlike Priscilla's husband, Alain had escaped, but he possessed no documents.

Vernier had taken him to 'a specialist for identity papers', a family friend who owned a publishing company that printed directories for leather-workers and furniture-makers. On 18 October 1941, Daniel and Simone saw Alain off on a train to Toulouse in the free zone with a laissez-passer in the name of Daniel Vernier.

Vernier now moved with urgency, asking his friend to perform the same trick for Priscilla. The publisher pasted her photograph on to a pale blue concertina of ten pages, scuffed it with grease and sandpaper, and inserted it into a wallet beneath old cellophane, the Germans being suspicious of new identity cards. He also supplied her with a four-page laissez-passer. In both documents he entered Vernier's own address as her's: 12 Rue Beaujon.

The building which Priscilla gave as her Paris home provides an arresting snapshot of the limited world she inhabited. 12 Rue Beaujon was owned by a well-connected Nazi, thirty-five-year-old Freddy Kraus. The tall voluble Austrian who passed her in the hallway was a senior figure in Bureau Otto.

Miserly as his 'landlord's lights', which turned off after thirty seconds, are the details Kraus has left us, after disappearing in a flash at the end of the war. The image which stays is that of a man who knew how to exploit his connections. Kraus's contacts reached into the heart of the British government through Jacqueline, his twenty-five-year-old wife.

Jacqueline Kraus – lively, Heathfield-educated – was a second cousin of Winston Churchill. Priscilla had met her with Gillian and Vertès, who could not believe how much Gillian looked like Jacqueline, and also like another darkly attractive woman at the same party, dressed in a sequined jacket, with shiny make-up in contrast to everyone's powdered faces. This was Jacqueline's mother, Daisy Fellowes, a woman described to me by someone who knew her: 'No one was more despicable, nor was anyone better company.' Jacqueline was nicknamed 'Little Daisy' after her.

Now sitting out the war in the Dorchester as the mistress of Churchill's Minister of Information, Sir Alfred Duff Cooper, Daisy 'Wanton' Fellowes had been the inspiration for Schiaparelli's Shocking Pink; Vertès had painted her and illustrated a novel that she had completed in the sporadic intervals between lovers. Black-haired, high-cheeked, highly-sexed, Daisy, too, had seen herself mirrored in Gillian – who in turn wrote: 'Vertès delighted that Daisy Fellowes admired my looks.' Interestingly, Gillian also recorded that Cecil Beaton commented on her resemblance to Jacqueline.

To bump into 'Little Daisy' was to be reminded of Gillian at a moment when Priscilla missed her more than ever.

Did Jacqueline Kraus tell the German authorities who Priscilla was? Unlikely. Since 1941, Jacqueline had acted as a courier for the Resistance, collecting letters destined for SOE in London, and getting her husband to deliver them to a soap-manufacturer's office in Marseilles. Jacqueline also protected Allied pilots needing shelter, claiming that she was personally responsible 'for helping sixteen French and British aviators to escape from the Gestapo'. Freddy Kraus's untrustworthiness is easier to be sure of. He was discovered after the Liberation to have been a German intelligence agent: he had shown all of Jacqueline's letters to the Abwehr.

Kraus was not the only significant Nazi associated with 12 Rue Beaujon. Inhabiting the same building since 1942 was Henri Chamberlin's number two, Joseph Joanovici. The cliff-faced 'Monsieur Joseph' was a complicated character, a Bessarabian Jew and former rag-and-bone man who, while occupying a top position in the French Gestapo, later claimed like Jacqueline Kraus to have saved the lives of many people on the run. He rented a maid's room off Freddy Kraus and, according to his mistress, used it to hide refugees. 'He calculated that one will never look for a Jew, a resistant, or an American parachutist in the house of a German officer who runs a bureau d'achat.'

Simone Vernier's brother Alain was another fugitive who put down 12 Rue Beaujon as his address.

Priscilla, a visitor to this building since November 1940, bumped into all of these people. Through his immediate neighbours, Daniel Vernier had direct access to Brandl, Chamberlin and the apparatus of the German and French security services. It would have been simple to alert the Gestapo to Emile Cornet's transgressions.

* * *

More startling than the identities of those who shared Priscilla's new address was to discover her new name: Simone Vernier.

Gillian was the only one to whom Priscilla confided her wartime persona. 'Through a very rich French lover called Daniel Vernier, she obtained an identity which was the exact replica of Daniel's wife Simone, who was also fair and blue-eyed. He pretended his wife had lost her papers – so there were two Simone Verniers.'

It simplified matters that both women looked alike and were fond of each other. But was Simone in the loop? Did she have any inkling that Priscilla was bicycling around Paris pretending to be Madame Vernier and dressing like her? Gillian wrote: 'Every time Daniel gave Pris a piece of jewellery he gave the same replica to his wife.' Priscilla herself was never sure to what extent Simone was aware that Daniel and she had been lovers. 'Simone was very sweet to me during the whole of this time and I couldn't make up my mind whether she knew about Daniel and me or not. She must have known that he was unhappy.'

I telephoned Simone and Daniel's daughter to see if she could solve the mystery of the two blonde Simone Verniers who ventured out in matching jupe-culottes, wearing the same brooches. She could not. 'I'm busy, the story doesn't interest me, my parents never spoke to me about it, I'm sorry, goodbye.'

'Aren't you interested in looking at photographs?'

'No.'

'Your parents saved my aunt's life during the war.'

The line was dead.

It might have consoled her to learn that her father was never in danger of squandering the Vernier fortune on Priscilla. 'When Pris tried to sell a sapphire ring in London,' Gillian wrote, 'she was told it was phoney, very good imitation.'

One needed to be a good imitation to survive in the spring of 1943. Becoming Simone Vernier took getting used to. Priscilla had to guard her response when someone hailed her who knew her from Boisgrimot or who had studied at the same lycée. And never a word of English. Although once or twice she thought of England and the past came back with a sharp pang, and she was Priscilla Mais again.

Everyone she knew masqueraded. Her mother had changed by deed poll from Mais to Ommaney-Davis. So had Priscilla's great rival for her father's affections, Winnie Doughty, changed her name – to Mais. It was a period which encouraged doubles and pseudonyms. Arthur Koestler emerged from the French Foreign Legion office as Swiss taxi driver Albert Dubert. In London, Gillian's boss at BCRA, André Dewavrin, adopted the nom de guerre of the Passy Métro station. In Paris, Gillian's previous upstairs neighbour in Boulevard Berthier, Leonie Bathiat, transformed into the actress Arletty.

The Gestapo were not infallible. They never found out that Vercors, pseudonymous author of *Le Silence de la Mer*, was Jean Bruller. Or that Priscilla's fellow internee at Besançon, Drue Tartière, was the broadcaster Drue Leyton of Radio Paris-Mondiale; or that Marie Cornet was another Besançon inmate, Antonia Hunt. And they failed to associate Priscilla Doynel with SPB Mais, at least for a few more months; and never with Simone Vernier.

'I have got false papers, but I feel like a hunted animal,' Priscilla wrote. She had become like Richard Hannay in her father's favourite book – 'going off to hide instead of going to the police', as SPB scribbled in a stage direction for his radio adaptation of *The Thirty-nine Steps*.

As 'Simone Vernier' Priscilla could appear genuinely French. It allowed her to be in the street on a day-to-day basis, pass through checkpoints and travel where she wanted, which would have been impossible with a British passport. Even so, it is hard to explain why the authorities did not pursue Priscilla once her French identity card expired. Perhaps they accepted she was safely tucked away in a nursing home and ill. Or maybe they presumed that she had escaped France, like Jacqueline Grant, Elisabeth Haden-Guest, Rosemary Say. A lot of this is unknowable.

She could move about freely, although she avoided Cornet's apartment. For the next three months, she slept at the nursing home in Ville d'Avray. But she had to support herself, and it was risky to apply for a job as the false 'Simone Vernier'.

Priscilla had not needed to work since leaving Robert in May 1942. Cornet covered the costs of everything with his boundless supply of new banknotes. She had lived well. 'You could buy anything if you had money,' she told her AA meeting twenty years later. 'Food and clothes were terrifically expensive, but providing you were willing to pay you could get anything coupon free. Before the Americans arrived, a packet of Chesterfield cigarettes cost £2 [at least £75 in today's money]. One never saw any milk. Coffee and tea were almost impossible to get even on the black market. Clothes were easy if you went to Paquin, Worth or Molyneux. You needed no coupons ... you merely had to pay!'

But she had no money and Cornet had been expelled to Belgium, and she could hardly go looking for work if she was supposed to be ill.

John Sutro's view on Priscilla's activities in France, wrote Gillian, was 'that people who had not gone through the Occupation should not judge those who had. Even today, new facts emerge which are not to the credit of certain people, but it's only the tip of the iceberg. There were heroes and there were traitors, there were brave men and others who preferred to make a great deal of money out of the black market. An enemy occupation does not always bring out the best in people. But who can tell what would have happened in England had we endured an occupation? No one can pretend there was no black market in London during the war. It was just a question of money.'

With money, you could imagine that nothing had changed. A German officer passing through Paris in October 1943 sat in the Ritz and rubbed his eyes at the wealth of luxury articles on display. 'People here live as though there had never been a war, and certainly not a war that France had lost!'

But Von Studnitz spoke for a mere handful. If Cornet, Stocklin, Chamberlin and Brandl formed one distorted and privileged part of the black market, on the other side were the majority who found it impossible to keep within the law and make ends meet. In London, Simone Weil famously starved herself to death when she tried to live on the official rations permitted to Parisians. After the Allied landings in French North Africa in November 1942, cutting off an estimated 40 per cent of foodstuffs from the African continent, the French suffered even greater food shortages, Parisians in particular.

Suddenly on her own, Priscilla no longer had access to Robert's food parcels or to Vernier's largesse. Vernier refused to assist further unless she came back to him, which she resisted. Her relationship with him on hold, she made her life day by day, as best she could.

Getting up early for bread with the little money she had left, she might have been back at Besançon. And, anyway, had her departure from there made any difference? The bartering, the queues, the clogs, the green clay soap that never lathered, the ersatz food and cigarettes made from Jerusalem artichokes – all were familiar from the internment camp. Priscilla had learned at Besançon that to survive one had to behave in an extraordinary way, and that everything was ersatz.

She had gone underground, but not to join the Resistance; rather, to dissolve into the crowd. And if, to keep warm and secure a meal, she did things that Priscilla Mais or Priscilla Doynel might have known in their inward conscience was wrong, then she was also part of the mass. She was not unique in the painful choices that she faced, the compromises she made, but representative.

'To be a hero is honourable; not to be one is not necessarily dishonourable,' wrote the Swiss historian Philippe Burrin. At first glance, I found it embarrassing to discover what Priscilla got up to. Of course, I wished for my aunt to be heroic. I wanted her to be an exception. But she was not an exception, she was an ordinary woman in extraordinary circumstances. Her struggles, bizarre as they are, were not heroic, like the famous Odette Hallowes; or like Yvette Goodden who sheltered a downed Canadian pilot. Neither was Priscilla a grasping tart who sold everyone down the river. Like the Doynels, she was bang in the middle.

This is not a criticism or disparagement. The impulse to cast people as heroes or traitors ignores the muddled and shifting reality of the overwhelming part of the population who drifted nervously with the stream; prudent, unaffiliated, not committing themselves to resistance or collaboration, not fitting into a neat moral category, playing a number of ambiguous and provisional roles, ready at any instant to change direction with the current. At this dark moment in France's history, a friend of André Gide said that he felt 'like a cork floating on the filthiest water'. That summed up Priscilla.

She was one of remarkably few English women to have lived in Paris through the Occupation – perhaps one of less than two hundred. She learned what it was to be faced with decisions that her family and friends in England never had to confront, and yet which they judged others for having made.

'Everything we did was equivocal,' Jean-Paul Sartre wrote, 'we never quite knew whether we were doing right or wrong; a subtle poison corrupted even our best actions.' Once you opted for Système D – after 'se débrouiller': in this case, getting yourself the best deals and out of trouble by whatever means – there were no rules about how to act.

With Cornet gone, Priscilla had to be exceptionally débrouillarde. The lack of options open to those, like her, who had no formal education and no political power – women in France could not vote until 1946 – meant that she had to use her body for survival. To ask the question 'Did she have to sleep with all these men?' is to see it from the wrong angle. Her body was what she had, and it dominated her life in a way that no man's could dominate his. A Frenchman in her position would have had a different experience.

Priscilla's constant need to reach out to men to look after her can seem like sluttishness to an outsider, but it flowed from the unsexual side of her nature. All her affairs were similar in a way, subject to the vagaries of a man and in his slipstream. Although as a woman she formed the majority of the population, she did not enjoy the same choices as Robert or Vernier or Cornet. In the choices that she was forced to make, she was not so different from her female friends and contemporaries who dressed in clothes made of wood pulp – 'it looked like tweed and dissolved in the rain,' said Yvette Goodden – or smoothed a flask of tinted Ambresoie into their white legs (to 'give the illusion of the finest silk stockings' promised the advertisement) or dyed their ankles, as did Goodden, with iodine. Morality, truth, love – these values were no less ersatz. Margaret 'Bluebell' Kelly was aware of the falsehoods that she had to utter after she was accused of supplying false documents. 'I don't know how I could lie so convincingly. I think it was because we were living under such tension then that life and death were unimportant.' Their fellow inmate at Besançon, Elisabeth Haden-Guest, also lied: 'What people call "lies" are substitutes for basic rights. You lie, sure you lie, you might kill to stay alive, women might sleep with men to stay alive (they did in the camps) – you might betray your best friend, your closest family, for your own survival.'

Nothing is easy or completely clear. All I know is that Priscilla, the little cork, made it through the Occupation. *Fluctuat nec mergitur* – storm-tossed but unsinkable.

Now that Daniel Vernier had banished Cornet and secured Priscilla a new identity in his wife's name, he was desperate to resume their affair.

Priscilla kept him at arm's length for as long as possible, but she was in no position to bargain. When she cast around for someone to support her, to provide food and clothes, fuel for her stove, it boiled down to two men: Vernier and her husband. 'I had the choice of going back to Robert who refused to divorce me, or becoming kept by Daniel. I had no other alternative.'

She had encountered Robert one morning in the street. He lashed his arms around her. How his voice rose. She knew that he was not as dull as he sounded. At least he did not make the baleful demand to know what she had been doing.

Priscilla hated to hurt him. She could sense his terrible unhappiness and did not want to see his eyes looking at her. Neither of them said much. Their meeting was like any meeting between two parties one of whom has fallen out of love. When Robert appealed for Priscilla to return to Rue Nollet, Priscilla told him that she didn't think she could bear it.

'So the inevitable happened. I went back to Daniel.'

Daniel Vernier rented a garçonnière at 11 Place Saint-Augustin where they could meet when Priscilla was not at the nursing home. He pretended to Simone that he was playing poker, something that he was known to do all night, 'and quite often poker was an excuse to stay the night with me'. Simone hated the horses, so at weekends Vernier took Priscilla to the races. He introduced Priscilla as his wife while grimly parading her as his mistress. He knew that he could not make her love him. He was making her pay.

It pained Priscilla to betray her doppelgänger. The real Simone Vernier had five children by now. 'I was in an awkward position as I was always being invited to their home. In fact, I was treated as one of the family. Daniel seemed to have no sense of shame or guilt where I was concerned, but I suffered enough for two.'

Priscilla now existed on the margins: shuttling between Dr Devaux's nursing home and Daniel Vernier's garçonnière. Frightened that everything she said or did was observed, she learned the trick of the trout, to sneak out of sight behind stones. She avoided people's glances. If she suspected that she was being followed, she darted into a shop and out of the employees' entrance.

Vernier gave her money. She read. She slept. She kept her head low as Simone Vernier. She remembered the two rules of concealment that John Buchan imposed on his hero Richard Hannay: 'If you are playing a part, you will never keep it up unless you convince yourself that you are it.' And the second: 'If you are hemmed in on all sides in a patch of land there is only one chance of escape. You must stay in the patch and let your enemies search it and not find you.'

The things that she missed were English films and taxis. 'There were a few soap-boxes in which one could sit and be pulled along by a bicycle, but the price was colossal' – and she never had the heart, the men were so thin. Without Cornet to drive her, she reverted to cycling everywhere. She had to have a numberplate and a licence; if you could not produce the licence, the handlebars were confiscated.

Fear thickened the air. Everyone hurried and yelled out commands. In July, a grenade had been tossed into the car of the Commandant of Greater Paris; in September, more 'terrorists' gunned down the SS colonel in charge of the STO. Hitler ordered reprisals. Suddenly, there were many more Germans in uniform.

She concentrated on what was immediately in front of her. One morning, she wheeled her bicycle through the Jardin de Luxembourg where she had discussed her pregnancy with Gillian. Gardeners had raked the leaves into rusty heaps. A cart rattled by with a girl on it, undernourished and grey-faced; the age her child would have been.

'One didn't think,' said Yvette Goodden. 'One lived without really analysing anything. One lived from day to day. The main thing was to live. To have enough clothes, food and not to get into trouble.' These were Priscilla's ambitions. Except that she did get into trouble.

26.
KESSEL

In London, Gillian pursued every lead. She had achieved one modest break-through. 'Through Free French friends, I managed to find out about Zoë whose husband (a naturalised Jew) had been imprisoned in a Stalag; through the Red Cross I sent him parcels.'

But about Priscilla Doynel, her fate: nothing.

On the assumption that the Germans had interned Priscilla at Besançon, Gillian questioned former internees who had escaped back to England through Spain. Some came to work for the Free French in London, among them Rosemary Say and Frida Stewart. But neither they, nor Elisabeth Haden-Guest – who returned in April 1942 – had information.

Gillian pestered her Secret Service contacts. She was most dependent on her thirty-four-year-old pilot, Edouard Corniglion-Molinier. One morning, she heard that he had suffered an accident during a mission and was in a London hospital. Gillian telephoned him and they talked, the Colonel his usual ebullient self: 'Tu verras que tous fonctionne à merveille – you'll see, everything is working marvellously.' Gillian took him some apples, hoping for a discreet conversation and news of Priscilla. 'I walked into his room and there lay Edouard surrounded by women, about three or four. "C'est le harem," I said, dumping the apples on his legs. I pretended the car was waiting outside and wished him a prompt recovery and hopped it.'

Gillian now shifted her attention to a friend of Edouard and Vertès, the novelist Joseph Kessel, whose undercover work also took him into Occupied France.

Kessel had escaped from France to England in January 1943. He impressed Gillian on the evening she met him as 'a Dostoyevsky figure': a big-boned 'peasanty-looking' man in a badly cut suit with a shy, gap-toothed smile. Over the sobs of a violin she heard the sound of glass breaking. 'The waiters seem rather clumsy,' she murmured. But it was Kessel – 'doing his Cossack number'. His party trick was to chew wine glasses, hurling the broken stems over his shoulder.

They hit it off at once. 'My deadpan look generally freezes up people famous for their wisecracks.' It had the opposite effect on the Russian. 'I made Kessel laugh, which is why all his letters started "My little clown".'

Kessel was not then widely known for *Belle de Jour*; the novel was not published in English until 1962, and then without Vertès's illustrations. But he became celebrated for the words of a war-song that he composed in the course of a few minutes on a Sunday afternoon shortly after his arrival in England.

A favourite haunt in London was Le Petit Club Français off Hyde Park, where he took Gillian. There one night they heard a guitarist, Anna Marly, sing a Russian melody. On 23 May, Kessel was staying in Ashdown Park Hotel in Sussex when, after waking from a nap, he remembered Marly's tune. Phrases surged into his head. 'Come up from the mines, comrades. Come down from the hills.' With the assistance of his nephew and the hotel's out-of-tune piano, Kessel wrote the words of 'Le Chant des Partisans', which became the instant anthem of the Resistance.

In London, forty-three-year-old Kessel served as one of de Gaulle's aides-de-camp. He flew to Algeria with him and later joined 'Operation Sussex', based at a secret location in Hartford Bridge. Kessel was one of fifty agents who took off on midnight flights to gather information from Occupied France. His job was to liaise with agents on the ground, bring back their coded messages and translate these on the flight home, often as the plane was weaving to avoid flak.

Gillian, who sent him to find Priscilla, wrote that Kessel was 'a brave man when it came to going to dangerous places, but quite incapable of ringing up a woman he fancied in case of a rebuff'. Lovable, naïve, strangely innocent, he had made his initial approach to Gillian through an intermediary, 'to find out if his advance would be welcome'. Out of some complicated revenge on Vertès, Gillian gave Kessel the green light. But the amount of vodka he consumed was not conducive to a memorable sexual performance.

On the first occasion when he came back with Gillian to her house, he fell asleep in his underwear on the sofa. In the morning, he could not remember a thing. 'Est ce qu'on a chuté? Did we do it?' with a sheepish expression.

'Not exactly.'

She served him breakfast in her kitchen and left. 'I said I had to rush off to BCRA to draw maps for bombing targets.'

Gillian perceived Kessel as a masochist who enjoyed carrying his cross, and he viewed her in a similar light – 'We're from the same tribe.' She wrote: 'Kessel and I shared a common kink. He wrote *Belle de Jour* because he loved his wife, but had not lust for her. It was the same situation as I had, which was one of the reasons we understood each other so well. We knew that one could love without desire and desire without love.' For Gillian, *Belle de Jour* was Kessel – as in pre-war Paris it had been Priscilla.

When Gillian looked back at their affair, she was grateful. 'Kessel was responsible for my writing career. He loved my letters, said I had a style of my own, colourful and sharp – probably because I am a spectator as well as wanting to live my life, which I did.'

Furthermore, it was Kessel who would eventually track Priscilla down in Paris. But that was still eighteen months away, by which time Priscilla had got herself into an awful lot of trouble.

All of a sudden Emile Cornet was telephoning her. She had not seen him since the morning when she heard the Gestapo coming up the stairs and escaped through a back door; had decided, in fact, 'to have nothing more to do with him'. Then there he was, in Paris, calling her from a small hotel on the left bank, pleading in a thin unfamiliar voice, needing help.

Without a word to Vernier, Priscilla bicycled to Cornet's hotel. 'He was ill and had abscesses all over his back.' She stayed and nursed him for three days. She felt sorry for him, was how she explained it. Deliberately, she had left behind her French identity card in the name of 'Simone Vernier': she feared his violent response were he to discover that she was now passing herself off as Daniel's wife.

Evicted by the Gestapo to Belgium, Cornet had honed his jealousy to a trembling point, and blamed Vernier for his arrest: 'He always vowed that Daniel did this to him.' But that told only half the truth.

Cornet's expulsion had followed Göring's decision in early 1943 to suppress the black market, after the French Ministry of Industrial Production informed the German authorities that contracts could not be honoured without long delays, owing to incredible corruption and rampaging inflation. Anyone who worked for Bureau Otto had to close their offices and suspend contraband activitities. The docks and warehouses in Saint-Ouen were shut down. Trafficking was made illegal – for everyone, 'without any exceptions'.

Only the creator of Bureau Otto remained immune. A grey and protean ectoplasm, Hermann 'Otto' Brandl drifted above the sparring factions of Göring, the Abwehr and the ultimately victorious Gestapo, and continued to sell gasogenes across the border into Spain under the protection of the German War Office. But those who had worked for Brandl were not so fortunate. It shocked several of his suppliers to find themself thrown into Fresnes – notably Brandl's 'principal agent' Max Stocklin, who, like Cornet, had flouted Göring's injunction; Stocklin was reported by Allied Intelligence to be engaged in 'a big smuggling racket in German foreign exchange' after the Gestapo found 'a large amount of gold on him'. Stocklin was one of 1,859 arrested.

All of which makes it hard to explain Cornet's decision to return to Paris other than his obsession with Priscilla. He knew the dangers: the Gestapo had warned Cornet upon ejecting him the first time 'that if he set foot in France again he would be shot'. He was taking his life in his hands – hers too – when he arrived from Belgium, lovesick, broken in health, and begged Priscilla to come to his hotel. How petrified both must have been at the appearance of two men in SS uniforms with SD on their sleeves who entered his room without a word of introduction and levelled sub-machine guns.

Priscilla and Cornet were driven to the Gestapo headquarters in Rue des Saussaies. Cornet was cross-examined and transferred to a cell in Fresnes. Priscilla was questioned closely for nearly two days – then suddenly and wholly unexpectedly released.

Had she had her false papers on her, Priscilla believed that she would 'no doubt have been shot' for suspected espionage or abetting the enemy. It is impossible to know. But even if she did make the right call in shedding the identity of Simone Vernier when she visited Cornet, it fails to explain the Gestapo's behaviour.

Think of it: an Englishwoman, daughter of a prominent BBC broadcaster, let out of Besançon to have a baby, who did not have that baby, who had already committed a serious breach of her conditions by not signing at the police station in Batignolles, who against Vichy law had abandoned her husband and home, who had been living in adultery with one black market trafficker that we know about, and associating with several others. Whatever light Priscilla is held up to, she does not look like someone whom the Gestapo would let go easily. To persuade them, it needed a person of influence.

Max Stocklin? Conceivable – at the time of her release by the French police. Now it seemed less likely. Freed on bond, Stocklin was on no better terms with the Gestapo than Cornet. Stocklin's other protégé, Henri Chamberlin? A distant possibility. He had sensibly detached himself into the Gestapo camp and had a record of bribing them to set free at least two women he was involved with. But this does not mean that Chamberlin achieved the same result for Priscilla, and nothing in the available records connects him to her release.

Gillian Sutro believed that someone very high up had arranged matters with the Gestapo. In her opinion, the evidence pointed to another lover of Priscilla, who – in the photograph that I had seen in Priscilla's papers – sat waiting for her beside a warm fireplace in an apartment hung with Impressionist oil paintings. The man who signed himself in his only surviving letter to her: 'Otto'.

27.
'OTTO'

The address had been typed over with XXXs. When I rubbed a crayon across the thin blue paper, I could make out 3 Mozartstrasse, St Moritz. The date was '4-3-1947'. The letter was typewritten, in English:

'My darling little Pris!

'Since I came home from France in June 1946 what they did with me I will tell you when we meet again. I am searching for you little Pris all over Europe. Nobody has seen you any more and your last letter which I got is dated November 44. All my notices they took away and so I haven't had no addresses of you or your family in England.

'First of all, how are you? What have you done in all these years? I have the feeling that you are living in England? Is that true. And your health? Poor little thing had to suffer so much while living in Paris. Everything turned out well? Pris – darling, how much I have thought of you all these 2 years. We were so sweet together and Pris is carved very deeply in my heart. Do you remember when we drove with the bikes to town having lunch together or seeing your friend Zoë (I wrote several times to her and no answer). What a shame I was always in a hurry, but when I tell you why you may understand it now.

'Now I tell you a little bit of myself. I am very well with the French and Americans. Nearly all my property is intact and the factories working on full capacity. I am one of the rare ones who got already several times a visa to Switzerland. My health is better than ever and I am full of ideas for the future. One of it is to live in England.

'In May I come to Paris. Couldn't we meet there? And how are your friends Daniel V. and all the others? Poor little Pris she was always surrounded by too many people. And Emile? Poor boy had also to suffer. You don't know that I helped him sending him parcels to Fresnes...

'Now darling let's get in touch again. I know that I'll meet you very soon again. We have so much to talk and I love to see you on the bike or swimming or guiding the car from Dijon to Paris. In my thoughts I took you so many times in my arms – oh Darling Pris. Whenever I can do anything for you just let me know. You are still a little baby and I must take care of you.

'Heaps of good wishes, so long little Pris.

'Otto'

The Rue des Saussaies is a short street. The building where the Gestapo had interrogated Priscilla curves into Rue des Cambacérès with its maison de passe where Gillian first made love with Marcel Vertès. At the end of her life, Gillian came to believe that to the same maison de passe, no more than a few yards from Priscilla's cell, Vertès took Priscilla after painting her portrait in 1939.

Priscilla declined to go to bed with Vertès in the version which Gillian first heard from Zoë Temblaire. In her Iago-like way, Zoë later radically altered her account. In the 1960s, following Vertès's death, she wrote Gillian a 'nasty' letter, insinuating that the pair had indeed slept together in Rue des Cambacérès; moreover Priscilla had boasted about it. Greatly upset, Gillian tore the letter into pieces and tried to forget Zoë's damaging claim, but she could never snuff out entirely the punishing image of Priscilla's transgression. 'I discovered that in the Thirties Vertès had gone to bed with Priscilla. Neither came out well. He half-lied and only admitted in a roundabout way by saying she was frigid. After the war, I mentioned the Priscilla episode in a letter and he answered that he had swallowed far more unpleasant affairs than an hour at the Cambacérès with my closest friend. True. Nevertheless I was disappointed with both of them.' Gillian felt that Priscilla's behaviour had been disloyal, treacherous and 'very shabby'; further, it broke the two girls' cardinal rule. 'Had I known, I would *never* have put her up for months at Lees Place after the war.'

Priscilla's suspected fling with Vertès was one of two posthumous grudges that Gillian held against her best friend. 'What distressed me was that she had betrayed me twice. Once before the war by going to bed with a man I loved, and bragging about the fact to Zoë quite cynically. Then during the war, while I was working for my country, she in Paris was going to bed with a well-known Nazi close to Göring and Hitler.' The man's name was Otto.

Gillian remembered how Priscilla was 'very cagey about this Otto character which struck me as odd. I had always suspected the worst about Otto when she first mentioned him. It took me a long time to drag the truth out of her, bit by bit, year by year. She did not want to talk about Otto. I was determined to know ...'

Priscilla had volunteered few details. Otto had offices off Avenue Foch 'dealing with export/import of various goods'. Maxim's was his regular canteen. He had plenty of money, was not in uniform and had access to high-ranking Germans. 'Pris told me that he presented himself to her as a Swiss businessman, a fact I never believed.'

On holiday together in Sainte-Maxime, Priscilla let slip that Otto was Swiss-German. But this was not enough for Gillian. 'I went on until she admitted he was a German. He was married and had a child. "Otto" was a code name ...' That he was 'very present' in her life during the Occupation was the most Priscilla allowed.

It was their last conversation on this subject. Gillian put Otto aside for forty-five years, until my two sentences about Priscilla in the *Telegraph* magazine goaded Gillian to pick up where she had broken off. Gillian recalled Priscilla's words when they embraced on the Sutros' doorstep in October 1944: 'I got out just in time.' She reflected: 'She had the fair hair and blue eyes that the Nazis admired.' Determined to nail Otto's identity once and for all,

Gillian contacted those who had known Priscilla in Paris, among them Gillian's sister Jacqueline and Harold Acton. 'Next I interrogated Zoë who had met Otto. She filled in the missing facts.'

The interview with Zoë Temblaire took place over the telephone, the first time they had spoken since 1963. 'I told her my grievance over her deviousness between Pris and myself, telling each one nasty facts about the other. She remembers nothing. Anyway, whatever she said she regrets. She remembers Church Farm. We discussed Priscilla's character. Zoë said, "Elle était insaisissable – she was impossible to pin down."'

Otto was the only lover of Priscilla that Zoë had liked. He was 'très distingué'. Zoë had met him 'quite a few times, always in the evening for drinks and delicious amuse-gueules and canapés, which Otto prepared.'

'Where did he live?' He had a splendid flat in Avenue Bosquet ('probably belonging to the Jew who had fled'). There was never a maid in sight, Zoë said. 'I imagine the flat was cleaned during the day.' Paintings hung on the walls, she remembered. 'They were pretty, but I did not recognise any old masters!'

'Did Pris live there?'

Zoë did not know. 'Pris seemed to move from one place to another.'

'How did she meet him?' In Maxim's, Zoë thought. 'Priscilla was with her friend Emile. Pris polished off her caviar then did her usual act of going to the lavatory where she exchanged telephone numbers with her new admirer who had been staring at her with great interest.'

What was Otto's profession? 'His work was to bring paintings and works of art for export. His office was near the Etoile.'

Then, in another notebook: 'Have discovered who "Otto" really was through reading Gilles Perrault's book on the Occupation.'

Published in 1989, *Paris Under the Occupation* provided Gillian with certain names and helped her to find out 'what Priscilla did not want me to know'.

Then this: '"Otto", an Abwehr spy; real name Colonel Hermann Brandl. He was in civilian clothes and worked for Göring, collecting pictures with Paco, a Spaniard. He frequented the One-Two-Two' – and pages enumerating

Otto's alleged activities, including 'La "Liste Otto" of 28 September 1940 which resulted in 842 authors, Jewish or anti-fascist, having their books destroyed and blacklisted.'

The former boiler-maker and bon-vivant. The all-powerful employer of Stocklin and Cornet. The Abwehr capo who for twenty months controlled the black market in France and sponsored the French Gestapo. The confidant of Marshal Göring. Gillian was convinced that in Hermann 'Otto' Brandl she had found the name of Priscilla's 'Swiss' lover and protector. A photograph would clinch it. 'I think I am right about Otto. If only I could have seen a photo of him it would have proved me 100 per cent right. Zoë said Otto was fair and blue-eyed. Obviously, if the Otto mentioned by Perrault was dark and brown-eyed, I would be proved wrong. But there seems to be no photo of Otto.' Then she crossed out the previous paragraph. '*Found photo – fair and elegant.*'

Gillian rang Zoë in Paris to tell her. 'Zoë nearly collapsed at the end of the phone.'

In the Bodleian Library in Oxford, I did not leave my chair after I read what Gillian had written. That night, I came home and telephoned my mother. I said that it looked as though her sister's penultimate lover in Occupied France, who would invite her to dine at Maxim's and dress her in Schiaparelli and Patou, may have been the prominent Nazi official believed by Gillian to have been responsible for naming and enforcing the 'Otto' list, in which the works of authors like Thomas Hardy, Virginia Woolf and Margaret Mitchell were proscribed and pulped as 'undesirable'. Additionally, in his role as the Military Intelligence colonel in charge of 'Bureau Otto', he had overseen the systematic plunder of France and the transportation of French art collections to Germany, cherry-picking the best paintings and sculptures for Göring's and Hitler's private collections, and, in Gillian's words, 'seizing paintings from requisitioned apartments deserted by Jews who had fled'. He was the man in the photograph seated beside the open fireplace.

My mother heard me out. Her reaction? 'Nothing would surprise me in the war. Absolutely nothing. It's a question of survival. You never knew who you were going to meet and you lived from day to day. I'm sure that you would have collaborated if you had wanted to live.'

I have no idea where Gillian found her photograph of 'Otto' Brandl: I have not yet seen one. She described him as fair and elegant, but there is dispute over his appearance. One source makes him tall, good-looking, with silver-haired locks curling from the collar of a naval uniform. This is not how he struck Fabienne Jamet, proprietress of the One-Two-Two. 'A little tubby man he was.'

In another glimpse, a rich diet gave Brandl big bones, a rubicund complexion and an incipient double-chin. Sometimes his eyes were small and black. Sometimes pale blue, concealed by puffy lids and set in a round pasty face. Sometimes his face was oval. A colleague in the Abwehr recalled him as 'short, stocky, grey hair, slight lisp'. In one depiction, his hands smelled of cocoa butter.

The same contradictions clouded his character. His manner was sober, refined, especially in female company. He spoke little, observed and listened a lot. He loved art, fine wine, rare stamps. But he could be violent. In June 1943, his number two, Alfred Fuchs, spent three weeks in hospital following an 'amicable disagreement'.

He worked for the Abwehr, the Gestapo, the SS. Sometimes he was a colonel, sometimes a captain. But rarely in uniform – he preferred the civilian anonymity of a blue suit. Practically always he was someone else. Harry Brandt, Helmut Brandt, Helmut Steir, Monsieur Otto, Doktor Otto, Otto. The characteristic that bound these personae was a formidable organising skill; plus a fondness for women.

A notable seducer, he brought with him to Paris his multilingual secretary, a ravishing half-English girl with a Cape Town accent called Mary Jacobson. But his 'famous generosity' secured him other conquests. He rarely entered a nightclub or his favourite restaurant, Joseph in Rue Pierre-Charon, without an actress or a model on his arm. Some of his mistresses were Jewish whom he protected with false papers. All agreed on his fine manners. He never failed to kiss the back of your hand when he left your apartment. The mistresses we know about: Genia Roenthalis, a Russian who called herself 'Madame Otto'; Dita Parlo, the German actress who had starred in *La Grande Illusion*. And also, according to Gillian Sutro, my aunt Priscilla. 'Odd to think that both Otto and Priscilla were going around together with false names.'

Gillian thought it even odder that Priscilla sometimes took pity on Zoë, whose husband Gustave, a naturalised French Polish-Jew, was a prisoner in Germany. Zoë was bored and hungry and clung to Priscilla. 'So Pris would ask "Otto" if she could bring along her unfortunate girlfriend to Maxim's for a good tuck-in. The image of that trio sitting together is my idea of black humour: the German spy, his English mistress and the French wife of a Jewish prisoner of war make a rum threesome. I'm sure Zoë suspected that "Otto" was not Swiss, but a good meal was not to be sniffed at in those difficult times.' Gillian ascribed the same motivation to Priscilla.

Gillian was convinced that she had discovered the answer to those discrepancies in my aunt's story which had continued to bother her, not least Priscilla's hurry to leave Paris after the Nazi departure. 'Otto was the reason why the FFI were trying to get hold of Priscilla in 1944 ... She only fled to England at the Liberation when the men of the Epuration were hot on her heels.'

Even though altered and rearranged many years later than the events, Gillian's perceptions made a dreadful sort of sense, and I began to wonder if Otto was the troubling secret that Priscilla had lived with after the war. Once she had found security in her second marriage, it became easy to understand why she never breathed a word to Raymond about her liaison with an influential German Intelligence officer. When I told Gillian's theory to Priscilla's stepchildren, they agreed. Tracey said: 'Raymond was in Intelligence. If he had found out about Otto, he would have exploded,' and recalled how Raymond had once stomped off in Split, preferring to go hungry rather than to sit at the same table as a German. Carleton was more emphatic. 'If Father had known, he'd have kicked her out.'

Which was what Gillian retrospectively did.

She wrote: 'What I find sad is that the childhood friend I had loved never existed. She had no ethics. Slowly, I discovered her disloyalties, her lies, her war record in Paris during the Occupation.' Priscilla was dead, unable to defend herself, but this did not prevent Gillian from dismantling their friendship of fifty-seven years. She remembered the way Priscilla had touched John Sutro on the evening of her arrival in London. 'Years later, after her death, thinking about Pris during the Occupation, I felt a definite retrospective malaise that the same beautiful hand stroking John must also have caressed Otto the Nazi secret agent recruited by Göring.' And all at once, it was too much, Gillian could no longer swallow Priscilla's affair with the famous Otto. 'In view of her deplorable war record in Paris during the Occupation, my childhood friend Priscilla Doynel certainly deserved a stay in prison.' Gillian now regretted the years when she had worried about Priscilla. 'I was sorry for Pris, never realising that it was like being sorry for a cobra.' She recast Priscilla as cunning, stupid, totally devoid of loyalty, frigid but also the polar opposite: she had la cuisse légère – light thighs, an easy lay. 'Looking back, I realise she was just a lazy slut who went from bed to bed in order to be kept in style. Une pute de luxe. If necessary she would have had sex with a dog, was my conclusion.'

But how correct was this posthumous account? Had Gillian documented it with a historian's thoroughness? Or was the harsh and derogatory portrait too implausible to be true – the fruit of an unstable cocktail of alcohol, late-flowering speculation and groundless jealousy? I thought of Harold Acton's remark when staying with Gillian and John Sutro at the same hotel in Paris. 'I must say that with Gillian life takes on an extra dimension. She has a way of adding drama to everything. Even very uneventful things become interesting.'

Few details are known about Brandl. The whereabouts of his fabled treasure is likewise a riddle, allegedly hidden in safe places all over Europe and South America and plundered with success only by thriller writers. In Robert Janes's *Carousel*, Otto Brandl is a figure of 'supreme power, supreme graft and everything else that went with it' who syphons off a dozen personal fortunes and guards them with ruthless tenacity. One character warns: 'No one crosses Otto Brandl.' In another thriller, Michael Bar-Zohar's *The Phantom Conspiracy*, Otto Brandl is responsible for 'the biggest robbery in history…In three years 158 railroad cars laded with 4,174 crates of objets d'art had been sent by Otto to Göring…Where was the treasure?' In these books, Brandl is the only person alive who knows the location of the Reichsmarschall's spoils, following Göring's unexpected suicide and the assassination of Brandl's right-hand man in Spain. In Bar-Zohar's menacing reconstruction, anyone trying to find out about Brandl or his treasure reaches the same grisly end, including, ultimately, Brandl himself.

In death, 'Otto' Brandl was not spared the contradictions that striped his life. Brandl's madam at the One-Two-Two believed that the calm, unruffled Brandl was killed at the Liberation in late August 1944. 'He really oughtn't to have been killed. Not him. He loved Paris so.' But French historians like Jacques Delarue were swift to resurrect him. According to Delarue, Brandl had tried to cross the border into Spain in early August. After being turned back at the frontier, he returned to Paris and on 12 August drove to Germany in a lorry full of valuable objects, settling, very much alive, in Karlsfeld, in an apartment which he shared with his polyglot secretary Mary. Over the next two years he liquidated and dispersed his assets. Precious stones and gold were concealed in fire extinguishers in a chateau in Champagne. Share certificates worth 60 million francs were safe-housed in Lisbon. Fifteen canvases by Monet, Corot, Sisley, Courbet, Cézanne and Renoir were hidden in a box on a relative's farm near the Austrian border. Jewellery was buried in Munich in buckets of cement. Then there was the gold bracelet and 300-piece silver service that he distributed to his last mistress Elisabeth Pertl ('an intelligent woman and without any scruples' according to her interrogator), who did not suspect that US agents had placed her under surveillance. On 6 August 1946, she carried a bag of food to 317 Fürstenrieder Strasse where he was discovered.

'What a shame I was always in a hurry,' he had written to Priscilla, 'but when I tell you why you may understand it now.'

Was this the voice of an Abwehr colonel? Was my aunt an English 'tondue', fleeing vengeful Parisians who wanted to shave her blonde head? Did Otto, his factories working at full capacity, ever come to live in England?

Gillian died in 1999 before she could find out more, her account still unfinished.

In Oxford, I slept on Gillian's revelations. The following morning, I googled Hermann Brandl and read that he had hanged himself in Munich's Stadelheim prison on 24 March 1947. In Bar-Zohar's thriller, his still-twitching body was discovered hanging from a rope in Cell 35 in the eastern wing. Suicide seemed improbable. 'His mouth was gagged and his hands were tied behind his back. His head was already dangling at an impossible angle from the limp, broken neck, while his legs weakly kicked the air for the last time, in the final convulsions of a dying man.'

I looked again at Otto's letter to Priscilla. 4-3-1947 – the date teasingly ambiguous, as so much in her story. It was an extremely perky letter for someone to be writing from prison. What could be his motives for pretending that he was in St Moritz and that everything was fine? The practice on the Continent of placing the month before the day meant that Otto could have written to Priscilla either on 4 March, three weeks before his death, or on 3 April, one week after it. Were they one and the same person? If so, what was Otto doing still alive on 3 April? If they were not the same person, then who was Priscilla's Otto?

Printed at the top of his letter to Priscilla was a name: Otto H. Graebener.

It appeared in no history of the Occupation. Nor was there a record of any Otto Graebener in the Bundesarchiv in Koblenz. At first, I wondered if the name was a pseudonym like 'Simone Vernier': another cloak for Hermann 'Otto' Brandl and his extensive assets to hide under. Then in the National Archives in Kew I found a trace.

The confidential report was dated 4 December 1944 and written by R. C. Fenton from the British Ministry for Economic Warfare. I was permitted to read it in a locked room.

Fenton's report on 'Looted Art in Occupied Territories, Neutral Countries and Latin America' concerned a wanted German banker, Alois Miedl, who in August 1944 was stopped by Free French officers on the Franco-Spanish border. 'He, and a companion named Otto GRAEBENER, alleged to be a Gestapo agent, were arrested by the Maquis, but Miedl escaped the next day.'

It was exciting to know that Graebener might not be a pseudonym, but there was no further reference to him other than the phrase: 'Implicated in the Miedl case'. If I wanted to pin down Priscilla's German protector, I had to find out about 'the Miedl case' – whatever that was.

Otto Graebener's identity unravelled from a single loose strand, as had Max Stocklin's. His solitary mention in a file in Kew, his fate left dangling, led me to another confidential report in the National Archives in Washington, and to a filing card in the same Paris police archives where I had found Priscilla's dossier. Document by document, his cover peeled back.

28.
THE MISSING BOX

Three weeks after D-Day, on 28 June 1944, Alois Miedl, a man 'as bulky and as powerful as an ox', fled Amsterdam in a high-powered American Mercury, and drove to Paris. The German Military Command interrupted everything to facilitate his onward journey.

In Paris, Miedl took possession of up to a dozen new pinewood crates which had been shipped out of Holland via Le Havre. Marked 'FRAGIL' in brown paint, the crates and their immeasurably valuable contents had been entrusted to him by Hitler's deputy, Hermann Göring. Miedl loaded them on to his convoy and continued south to Spain, having obtained three-month entrance visas for his family.

Few people might have heard of Miedl again after he passed unnoticed into Spain. But on 20 August, Miedl recrossed the border and was chauffeured with some haste to a villa a mile away in the French town of Hendaye. Travelling with Miedl in the back of his green Mercury was a reddish-haired man with different-coloured eyes and dressed in an elegant double-breasted grey worsted suit and spats. This was Priscilla's lover, Otto Graebener, who had earlier accompanied Miedl from Paris and organised his passage into Spain on 5 July. Their intention was to bring back a second Mercury from Hendaye and, according to Miedl, 'a box' that he had left behind as security.

The box must have been important to warrant the journey to the villa of Jean Duval, a Corsican specialist in shifting paintings, jewellery and cars across the Spanish border. Paris – where days before, Graebener had said an emotional goodbye to Priscilla – was in the throes of self-liberation; and in the south, forces of the Free French, which had landed on 15 August as part of Operation Dragoon, following the BBC message 'Nancy has a stiff neck', scrambled to regain control of the country. Miedl and Graebener were delayed 'for various reasons' and did not return until the next day, by which time German troops had withdrawn from Hendaye. 'When they reached the frontier they found it occupied by the French FFI who arrested them.'

The convoluted report received by Allied Intelligence three weeks later reveals that the Free French unit expressed notably less curiosity in Miedl and his box than in Priscilla's lover: they did not believe who he claimed to be – a businessman living in San Sebastian. 'Graebener, in whom the French were apparently very much interested, was immediately isolated from the other prisoners.'

Miedl was then interrogated. 'He was asked questions about himself and more particularly about Graebener whose real identity the French were particularly keen to learn. Miedl replied that he had always known him by that name and that furthermore he believed it to be authentic because he knew many people in Spain who did business with Graebener and who knew him by that name.'

At 3 a.m., Miedl was taken out of the common cell where he had been locked. His handcuffs were removed, his car and his box returned to him without explanation, and he was escorted over the international bridge by a French officer who asked – again – what he thought of Graebener. 'Miedl answered that he would "... put both his hands into the fire for him" to which the Frenchman replied that he would not expose so much as his little finger.'

Otto Graebener was taken to Paris to be interrogated. He did not resurface for another two years, typing to Priscilla from Switzerland: 'Since I came home from France in June 1946 what they did with me I will tell you when we meet again.'

The Free French were convinced that in Graebener they had captured a figure of the utmost importance. But who? The likeliest interpretation is that they had mistaken this suave-talking round-faced sophisticate for none other than Hermann 'Otto' Brandl, who had attempted to cross the border two weeks before. Gillian Sutro may not have been alone in confusing their identities, and it is easy to see why: the hands of both men were plunged in the same contraband pies. Otto Graebener knew Brandl and other senior figures in Bureau Otto – which ran a section specialising in the traffic of looted art. Graebener also knew Max Stocklin and Daniel Vernier and Priscilla's imprisoned lover, Emile Cornet: 'Poor boy had also to suffer. You don't know that I helped him sending him parcels to Fresnes.'

But who could tell me about Graebener?

Tell me who you are with and I will tell you who you are. The circumstances of their arrest indicated that Otto Graebener and his bulky German friend were thicker than average thieves. Graebener was Alois Miedl's 'supposed associate' in the assessment of Allied Intelligence, and featured in the following months on a list of German nationals 'believed to have been involved in the looting of European art treasures'. But then Graebener's trail goes cold.

To pick it up, I had to turn to the passenger weighing down the springs beside him in the back of that green Mercury.

The big rat that got away at Hendaye was the German banker from Amsterdam, Alois Miedl.

Ten months later, unable to arrest Miedl in neutral Spain, an American Intelligence officer, Lieutenant Theodore Rousseau, spent time talking to him in his Madrid hotel room. He described Miedl as: 'A typical south German, 5'9", brown hair, brown eyes, ruddy complexion; young-looking for age, rather fat, but strong; used to do great deal of mountain-climbing; when talking looks straight in the eye and gives frank open expression.'

Otto Graebener's interrogation in Paris has not come to light. But his character is there to read between the lines, in the interviews that Rousseau conducted over a brandy with Graebener's friend Miedl during the same period. To understand Graebener's 17-stone Bavarian associate is to understand Graebener, but also the sort of people Priscilla mingled with in Occupied Paris; men and women whose activities brought them – and Priscilla – into close contact with Nazi leaders. Miedl positioned Priscilla and her German lover just one step away from the figure whom Himmler called 'the king of the black markets': Hermann Göring, Hitler's second-in-command.

The sociable Miedl was born in Munich in 1903 and shared a birthday, 3 March, with Priscilla's husband. Although a strong Catholic like Robert, Miedl had a Jewish wife, who waited anxiously to receive him on the far side of the bridge at Irun. It was a tribute to Miedl's friends in high places that he had been permitted to scale the peak he had in the Reich while married to Dorie Fleischer.

Not for another three weeks did British Intelligence learn of Miedl's 'evasion' at Hendaye, and they were apoplectic. Agents had been tracking Miedl since April 1940, when the British Consul General in Amsterdam reported that 'A.M. should be watched very closely and with great suspicion.' Miedl was not just any German banker: he was Göring's financier. Not only that, he was the most active of Göring's art agents, and regarded at the end of the war as one of only five confidants who had knowledge of both the inventory and location of the Reichsmarschall's treasure.

In the view of Allied Intelligence, Miedl was the person instrumental in helping to amass the Hermann Göring Collection, including the Reichsmarschall's favourite of all his paintings, Vermeer's *Christ and the Woman Taken in Adultery*. Miedl was also involved in building up the collection of Nazi-approved art in Hitler's vast museum complex in Linz. The value of this stolen European treasure is unknown, but in August 1946 the Director of the Metropolitan Museum calculated that it was worth 'more than the value of all the works of art in the United States'.

Otto Graebener's thwarted journey to retrieve Miedl's box from Jean Duval's villa on Boulevard de la Mer took on immense significance for one reason: it alerted the Allies to Göring's booty. The Miedl Case became the first report issued by the Art Looting Investigation Unit in February 1945. A direct consequence of Graebener's arrest, this was the keystone of an investigation that raised the rock on how Göring and Hitler had put together their art collections, and afterwards tried to dispose of them – with input from Miedl, plus Priscilla's 'chums' Max Stocklin and Otto Graebener. The paintings on the wall above the fireplace in Otto's photograph to Priscilla were not any old paintings.

When on 14 September 1944, a branch of the Supreme Headquarters Allied Expeditionary Force (SHAEF) received a report of Miedl's brief detention at Hendaye with Graebener, the combined forces of British, American, Dutch and French Intelligence were unleashed.

Miedl had walked over the bridge at Irun, and back into his wife's arms, on 22 August 1944, a free man. His last sighting was on the balcony of the Pension Ursula. Then, on 28 September, an undercover customs officer came across three packing cases in the port of Irun. The cases, 'made of pinewood very new and clean', contained twenty-two paintings shipped from Holland in June. Packed in sawdust, the paintings were wrapped in coarse brown paper with 'Miedl' written on the outside in blue pencil together with the names of Van Dyck, Corot, David, El Greco and Thomas Lawrence. Two of the pictures were protected in grey blankets with black stripes. Every single one was stolen.

Sequestered, Miedl's dubious consignment sparked a gunpowder trail that led back across Europe to a seventeenth-century mansion in central Amsterdam, and a smuggling network with long-established branches in Germany, France, Belgium, Switzerland, Spain, Portugal, South Africa, Brazil and Argentina.

The hands that Miedl was prepared to put in the fire for Priscilla's German lover could not have been more compromised. They had been clasped to Hitler's deputy since the 1920s. Miedl's Swiss lawyer 'somewhat naïvely' disclosed the fact that Miedl and Göring used 'Du' and not 'Sie'. Miedl admitted to his American interviewer 'that Göring was his chief client and that he both admires and likes him ... and every year gave him a birthday present'.

Miedl and Göring were closer than mere business partners: they were 'great friends'. Their relationship went back to the days when Miedl was a Munich banker 'helping to finance the Party'. In 1932, Miedl moved to Amsterdam. Impressed by the role that Miedl had played in a campaign for 'the return of German colonies', Göring provided funds for Miedl to buy his own Amsterdam-based bank. He entrusted Miedl with money 'to be deposited abroad' and financed several Miedl ventures, including a geological survey to Canada with the aim of purchasing a section of the Labrador coast; the authorities in Montreal blocked the sale because they 'suspected its real purpose as being the establishment of a German outpost'. Elsewhere, Miedl and his silent partner Göring bought up sisal plantations in East Africa, palm-oil factories in Cameroon, cement works in India, and the German Asiatic Bank in China. Miedl's network of shipping agents laid the base for a formidable contraband operation.

Miedl was even more intimate with Göring's widowed sister Olga, whose visits to Miedl's homes in Munich and Amsterdam were the subject of hot speculation. But when Göring suggested that Miedl divorce his Jewish wife, saying she was a liability, and wed Olga, Miedl refused. He remained steadfastly married to the neurotic Dorie Fleischer. His loyalty made him vulnerable to Göring and beholden to him in the area that Göring was most rapacious to exploit: the art world. In return for protecting Dorie, Göring 'the art lover' expected Miedl to satisfy his aesthetic cravings and assist him in putting together the collection on his estate near Berlin that he was dedicating to the memory of his late wife, Karin.

With Göring's shadow behind him, Miedl was unassailable. The SS knew that 'he could always get to Göring personally as a last resort. Which always protected him.' Göring in return called on Miedl to talk 'as a businessman' to Jewish collectors reluctant to sell. Göring allowed Miedl to augment his own art collection, provided that Miedl offered him the best pieces first.

Like Max Stocklin, Miedl had no scruples about selling both to Göring and to Hitler. His main conduit to Hitler was Hitler's photographer, Heinrich Hoffmann – 'an honest and good man', in Miedl's opinion. But Miedl's willingness to feed simultaneously Nazi Germany's two rival buyers caused resentment in Göring's circle, and with the director of Göring's private museum at Karinhall, Walter Andreas Hofer. Matters came to a head over the sale of what was to become the undisputed jewel of Göring's collection, *Christ and the Woman Taken in Adultery,* a painting signed on the upper left side by Vermeer.

The story is well-known. Miedl told a self-serving version to Theodore Rousseau in Madrid. 'One night,' wrote Rousseau, 'a man who he knew was in the Resistance came to him and said "Mr Miedl, I know you buy paintings for the Reichsmarschall and I have a picture for you. But I will sell it to you only on one condition. And that is that you don't inquire where it came from. Because it belongs to an old Dutch family who want to give the money to the Resistance."' The anonymous elderly widow wished to sell for the astronomical sum of two million Dutch florins. Miedl had Hoffmann staying at the time. 'Miedl took the painting up to Hoffmann, who said, "Why it's a Vermeer! I want it for the Führer."'

Rousseau warned that Miedl would 'never tell a complete story unless under proper control'. What Miedl omitted to say was that he had all but agreed to let Hoffmann offer the painting to Hitler when Hofer stepped in, with a cold reminder to Miedl of his obligation to allow Göring first refusal. Miedl could not afford to antagonise Göring and in September 1943 he brought the Vermeer, nailed in the bottom of a case, to Berlin. Göring inspected it in the vault of the I. E. Meyer Bank and scooped it back to Karinhall, at last offering 1.65 million Dutch guilders – then the highest price paid for a single object of art.

The bogus heart of the Nazi regime was nowhere better on display than in this Vermeer – the showpiece in the grand gallery at Karinhall. An Allied officer who inspected the painting after its capture, Lieutenant Craig Smith, was among the first to express doubts. 'One morning as we unloaded a truck from Berchstesgaden in the bright sun, we came to Göring's Vermeer. It looked untrustworthy to all who were unsupervising the loading.' This was hardly surprising in view of the fact that the artist had used a cobalt pigment not invented till the nineteenth century and, for the craquelure, a substance like Bakelite. Interviewed in his Madrid hotel room about the Vermeer's provenance, Alois Miedl said that he had bought it off a Dutchman, and gave his name. Three weeks later, a morphine-addicted forger called Van Meegeren was arrested in Amsterdam, confessing all. Asked where he had got the Vermeer from, he said: 'I did it; I painted it.'

But what of the authentic masterpieces? Göring boasted that his collection was 'the most valuable art collection in the world'. When the tally was made, hundreds of Old Masters were still missing. A report in 2000 computed at $30 billion the value of unaccounted stolen art. Where did it all go? The answer was contained in the Allied Intelligence report that I had read in Kew. 'There is a great body of evidence to show that men like Göring and Ribbentrop have taken steps to transfer some of the most important items in their collection to neutral countries. Switzerland and Spain in particular, though the Argentine has been mentioned.'

The Nazis took care to not to leave behind any traces. The only tangible evidence of art-smuggling from Holland was Miedl's personal consignment of twenty-two paintings held by the Spanish authorities. But SIS sources in

Madrid discovered that this accounted for only a small fraction of the original cargo; furthermore, Miedl had already transported the bulk of it into Spain on 5 July. Packed in the dozen pine crates marked in big brown letters 'FRAGIL' had been 200 canvases that belonged to Göring, plus 4.2 million pesetas in bonds. 'It was suggested that Miedl was acting under orders from Göring to sell the paintings and keep the proceeds for him.' This was why Miedl and his luggage had been fast-tracked through Paris.

On 26 October 1944, two months after he was arrested with Graebener at the Spanish border and released without charge, Miedl reappeared in Madrid, staying at the Ritz. Snippets of information reached London. He had seen a representative of the Prado who might be interested in buying a Goya for two million pesetas. He planned to auction the remaining 199 canvases, which were, by his account, extraordinary – works by Rembrandt, Rubens, Van Dyck, Cranach, Van Gogh, Cézanne, Titian and El Greco. 'Miedl had distributed a catalogue of them. He had boasted of his connection with Göring and of the commission he would receive upon the sale of the paintings; German circles in Madrid believed his boasting to be justified.'

The sale never took place. A furious German air attaché alerted Göring to Miedl's undesirable publicity, and on Göring's instructions took the paintings into care. Rumour was that the air attaché gained permission to conceal them in the embassy of Germany's ally Japan, from where they vanished. There is no record to this day of their fate.

Miedl was not located by the Allied Intelligence services for another four months. At 6.30 p.m. on 12 April 1945, he opened his door in Madrid's Hotel Capital to someone he had been told was interested in buying his twenty-two pictures. The young man who stood there was an American Naval Intelligence officer. Lieutenant Rousseau 'at once informed Miedl of the situation'.

A communiqué to the American Embassy in Madrid hoped that 'we may be able to list him as a War Criminal or at any rate as a near War Criminal.' But Miedl was never extradited, and continued to live in Madrid with Dorie. Placed on the Allied Expulsion list of Germans to be repatriated from Spain, Göring's great friend and banker knew how to defend himself and his fortune.

He spent time in Switzerland and South America and died on 4 January 1990 aged eighty-six.

'Miedl has up till now only told part of the story.' Not once in all their 'brandy-laced' discussions did Miedl disclose to Rousseau what was inside the box that he and Otto Graebener had crossed the border to collect; what paintings, what diamonds, what gold and securities. But Allied Intelligence believed that Miedl and Priscilla's lover were 'connected with a scheme to finance the future operations of German subversive organisations or to find a safe haven for Göring's fortune'. One source speculated that Göring had dipped deep into funds connected with the Four Year Plan, and these may have been in the box, and that Miedl's intention was to 'start a bank or some other kind of business organisation' – and to launder looted art into cash 'to finance the Nazi's Abwehr espionage ring'.

Rousseau was driven to speculate what had happened to the box. Argentina was a likely destination. Miedl had used a firm in Irun, Baquera Kutsche y Martin SA., which shipped to the River Plate. In Buenos Aires, a German banker sold pictures on Miedl's account. It is easy to imagine the contents dispersing south to hang on remote walls in the dust bowl of Rio Pico, or north to Cordoba where another of Göring's friends, Friedrich Mendl, owned a castle.

All these improbable elements combined in the Occupation. When Louis Malle consulted an historian of the period before making *Lacombe, Lucien*, he was advised that he could put anything he wanted in the film '*because everything happened*'.

29.
GRAEBENER

'In my thoughts I took you so many times in my arms – oh Darling Pris. Whenever I can do anything for you just let me know. You are still a little baby and I must take care of you ...'

Otto Graebener was not so high in the Nazi pecking order as Alois Miedl or Hermann Brandl, but his connection with the German administration in Paris was influential enough to secure Priscilla's release from her SS cell in Rue des Saussaies and to protect her until the Liberation.

Graebener was forty. A friend in the Abwehr described him as 'about 1.60 m tall, medium build, light red hair, left eye brown, right eye green, round face, pink complexion, married, one daughter'. Priscilla was twenty-seven when they met.

He was the son of a well-heeled German family who owned food stores in Karlsruhe. His English was fluent, the product of two years at an exclusive boarding school in Zuoz, 'the Swiss Eton', modelled along English lines, where he learned to play fives and cricket, and was a member of a dining club, the 'Heidelberger Kreis', which held annual asparagus dinners. The motto of the Lyceum Alpinum was 'Mens sana in corpore sano'. Over a lunch facing Lake Geneva, the oldest alumnus told me: 'We didn't have a song.'

Graebener was one of those who came behind the Panzers, hastening to Paris after the German Occupation to buy up food for the Reich. He acted as a top purchasing agent for Bureau Otto, taking Robert Doynel's milk and grain to Germany after first transporting it to Spain to be dehydrated in a factory that he part-owned in Navarre. His filing card in the Paris police archives notes that he was a member of the Cercle Européen and an 'important industrialist involved in the manufacture of concentrated food products – powdered cream, soup cubes, flour'. He had offices in Karlsruhe, Hamburg, San Sebastian, Lisbon, Paris, and an apartment at 3 Avenue Bosquet. A one-paragraph report on him by Allied Intelligence mentioned simply the date of his arrest with Miedl, and confirmed his cover: 'In business with Trebijano Company in Spain. Had an Abwehr Ausweiss to get him out of fighting forces. Miedl says he is anti-Nazi.'

He had powerful links with the Abwehr, though. One of these was an Abwehr art trafficker, Wilhem Mohnen, whose chief activity was to buy paintings on behalf of Göring and Hitler's principal scouts in the Paris art market. Mohnen regularly met up with Graebener at the Hôtel Lutétia, where he boasted of having an 'unlimited amount of foreign funds at his disposal'.

Which begs the obvious question: was Otto Graebener's snout in the same trough? Zoë Temblaire had visited Otto's apartment with Priscilla and observed the canvases on the walls. 'He told Zoë he dealt in pictures,' wrote Gillian. 'He certainly did! All the loot went back to Göring & Co.'

'Please wire collect immediately whereabouts of goods.' The depth of Graebener's involvement in Nazi art-trafficking is suggested by this frantic message made to his office in San Sebastian in January 1945 – six months after he had organised the passage of Göring's crates into Spain. Graebener was in no position to reply, still under interrogation in Paris. But it hints to why he might have become such a close associate of Göring's banker Alois Miedl – and why the Free French lieutenant at Hendaye told Miedl that 'he would not expose so much as his little finger' for Otto Graebener.

All this allowed Priscilla to have the lifestyle she led with Otto.

'We were so sweet together and Pris is carved very deeply in my heart.' Their affair began in the summer of 1943 and continued into the following year. Emile Cornet was conveniently imprisoned in Fresnes. Graebener's wife had returned to Karlsruhe with their six-year-old daughter. Priscilla and Graebener were free to ride bicycles into town and take lunch with Zoë. With Graebener's car and Ausweiss, they went further afield than Priscilla's conditions would have permitted. 'I love to see you on the bike or swimming or guiding the car from Dijon to Paris.'

The precise development of their relationship remains unclear. Graebener complained that Priscilla was always surrounded by too many friends, and yet he introduced her to his. A man called Johnny (Jean Duval?). 'Just think of it, our old good friend Johnny is dead. While driving his car, very lately, in 1945, he had an accident and was instantly killed. I know you liked him so much. *We*, you and I, lost a really good friend.' Another man called Wolff (Marcell Wolff, picture dealer in Spain, close contact of Miedl and Hofer?): 'Once he told me you are a remarkable young lady – and he was right.'

Did Otto escort Priscilla to auctions at the Hôtel Drouot in Rue Rossini, or to Serge Lifar's ballet evenings, or to dinner with Alois Miedl – when Miedl came to Paris in April 1944 to arrange his Spanish visa? Compared to Priscilla's other love affairs, we have very few documents from Otto Graebener: a letter, three photographs (even though Germans were forbidden to give girls their photos), but nothing more. Most of my information comes from Gillian's interview with Zoë Temblaire.

According to Zoë, Otto often invited Priscilla to Maxim's in Rue Royale, the preferred dining place of the Nazi elite, where one had to book a week ahead and meals cost 1,000 francs. I imagine Graebener transferring Priscilla from one arm to another so that he can give the Heil Hitler salute. I see men coming in, shaking hands with him, greeting Priscilla who sits there in the navy dress that he has bought her – feeling what? Shame, fear, sickness? Or does part of her enjoy the frisson of being saluted? I see women at other tables, the clandestine bend of their necks, their glances of envy or commiseration. Or do they avert their eyes, like women meeting in a brothel? I see her trying not to look around, concentrating on the caviar brought back from Russia. I wonder if she recognises from a snow-covered courtyard in Besançon the tall black man in an apple green turban who brings Priscilla her coffee. And if so, what does she say?

The whole nation was up to it, if you believed one of France's most famous journalists, the anti-semitic writer Robert Brasillach. 'Whatever their outlook, during these years the French have all more or less been to bed with Germany.' And the memory of it remained sweet, he added. That was in February 1944. One year later Brasillach was executed as a collaborator. After the war, it became necessary to play down any connection with the Germans to save your skin.

What inferences would Priscilla's friends have drawn had they spotted her in Maxim's with Otto Graebener? Pass by stiff-necked, without a nod? This was not Zoë Temblaire's reaction. Her Jewish husband was a POW, but Zoë was happy to enjoy Graebener's hospitality when Priscilla invited her to join them; by accepting Otto's story that he was Swiss, she participated in the same deception and self-deception as Priscilla. The neutralising choices that both of them made were not innocent, more a matter of selective ignorance.

Generally speaking, it would have been considered compromising to be seen at the same table with a German. On her return to Paris from Boisgrimot in October 1940, Priscilla had picked up a leaflet in the Métro which enjoined every self-respecting Frenchman to slap a woman who paid too much attention to a member of the occupying forces. In February 1942, another underground newspaper, *Défense de la France*, warned those who slept with the enemy: 'You so-called French women who give your bodies to a German will be shaved with a notice pinned to your backs "Sold to the Enemy"!' In November 1943, armed men burst into a café in Plouhinec south of Boisgrimot, disarmed a German officer and shaved the head of the girl sitting beside him.

Between 1940 and '41, the writer and biographer Gitta Sereny worked as a nurse looking after abandoned children at Château de Villandry in the Loire. 'The atmosphere of Occupied France was very tendu, very tense,' she told me. 'It was important not to be seen talking to a German, oh my God.'

After 1941, the same rule applied to the occupying forces. The Wehrmacht introduced tough measures following the first attacks on Germans. No overly intimate relations with French women. No taking the arm of 'any female person' in public. No riding with a woman in a vélo taxi. No exchange of photos. No marriage.

Sereny examined two figures at the core of the Nazi regime: Franz Stangl, Commandant of the Treblinka extermination camp, and Albert Speer, Hitler's chief architect and Minister for Armaments whose Organisation Todt oversaw the building of the Atlantic Wall. She knew personally both men and in writing their biographies had the courage to explore their good qualities as well as their faults, Speer in particular.

I had sought Sereny out before when in search of an explanation. She was the one I trusted most to place Priscilla's situation in context. The experience that Sereny shared with me of her time as a young Hungarian nurse in Occupied France, living in the same chateau cheek by jowl with German soldiers, and accepting invitations to dine at Maxim's, was illuminating.

'The Occupation was quite dangerous. It was also exciting in its own way. If you were against the Germans in your mind but able to communicate with them, you were in a good position. If you were polite, they readily gave you food, medicine – anything. I was looking after children, sixteen refugees. They gave sweets to the children and the children backed away and finally put their hands out.' It did not disgust Sereny to observe herself mimic the children. 'The Germans were very strong, very sure, very handsome. They were well dressed, in uniforms that were always fitting, and never looked untidy. They were everything that the English, so far as we knew, were not. And they had won the war. I had quite a life. I didn't sleep with them. But I was on good terms with them, both officers and men, and they were happy to listen to a young Hungarian aristocrat. They were lonely, everyone loathed them. For an attractive young girl to talk to them as human beings and take their minds off what they were doing was a thing for them. Let's face it, the Germans were actually quite nice, you know. I quite liked the Germans.'

A surprising number of Frenchwomen liked the Germans. The actress Arletty: to whom was attributed, probably wrongly, the saying 'My heart is French but my arse international', and who lived in the Ritz with a Luftwaffe colonel. The couturier Coco Chanel: who in a small room also at the Ritz conducted her affair with an Abwehr officer in charge of pricing textiles for Bureau Otto. By October 1943, some 85,000 French women had children fathered by Germans – 4,000 in Rouen alone; enough to populate a town, or go on the First Crusade.

There was a dearth of available men, for one thing. More than a million had died in the First War. Nearly two million were prisoners in Germany. Young Frenchmen were most lacking in those areas to experience the largest influx of Germans – Paris, the north and east, the Atlantic coast. 'The prestige of the stranger, the hint of perversity and adventure, the persuasive white dress uniform of a Luftwaffe pilot, the dinner in sumptuous surroundings – a German boyfriend offered immediate and solid advantage', argued the historian Hanna Diamond. She quoted a woman in the Toulouse resistance who remembered how women 'wanted to enjoy themselves, to make the most of their lives, because they saw that the years were passing by and that things would not change.' Going to bed with Otto Graebener did not make Priscilla anti-French or anti-English; it was not proof of political affiliation. It made her a woman who wanted, in the drabness of that moment, to be a woman. In the memorable words of Joseph Paul-Broncour, France's representative to Switzerland, to his mistress Marga d'Andurain (alias Magda Fontanges, alias Madeleine Coraboeuf, alias Baronne Thévenin), a woman of charismatic liability who seduced Mussolini and later became Henri Chamberlin's mistress: 'When I think of your lovely body, I don't give a damn about Central Europe.'

The pressure of wartime meant not only French and Germans jumped into bed. Most Englishwomen imprisoned with Priscilla in Besançon took comfort in physical relationships.

Jacqueline Grant before her arrest had a lightning affair with an English Spitfire pilot based in Le Touquet – 'very good-looking, I can't remember his name, the quickest love affair on record'.

Some affairs were even more peremptory. Rosemary Say was seduced by a young French soldier on a train from Dijon to Paris: 'Our conversation had run its course. He rose and jammed his heavy kit bag up against the carriage door. The blinds were still down, so no one could see in from the corridor. He sat next to me and gently lowered me on to the carriage bench without a word being said. We made love. It was brief, perfunctory and almost totally silent. We both felt comforted.' She made love on another occasion in a brothel in the Septième, with a tall, fleshy police officer from Toulouse, moustached, who had agreed to post a letter to her parents. The price was to go to bed with him. In the charged atmosphere of the Occupation where so many interests coincided, Say's Besançon friend Sofia Skipwith had fleeting sexual encounters with numerous strangers. A relative of Skipwith elaborated on her promiscuity: 'When I say promiscuous, I mean the sleeping-with-the-window-cleaner-and-postman-sort of promiscuous.'

At least two fellow internees shared Priscilla's experience of falling for the enemy. Antonia Hunt was arrested by the SS following her release from Caserne Vauban and, like Priscilla, felt a debt of gratitude to a member of the Gestapo who had been tactful. Starved of affection, and believing that she owed her life to him, Hunt encouraged her German interpreter at Rue des Saussaies, Karl Gagel, to fall in love with her. 'I was content to let each day happen. With my naturally affectionate nature, I trusted him and thought I loved him too. He kissed me … it was in the Tuileries Gardens. There was nothing unusual in France about a young man and a girl kissing each other in public, but I wondered what on earth they would say if they knew that one was a Gestapo interpreter and the other an English prisoner.'

Elisabeth Haden-Guest courted greater risks with a young SS officer billeted on her in a chateau near Saint-Briac. In his scarlet-lined cloak, black boots and with a book of poetry in his hand, the 'more than handsome' Fritz Reinlein was irresistible. 'We became lovers: it was his first time. We made love often, with urgency and passion.' If discovered, she knew that it might mean death for both of them. 'I remember so well how death seemed worth it …' Her love life, as with two of Haden-Guest's previous lovers, both French, was predicated, like Priscilla's, 'on the fact that we had no hope of a future because in the future there was war and death. My relationships with them were entirely based on catching the last bit of life and poetry and music and Christmas, drinking it in and storing it up for the time to come of coldness and aloneness. I shall never forget or regret the intensity of those lovers born out of despair.'

Few women embodied these contradictions more succinctly than the double-agent Mathilde Carré, the Kleines Katchen of the Abwehr of Saint-Germain-en-Laye. Priscilla was seven months into her second marriage when she had to endure the details of Carré's trial in January 1949, after Carré was charged in Paris with the crime of Intelligence with the Enemy. How many of the 'little cat's' experiences did Priscilla recognise? The effect of Stuka dive-bombing near the Maginot Line, where Carré had worked as a nurse – 'in moments of great personal peril a person's entire being responded with almost sexual anticipation'. The ride back in the rear of an unmarked Abwehr car. The villa in Maison Lafitte. The seduction by the Intelligence officer – in Carré's case, a short-sighted sergeant called Hugo Ernst Bleicher, who entered her bedroom, locked the door.

'Nevertheless you went to bed with him,' chastised the Parisian judge. 'Well, what else could I do?'

Carré's answer to her own question: 'What must be done; survive, of course.'

The best thing to do was eat the bacon. Only those who were there at the time undertood this. Priscilla understood. Her friend Zoë understood. And so did Gitta Sereny. 'I was never hungry,' Sereny told me. 'I went to Maxim's time and again. It was Maxim's or Flore. You didn't eat in Flore; in Maxim's you ate.'

'Well, here it is – your beloved open fireplace.' Otto Graebener's snug drawing room at 3 Avenue Bosquet was a tempting sanctuary when Priscilla compared it with her unheated, airless Gestapo cell in Rue des Saussaies. Hardened by her losses in love, she took a pragmatic attitude to this educated German who played cricket and fives, and spoke fluent English; who had galloped to her rescue.

Perhaps later there was a bitter aftertaste mingled with shame, but at the time she hid her face in his mane. She accepted Graebener's gifts; his 'exquisite cigarettes' and couture dresses. She invited Zoë to join them for canapés in his apartment. She stayed with Graebener in between his business trips to Spain and Germany, on the understanding that he shielded her from the Gestapo. But her heart was not scratched. This was about to change.

To recap. In the winter of 1943, her possessive lover Emile Cornet was in Fresnes prison, and Priscilla was under the Gestapo's instructions not to communicate with him. Robert remained based in Boisgrimot, impotent and neurotic and refusing to divorce. Daniel Vernier continued to take her to the races at weekends, seeing Priscilla on his own at 11 Place Saint-Augustin when he was meant to be at a 'poker evening', or inviting her to a family dinner like the one on that cold December evening.

In the years ahead, she would once or twice find herself going back to this moment when something in her chest slid sideways.

30.
PIERRE

A wind was blowing and there was no one in the street as Priscilla bicycled to the Verniers for dinner. She was tugging off her ski-gloves when a man entered the room, quiet, watchful, blue intelligent eyes, a mocking smile. He wore an English suit and a shirt monogrammed with the initials PD.

Simone introduced her eldest brother Pierre.

He had arrived from Annemasse on the Swiss border. In October 1940, following their ejection from their home in Tourcoing, the family had bought a factory manufacturing nylon stockings under the brand name 'Callipyge'. Soon after his meeting with Priscilla the emblem for these stockings became a blonde in a tight-fitting dress, and parading the unofficial motto, 'La déesse aux belles cuisses': the goddess with beautiful thighs. The image was painted on mirrors and showed the young woman's long hair piled high, just as Priscilla wore it at this period because of electricity cuts.

Pierre was thirty-two, married with three small children, a practising Catholic, Anglophile, upper class. His father was a Viscount to the Holy See and the Vatican's ambassador to Monaco, a title that Pierre inherited after the war. But on that December evening in 1943, all consideration of family, class, religion suspended itself. Simone explained how Priscilla was an English friend living precariously in Paris. With the stillness that anticipates a light going out, Pierre stood there helpless, Priscilla too, in her divided skirt. 'That meeting of you was a so marvellous thing,' he wrote to her in English.

A song half-buried came back, the sound of her abusive 'stepfather' Boo humming 'I never seemed to know what love meant, dear, till I met you/I never thought that two hearts as one could beat so true.' She had been mistaken before, but not this time. For the next eight months, Priscilla came to feel emotions different from any that she had experienced hitherto. In Pierre's presence, she felt her full height, as if the tips of two searchlights had met.

A property of his stockings was that you could rip them off without tearing them. With Pierre, Priscilla hoped to have the daughter that both of them craved. But from the outset they had to proceed with care, less out of concern for Otto Graebener than for Pierre's envious brother-in-law, whose desire for Priscilla had not slackened. According to Gillian: 'Daniel was mad about Pris who in turn was mad about Pierre.'

He called her 'Petite Pris de mon coeur'. They spent their first night together on 8 December. The letter that he wrote next day makes it unlikely that Priscilla was frigid. 'It's in our bed that I'm writing to you and I imagine your body that I love so much is lying next to me, pressing up against me. What a miraculous night, chérie, and I have only one desire: to start it all over again. What a marvellous day it's going to be when we're both once more on this bed which has obligingly offered itself up to our revels. Then it won't be only one or two hours, but four or six hours of unsatisfied desires, and finally the total communion of our two bodies. I love your eyes, Pris darling, I love your mouth, your ears, your breasts on which I adore to rest my head, your shapely legs, your chest . . . there's no part of your beautiful body which I want to leave alone.'

Pierre was back in Paris the following weekend, meeting her in the apartment of his great friend, the publisher Henri Johanet, now working in Annemasse for the Red Cross. Johanet – nicknamed 'Kikki' – had escaped his POW camp and felt unable to live in safety in Paris, but he had kept a third-floor garçonnière in 28 Rue de Turin. He offered it to Pierre and Priscilla as a bolt-hole. Johanet was the 'specialist' who had provided Priscilla and Pierre's brother Alain with false papers. And Johanet helped further: as a 'pigeon' to deliver Pierre's letters from Annemasse to Priscilla.

Pierre's letters are remarkable for their candour. This was a period when everyone in Occupied France talked in a furtive way around subjects, weighing every word that they spoke in public or over the telephone, or wrote down on prized sheets of paper. Yvette Goodden exchanged three typed sentences with her husband during the entire Occupation. Their letters took five months to arrive and had to remain open for the censor to read and, if necessary, to scissor out offending words.

No such restraint hedged Pierre's correspondence. He knew about Daniel. ('Understood about D.'). He knew about Otto. ('O. back, you must now lead a quieter life'). It had no effect on his feelings. 'Oh my love how I miss you.'

In Paris, her emotions were twisted, confused. First, she had stolen the affections of Simone's husband; now of Simone's brother. She thought of Emile in Fresnes, Robert in Boisgrimot, Otto in Avenue Bosquet. She wrote to Pierre: 'Je suis aimée, mais par qui???' She was loved, but by whom? 'I'm frightened of loving you because I know it will make me suffer.' She alluded to Pierre's mocking smile. She was careful to play down what they had as 'a loving friendship'.

But Pierre swept aside her concerns, writing from his bed at 5 Rue du Faucigny in Annemasse: 'My body is avid for your caresses – my hands look for your body because they love to wander over their property – I love every bit of you and I'm happy and proud to think that you have made me a gift of yourself and that you belong to me in your entirety. For my part, I offer myself to you body and soul. I am really desperate to see you again because without you, my love, I can't go on living. I often think of our love. I find it beautiful and pure. No one can trouble it. Until very soon, petite Pris Chérie. How I envy this letter which tomorrow will have the great good luck to be in your hands. I love you, I love you, I love you. My love. Me too. P.'

'Me too' was Priscilla's expression. In the beam of Pierre's beautiful pure love, she conquered her reservations. 'I fell madly in love with the one person I should have avoided at all costs. He knew about Daniel and me, and yet he made love to me.' He was stuck in a marriage de convenance, he told her, but he planned to begin another life with Priscilla. 'He gave me every encouragement. In fact, we often talked of where we would live and what we would do.'

First on their wishlist was a child. Both of them wanted a daughter. They had a name for her: Carole.

What Priscilla delayed telling Pierre until the New Year was that she had undergone an operation in September to drain a cyst on her right ovary. Their daughter might have to wait until Priscilla's ovary had healed. Pierre was reassuring. 'How hurt I was, my love, to learn that for the moment there's no hope for our girl. I had already got used to the idea and was so happy. Fate does everything for a reason, and perhaps fate is making us wait for her a little more before giving us this great joy.' When she received this letter, Priscilla at last allowed herself to trust in Pierre's declarations that once she was pregnant with Carole he would leave his wife and 'run away with me'. Meanwhile, she tried to conceive.

At 11 a.m. on 27 January 1944 Pierre arranged to meet Priscilla at a racecourse near Paris, in the Yearling section. 'Believe me, little Pris of my heart, when I say: satisfy yourself by looking at the horses, but don't place any bets. Our love is too great and precious to risk losing a fortune.' To play Cupid,

Pierre relied on Zoë, alibi in all Priscilla's relationships at this period. 'Tell dear Zoë to go there and she will lead me to you.' He proposed that without wasting time at the races he and Priscilla install themselves in Zoë's apartment.

After a weekend in Boulevard Berthier, he loved Priscilla even more. They met throughout February, March, April, lodging with Zoë or shutting themselves up in Kikki Johanet's bolt-hole. 'There we would stay for two or three days,' Priscilla remembered, 'never going out, eating cold things brought up by a restaurant, and making love.' Priscilla was responsible for bringing clean sheets. In the blackouts they lit candles. The flirtatious Kikki, under the self-appointed guise of her 'guardian angel', wrote to Priscilla on his return to Annemasse: 'You tell me you're living without electricity, but intimacy is much nicer and sweeter by candlelight, as many demonstrations have convinced me!'

Pierre repaid Zoë her discretion, using Kikki's connections with the Red Cross to trace Zoë's husband, who remained a POW in Germany. Pierre wrote to Priscilla: 'You can tell her that for more than two months no one has received news of the prisoners. But I hope to be able to give you more information when I come.'

All through this time, Pierre was mindful of Otto in the background. Taking Priscilla to Dijon. Taking her for a golfing weekend to Louvain ('I imagined you, my love, at your first golf lesson'). Taking her to see Max Stocklin – whose role in buying up textiles for Bureau Otto may have brought Stocklin into contact with the Duboyon family (the cloth from whose three factories near Tourcoing was sent back to Germany to make uniforms). Taking Priscilla to meet Johnny and Wolff and perhaps Alois Miedl. Above all, protecting her from the Gestapo: in February, the Gestapo had started rounding up married women without children for compulsory labour service in Germany. Pierre wrote respectfully of Priscilla's German guardian: 'O. back, I hope that nothing's going to alter our wonderful plans.'

Their latest plan was to marry.

On 4 May 1944, Priscilla angrily petitioned Robert a third time. Again, his lawyer turned her down. 'In the hope of returning his wife to the family home, in spite of her conduct and the particularly harmful character of things said at their meeting, Monsieur Doynel opposes the demand for a divorce.'

Three weeks later, on 24 May, Robert sent Priscilla a passport photograph of himself taken at the time of their encounter at Victoria station in 1937. The message on the back is hard to read, but it stops the heart. 'Your poor little Poppet who wishes that you did not [illegible] for one day. Thanks for the memory.' He was smiling.

This was not how he appeared to Zizi Carer at Boisgrimot. The steward's daughter had a powerful recollection of Robert slumped in an armchair in the drawing room. 'I looked through the window and I thought, "Is he sleeping or praying?" He prayed a lot.'

31.
CHANSON D'AUTOMNE

The announcement of the D-Day landings was first picked up by a German wireless operator in a reinforced bunker right next to Pierre's family home in Tourcoing. The phrase was broadcast over the BBC at 9.15 p.m. on 5 June, and logged, apparently, by Horst Wenzel. 'Second half of message, *Blessent mon coeur d'une langueur monotone*, recorded.' The words were the most important that German Intelligence had intercepted since Max Stocklin installed his clandestine transmitter in Saint-Cloud. After writing them down,

Wenzel snatched off his headset and called out to Colonel Helmuth Meyer, head of the radio-team. Seconds later, Meyer emerged from the bunker and walked fast across the lawn.

The German general who requisitioned their large house on Avenue de la Marne had thrown out the grand piano when he evicted Pierre and his parents in 1940. He required his men to tune their ears, but not to Schubert. In September 1942, he ordered Organisation Todt to construct, as part of the Atlantic Wall, a thirteen-room brick blockhouse in the neighbour's rose garden, dividing the tennis court where in childhood Pierre had played with Simone and Alain. This was the Wehrmacht's listening post for broadcasts originating from England. A team of 30 translators and technicians monitored goniometers and oscilloscopes in two radio rooms, recording all messages, friendly or hostile, within 1,000 kilometres. The equipment was sensitive enough to eavesdrop on air raid wardens chatting to each other on the South Downs. Several of the programmes recorded by the Germans featured Priscilla's father.

But it was not SPB's voice which Horst Wenzel had heard declaiming the second half of a verse from Verlaine's 'Chanson d'Automne'. The first line – *Les sanglots longs des violons de l'automne* – had been broadcast by the BBC successively on June 1, 2 and 3, and meant that the Allied invasion was imminent. The second line signalled that the invasion was to begin within 48 hours, according to an Abwehr informant in the Resistance.

Also cupping their ears for Verlaine's text on this windy Monday evening were SOE saboteurs and regional leaders of the Resistance. Upon hearing the B message, they were to start blowing up railway stations, main lines, bridges and viaducts.

Clutching Wenzel's transcription, Colonel Meyer burst into the Duboyons' dining room where General Hans Von Salmuth sat playing bridge. The bluff Von Salmuth said 'I'm too old a bunny to get too excited about this,' and went back to studying his cards.

Meyer sent a teletyped message to Field Marshal Von Rundstedt in Saint-Germain-en-Laye, but the elderly Commmander-in-Chief did not believe the report. 'As if General Eisenhower would announce the invasion over the BBC' – and in a poem! The information was not passed on to his subordinate Field Marshal Erwin Rommel, who might have acted.

Since December, Rommel's black convertible Horch had been a familiar sight at 8 Avenue de la Marne, an imposing Edwardian pile modelled on the Petit Trianon. Rommel had taken to driving to Tourcoing every two weeks and disappearing into the radio room followed by his dachshund puppy Elbo. Alerted by headlights from convoys of lorries moving at night on England's south-west coast, Rommel expected an attack very soon; the likeliest location was between Calais and Le Havre, the narrowest part of the Channel.

The recalcitrant Von Salmuth was in charge of this stretch. In January 1944, Rommel had stood in the Duboyons' wood-panelled drawing room – where Daniel and Simone had held their marriage reception – and ordered him to lay a mine every ten yards along the coast. Von Salmuth, 'a thoroughly rude fellow' in Rommel's opinion, blustered that this would take a year and anyone who tried to tell Rommel different was 'trying to flatter you or was a pig idiot'. Rommel quietly asked everyone in the room to leave and then, on the Persian rug in front of the black marble fireplace, gave the Commander of the 15th Army the carpeting of his career.

But on that drizzly June evening of the landings, Rommel was away in Germany, and no further action was taken. Four hours later, at 1.11 a.m., came news that Allied paratroopers had begun dropping over Carentan. At 5.20 a.m. the garrison on Pointe du Hoc reported the presence of four cruisers. The wet fog concealed that they were part of a fleet of 5,000 ships and landing craft. At 6.30 a.m., 132,000 British, American and Canadian troops began streaming ashore on the north Normandy coast in the largest maritime invasion in history.

In Boisgrimot, Priscilla's husband woke up on what had become the front-line, his sleep interrupted by explosions in the marshy fields north of Sainteny. Dropped in a Force Six wind, the dummy rubber parachutists or 'explosivpuppen' detonated as they landed. Dawn exposed them for what they were:

floating scarecrows designed to maximise confusion. Lured by the spectacle of tattered parachutes in the hedgerows, farmers' wives ran outside to shear off the silk.

D-Day caught Priscilla in Le Havre, sixty miles away – with Otto Graebener. He had hastened to the port to supervise the onward passage of Alois Miedl's precious cargo of paintings, transported out of Amsterdam by a Dutch shipping company.

There was a power cut that day and the next. With Otto down at the docks, Priscilla sat in the dark and listened to the distant concussion. 9,210 aircraft had left Britain in the early hours. By the day's end, they had dropped nearly 12,000 tons of bombs, most of them on Saint-Lô and Caen. Leaflets swirled down, urging citizens to abandon Le Havre and find refuge in the countryside. But Priscilla was too frightened to step outside.

The Resistance had cut telephone lines. In the news blackout, neighbours turned to each other for information. In Sainteny, it was forbidden to talk in more than groups of three. If Yvonne Finel saw villagers assemble, she strode up and demanded to know what they were discussing. Monsieur Philippe had draped white nets over his gooseberry bushes. The Germans suspected that he was signalling to enemy pilots and arrested him, summoning Finel to judge. He explained that he was putting up the nets to stop birds eating the gooseberries. True or false? the Germans asked Finel. 'No, he's lying,' she replied. Monsieur Philippe was executed.

A curfew was in force. Soldiers shot at anyone.

In Normandy, they talk of that summer as 'the time of bombardments'. Saint-Lô, 13 miles south of Boisgrimot, was christened by Samuel Beckett 'the Capital of the Ruins' after the RAF and USAAF flattened nine-tenths of the city on 6/7 June. The Allies planned to capture Saint-Lô in nine days. In the event, it took them 43 days. The main reason: the bocage, those compacted mounds of earth used by Robert's family since time immemorial to partition off land and encourage game, on top of which abundant greenery, trees, bushes, brambles, intertwined.

The foliage of the bocage was at its thickest in June, providing concealment for German anti-tank guns and troop movements. Allied soldiers had expected small hedges as in Bodmin, where they had trained, but these hedgerows were three times higher and too dense for tanks to push through. An American general found the bocage to be more impenetrable than anything that he had experienced in Guadalcanal. Confronted by this untidy maze of small winding tracks sunk between broad banks of tangled roots, and swarming with large mosquitoes, General Omar Bradley judged it 'the damnedest country I've ever seen'. His troops named it 'The Green Hell'.

Boisgrimot lay in the middle.

Robert's chateau was a symbol of the frustrations encountered in bocage country. 'The fear aroused by fighting in the *bocage* produced a hatred which had never existed before the invasion,' wrote Antony Beevor in his classic account of D-Day. The German defence of Sainteny was bolstered by tanks of the 2nd SS Panzer Division 'Das Reich', which one month earlier had murdered 642 villagers in Oradour-sur-Glane. In the decisive days between 3 and 11 July, 7,000 GIs were killed within a three-mile radius. The Doynels' house was a target for both sides as a potential observation post or sniper base. German snipers were particularly lethal. An American sergeant remembered: 'They used every bit of debris, hedge corner, and bush to hide in, under, or in back of.' German and American tanks blew off the church tower and cracked apart the Doynel family crypt, exposing the bones of Robert's parents. The chateau and pigeonnier met the same destruction. 'Liberation' in Robert's case meant the Doynels having to evacuate their family seat and the loss of almost everything.

The intense attacks and counter-attacks reduced Sainteny to piles of rubble; 2,500 cattle died. Jacqueline Hodey took part in the village exodus towards the end of June. She was led out by French veterans of the First World War who warned what noises to be alert for. She witnessed Boisgrimot and the surrounding estates exchange hands five times in three weeks. She said, 'I fried potatoes at Les Landes farm. One day it was for Americans, next for Germans, and some days for both.'

* * *

Otto Graebener never revealed to Priscilla anything about Göring's pine crates marked 'FRAGIL' – and it is unlikely that Priscilla would have paid attention. Once the bombing started, her priority became to leave Le Havre, where she had travelled in a great state of anguish and confusion after receiving Robert's latest refusal to divorce. 'I had driven out there at my own risk as I was not allowed to be there at all. When I found that the Allies were not advancing as quickly as I had hoped, I thought it wiser to go back to Paris, so I cycled just over 100 miles in a day and a bit.'

Graebener's last protective act was to deploy a young Spaniard to accompany Priscilla on her epic bicycle ride. Almost all that is known about Graebener's associate is his name: Paco Diez. It was a terrorising journey, recollected in a succession of staccato images. Wounded cows waiting in corn fields. A woman tugging a sock off a swollen German corpse. And everywhere, lorries on their side, smoking, and the smell of putrefying flesh and cordite.

As Priscilla pedalled south, there was a thunderous roar over the trees that hid the horizon. RAF Typhoons whined up from behind and strafed the road with 20-mm cannon fire. The pilots in their overheated imagination may have mistaken Priscilla for a retreating enemy sniper. Beevor described how a most unconvincing although widespread belief developed among American and British troops 'that Frenchwomen, supposedly the lovers of German soldiers, acted as snipers'. Suspected snipers were rarely taken prisoner. A sergeant in the 6th Engineer Special Brigade reported seeing dead French girls and German soldiers in the ditches near Omaha Beach. 'They were killed by our planes and they were found lying side by side.'

The decision to bicycle probably saved Priscilla. One month later, at 4 p.m. on this same road between Livarot and Vimoutiers, two fighter bombers spotted Rommel's open Horch driving south, and attacked. Rommel was hit in the temple and thrown from the car, fracturing his skull. Priscilla and Diez were lucky to escape a similar fate: 'We were machine-gunned most of the way by the British, and that was why we had no intention of taking a lorry, as one could at least see aeroplanes and hear them in time to get into a ditch.'

Crouched in a ditch to avoid the bullets, Priscilla understood what Robert had endured in the trenches. Beevor quotes a Gordon Highlander in Normandy that week on the effect of having shells explode around him. 'All that shrieking, whining venom is directed at you ... Involuntarily you curl up into the foetal position.'

At nightfall, Priscilla and Diez crept into a barn. 'We had to sleep in a loft on some hay as there were refugees everywhere and no rooms to be found.' Was this when Priscilla was photographed lying back in the straw? Was Diez the photographer? Were they lovers too in this dirty corner of the hayloft? Or was the photograph taken somewhere else and was Otto the one with the camera? Or Emile? Or was it Pierre, and, if so, was Priscilla dreaming of him and of their daughter?

I have no answers. Her serene expression has a post-coital languor – at least, this was my initial reaction. But tilt the photograph and the way that Priscilla lies back could suggest simply that she is shattered after her exertions of pedalling all day under fire, and in the heat of summer. Viewed from this angle, her posture is more convulsive, more like a crucifixion, as if she has a premonition of what lay in store for her in Paris.

A fortnight after the Normandy landings, the RAF bombed the oil depots at the docks in Saint-Ouen, once the centre of Bureau Otto's operations. Clouds of thick smoke drifted over the sun, smelling of burning rubber – and bringing back to Priscilla the greasy black clouds that had mushroomed out of Rouen four years earlier; only, now, everything was in reverse.

Priscilla told Gillian that during the Occupation French women relieved at the appearance of their periods would say: 'Les Anglais sont débarqués' – the English have landed – an allusion to the red coats formerly worn by British soldiers. This stopped on 6 June 1944 – and for Priscilla too. She may have escaped the bombs, but she could not escape what was waiting for her at the end of that 'Liberation cycle ride', as she called it. Her body, still weak from her operation in September, was not up to pedalling non-stop for so many hours, all the time having to dodge incendiary bullets. She had made a colossal effort to reach Paris, but at a cost. 'I became ill and had to have an operation shortly after.'

When he heard the news, Pierre set out from his home in Annemasse. Kikki Johanet alerted her that he was on his way, and imagined the wonderful moments that she and Pierre would enjoy together. 'My very dear and charming Pris, I see you from here as a valkyrie, launched over valleys and hills to find your Tristan all alone.' Speaking in the capacity of her 'ange gardien', Johanet regretted that he did not himself possess a pair of wings, that he was not a pure spirit. But he was content all the same, 'because I see that I have generated plenty of pure spirit in you both!'

One morning in early July, a knock on her door at her clinic in the west of Paris. Pierre. Holding a cage with a canary chick inside.

Pierre slept in Priscilla's room, the tiny yellow bird shuttling from its perch to the bars, watching them. She wrote of the scene: 'Where else could this happen but in France? The nursing home was very comfortable and the nurses were very kind and efficient. The rooms were large and were all named after flowers.'

The diagnosis came. The cyst on her right ovary, aggravated by the cycle ride, had grown 'to the size of a grapefruit', according to Gillian. What Priscilla was afraid of most had overtaken her. On 29 July, Dr Sicard performed a hysterectomy. Priscilla would never have children.

Her illness, operation and convalescence played out against the Allied advance. A nurse smuggled in a wireless so that Priscilla could tune in to the BBC. On 12 July 1944, she had learned that Carentan had fallen to the Allies. On 18 July, Saint-Lô. The 83rd Infantry Division finally liberated Sainteny on 21 July.

The power cuts in Paris lasted all day, the lights burning for one hour at dawn and another hour at 11 p.m. Priscilla lay back on the pillow, listening to Pierre's bird cracking seeds. She was too frail to move. 'Poor little thing had to suffer so much while living in Paris,' Graebener had written.

She had pinned her future on Pierre. He appeared when no one was around. 'The nurses all adored him and helped to keep the doctor in ignorance of his sharing my room.' He was out during the day, visiting friends. Paris was becoming sadder, quieter, he reported. All cinemas and theatres suppressed. Bread queues getting longer. Only the no. 1 line to Neuilly working normally, with one station in every two closed. She waited for his return. Over the canary's baby song she heard firing.

Pierre brought back scraps of news. The streets hummed with rumours, or Blue Pigeons, as P. G. Wodehouse, now living in the Hôtel Bristol, called them. Hitler – last seen in France in 1943 buying fish in Saint-Brieuc market – had joined a Japanese suicide cult. Other stories had firmer foundations. A Panzer division was on its way from the north. German sappers were laying dynamite under the bridges, following Hitler's orders to reduce Paris to 'a pile of ruins'. The Americans were approaching from the south-west.

There was the creak of tables being overturned. Pierre watched from a café near the Ecole Militaire, sipping his ersatz aperitif, the German ambulances returning from the Falaise plain, the wounded on stretchers, the unseeing eyes; he was unable not to gloat.

On 25 July, Chartres was taken. On 31 July, General Patton's 3rd Army broke out from Normandy. Lorries in black and green camouflage started to remove boxes of files from 11 Rue des Saussaies. Three years before, Lieutenant-

Colonel Blake, former British Military Attaché in Belgium, told the Joint Intelligence Staffs: 'Even the Germans say that if they entered France at 60 km an hour, they expect to leave at twice the speed.' On bad terms with the Gestapo, Max Stocklin had reached Switzerland at the end of July. Early in August, Hermann 'Otto' Brandl departed with his lorry for Spain.

One morning, a reddish-haired man with different-coloured eyes appeared at Priscilla's bedside: Otto Graebener, to say goodbye. He had come from Hendaye, after organising Alois Miedl's passage across the Spanish border, and was shortly to rejoin Miedl in San Sebastian. Before quitting Paris, he wanted to check up on his 'darling Pris'. The scene in her room astonished him.

Priscilla had relied on friends to ease the emptiness after her womb was removed. Her room was 'always full of people', she wrote with unconvincing jauntiness. 'As soon as I was well enough to have visits, my bedroom became bedlam. It was not rare for me to have ten or twelve people all sitting round my bed and the nurses seemed amused by the various dramas going on. Of course, everyone was abnormal and excitable because of outside events.'

This was the first time that anyone aside from Zoë had met her 'Swiss' friend Otto. To Graebener, it all seemed very hysterical. 'Poor little Pris,' he had written to her, as though describing a third person, 'she was always surrounded by too many people.'

On another day, Robert appeared and made a scene. He had returned to Paris. His club remained open in August because no one had gone away. He brought news of Boisgrimot, the unrecognisable skyline. Sainteny was in the hands of the US VII Corps. American soldiers, hoping to endear themselves to the scattered population, were using phrases provided in the US Army newspaper *Stars and Stripes*. One phrase was: 'Are you married?' Another: 'My wife doesn't understand me.'

No one was more upset with Priscilla than Daniel Vernier. He walked in unannounced with Simone – to catch Priscilla in the arms of Pierre. Vernier was speechless. This was the first time that he had suspected anything between Priscilla and his brother-in-law. Pierre pulled away from her, 'sheepish at first and then with an increasing bright manner'. He chastised Vernier for avoiding him lately. He had been trying to get in touch to invite him to dinner. He was very excited. He wanted Daniel and Simone to be the first to know: Priscilla and he were getting married and they were giving an engagement party next week. Vernier rushed from the room.

Troop movements prevented Pierre from returning to his home in Annemasse. What he intended to say to his wife is anyone's guess. He wrote to Priscilla eight months later: 'We spent six marvellous weeks together during which we got to know each other better.' But it had weighed on him that she would not now be able to bear their daughter.

Priscilla loved Pierre. Wishbone thin, she lay stretched out on her bed, staring at everyone and no one, thinking of him. But their time together was almost up, their engagement party postponed indefinitely by spontaneous street celebrations featuring columns of excitable young men chanting the Marseillaise – alternating with the crack of rifles from Laval's pro-German paramilitary force, the Milice. Chamberlin's French Gestapo eliminated 110 people between 17 June and 17 August, dumping their tortured bodies on the pavement, eyes ripped out, fingerless. Loudspeakers ordered Priscilla to be indoors by 9 p.m. Yvette Goodden did not dare leave her apartment for four days following an encounter with the Wehrmacht. 'They are in a devilish temper,' she wrote after bicycling to Montmartre. 'The Germans were emptying out a big shop and were shooting at everyone who drew too close.'

On 12 August, as the Abwehr began shredding its secret files, railway workers went on strike. On the same platform at the Gare de l'Est where Priscilla had waited to be transported to Besançon, German women and whimpering children assembled in scared groups, not knowing how they were supposed to leave Paris. The Métro ceased working altogether on 15 August. The boulevards were choked with hundreds of vehicles departing for Germany, their roofs covered with branches for camouflage, and weighed down with bottles of wine, bidets, whatever the drivers had managed to grab. Trucks piled with stolen valuables rolled in a clanking procession down Rue Lord Byron, tyres flapping and tense men perched on the mudguards. As in June 1940, everyone was taking to the road. The city was falling as it had been captured, the chorus line of handsome youths which had entered Paris four years earlier now resembling the bedraggled French soldiers that they had routed.

Parisians cheerfully waved the Germans off with lavatory brushes. 'We shout insults and sometimes an angry driver swerves and knocks us down,' wrote Antonia Hunt. But it was dangerous to be associated with the scornful crowd, as it was for Priscilla to stand at her window in case she was mistaken for a sniper. 'People who visited me took risks as the Germans were trigger-happy and a girlfriend of mine had a narrow escape one day when bullets whizzed past her.' Zoë was on her way to the nursing home when a garbage can on the pavement sprang back, hit by a bullet.

On the radio, a woman sang Joseph Kessel's words that he had composed at the Ashdown Park Hotel in Sussex: 'Take the guns, the munitions and the grenades from under the straw...'

The Allies had landed unopposed in the south of France; five days later a Free French unit swept into Hendaye, in time to stop the green Mercury containing Otto Graebener and Alois Miedl. On 18 August, Annemasse fell.

Pierre was agitating to get back to his wife and children. He reported news of fighting outside Fresnes prison, where Cornet was still incarcerated. He had seen bonfires of uprooted German street signs, with people feeding torn-up photos of Hitler and Göring into the flames, after carefully removing the glass from the frames. Priscilla watered the canary.

On 19 August, the BBC prematurely declared Paris's liberation – but with the peals of St Paul's rather than Notre Dame. Not for another five days did Priscilla tune in to a radio announcer, who was about to speak live to a captain of the Free French. He had arrived in the courtyard of the Hôtel de Ville, his shabby column of eleven half-tracks and three Shermans safely guided through the back streets by an Armenian on a moped. The announcer said: 'I have in front of me a French captain who is the first to arrive in Paris. His face is red, he is grubby and he needs a shave, and yet I want to embrace him.'

Two hours later, at 11.22 p.m, a large bell started tolling: the 13-ton Gros Bourdon of Notre Dame – the first time that Priscilla had heard its F-sharp since 1940. Soon, other church bells rang out over the darkened rooftops. The sound reached the Hôtel Meurice where General Choltitz, Military Commander of Greater Paris, was speaking to Berlin. He held the telephone to the window just as, five years before, an English correspondent had raised her receiver to catch the grinding of German tanks crossing the Polish border. Choltitz explained: 'What you are hearing is that Paris is going to be liberated and that Germany without doubt has lost the war.'

No one in Priscilla's nursing home slept that night. Elderly patients pinned medals to their nightgowns. Excited nurses, with tricolour cocades in their curled hair, stitched flags from sheets to hang from the balcony. A thin old man smelling of ether was carried into the main entrance on a stretcher so that he could hear the singing in the street. He repeated over and over: 'They're here.'

Yvette Goodden wrote in her diary: 'We're going to go for a walk and we sing bare-headed with the crowd, Marseillaise, Tipperary, the Chant du départ, À bas les boches, Hitler au poteau. We climb on to the roof and there's a magnificent crescent moon, to the west an immense conflagration, also to the east, the race course at Longchamps, the Germans firing on 2nd Arrondissement. We see tracers in the sky.'

De Gaulle arrived next afternoon. Bed-ridden, Priscilla could not join in the delirious crowds of more than a million who cheered him on foot down the Champs-Elysées on 26 August 1944. She lay in the almost deserted nursing home knowing that among the faces milling outside there would be English and American soldiers. In her apartment at 37 bis Avenue du Roule, Yvette Goodden would hear a commotion on the stairs and see a white cap coming up the steps, her husband. 'I just felt panic-struck that this stranger was my husband. We clung to each other speechless.'

When dusk fell, men and women paired off. In tents and vehicles or in the open, around the tomb of the Unknown Warrior, beneath the chestnuts in the Bois de Boulogne, on the warm grass in the Jardin des Plantes, couples made love. A female soldier remembered how everything was quiet in the Jardin des Plantes ... 'or at least, almost quiet ... from all around there were stifled sighs and ticklish giggles. Many Parisian women were too charitable to let our lads spend their first night in the capital alone.' Gilles Perrault stopped in his tracks to absorb the stifled cries. 'Transfixed – God forgive me – with near-religious feeling, I spent a long moment there listening to Paris make love.' A Frenchwoman explained this precious moment, the end of 1,533 nights of occupation: 'You cannot understand how wonderful it was to fight finally as free men and women, to battle in the daylight, under our own names, with our real identities, with everyone out there, all of Paris, to support us, happy joyful and united. There was never a time like it.'

And yet my aunt could not enjoy any of this. On the night when Paris made love, Priscilla was alone in her room. Pierre had returned to Annemasse.

32.
TONDUE

Suddenly next morning everyone woke up in the Resistance.

'Were things getting a bit dodgy for her towards the end of the war?' Gillian asked in a notebook. 'YES. EPURATION. FFI came to the clinique; she might have been jailed or had her head shaven.'

The existence of the Forces Françaises de l'Intérieur had passed unnoticed by Priscilla until a few days earlier. All changed with the German exodus. Outside her window roamed up to 60,000 ill-disciplined men and women, dressed in white armbands with the initials FFI embroidered on them, clutching guns, animated by the slogan: 'A chacun son Boche' – each person should take out a German.

A large proportion of these 'volunteers of the thirteenth hour' were mockingly rebranded members of the RMA – Resistants of the Month of August. They strutted about in uniforms which they had jettisoned in June 1940, giving rise to another name: 'mothball men' or Napthalinards. The writer Paul Léautaud called them 'nothing but a "gang of Apaches"'. Their vindication was to chase down anyone who had not maintained 'a sufficiently independent attitude with respect to the enemy'. All it required was a stabbing finger and the shriek of 'collaboratrice!' for a frenzied crowd to start tearing at your clothes. On 25 August, Léautaud wrote: 'It's a chase; it's a bloodbath; it's a bloody hunting party.'

In a broadcast defending P. G. Wodehouse, who was one of those arrested, for having delivered six radio talks on Radio Berlin, George Orwell argued that 'few things in this war have been more morally disgusting than the present hunt after traitors and Quislings. At best, it is largely the punishment of the guilty by the guilty. In France, all kinds of petty rats – police officials, penny-a-lining journalists, women who have slept with Germans soldiers – are hounded down, while almost without exception the big rats escape.'

The first victims were young women. On Gillian Sutro's refectory table in 58 Rue de Clichy a group of men with FFI armbands raped a German girl in uniform. Women who had slept with Germans presented the readiest target for a nation in need of a symbolic act of purification. Anyone guilty of 'relations with the Germans' was labelled a prostitute, standing in for the dishonour of France. In the Lot-et-Garonne, an Englishwoman known as 'Miss Betsy' was shot when she refused to confess the reason behind her frequent travel with Germans. But summary executions were not the norm. 'The violence has been mostly haircutting,' observed an OSS agent in Normandy.

Up to 20,000 women that summer had their lives fractured by a pair of scissors. 'The first thing they did was to shave heads,' Shula Troman told me. 'I saw it at Vittel, the tondues, it was disgusting, and it happened immediately.'

Yvette Goodden had returned to her apartment after cheering de Gaulle when cries from the street drew her to the window. A dense crowd advanced along Avenue du Roule, screaming deprecations. 'As they approached, we saw two women with shaved skulls carrying their hair in their hands with swastikas on their cheeks. The crowd hemmed them in and stopped them from putting their hands in front of their faces and hurled the grossest insults at them. This was the punishment for having slept with German soldiers. From Batignolles they were.' The two women were jostled through Saint-Cloud, where Priscilla's nursing home was, the crowd kicking at them and scratching at their faces and earrings with long fingernails to make them stumble along faster.

Most tondues came from Robert's area of north-west France, home to the least number of available Frenchmen and the largest concentration of Germans, or 'fridolins' as they were sometimes known. In the Manche department, 621 women were arrested for 'collaboration sentimentale' – a crime punishable by forced labour and imprisonment. So incensed was one FFI interrogator that he slapped an accused woman, then produced a ruler, demanding to know about her fridolin's performance in bed.

In Robert's village of Sainteny, a community of less than 800, twenty girls were known to have slept with Germans, including one who had borne two children by a Wehrmacht soldier. Sainteny having been razed to the ground, there was no haircutting party. But up the road in Carentan, the reprisals began with the arrival of the 101st Airborne on 12 June. Twelve women, stripped half-naked and with their breasts exposed and slogans scrawled in lipstick over their torsos, were dragged by neighbours to the town square. In some cases, a father would cut off his daughter's hair. More often, the local hairdresser wielded the clippers.

'Their look,' said an American soldier watching, 'was that of a hunted animal.'

Afterwards, bald craniums daubed with mercurochrome, and to the dirge of a drum, the women were pushed roughly through a gauntlet of men who struck them on their bare bottoms shouting, 'Putains des fridolins, filles aux boches!'

In Germany, a surprising number of France's 1.8 million POWs had liaisons with local girls – in particular those prisoners sent, like Robert's brother Guy, to work on farms – but not one Frenchman had his head shaved for sleeping with a German woman or was condemned for this. Horizontal collaboration was a crime uniquely pinned on French women, for whom sleeping with the enemy may have been the only way to feed their children. In the expiatory fervour, it was as if the male population, who had humiliatingly failed for four years to protect their families, were battling to reclaim a moral authority they had lost in the stupendous defeat. Something about the degradation made them feel respectable again.

The liberation caused many who had supported Pétain to change their tune. But it was the same siren song of expediency. The music written to accompany Pétain on the pro-German newsreel agency France Actualités – and which resulted in the arrest of its composer – was exactly the music used by France-Libre-Actualités to follow de Gaulle on screen as he walked down the Champs-Elysées. And yet even for de Gaulle, in his speech on that day, it was necessary to absolve the hysterically cheering crowds and to stress the fiction that collaboration was merely the work of 'a few unhappy traitors'.

A woman's shorn hair was nailed to the front of her house, or burned in large heaps which could be smelled for miles. Some women committed suicide from the humiliation. Others shunned public contact. In 1983, the year that the last collaborator was released from prison, a former tondue was discovered in the Auvergne still living as a recluse nearly four decades on. The majority of women dared to hope that once their hair sprouted back, people would forget the shearing and there would be no necessity ever to speak or think of it again. This was what another tondue, Marie-Rose Dupont, fervently believed when she reopened her hairdressing salon in Moissac – until the morning she walked into the salon and saw her traumatised eight-year-old son seated in one of the chairs, bald.

Her hair, her famous hair. Priscilla was thrown back to the last time it was scissored off, when she was fourteen, and Gillian had hauled her around the floor of Doris's studio on a Persian rug. Stretched out in her room at the nursing home, she was constrained in her movements, like Pierre's fidgety bird. Pierre had promised to look after her. Where was he?

'It was very unfortunate to be bed-ridden at such a time,' she wrote. If not for Emile Cornet and Max Stocklin, they would be after her for Otto Graebener.

Without Pierre to tell her what was going on, she relied on the nurses. It was clear that everyone was living in terror of denunciation, no matter how high up you were in the gratin. Prince Jean-Louis de Faucigny-Lucinge, a member like Robert of the grand social and dining club Cercle Interallié, had, apparently, witnessed an impromptu FFI tribunal interrogating a dishevelled Duchesse de Brissac, a fur coat like Priscilla's hastily thrown on over her underclothes; the Duchesse was known for her romantic attachments to

German officers. Another fashionable tondue was the woman who had shared Priscilla's address, Gillian's lookalike: Jacqueline Kraus had her dark hair shaved in the streets.

'Accusations rained on people,' Gitta Sereny told me. 'Everyone was in danger of going to prison' – like Isabelle de la Bouillerie, president of Sereny's charity. 'She was sent to Santé and died there. She was not pro-German, but she was not beyond getting help from Germans when she needed it. And the Germans were the only people who could give this help.'

Overnight, the men who might have helped Priscilla had melted away. Otto gone; Pierre gone; Emile, still in Fresnes; Daniel and Robert hurt beyond measure. She was an obvious target for revenge: not of French origin, well fed and dressed because of her association with Germans. She had lain beside Otto Graebener's warm fire while the rest of France shivered.

Priscilla was in her room one evening when she heard raised voices in the corridor. She gripped the iron frame of her bed.

The door was flung open and Daniel Vernier marched in, dressed in a tight-fitting uniform that she had last seen him wear in Rouen during the Phoney War, and produced, with an extremely shaky hand, a revolver which he pointed at her. His gloomy face trapped in a big beret was white. 'I had not noticed the FFI band on his arm until then and thought he had come to murder me.'

There was a ring of absurdity about the scene: the demented ex-lover smelling of camphor, the petrified convalescent – and between them that canary.

She stared back into the muzzle of Vernier's trembling gun and dreadful images flashed through her mind.

If Vernier did not pull the trigger, then more than likely he would insist on taking Priscilla to Fresnes where a grisly pageant was unfolding.

The crowded cells mimicked the recent bedlam in her room. One woman staring out between the bars was the actress Arletty, arrested because of her relationship with a Luftwaffe colonel. 'What kind of government is this,' she complained, 'which worries about our sleeping arrangements!' It was being whispered in the nursing home that her breasts had been cut off.

Jacqueline Kraus's sister was in Fresnes, and the well-known opera singer Germaine Lubin, whose crime was to have sung for Hitler. 'Except for having eaten the flesh of children there was nothing I was not accused of.' She shivered at what she was compelled to witness: 'In the corner, garbage was mixed with the hair of women who had had their heads shaved the night before. During the course of the day another four were shaved completely bald except for one on whom, for laughs, they had left a tug in the middle of her head which hung down like the mandarin's pigtail.'

It was not only bald women who were jammed into the cells and prison yard. Albert Blaser, the head waiter of Maxim's who had led Priscilla to her table, was arrested. And Maurice Chevalier, whose manager had been engaged to Gillian's sister; Chevalier had sung on the German station Radio-Paris. Otto Graebener, arriving from Hendaye for further interrogation, brushed shoulders with his rival Emile Cornet. Arrested on the Swiss border, Max Stocklin arrived in Fresnes on 17 November. He joined 4,500 inmates.

In Sainteny, the rumour spread like pink-eye that Robert's brother Georges had spent time in Fresnes.

No one in Sainteny considered Georges Doynel a collaborator, and his son Dick denied that he was ever arrested. But when the wind blew down the oaks in the avenue in the winter of 1940, Georges had summoned a forester who owned a sawmill at Le Chalet des Pins. Joseph Carer, the steward's son, was one of those called upon to clear the fallen branches. 'I saw the tractors pulling the oaks, but the tractors broke down because the woodcutters sabotaged them, so the Germans came in half-tracks and dragged the trunks to the mill.' At least fifteen sawyers were involved in cutting the estimated 5,600 trees into planks, some of which went to Cherbourg and Speer's Organisation Todt to make pill boxes and railway sleepers for the Atlantic Wall; the rest of the timber was burned into charcoal. Carer said: 'I helped cut the trees and load them into wagons, and also the charcoal that was sent to Paris for gasogenes. And that was the beginning of the problem for poor

Georges Doynel. It cost him dear.' Communists in the FFI accused Robert's brother of 'having participated in the war effort' and for sucking up to the Germans during their residence at Boisgrimot. After the war, Georges sold the gutted chateau in panic-stricken haste and was rumoured, inaccurately, to have fled to Bolivia. The last time Jacqueline Hodey saw him was during the 1960s, in the village square. Georges had turned up at the café run by her parents, to seek their support in his denial that he had been a collaborator. Reluctant to talk in front of others in the bar, he tried to persuade Jacqueline to go outside in private, using the over-familiar 'tu' instead of 'vous'. She said: 'He came to the café and knocked at the door. "Jacqueline, je veux te voir, I want to see you, come here," and I didn't go. Times had changed. He left without saying anything.'

In Priscilla's nursing home on that hot day in August 1944 Daniel Vernier turned on his heels, walked away.

Soon afterwards, a nurse came into the room with a letter. Kikki Johanet had dropped it off. Priscilla's guardian angel and carrier pigeon had lacked the wings to give her Pierre's message in person.

'My love, my love, my love. Blessed is he who has never known love. That's the state I'm in after fifteen hours of agony and having returned home. You wrote to me a while ago, "I'm frightened of loving you because I know it will make me suffer." I confess I didn't believe you, because, just like you, I felt that our love was so passionate a thing that it would be impossible for us to cause each other the slightest pain. But I'm feeling close to madness and intensely depressed. You, Pris, who knows the deepest part of me – you will know what it costs me to write this word of farewell. You took my heart. One only loves once in one's life. My heart has loved you above anything that you can possibly imagine. So I offer it as a parting gift – it's yours . . .' Pierre's letter trails off at this point, not even signed.

Nothing could be more awful than the fact he was not coming back. She sat erect and did not hear the nurse take away her tray and did not say anything. She just read it and closed her eyes and felt something inside her tear apart.

* * *

Priscilla abandoned the nursing-home and entered a clinic in Rue Mirosmenil. To protect herself from marauding FFI she sent out a nurse to bring an Allied officer to see her. 'I wanted an Englishman, but they were few and far between and I had to be content with an American' – a swaggering Texan pilot called Jimmy Richardson. 'I asked him about England as he had come from there and that was my first news of home for four long years.'

Paris continued to fill with Allied soldiers and diplomats. Early in October, Priscilla moved back into her garçonnière in Place Saint-Augustin. She shared it with Pierre's canary and Paco Diez, her companion on the harrowing bicycle ride from Le Havre. Graebener's associate in looted masterpieces now masqueraded as an art student at the Académie Julian. There was no fuel for the stove and the one electric heater worked on a reduced current. Priscilla was sitting in her coat reading beside the single bar, when there was a knock on the door. A tall officer introduced himself in a sing-song English voice as Harold Acton, a friend of Gillian's and best man at her wedding.

Acton was staying with the Sutros in London when the BBC announced that Paris had been liberated and he was ordered to the French capital with the SHAEF censorship unit. He asked Gillian if he might leave behind a suitcase containing his airforce uniform. Gillian sought a favour in return. She had no address for Priscilla, but she had – at last – a lead: Joseph Kessel had managed to get hold of a telephone number. Gillian begged Acton to use this to track Priscilla down and gave him a letter to deliver in the event that he was successful.

On 5 October, Acton flew to Paris. He observed in his memoirs: 'Externally Paris had changed far less than London during these tragic years. Externally … What of the heart?' From his billet in the Hôtel Chatham, he dialled the number that Kessel had supplied. Priscilla's laconic voice answered.

Over 'a big tin of caviar and champagne consumed in a freezing room', Acton told Priscilla of Gillian's concern for her during the last four and a half years, and produced the letter in which, Gillian wrote, 'I had offered to harbour her while she sorted herself out.'

The war was still raging. To leave Paris was very difficult. Acton passed on the message that if Priscilla needed assistance, she was to contact Gillian's sister, Jacqueline Hammond, at the British Embassy, now reopened in Faubourg Saint-Honoré.

Jacqueline had joined the Free French in April 1943, in Guildford, and was one of the earliest British diplomats posted back to Paris, after Duff Cooper arrived as Ambassador on 13 September. The last time Jacqueline had seen Priscilla was at Prunier's in May 1940, to celebrate her engagement to Max Ruppé. Jacqueline was still adjusting to the shock of bumping into Ruppé, wearing the same teddy-bear coat, at the Invalides Métro, and discovering he was married: friends had told him that she had died during an air raid. Almost her first task was to sort out Priscilla's expired English passport and 'get her an "exit visa"'.

Priscilla was among a group of 100 former internees, mostly men released from Saint-Denis prison, who were anxious to return to England as swiftly as possible. She owed her delay to RAF Transport Command at Le Bourget which had specific instructions 'not to transport female ex-internees'. On 25 September, the Permanent Secretary Sir Arthur Street wrote asking the Air Ministry to remove its objection to the carriage of women. 'Mr Eden considers that it is in the national interest that the British subjects concerned should be repatriated without delay … These people have for the most part endured incarceration by the enemy for several years and can rightly expect that HM representative will do everything he can to return them at the earliest possible moment to this country on their release. Some public outcry and parliamentary criticism may indeed be anticipated if this is not done.'

On 13 October, the Foreign Office sent a letter to Priscilla's father. 'Sir, I am directed by Mr Secretary Eden to inform you that he has received a report stating that Priscilla Doynel de la Sausserie may shortly be expected to arrive in this country. Arrangements have been made for the reception and assistance of persons repatriated from liberated territory, but it is regretted that in no circumstances can any further information be given as to date and place of arrival.'

One week later, on Saturday 21 October, Priscilla was driven out in an uncomfortable Jeep over a bomb-damaged road to Le Bourget. At 4 p.m., carrying a single suitcase (she had been forbidden to bring Pierre's canary), she boarded the King's Messenger's plane for Hendon. The service being a military one, she was not charged a fare. The plane was full and there were no seats. She sat on the floor.

Priscilla had packed Pierre's letters into her ochre suitcase, along with clothes which Graebener had given her, plus the intimate correspondence and photographs of the men she had known in the Occupation. She was obeying her father: not merely his private injunction when she was nine years old for her to keep a journal, but also in a series of broadcasts during the war – this time made to the world. On the radio at Boisgrimot, she had listened to SPB saying that one must never destroy letters and diaries because, though they may be just genial gossip and tittle-tattle, 'they can also be priceless, imperishable monuments to man's courage in the face of the worst that life can offer'.

PART FIVE

33.
LIVING WITH ANYBODY

Thinking about Priscilla on D-Day, her father placed a bet on a horse. 'I backed Hycilla because of Priscilla – and won £2. It's the first time I won a horse race for years.'

Eight weeks later, SPB wrote in his journal: 'PARIS REGAINED. After 4 years and 4 months, I hope to God she's free.'

A fortnight passed before he heard that she was alive.

On 9 September 1944: 'Grand day. News of Priscilla from Vivien. She's at 98 Rue de Miromesnil, a nursing home, after an operation. I wrote at once and found an airman press photographer going back to Paris to take letter.'

23 October: 'PRISCILLA at home again. 1st letter for years – a quite casual letter. Flew over from Paris day before yesterday. I phoned at once. Her voice sweet, low & staccato like a child's. Her writing carefree, neat like a child's. What have the bloody Germans done to her?' His first impulse was to write to his thirteen-year-old daughter Lalage. At her school in Cheltenham, Lalage who is my mother, learned that she had another sister.

9 November: 'An eventful day.' SPB took the train with Winnie to London where he gave a talk on the BBC about 'How I Failed to Find a Kite' and afterwards met Priscilla at the Great Western Railway Hotel in Paddington.

His daughter – 'looking younger than ever' – had a French intonation in her cigarette-furred voice. She had not spoken English since 1941.

'First time I've seen her for FIVE years. She told us her story at night. Three months in concentration camp. Then three and a half years on false papers living with Spaniards, Belgians, Swiss, and always the French Robert cringing in the background.' But SPB's elation was short-lived. Before the evening was out, a tremendous pity assailed him. In a moment of piercing realism, he wrote: 'She cares nothing for anything except having a good time. She'll probably end by committing suicide. I'm desperately sorry for her.'

Priscilla accompanied SPB and Winnie back to Oxford, staying for a week at 291 Woodstock Road with their eight-year-old daughter Imogen. It was the first time that Priscilla had slept under her father's roof since she was a teenager. She attended a performance of *The Mikado* and a Sunday service at the Dragon School, where SPB was teaching for £1 a week.

But the young woman who had reappeared in his life, showing the detachment that many people feel in moments of stress, was not a daughter he recognised. It shocked SPB to observe how Priscilla had returned home flaunting Arletty's international arse, and was 'still chasing after or being chased by men of all nationalities'. The Texan pilot she had befriended in Paris joined her in Oxford for the weekend – 'She lives with anybody!'

In marked contrast, Priscilla's attitude towards her father was 'cold as iceberg'. Her departure left SPB battling to pacify his troubled emotions. 'In all morning writing short story about Priscilla.' This missing story, out of all my grandfather's works, is the one I would most like to read.

Priscilla went on to Bath. Vivien, her sister, met her at the station. 'I saw this woman and I thought, "What the hell's my mother doing there?" – and it was Priscilla, looking exactly like her. Same build of face, same eyes – which I didn't have. She stayed a couple of weeks, we were sisters again, but she didn't want to talk about the horrors. She'd had France.'

It was a liberation to speak her own language – and to play the radio so loud; on 20 November, she listened to news of P. G. Wodehouse's arrest at the Hôtel Bristol. She felt relieved that no one had bothered to debrief her when she landed back in England or shown any interest in her knowledge of Occupied France.

In London, rare wild flowers bloomed in the rubble. The taxi drivers were politer than their Paris equivalents. Even the Underground was preferable to the Métro; there was not the suffocating whirl of hot air that hit her in the face when she went down the steps. She had forgotten how wonderful porridge, bacon and tea tasted. 'I was so thrilled at being home at last that everything looked good.'

There was one more family member to meet. One Sunday morning, Priscilla arrived at Cheltenham Ladies' College and treated my thirteen-year-old mother to lunch at a hotel. My mother said: 'I didn't query, which I think was very odd, that I had a new sister out of the blue. I was far more excited at being taken out to lunch. I was starving at school. I had to live on bread – that's why I never eat bread now – and French mustard, which I kept in the dorm under a loose floorboard, and spread on the bread. So to be invited out to a meal was quite something.' She got on well with her half-sister, despite their fifteen-year age gap. 'I thought she was beautiful. She had this amazing long blonde hair and attractive face, and an air about her, a confidence.' My mother told me that Priscilla was on her way to see a man, and the man was Robert Donat. 'She said he was a great friend.'

Priscilla had escaped Paris with a suitcase. Within weeks, she was in bed with one of most desirable men in England. Gillian Sutro worked hard to promote their romance, having introduced them.

Gillian at the time was having a snatched liaison with the film director Carol Reed, who had turned up on her doorstep one day at 1.25 p.m., when he knew that John Sutro lunched at the Beefsteak. Six-foot tall, blue eyes, aquiline nose, Reed took off his camel-hair coat and asked Gillian for a gin and tonic. 'As I put on a French record on John's cumbersome machine to remind me of Paris, he pushed his arms round me, clutched my shoulders, and tried to kiss me. "Don't be so silly." I pushed him off. He was behaving as though time was money.' Reed told her that his marriage was breaking down. 'Why don't we run off together? It will solve everything.' Gillian opted for an affair, to be fitted in during lunchtimes. 'For him it was like buying the rights to a book he wanted to direct. I never sensed passion; he kept that for films.' Reed, who went on to direct *The Third Man*, resembled Robert Donat in this respect.

Donat was forever following girls with fantastic legs and moulding them into an ideal of womanhood that he had conceived as a boy. He did this with Priscilla after meeting her at a party given by the Sutros in that first winter of her return in 1944.

He had come from the Westminster Theatre where he was producing a version of the Cinderella story. Gillian steered Donat into the drawing room to meet her long-lost best friend. She had a hunch the two might get on.

On that evening, Priscilla was never so alluring or so alone. She stood by the Sutros' fireplace in her Schiaparelli ivory silk dress that left her neck bare. Donat looked into her 'mild wild eyes, like a pregnant faun', and was, he afterwards confessed, 'enchanted'. They talked and the other guests receded.

The Germans banned English films in Paris, but Priscilla knew who Donat was. His hold on the public imagination is hard to exaggerate, even if his name does not register today. In 1939, Donat had pipped Clark Gable in *Gone with the Wind* to win the Academy Award for playing an English public schoolmaster in *Goodbye Mr Chips*. The role had strong associations for Priscilla; her father had been a teacher at Sherborne when she was born. And it makes me wonder if, in fact, SPB provoked Priscilla, having resampled him, to seek a father-substitute in Donat who, in his most famous screen role, had popularised the novel which SPB wished to have written more than any other.

It would be too much to say that Priscilla's affair with Donat was a deliberate strike at her father, but I notice that SPB in *I Return to Scotland* takes a derogatory swipe at Alfred Hitchcock's adaptation of Buchan's thriller in which Donat made his name. 'I remember how keen was my disappointment on seeing the film version of *The Thirty-nine Steps*. The film couldn't create in the way that Buchan had created that bold moorland, and failed to arouse in me that state of wild excitement and suspense that I felt all the time that Hannay was on the moors.'

Here, SPB was out on a limb. In this Golden Age of British cinema, Donat was England's leading man, and epitomised an effortless, understated charm. To Hitchcock, who directed him in *The 39 Steps*, Donat had 'a beautiful dry quality'. An unaccompanied young woman in a humdrum job, reclining in her velvet seat, might with Donat's assistance shrug off the anxiety of the V bombs and for ninety minutes imagine herself playing opposite a man who, in the opinion of one critic, 'can make you feel like he is in love with somebody, which few actors can'.

The problem was that the thirty-nine-year-old Donat could not spark in himself the same emotion. In 1940, concerned for their safety, his wife Ella had taken their children to Los Angeles. On his own for four years, Donat had rarely been so unhappy as on the evening he encountered Priscilla. He telephoned her the following morning at the Sutros, shaken by what she had unloosed.

Soon afterwards, Donat made a list of the qualities he sought in a partner. 'She must be physically attractive. How? Voluptuous ... capable of physical excitement, warm, soft-voiced. She must be capable of being satisfied by me alone.' Furthermore, he wished his Ideal Woman to be calm, warm in temperament, with an intellect superior to his. 'Conclusion: Happiness only possible if MARRIAGE is possible. Things against marriage – Divorce. 3 children. Ella.

Do I want anyone enough to justify the disentanglement?' His letters to Priscilla suggest that he did. 'Oh oh oh when am I going to see you?'

Donat bombarded her with letters between January and May 1945. Letters to Darling Priscilladimples; Blessedest babe; Dear Doynel Poynel. He ended one letter: 'Love and kisses all over the blooming place – I mean *especially* the blooming places.'

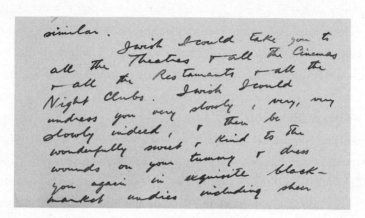

Their relationship mimicked the fate of the beard he was cultivating for his next role. 'The beard, dearest – your beard, darling, all yours – is rather tough and curly without much real shape to it.' Out of a romantic or superstitious habit, he used his/her beard as a barometer, wrestling to give his feelings for her a contour, a significance. 'I swore I would never again take any woman seriously – and here you are beginning to nestle down snugly under my skin, bother and confound you.'

Convalescing from asthma in Tring, Donat was concerned to hear of Priscilla's visit to a doctor – a complication arising from her hysterectomy in July. 'What did that doctor say about your poor little inside? I haven't heard from you for two whole days. No wonder I've had a relapse.'

Since her arrival at Lees Place at the end of October, Priscilla had been coy about the network of scars on her stomach and legs, as about her experiences in France. All that Donat had extracted from Gillian was that Priscilla wanted a divorce from the Vicomte. Donat tried to draw Priscilla out more.

'Why do you enchant me, dear one?'

He discovered her hunger for reading. There was nothing to do in Occupied Paris, she said, apart from read and read. It allowed Donat an entry: 'Do you ever read plays? I have masses of plays sent to me,' and asked if she would make notes on *Yellow Sands*, the Devon comedy for which he was growing their beard. 'It's difficult finding a play for myself. What should I do next? Writing to you has eased my wheeze a bit.' His nights, too, had lost their terrors. With her photograph propped up beside his bed, he assured Priscilla: 'I want a great blaze of sunshine and the good expanses of Somerset to show you on a breezy midsummer day with fat white clouds scudding along the horizon, sitting up beside me on a mountain side. And I want a hell of a lot else beside.'

Envisaging their future, he covered page after page in his green ink. 'I do miss you quite a little lot.' He wished that she were there right now to hold on to. 'I'd hold you ever so tight and ever so close and ever so long and ever so nicely.' He yearned to hear her voice, read her words. 'No letter from you all day Monday and no pigeon post Sunday. How on earth do you suppose I can carry on without you?'

And then a new note.

'I posted to you three times last week – all to Horsham. Did you get them?'

More days passed.

'I'm wondering are you at Depot Road or at Lees Place and where the hell shall I send this? ... I phoned you three times and had ordered supper for two at home. Bother you.'

What was distracting her? Why so moody all of a sudden?

He asked her to pass on his love to Gillian – 'I miss her *terribly*' – as if hoping to reel back Priscilla by invoking the person who had introduced them.

May arrived and the end of the war in Europe. The rest of the world danced in the streets, but Donat stayed indoors. 'I did not celebrate VE day at all – except with gramophone records. I was alone. Love to Gillian.'

His Ideal Woman, his Cinderella, had disappeared on him. Unaccustomed to rejection, he sensed a rival. It was a colossal letdown to discover that his rival was a pen.

'I have tried to dial THRU and get THRU to YU – and when I DU you are in a mood so I leave you to your writing – noting with relief and amusement that you are far too busy inking paper to miss anyone.'

Their love affair did not outgrow his beard. 'My beard will probably disappear Saturday morning … Could you bear that?' Once he shaved it, the relationship was over. Priscilla was involved with the secretive book she was writing. And on 1 July, the *Samaria* docked in Liverpool, bringing Donat's wife and children from America.

'Darling,' Donat wrote to Priscilla. 'We have come to the end of our tether and don't like to admit it to one another. Isn't that the truth? It is only sensible to end it now before it becomes too hurtful.

'Due in the main to circumstances you have had a pretty thin time of it, I know, and you have been so good about it and thoughtful and considerate, but my conviction has nothing whatever to do with circumstances and I should be a hypocrite to pretend that it had anything to do with the return of the family. It hasn't. I just feel, deeply and truly, that I am not for you nor you for me. I have always tried to be honest with you and I have never pretended with you – nor can I now. So please forgive me if I am hurting you (I would not willingly do so). And forgive me for all my shortcomings. And thank you from the bottom of my heart for so much. Robert.'

Even so, it rankled. What was she writing? How could it have been more important for Priscilla Doynel to put pen to paper than to be with Robert Donat?

Priscilla's husband continued to reach out during this hectic period. It was a measure of their deep affection that they kept up good relations and went on saying very tender things to each other, despite not having a physical relationship. After the war, Priscilla discussed her marriage with Vivien, who was left with the definite impression that once Priscilla's honeymoon was over she and Robert had not attempted to have sex again.

So often people escaped the stresses of the Occupation by going to bed with each other. But the war had cruelly exposed Robert's impotence. He was forced into becoming a 'wittol', a word presumed by Collins Dictionary to have fallen out of usage by 2011, describing a man who tolerates his wife's infidelity.

One can safely presume that Priscilla's situation was not unique in an era when few discussed what went on in their bedrooms. Alec Waugh's first marriage was never consummated, which drove him to seek a divorce. It would have been reasonable for Robert to be bitter when Priscilla did the same thing, but there is no evidence that he blamed her. On the contrary, he never stopped wanting to look after her, as if his failure to perform was the fuel for his tenderness.

Writing from Paris, Robert thanked Priscilla for wishing him a happy birthday on 3 March and bringing back happy years. He begged Priscilla to take care of her health. It concerned him how she was coping financially – in an emergency she must draw on funds that he had lodged with Samuel Montagu – and he advised her to buy 'a small detached house in London'. He apologised that his letters were thin on news, 'but as you know I see very few people'. Apart from Zoë's father, he mingled with none of Priscilla's Paris friends and rarely left his apartment. 'Two days ago I took my first taxi (50 francs to go the Champs-Elysées to see a film of Danielle Darrieux). It was all right, nothing special. Since the war, she's aged a lot and her face has withered.'

A visit to London in November 1945 persuaded Robert that Priscilla would never come back to France with him. With a sadness that he was unable to vanquish, he wrote that he had instructed his lawyers to draw their matrimonial affairs to a close. 'I don't have the heart to say anything more to you today.' On 11 March 1946, he attended a regimental reunion in Paris, the date coinciding with the anniversary of their encounter in 1937 on the boat-train from Victoria. 'What a lot has happened since that day. Despite all the sorrows, I don't ever forget the very great joy you have given me, for which I thank God every day.'

Soon afterwards, he dined with a neighbour who had hired as a servant a Hungarian prisoner of war: an aristocrat who, after dinner, played some Hungarian romances on his violin. 'He played very well, and for me especially the little air which they played in the boîte of the Rue Marbeuf where we went before the war. This air had a charming title. "Just one girl is in the world for me". In Hungarian: "Csak Egy Kislany Van a Vilagon".

1946 was a record year for the number of divorce petitions in France. On 16 July, Robert consented to a civil dissolution of their marriage. As a devout Catholic, he continued to think of Priscilla as his one girl in the world, but in so far as it concerned the French State, Priscilla was free. After eight and a half years of a celibate and childless marriage, she had reached the end like a train shunting into the station, slowing down, last roll of the wheel and shudder, release of steam, slight rocking back. Over.

Too many men passed though Priscilla's life in the months that followed. She was desirable and pitiless. Her womb removed, it mattered little whom she slept with, whom she hurt.

In the grey peace of London she and Gillian went out dancing, to the Milroy Club in Hamilton Place or the 400 Club in Leicester Square. 'Darling, you certainly have enough boy friends,' wrote one admirer. Her father put it down to 'having a good time', but there is something frantic and joyless about Priscilla's promiscuity, as though an essential part of her had not come back from France and there had never been any return. Some gate in her had closed with Pierre's desertion. She was free, and yet like Shula Troman her true imprisonment began the moment she landed in England. Troman said: 'I didn't cry on my first night of internment, but I cried on my first night of liberty. The war ended and it all came to me what I lost with my liberation, what I don't dare say to anyone: that the années de liberté were my four years in prison. In the camp I was free. How could I have known, how could I have been so deformed in my thoughts? It's complex, life, isn't it? Full of contradictions.'

After Donat came Edward Fay, a one-eyed American naval captain whom Priscilla had met in Plymouth when staying with Berry, her former room mate at Besançon. A disoriented Fay wrote to her: 'I feel completely lost – don't know which way to turn.' He thought of Priscilla every five minutes and lived for her letters. He treasured one sentence that she had written him: 'I love you more than words can say and nobody else exists as far as I am concerned.'

He wrote back: 'My darling, as you would say, me too.' Demobbed, Fay travelled from Boston to London fully expecting to make Priscilla 'Mrs Fay', and was miserable when she broke off their engagement. 'Frankly, the months I spent with you were the happiest in my life.' He had had no inkling that she was juggling other suitors.

Priscilla kept their letters, the bad things they wrote as well as the good:

There was Charles from University College, Nottingham, who composed a gleeful poem celebrating 'Your figure divine, your complexion so clear, your teeth so white and your eyes without fear ...'

There was Max, an emissary of her husband's, who dropped off at Gillian's house a pink dress and a pair of shoes that Priscilla had left behind in Paris. 'It's perhaps better I don't see you. The most beautiful memories have their price. I know that you continue to be terribly attractive and you are still young. If my friendship can be useful to you one day, whenever and wherever, let me know and I'll do everything in my power.'

There was François, a Yugoslav, who wrote from the Carlton Club: 'I cannot go on like this. Good-night, sweetheart, bon soir, gardez-vous bien; je t'embrasse et en fin je reste toujours ton ami devoué.'

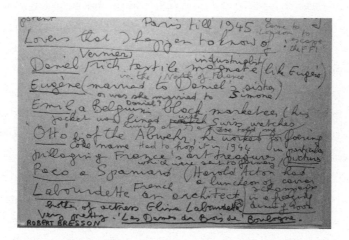

Gillian's notebooks mention two other men. The film director Anatole de Grunewald ('a proper shit, I warned her') who left Priscilla in the lurch at the

Mayfair Athenaeum with an unpaid hotel bill: 'She sold her jewellery to pay the bill' (and in the process discovered that Daniel Vernier's sapphire ring was phoney). And Jacques Labourdette, a French architect and brother of the famous French actress Elina Labourdette, who in similar circumstances abandoned Priscilla at the Mamounia Hotel in Marrakesh.

Priscilla was engaged at the time to her future husband Raymond. The wedding invitations had been sent out when, according to Gillian, 'she hopped it to France a day before, in order to go to Sainte-Maxime with Jacques'. Raymond came rushing after, and telephoned Gillian in Rue de Clichy, 'very pissed and agitated', shouting: 'I want to beat up that bastard!' Gillian tried to calm him, she did not know where Priscilla was. She advised him to go home.

A horror with a foxy face was how Gillian described Labourdette. She had been present in Paris when he promised to leave his rich wife for Priscilla, 'and coolly discussed in front of me on Fouquet's terrasse his plan to murder his wife by making it look like suicide. A plot to make her write some letters. I told Pris to be careful as I thought she could end up an accomplice.' But the melodramatic plan fell apart in Morocco after Labourdette's wife discovered his elopement and threatened to remove her dowry. 'Jacques packed his bags during the night and tore back to France leaving Pris with the hotel bill, no money for her plane fare. She rang up Raymond who behaved very well. He flew to Morocco, paid up the hotel and took her home. I don't think he ever forgot the incident.' This story doubly explained Raymond's possessiveness and why, once Priscilla arrived back in England with him and their wedding eventually happened, she did not leave his side for the next thirty-four years.

'I have always advised you to find a really rich man,' Berry had written from Plymouth. 'You could not be happy on small means. Believe me, it is not amusing to have to count pennies.'

The pennies that it required Priscilla to keep up her striking appearance were itemised in a bill, dated February 1947, for clothes from Betty Lyng's Exclusive Dress Agency in Knightsbridge.

1 black evening cape £10 [at least £330 in today's money]

1 black lace dress £10

1 tweed coat £10

2 black afternoon dresses £10

1 brown dress £10

2 bags £2

corset £6

1 black shoes £2.

Marriage to Raymond Thompson – a thirty-three-year-old divorced Englishman who sailed his own yacht and owned a Lancia Aprilia – guaranteed Priscilla financial and emotional security. After being rejected by her father, here was a man absolutely anchored to her. It was his one overwhelming virtue: he was dependable to be there, shouting and screaming maybe, but he was never going to leave her.

'She met Raymond in Paris.' Gillian was present. In October 1947, she and Priscilla took the Golden Arrow to Sainte-Maxime for a fortnight's holiday, stopping off in Paris. It was their first time together in France since 1940. They slept on camp beds in Gillian's apartment and dined at La Crémaillère. At a party, Priscilla came under the scrutiny of a dark-haired Englishman wearing a cravat. He looked at her through thick black-framed spectacles, not taking his eyes off her.

Poor eyesight had thwarted Raymond Thompson's ambitions to be a pilot. Demobbed from Air Force Intelligence, he had followed his father, a wealthy insurance broker, into Lloyd's, but resigned shortly before meeting Priscilla; he was still jarring from the shock of his failed first marriage in 1946, after his wife, according to Gillian, 'ditched him for his best friend at an airport leaving him with the children' and went to live in Guatemala. Professionally and personally speaking, Raymond was in a terrible state when he introduced himself to a tanned Priscilla. Gillian recalled: 'We were sunburnt, slim, and wore the minimum.' While Gillian went on exhausting walks through the streets of Paris with her new lover, film director Henri-Georges Clouzot, Priscilla was left on her own with Raymond.

He told her of his marital situation, how he had escaped into drink and gambling, his passion for sailing, his abhorrence of the City, how keen he was to start another life in the Sussex countryside, this time as a market gardener.

Priscilla gave him the sketchiest account of her life in France. Like everyone she knew, she talked of anything but the Occupation. 'One asked nothing in Paris in those days,' wrote Martha Gellhorn. 'There was a terrible discretion between friends, after the years of separation, and not knowing what the friends had thought or done or where they had been.' Even so, it touched Priscilla to discover their overlapping histories. Raymond's ex-wife, Carmen Hochstetter, had attended Priscilla's cookery school in pre-war Paris. Carmen's mother was Doris's ex-bridge partner. Carmen's elder sister Sylvia had been seduced by Priscilla's first love – Gillian's brother Nicky. And a connection closer to home: Raymond and Carmen had rented a cottage during the war in the same Sussex village where Doris had come to live. They had Paris and Bosham in common.

After a few days in Paris, Priscilla and Gillian continued on to the French Riviera. A smitten Raymond wrote to Priscilla from his hotel in Rue d'Alger. 'I don't often write letters unless I have to – (& this is not a "have to" letter in the accepted sense) – consequently I'm not much of a hand with a pen.' What he wished falteringly to say was that 'Paris is very empty and autumnal without you' and that 'I can't help thinking of you lying in the sun building up that "honey-brown" tan & wishing that I were with you.'

Back in England, Raymond could not erase Priscilla from his mind. 'The other day I saw "2000 Women". Have you seen it? A film of life in a German internment camp for women in France. It made me think of you & wonder what it was really like.' Priscilla had been due to return to London with Gillian the following Sunday. Anxious to speak to Priscilla on her way through Paris, he booked a call to Gillian's apartment – but no response. 'Have I got the number wrong or have you escaped again?' He tried several more times. Then, ominously: 'I shall have to put you on a chain!!' She had arrived back at 5 Lees Place when he wrote inviting her to a race-meeting at Fontwell Park ('We could go together? Why not? Why not?'). Although Priscilla did not enjoy horse racing, she accepted.

Tough-as-teak, upright, unswerving in whatever course he set himself, Raymond had the attributes of his cross-Channel ocean racer, *Mary Bower*; and he adored Priscilla until her death. But in an adverse wind, he could be dictatorial, intractable and jealous. His manager at Church Farm, John Bevington, described him as tunnel-visioned on certain things – 'and very bad-tempered if you didn't do what he wanted. Once he'd gone off the boil with you, you never got back into his good books.'

Introduced to Raymond, Vivien found him prickly. 'He was atheist, domineering, and had a chip because his wife had left him. And Priscilla was still always frightened, hated rows and generally a timid sort of person.' Vivien advised Priscilla to take more time before deciding to commit. Raymond might offer long-term security; but he might prove to be a most unsuitable liaison.

Gillian was warmer in her encouragement, writing to Priscilla in the New Year, after Raymond threw a party in Paris for Priscilla's friends: 'I thought Raymond quite human. He is not ugly either. I rather admire his "hawk" profile and I like the way his hair grows. You were looking pretty and very happy.'

Raymond was convinced that he had found a stepmother for Tracey, born in 1942, and Carleton, born in 1944. He had agreed to a divorce on condition that he had custody, but his wife refused to give up the children unless there was a woman in the house. Vivien said: 'He was looking for a mother for them and this is exactly what Priscilla was looking for: two children to mother – and so, eventually, they got married.' The reaction of Raymond's mother clinched it. 'Priscilla will be wonderful with them,' she decided after meeting her. 'She has a face which shows truth and sincerity.'

Their marriage on 4 June 1948 at Caxton Hall Register Office in Westminster attracted headlines. 'VICOMTESSE WEDS'. 'BRIDE WAS IN GESTAPO GAOL'. 'She was Nazis' captive who was arrested by the Germans and kept in a concentration camp.' The French press joked that she was exchanging one set of chains for another.

Afterwards, the couple assembled for a group photograph with their witnesses. Gillian was in Paris, but John Sutro was there, and Vivien and Doris. Once again, there was a father-shaped absence. 'The 31-year-old bride is a daughter of Mr S. P. B. Mais, the author.'

Priscilla wrote only one sentence about her wedding day. It hints at a pattern of hard drinking and horse racing: 'Couldn't get out of bed until Ray fetched me Amber Moon' – a pick-me-up of Tabasco, raw egg and whisky. It was also Derby Day, and directly after the reception they went to Epsom to watch the race, won by My Love.

In the evening, Raymond drove Priscilla in his silver Lancia to their new home in Sussex by the Sea.

34.
LIFE AS A MUSHROOM FARMER'S WIFE

Wittering was where the Saxons first landed in England, a village of thatched cottages with small gardens that smelled of honeysuckle, mud and rotting seaweed.

Inevitably, SPB had written about it, after taking the inward journey by boat from Bosham. 'I disembarked on a long sea wall, fringed with tamarisk and gorse. There was a gorgeous medley of inland and marine flowers, of land and sea birds, of marsh and meadow.' From near here, Vespasian began the conquest of Britain, King Canute defied the waves, and Harold spent the night before making his unfortunate visit to William of Normandy. Twinned with the French village of Moutiers-les-Mauxfaits, Wittering was a reminder that Britain was occupied too, but never had to process the trauma since the occupiers had never really left. 'From the point of view of history you could not hit on a better place,' SPB wrote in *It Isn't Far From London* (1930). 'Pitch your tent or stay your caravan in the Wittering fields and you will find yourself transported not seventy miles or seventy minutes from Hyde Park Corner, but back to AD 700 in the days of St Wilfrid of York, seven million miles away from the noises and odours and distractions of a civilised world.'

But not even this distance proved far enough for Priscilla.

Raymond had bought a seven-bedroom red-brick Georgian house next to a grey stone church. Church Farm was originally the beach cottage for the Dukes of Richmond. It was ramshackle, with an untended walled garden and a view of the Isle of Wight. There was no furniture. They ate their meals sitting on packing cases. Priscilla laid felt on the staircase and stained the floorboards in their bedroom. She found the all-important padded chest in an antique shop in Peacehaven.

To make the place homely for their house-warming party, Priscilla's mother Doris came over from Emsworth, where she was now living, and sewed the curtains.

Doris had been abandoned – again. She had spent the war in Bosham, pretending to be the wife of Surgeon Lieutenant-Commander Bertie Ommaney-Davis. Then in March 1948, Bertie asked Vivien, whom he called Widge, because she was quite small, to visit him at the Royal Naval Hospital Haslar, where he worked. 'Widge, I've something to tell you. I simply can't stand your mother another minute. I've been appointed to Malta and I'm not going to take her with me. I'm going to buy her a cottage in Emsworth, with an allowance.'

The cottage into which Doris had since moved was less than six miles from Wittering. A dutiful Priscilla used to drive over with Tracey and Carleton for lunch. The atmosphere was formal, Tracey remembered. 'We knew her as Mrs Davis, and she served stewed rabbit.'

Vivien told me about the rest of Doris's life. In Malta, Bertie got married to a South African with an enormous nose, but appointed back to Haslar four years later, he decided that he needed Doris's cottage for himself and his new wife, and turned Doris out. Vivien wrote to him: 'That's a shit's trick' – and never spoke to him again. Homeless once more, and still legally bound to SPB, Doris went to stay with her mother in Horsham, thirty miles away.

Vivien said: 'At some point she met Lambert White, a married fruit importer in London. He fell for Doris and bought her a flat in Shepherd's Bush.' When his wife died, Lambert moved in with Doris. They had boiled eggs for supper and lunched every day at the Portman Hotel. 'After one lunch, Lambert says he has to go and have a pee. My mother waits in the hall. The porter, not looking, crashes into her with a huge suitcase and breaks her hip. She's eighty-three.' With Vivien's help, Priscilla put Doris and Lambert into a nursing home in West Wittering, one room with a wide bay-window and a brass plate on the door: 'Colonel White & Mrs Davis'. There, just up the road from Church Farm, Doris drank gin, played bridge and did the hard *Telegraph* crossword, but she failed to complete the puzzle of her relationship with Priscilla, despite their proximity. Vivien told her son: 'I never want to be like my mother who was so cold-hearted and selfish and when she had money never helped anyone else out.' Priscilla felt the same.

It was at Priscilla's house-warming party at Church Farm on 8 September 1948 that my mother came face to face with Doris. 'I met her in an upstairs corridor. I was seventeen and staying there. "Who are you?" she said. I told her, and immediately she turned the other way and walked on without a word, not even hello.' It was the first and last occasion when Doris set eyes on SPB's 'other' family.

Raymond had hated working for Lloyds. 'I love the open air,' he had written to Priscilla, 'and it will certainly take a lot to make me incarcerate myself in some bloody office again fifty feet underground.' At Church Farm, he remade himself – first, growing strawberries and tomatoes; then as a mushroom farmer.

The business expanded from four mushroom houses to thirty, producing 35,000 lbs of mushrooms a week. Priscilla was the company secretary. She learned terms such as turning, spawning, beds, La France disease. The faint sweet smell of horse manure pervaded everything. There was mud on the stairs, indeed in all the rooms. After a weekend visit, Gillian sent a description to Vertès, who shook his head. 'What a funny idea, darling, that while John is away you should want to live in the countryside with Priscilla in a chaotic and no doubt badly-heated household full of children among the mushrooms … Why?????'

Zoë also came to stay, bringing her baby son, who was Gillian's godson, and news from France, none of it heartening. Her mother had disappeared one night, announcing that she was going to watch a film, and flung herself into the Seine. Zoë's badly shaken father identified the body at the morgue. Zoë heard about it while on a delayed honeymoon with her husband, recently released after five years at a POW camp in Münster.

With Gillian, Zoë had refused to speak about the Occupation. Gillian assumed that the subject was too painful, too recent to bear discussion. 'Later it struck me that a certain unease floated whenever I brought up the subject. I remember hearing, "C'était une grande tragédie ... nos pauvres prisonniers ... les fridolins ... les privations ..." I never heard the words "la résistance, le maquis, radio-Londres".'

Not in Paris, nor in London, only in Wittering with Priscilla, who had lived through it with her, did Zoë open up.

They went on walks where Raymond could not overhear, multitudes of gulls standing in the mud and a restless band of oyster-catchers scurrying up and down. Beside a landward marsh, they watched red-sailed fishing boats wind their way up the estuary, and to the sonorous bubbling of a curlew caught up on the years.

On 26 December 1944, a Free French firing squad executed Henri Chamberlin and eleven members of his gang at the Fort de Montrouge; they had been betrayed by Priscilla's neighbour in 12 Rue Beaujon, Monsieur Joseph. In the puritan flood, the ban on dancing which coincided with Priscilla's hasty departure from Paris had extended to brothels. The Panier Fleuri had closed, and the One-Two-Two was now the Union of Leather and Skin Trade workers. Arletty's three-year acting ban had come to an end. Albert Blaser was back at his old job at Maxim's. Stocklin's friend Comtesse Marie Tchernycheff-Bezobrazoff, the 'Red Princess', had been released from Fresnes and declared bankrupt. That was two months before.

Seated on the flower-covered sea wall, the two friends remembered Max Stocklin, in Fresnes prison. Otto Graebener – in Switzerland, last they heard. Emile Cornet, ensconced in the royal palace in Monte Carlo after winning the

Belgian Grand Prix ('To be sick, broken-hearted and jailed was a maximum!' he had written to Priscilla. 'I got over all that! I have become very friendly with the young prince of Monaco, who is an enthusiast of all things to do with car racing etc...'). Daniel and Simone, still together in Paris (Cornet had bumped into them, in a restaurant where he had gone with another racing-driver. 'He didn't understand why we weren't put at the same table!'). Pierre, now in Tourcoing. It all seemed so remote and so foreign that they began to laugh. And tears filled their eyes.

Suddenly, Priscilla found herself responsible for two small children who were upset by their mother running off and puzzled by Priscilla's relationship with Raymond, wanting to know: 'Why do you sleep in Daddy's room?'

She struggled in the role of stepmother. Tracey remembered walking into Priscilla's room each morning to ask what to wear. 'She was terrified of us to begin with. She didn't know how to be a mother because she'd never been mothered or had children.' Panic seized her if she had to organise a party. The children's big treat was to dance after tea or sit quietly by the drawing-room fire.

Priscilla found Tracey complex, observant, with a phenomenal memory; also lazy, a beater-around-the-bush who never asked for anything outright and 'generally tried to curry favour because she feels her brother has more charm'. Carleton stuttered, spending ten seconds on a word, burst into tears easily, had no memory and could never find anything. 'Always has hair in his eyes,' she noted, describing him also as 'hardworking, shy, obedient, affectionate, loves soft things such as animal fur or skin.'

Although never a convincing maternal figure, Priscilla was there for them and cared about them, and it was not long before both of Raymond's children, having initially addressed her as 'Aunty Priscilla', started calling her 'Mummy'. Carleton was once taken to hospital with earache. Priscilla was allowed to visit only on a Sunday. When finally she was with him, he said, breaking her heart, 'I didn't think you were ever coming back, Mummy.'

Their real mother's departure continued to unsettle them, and for several years they had trouble sleeping. Priscilla would leave the radio on in the passageway, playing music, and quietly come back to check if they were asleep, and turn it off.

'I doted on my stepchildren,' she wrote. 'However, I found that I had too much time on my hands when they went to school, so I took up writing.'

She started to write after an embarrassing stab at modelling. Priscilla had been back in London less than two months when Gillian organised a photoshoot for her at *Vogue*.

Everyone agreed that Priscilla was beautiful, but the stilted portraits that resulted from her *Vogue* audition failed to bear this out. She presented two to Robert Donat, who claimed to love both unconditionally, before backtracking, saying of one that it 'lowered my blood considerably' – she looked like a gangster's moll. Pierre was unimpressed by the portrait chosen for him: 'I find it photographed from a bad angle.' Gillian posted a copy to Vertès in New York. His reaction – 'I would never have recognised her.' A French admirer called Bernard remarked only that she possessed remarkable hands.

Priscilla's first husband spoke for all those sceptical that her future lay in modelling. 'I want to say how happy and touched I am that you sent this photo. It is beautiful and you are beautiful.' Nonetheless, he would have chosen her portrait taken before the war in Avenue de l'Opéra. He wrote diplomatically: 'One is a little cork, the other is a woman of character. What a mixture you are ...' He wondered if the English weather was making her so sad.

Her eyes had enchanted Robert Donat and numerous admirers, but Priscilla saw nothing when she looked into them. The urge to break the mirror on her dressing-table to see something – to be present to herself – lay behind her redemptive compulsion to write. She wanted to straighten out her thoughts in the hope of understanding those things which had always troubled her.

Priscilla's French husband had tilted her in the direction which she now took. 'If you're going to work in the future, I think you would have greater success in writing articles.' He advised her to buy some magazines, study the articles, their construction, and copy them, but making sure to inject a personal and original tone. 'Your father could give you a serious helping hand in this area and open some doors. All this advice is given out of concern for your future and your happiness in which I hope, whatever happens, I shall always remain interested. I hug you with all my tenderness, R.'

Every day she sat and looked down at the yard. She watched Raymond's workers stack the boxes, spade the compost, tug on plastic gloves before disappearing inside the sheds, canisters of fungicide strapped to their backs.

Priscilla titled an essay that she wrote at her dressing-table 'Life as a mushroom farmer's wife'. It is hard to tell from this whether she had a developed sense of irony, but elsewhere she could be drily droll in her writing. It is also possible that when observing the struggles involved in growing Raymond's champignons de Paris (not only protecting them from La France disease, but against the ink caps that caused the mushroom spores to disintegrate into a black squidgy mess), Priscilla may have reflected on certain parallels with what she was doing, and with her long losing battle to produce an account of a life that was now so ordinary but had been so extraordinary.

Raymond fulfilled his emotional function for Priscilla. Terrible though his possessiveness may have been, it was something that she needed. But in order to keep his protection and security, she had to remain mute – and in a place called Wittering. The only thing to do if she wanted to express herself and disinfect the past was to write it down. Even so, she kept this under wraps. 'I never knew she was writing or wanting to write,' said my mother. Not even Gillian suspected. 'I often said to Pris that she should write about her years in Paris as they were very strange, but she showed no desire to put pen to paper.' Only in her bedroom, in secret, did Priscilla try to repair and stabilise her life by indexing what had happened. After her travails, it was a way of affirming her will and character; a way of shouting 'I'm here, I haven't vanished!'

Many of the significant emotional moments of Priscilla's life had occurred in wartime France. It was a period which she came to regard as separate from the rest of her life. An interval which Simone de Beauvoir called a 'no man's land' in time – when Priscilla had lived on another level and according to values which had little in common with her previous existence.

But the entr'acte was over, and Priscilla had no continuity to slip back into. Her French years fell suddenly into the category of a shameful subject not to be spoken about, like Vichy. 'But why should we proclaim the Republic?' was de Gaulle's testy reaction on the day after Paris's liberation: 'She has never ceased to exist.' Priscilla's time in France was another non-dit. It belonged to a null and void piece of history, to be treated as though it had never actually taken place.

In any case, by September 1945 the war had ended. No one having just gone through the past five years wanted to read about it. 'There is at the moment a great resistance to books dealing with any aspect of the war,' was one publisher's response when rejecting the memoirs of an American woman who had fought in the Resistance. This indifference was the same whether you were a hero or a victim. Even if, like Primo Levi, you did find someone to publish your story, you could not expect a large readership: his masterpiece *If This Is a Man* sold less than 1,500 copies.

In particular, no one was going to want to read about Priscilla's war. As Gillian pointed out, Priscilla had not been in a camp like Levi or Jorge Semprún: Besançon was not Auschwitz, nor Buchenwald. Her experience was not one of victory over the enemy, but of personal defeat and a sense of shame. Priscilla's need to piece together a narrative which could make sense of her life was therefore at odds with everything that most people were prepared to accept. The British view of adultery was *Brief Encounter*: a clandestine handshake on a railway station. The story of Priscilla's adulteries would have been incomprehensible. After Belsen was liberated in April 1945 and the public saw the newsreels, it became even harder to accept the Germans – and more or less unthinkable to admit to any intimacies with them. In Paris at the time, Gillian reported back how the pianist Alfred Cortot was cat-called at a Chopin recital at the Théâtre des Champs-Elysées after someone in the audience yelled: 'Do you dedicate that to your friend Hitler?' Cortot fled to Switzerland, and in the opinion of a friend would sooner bite off his tongue than speak about the incident. The majority of Englishwomen interned with Priscilla in Besançon opted for silence over honesty. Rosemary Say wrote: 'I had learned to keep my mouth shut about the survival tactics of those I knew.'

And there was an extra worry. Raymond.

When, aged fifty-seven, Gillian went to live in Monaco, she often visited Graham Greene in Antibes to seek advice about her memoirs. 'Tell all,' he said. But if Priscilla did tell all, if she did succeed in facing what was most difficult to face, and exposed what Semprún called the 'truest and deepest part, the opaque, unspeakable heart of the experience', would she be able to show it to her husband?

Priscilla's predicament was her father's: SPB could not in his diary speak of his feelings for Priscilla in the knowledge that Winnie was going to type it up. Nor could Priscilla, aware of Raymond's intolerance of Germans, aerate – to use a composting term – certain episodes. 'If she had told the truth,' said Carleton, 'my father would have been destroyed.'

To cover or to expose. She had learned from SPB how Jane Austen pushed her manuscript under the blotter if anyone came into the room. From her late twenties up until her early forties, Priscilla was torn between two opposing impulses; between feeling that she had to shut away what she had written – in the chest beneath the television which Raymond watched every night, with a tray on his lap containing a baked egg and cream – and wishing with every particle for it to be broadcast.

This complicated mixture of shame and embarrassment on the one hand, and, on the other, bloody-minded determination, touched the deepest springs of Priscilla's feelings about her father. While it was not the only reason she wrote, her writing became more and more what earlier she had used her body for: a means of establishing a relationship to save herself.

Priscilla completed her first article, describing her imprisonment at Besançon, six weeks after landing in London. She sent the manuscript to SPB, hoping that he might bring to it the transformative magic he had performed thirty years before on Alec Waugh; encourage, criticise and find a publisher. Her father had been a genuinely legendary teacher – not merely to Waugh, but to writers like J. R. Ackerley, Brian Aldiss and Jon Stallworthy. He was the one person who might have taught Priscilla how to write. Had he taken the time to sit down and help her, he might also have started to understand what she had gone through.

Priscilla's story was her heart's blood and she felt brutally rejected when she received a reply not from SPB, but from Winnie. 'Daddie is ill again & has been in bed since Thursday. He sends his love & says he should think the *New Statesman* the best paper to send your story.' Winnie's disabling brush-off set the tone for Priscilla's post-war dealings with SPB and was one more instance of their not communicating successfully. It was a completely missed opportunity, the last hope he had of reconnecting with his eldest daughter. Her father's rejection was the most cruel, but it anticipated the reaction of each and every agent, magazine editor and publisher to whom she offered her work.

Paper-clipped together in chronological order at the bottom of Priscilla's papers was a neat stack of rejection slips. They painted a caricature of the struggling writer and attested to her persistence in the face of continual disappointment.

She submitted her first manuscript in December 1944, when she was involved with Donat; her last, in March 1957. Again and again, what she had written had 'not been found quite suitable' – by the editors of *Home Chat*, *Modern Woman, Woman's Own, Queen*, even *Yachting Monthly* (although the latter did express interest in her sketches, 'which show promise'). The reasons for turning her down: 'Stories bringing in the war are not liked now ...' 'Anything morbid or sordid is no use at all ...' 'The sustained amoral atmosphere will, I fear, put it out of court for most publishers ...'

Everything that Priscilla was obsessed to gather together in her padded chest braided into the same story: the drama of a woman with a past nobody was interested in – not even her own father – but who was compelled to write it down, however incriminating.

Priscilla had been writing for nine years when she started a diary. Her life was boring and dull. She and Raymond had argued about money. 'Yesterday I posted off a short story which I have high hopes for. If only I could earn some money I should feel more independent. It is hell for a woman to have to beg for every penny.'

12 November 1953: 'High hopes for story end in dismal failure. It has been sent back and obviously not read by my agent. Generally she keeps a story for a month. This time it is back in two days.'

Her writing and its subject repudiated, she sent one of her stories to a friend who was a popular author, soliciting his advice. Geoffrey Willans was the creator of Molesworth and author of *Down with Skool*, who in 1958 dedicated *The Dog's Ear Book* to Priscilla's schnauzer Viking – pencilling on the title page: 'who undoubtedly has the dirtiest arse in West Sussex'. His tact was exemplary. 'My dear Pris, I've read the short story and dear Pris, I know you're going to hate me for this but I don't think you will sell it, not because it isn't interesting and well-written, which it is, but because it breaks a fundamental rule of the women's press. This is that a woman may have lustrous gold hair, trim ankles, shapely legs BUT, for this kind of work, she *stops* below the shoulder and above the knees. In other words, any heroine loves romance, music, a glamorous man but she can't even go to bed with her husband, let alone take a lover. In other words, you can deal with love and even the very slight temptation, but never with the basic result of it, which isn't even admitted.' He concluded: 'You might get away with your story in a novel, but never in a woman's paper.'

Priscilla's story may have been too saucy or unsavoury for most contemporary publishers. And yet it would probably never have been published anyway, even with her excellent literary contacts. The pile of rejection slips that she so assiduously kept told a truth about her writing talents – a truth that she must have found excruciatingly difficult to reconcile with her ambition, or for that matter her need. Her writing was just not very good.

The novel that Priscilla started on Willans's advice was her third – the other two are lost. Once again, she took for her model Alec Waugh's first autobiographical novel which, if little read today, enjoyed a succès d'estime (and de scandale) for its portrayal of homosexuality at an English public school. *The Loom of Youth* – in which Priscilla's father featured prominently as the 'great god' of Waugh's soul – was a fictionalised account of the author's time at Sherborne under SPB's inspirational tutelage. Turned down by several publishers, the manuscript was accepted by Grant Richards, mainly thanks to SPB and Doris, and on publication became as famous as *Tom Brown's Schooldays* a century before. 'My dear Alec,' SPB wrote to Waugh in October 1917, 'Your book on every stall & in the mouths of every one who matters.' Forty years on, Priscilla wanted the same reception.

She regarded Waugh as her literary godfather ever since reading 'To Your Daughter', the poem he had composed for her birth. Like *The Loom of Youth*, her book would be an autobiographical Bildungsroman, taking in its sweep her upbringing in Sherborne and Hove, her move aged nine to Paris, her life during the Occupation. At its core would be her four and a half years in Nazi France.

When Priscilla flew back to England in October 1944, she had learned to distrust what she had been taught and not to depend on what anyone told her. And yet about one thing she was clear-sighted. She had brought with her out of France material for a cracking story, not about an elite coming to terms with fascism, but about ordinary people – ordinary women especially – adjusting, screwing up, and developing survival skills of a deeply primitive and totally understandable, if ruthless, kind. It was a story that would give Alec Waugh and even John Buchan a run for their money, and compete with any novel that SPB had written. In Priscilla's Electra-like struggle with her father, her book would be a way of communicating and identifying with him, and also her weapon and revenge.

Priscilla narrated her story through the eyes of two young women: Crystal, based on herself, and Chantal, based on Gillian. In one of those coincidences which make their relationship even more poignant, Gillian had, unknown to Priscilla, decided to write about her own life in pre-war Paris, with a character based on Priscilla. Gllian's novel, written in French and also the first of several attempts to shape the material that they shared, received the same rejection. 'My novel went to 5 publishers, nearly taken by Gallimard, one vote missing.' Gillian at least finished *Un Etrange Maître*, on 17 March 1957. When Priscilla's 'novel' reached the scene where Daniel Vernier lowered his pistol inside the clinic in Saint-Cloud, it disintegrated into a mass of notes and scribbles.

35.
TOO MUCH GIN

Survivors pay with their conscience. Not to Raymond, not to Gillian – not even to Zoë – did Priscilla admit the extent of her friendships with Emile Cornet, Max Stocklin and Otto Graebener. Nailed to the cross of her secret past, she preserved the silence of Garbo on her years in Occupied France.

Once, Priscilla was rereading *Candide* and noticed she was eating all the time, and realised that she had read the novella in a state of semi-starvation at Besançon. There were triggers she tried to avoid – being jostled in the Underground or anyone in uniform. But her past was a phosphorus that continued to burn. A breath of cool wind over the Nissen mushroom sheds goose-pimpled her bare arms, and at its touch she was back in a freezing courtyard, back with the noise and snow and queues, the eye-stinging smell of the stove, the bitter taste of the soup, the clop of the wood-soled boots on the long stone corridors, and the piercing toot of the trains at night in the remoteness of the town.

Arthur Koestler said that guilt should be forgiven but not hushed up. Priscilla had held her shame at bay through the 1940s and 50s, but it was eating away inside, and finally it overwhelmed her. Unable to relieve the pressure through writing, unable to speak out candidly, she resorted to Gordon's gin. From about the time that she abandoned her third attempt at a novel, Priscilla, the once-priggish young woman who for many years never sipped anything stronger than milk, was to her intimate friends a drunk.

It was a refrain of guests at Church Farm: 'Oh, where's Priscilla, I'd like to say goodbye.' My mother admired the way that she stood up in the middle of her own dinner party and went to bed. 'I wished I could do that.' She never knew that Priscilla had become a member of AA. 'I was just aware of everyone drinking like mad.'

Upstairs, Tracey remembered her stepmother weaving down the passageway to get to bed. 'She was very clever at disguising it. She thought we were asleep.'

Her father could tell, though. After a visit to Church Farm, SPB wrote in his diary: 'Too much gin as usual.'

Priscilla and Raymond were part of a circle of friends who were hard drinkers. And yet she paid a ruinous price. She had resembled Grace Kelly for so long. Now alcohol put lines beside her mouth; her skin grew blotchy, her neck thickened, the once-blue eyes that looked at you were blood-shot. She broke out in excessive sweats, making her blonde hair damp and stringy.

John Sutro loved Priscilla, and invited himself to stay whenever at a loose end during Gillian's absences. He was struck by Priscilla's deterioration: 'She's lost all her looks poor thing.' After seeing it for herself, Gillian wrote to Vertès that their friend had become fat. Vertès's reply: 'Priscilla fat? That doesn't surprise me. Already in December, I found her quite voluminous. She's soon going to be a very obese woman. That shouldn't make her unhappy since she has the character of a fat person.'

Ravaged by an inner despair, her health suffered. She had aches and pains. She stopped going to the cinema after she began seeing double. She lost interest in driving; even in reading. Her sole interest – to 'get at the drink quickly'. And yet for all the cunning that she deployed to get drunk, Priscilla could no longer hide the effect. From the early 1960s, the sadness that I had picked up on as a child started to reveal itself.

One afternoon, she went to tea with Gillian and passed out. On coming-to, Priscilla lurched against a table, smashing an antique vase. 'When Gillian remonstrated with me, I roared with laughter, thus adding insult to injury.

Appalled by this story I decided that something had to be done. After all, I had known her all my life and she was closer to me than my own sister. This is when the idea of AA first entered my mind.'

In December 1963, Priscilla stood up to address her first AA meeting in London, afterwards writing in her notebook: 'Resolutions: to save my marriage, to save my health, to save my looks.' Throughout early 1964, she attended meetings in Brighton, Bognor and Swiss Cottage, where her fellow members were: a delightful woman called Nina, a foul-mouthed Soho greengrocer, two burglars, and some hold-up men.

By April, Priscilla had been dry for two months. She enjoyed reading again, watching films. 'I felt a new lease of life.' She looked forward to a sailing holiday with Raymond. 'My life is full of excitement and our new boat "Drusilla" was acquired at just the right moment for me. I no longer spend my "all" in pubs and secret bottle-hoarding. Perhaps I shall be able to take up writing again and fulfil my ambition to have a book published. I am happier than I have ever been and am full of hope instead of despair.'

Then on 2 May, Priscilla suffered a terrible 'defeat'. Committed to go to an AA meeting in Bognor, she did not attend 'because of bloodcurdling row with SPB'.

Priscilla's last and most dramatic rift with her father had its origins six years earlier, when he asked for money.

SPB was one of the radio casualties that failed to make the transition into television. A pioneer of television, he had come off screen when transmission ceased in 1939, when there were only 18,000 sets in Britain. By the time the service resumed in 1946, he was, at sixty-one, too old. He had to fall back on his voice and his pen, but he found it hard to earn a living.

Not one of SPB's novels sold more than 5,000 copies. *It Isn't Far from London* sold 2,765 copies and earned £77 in royalties [£2,000 in today's money]. The most he earned from any book was £850 – for *I Return to Scotland*.

Unable to support himself and Winnie through writing and broadcasting, and lacking a pension, he was reduced to the humiliating tradition of sending out begging letters. Until well into the 1960s, SPB continued to importune friends like Henry Williamson and Alec Waugh.

A fairly typical SOS was one written to Waugh in June 1965, from SPB's final address, Flat 20, Bliss House – a modern low-rise building owned by the Samaritans in the Sussex village of Lindfield. 'Dear Alec, you were kind to me when I was last in touch. Be kind again. I have just moved into this doll's house of a flat which is really a superior old people's home, though the rent is £234 a year plus rates of £60. The government expects me to get by on my old-age pension of £4 a week. It doesn't keep me in cigars. I can't afford to get my hair cut, shoes repaired or shaving cream. I can't afford this writing paper ... But you made such a packet out of *Sunshine Island* [*sic*] I have no compunction whatever in asking you to help me pay rates & the bills that fall – money to beautify this cesspool of an asylum.' He referred to himself as 'the ghost of Mr Chips' and concluded with an appeal that he knew Waugh would find helpless to resist: 'I just want to remind people that I am NOT the author of *The Loom of Youth*.'

This sly reference to Waugh's first book was calculated to graze Alec's conscience: no one had contributed more to its success than SPB – or looked out for its teenage author with such boisterous care.

SPB had been a paternal figure to Alec Waugh after his expulsion from Sherborne, and a visitor to his home in North London during a period when Waugh was 'lonely and without a friend'. SPB had no son. Waugh came closest to filling this role. 'My good ox,' SPB called him. 'I say and I say again that you have it in you not to be merely clever but a genius.'

Their close relationship alarmed Alec's supersensitive father, who happened to be SPB's publisher at the time. If ever Arthur Waugh had a rival for his favourite son's attention it was SPB during 1916 and 1917. Arthur made a wounded observation to this effect in January 1917, after SPB went to stay with Priscilla at 'Underhill'. Waugh moved swiftly to reassure his father. 'Please don't think I put Mais before my family. I don't. He has no standards, often his opinions infuriate me, but he has the most wonderful personality. No one can understand him who has not come directly under it.'

Alec Waugh remained loyal to his old teacher, and to the end of his life appreciated SPB's central part in making *The Loom of Youth* a success. Furthermore, Waugh knew what it was to scrape professional and financial rock-bottom. He had faced exactly this situation in the early 1950s. The person who had guided Waugh from his 'all-time low' back to the surface, if inadvertently, was, for a second time, my grandfather.

Waugh's son Peter told me the background. 'In January 1953, Alec had the pills lined up. He was looking at the packet and thinking, "Do I do it now?"' But just when Waugh saw no option other than to swallow a mouthful of barbiturates, he recalled a story that SPB had told him years before at Sherborne: how SPB's great-great grandfather, a sugar merchant in Bristol, had eloped to Jamaica and raised a black family in Kingston. The vivid image of Harry Mais spawned the Fleury family and a novel, *Island in the Sun*, for which Waugh received what was then one of the largest movie advances ever. Within four weeks, Waugh had earned a quarter of a million dollars [several million in today's money]. A film was made starring Harry Belafonte and Joan Collins; the title song topped the charts and gave birth to the reggae label, Island Studios. Alec Waugh's life was not merely saved, but overturned. 'I had become overnight a different person.'

For these obvious reasons, Waugh was more than willing to help when, soon after the film came out, SPB approached him for financial assistance to cure Winnie of her depression. Winnie had lived with SPB for thirty years and her guilt at not being married, exacerbated by their constant lack of money, threatened to make her 'dangerously ill'. It appears from what happened next that Waugh's contribution was not enough, forcing SPB to reach out elsewhere.

He had already approached my mother. She told me: 'When I was seventeen, he said "We're desperate for money. Can we have your savings?" It was not more than £100, but it was all my savings since I was a child. I didn't ask what it was for.' Now that she was married to a *Times* journalist who earned only £500 a year, and had a baby, she had no spare pennies.

On a cloudless day in May 1958, SPB and Winnie joined my parents and Priscilla at Church Farm. My grandfather, in shorts, spent his time cutting wood, collecting compost and playing with his one-year-old grandson, Slogger, as he had decided that I was to be nicknamed. But SPB was 'worn to a frazzle' by Winnie's continued depression. 'She kept on saying "I want to die."' On 7 May 1958, SPB wrote in his diary: 'She thinks she is going mad. We walked to the sea. I rolled the lawn; borrowed £3 from Priscilla to get home.' The loan was an ominous prelude.

Back in Oxford, Winnie's doctors insisted that she undergo immediate electric therapy treatment. SPB could not meet the bills. In late November, he turned to the one person whom common sense ought to have warned him to spare.

I have their letters in front of me, three from Priscilla and one from Winnie. Together, they dramatise the proverb: 'When a father gives to his son, both laugh; when a son gives to his father, both cry.'

'29/11/58, Church Farm, Wittering
'Darling Winnie,
'Send me your bills and I will settle them by postal order, providing they don't exceed £20 as that is all I possess in the world and I *was* saving it for Christmas.
    'Priscilla'

'29/11/58 Church Farm, Wittcring
'Darling Daddy,
'I've written to Winnie about the money as this seems to be her main domain.
    'In return for my help you can answer me a few questions (although I don't suppose you will).
    'Why do you expect *me* to help *you*? What have you ever done for me except give me the "gift of life"? This can't have been too difficult for you – it was more troublesome for Mama, surely?
    'The one time I turned to you for help in 1937 you utterly failed me. Although you were famous and presumably well off you allowed me to go to France with £5 in my pocket *borrowed from a friend*! The sum of £50 then

meant more to me than any money can mean to you now. In fact it was my life at stake and you didn't give a damn. You had no pity and as far as I can see you have never cared about anyone but yourself.

'As for Winnie, why the hell should I worry about her? She broke up my home when I was 9 without hesitation, causing me great unhappiness and now she has the nerve to moan about her fate to *me*.

'You are both utterly selfish and irresponsible,

'Love, Priscilla'

'1st Dec 1958, 116 Woodstock Road, Oxford

'Priscilla (why do you hate me darling),

'The sting of your letter is very bitter and I wish I could talk, rather than write, this to you.

'You seem to have got the details in your life so mixed up that there is scarcely any truth left.

'1. You accuse me of breaking up your home when you were nine. The fact is that Doris and Daddy never got on, not even during their honeymoon, and by the time I met Daddy, Doris was living with, and planning to go to Paris with Bevan Lewis. Also Vivien was 5 or 4, the child of Neville Brownrigg and Doris, who incidentally left him, as indeed all her men have done, for another woman.

'2. In 1937, I believe that was the year you were pregnant by one of your many young men, and I vividly remember both Daddy and I imploring you to have the child and we would look after you. But Doris had already persuaded you to have an abortion and given you an address in Paris where it could be done.

'3. You accuse us both of irresponsibility. Daddy paid handsomely for your and Vivien's education and ballet dancing in Paris and we have always been delighted to have you stay, as a child, adolescent, & adult during which visits (as a child) I suffered considerably because your mind had from the start been poisoned against Daddy and me.

'As for the accusation of selfishness, may I say that I have remained faithful to Daddy since the day I met him, have given him two daughters and have slaved to give them a good education and a stable background.

'For years now I have worked in the house without help and taken a job outside and even the money I earned from that has had to go into housekeeping.

'I met Daddy with an overdraft and he has never been able to get free. Now in his old age he is still working for a pittance and I am still looking after him as well as I can, but I am also getting old and it is not easy to get jobs in competition with youth.

'Think again, Priscilla, for you have got such a cock-eyed idea of what has happened.

'Recriminations are not good and I am sorry you have had such a rotten home life as a child but remember it broke up long before I met Daddy.

'My love, Winnie'

'22/12/58, Church Farm, Wittering
'Darling Daddy,
'Your letter with enclosures arrived as I was leaving England. I had thought that you had found some other way round your problems, owing to your long silence. Meanwhile, naturally I had spent my 'worldly possessions' on Christmas presents. Therefore I had to ask Raymond if he could help and he agreed reluctantly to write a cheque for the smaller bill (the other one is out of the question – I told you that £20 was the limit). You put me in a very difficult position where Ray is concerned. He has enough responsibilities of his own without my adding to them.

'With regard to Winnie I would merely like to say that I consider her last letter to me (did you see it?) *unforgivable*, and I have no intention of ever seeing her again or mentioning her name. As far as I am concerned she no longer exists and that is final.

'As regards your wonderful kindness in paying for my education, thank you so much. Who else was supposed to do it? You can't just put children into this world and then forget about them… or can you?

'Love, Priscilla'

Upset, unable to see straight, Priscilla had reached for the strongest word she could find: unforgivable. But her father was the one she could not forgive, not her stepmother; and by proxy it was herself she could not forgive, for the mess she had made of her life.

Priscilla's savage disappointment in herself was the background to the bloodcurdling row which erupted in May 1964, causing her to fall, as she wrote, 'off the straight and narrow'.

It was raining hard on the day, six years later, when Priscilla met SPB and Winnie at Chichester station and drove them to Church Farm. She never disclosed what made her relent to invite Winnie for the weekend, after vowing never to see her again. Winnie, though, has left an account of the tirade to which Priscilla subjected them.

Ever since Winnie arrived in Hove and usurped the nine-year-old Priscilla, there had been a Greek element to their relationship. Both competing for the same unpredictable man, the two women were never likely to get on. Winnie resented Priscilla for being the legitimate daughter; Priscilla resented Winnie for replacing her as a pseudo-daughter – most hurtfully when SPB was invited in 1933 to make his ground-breaking broadcasts from America. According to Winnie, he and Winnie decided to risk travelling as father and daughter. It worked. President Roosevelt remained unaware that the attractive blonde introduced to him as SPB's daughter-cum-secretary was actually his inter-viewer's common-law wife.

Forty years on, each woman continued to feel an unbridled aggression. Their distress was compounded by a joint sense of exclusion that they were 'living in sin': Priscilla because she had remarried, Winnie because she was unable to marry and have the respectable life that she longed for.

The bloodcurdling row at Church Farm sprang from the usual conversation about money. Winnie and SPB had left Oxford four years earlier and were renting a flat in Hove. Before lunch, SPB revealed that he and Winnie were now going to have to move into the charitable home in Lindfield. He worried about what prospects he had at his age of ever earning enough to live on. His financial irresponsibility, on top of flashbacks to her Hove childhood, was the cue for Priscilla to bring up a subject which she considered one of the two misfortunes in her life.

Raymond served the meal that he had cooked, while Priscilla fatally broke her pledge and poured drink after drink for herself and guests and, according to Winnie, grew ever more aggressive and irrational. 'All her pent-up venom showed in her abuse of her father through life and in the fact that she was unable to have children after her abortion and consequent hysterectomy because we had not stopped her going to Paris for the abortion.' Winnie protested, reminding Priscilla how in March 1937 they had begged her not to go to Paris.

This was too much for Priscilla. She stood up over Winnie 'like an avenging angel', in belligerent fury blaming first her father and then Winnie for her unhappiness. Her ferocity was terrible. She was shaking like a piece of paper. What aggravated Priscilla's unreasonable hurt was to see Winnie's name flagged alongside her father's on his travel books, including the account of their journey through the Vosges, *Continental Coach Tour Holiday*, which they had dedicated to Priscilla – an unbearable taunt, given her repeated failure to find a publisher.

Winnie, unable to stand more abuse, burst into tears, collected her coat and suitcase, and with SPB walked out in the rain to wait for a bus to take them into Chichester.

This disastrous weekend was one of the last times that Priscilla saw her father and it pitched her back into despair. Soon afterwards came terrible news of her favourite AA member. '22 June 1964, Nina found dead in her flat – suicide. End of saga. AA.' Priscilla never attended another meeting.

'For the next 12 months I thrived on gin, vodka, brandy, Pernod, and I remember little of what occurred.' Each new stage of Priscilla's decline was inexorable. She was in an appalling state, drinking to the point of vomiting. She made a strenuous effort for three months to survive on wine alone, and failed. 'She was hooked,' wrote Gillian. 'She told me that unless she stopped drinking Raymond would end the marriage.'

The nadir was reached one October evening in 1965. Raymond was President of the Mushroom Growers Association that year and host of the annual dinner in Worthing at which Priscilla passed out with a black eye. 'Had a terrific row with Raymond at the end of dinner on the subject of my drinking and I feel our marriage may have been nearer to the brink than I thought. He thinks that some of our friends now shun us because of "unpredictable" habits.'

Gillian was reminded of her father hiding bottles. It seemed obvious what Priscilla was doing: 'She was punishing herself by destroying the only thing of value she possessed, her beauty.'

Why this self-destruction? A host of reasons suggest themselves. No children of her own. No luck with her writing. A fractious relationship with a father whom she still loved. The sheer impossibility of talking about the life she had led before she met Raymond. And boredom. 'Father kept her in the bedroom reading and drinking,' Carleton said. 'It was boredom that set the rot in.'

But there was a further explanation which Priscilla had long concealed from everyone: her genuine dread that redemption was impossible in any form.

36.
A SYMPATHETIC PRIEST

'Before returning home,' SPB wrote in *It Isn't Far from London*, 'it is worth going inland to see the village of Wittering, with its ancient church in the trees.'

If she opened her window and leaned out, Priscilla could see this over-restored Norman building contructed from random rubble. The church was tantalisingly close. It was also taboo.

Raymond never attended a service. He once donated land when St John's ran out of graveyard space, but he had no interest in God, and early on convcycd his astringent views to Priscilla. On the one and only occasion when Priscilla said she wanted to go to church, she was cowered by his reaction. 'Raymond went berserk,' remembered Vivien. 'He said she couldn't, and her being her she didn't.'

Even so, her stepson Carleton grew up aware that Priscilla was religious. He had cried a lot after his mother's retreat to Guatemala. 'So every evening as we went to bed Priscilla would insist on me reading the Lord's Prayer. I felt that she used the prayer as her guideline.'

Her god-daughter Annette was also conscious of Priscilla's spiritual side. 'She used to drive me to Chichester cathedral. "You're my god-daughter, we're *going to go* to church."'

Priscilla kept silent about her faith. Few people realised that she was to the end of her life a devout Roman Catholic. And yet for a mysterious reason, perhaps implanted in childhood by Boo, or later on by the Doynels, Priscilla came to believe that by marrying Raymond, while her first husband was alive, she had placed herself beyond the Catholic pale.

In Priscilla's mind, it was not Raymond who stood in salvation's way, but God. Her adulterous relationship with Raymond constituted a mortal sin in His sight, and Priscilla faced eternal damnation.

Once again, Priscilla confessed only to Gillian the reason why she drank. 'It was religion,' Gillian wrote. 'A convert to Catholicism, she was troubled to the end of her days by the fact she was living in sin when she married en secondes noces an Englishman.'

Priscilla's confession astounded Gillian, who up until this point had remained unaware what Priscilla's Catholicism meant to her. Quite apart from the strangeness of worrying about such a matter after the life she had lived, there was the peculiarity of her interpretation. Like her writing, Priscilla's apostasy was a deeply personal matter; her normal riposte – 'You wouldn't understand.' But it was evident to Gillian that religion was ruining Priscilla's life, not enhancing it. Gillian discussed the situation with John in December 1965, when they feared – correctly – that Priscilla was suffering a breakdown. 'He thought a priest might sort it out and promised to see what he could do.'

In the event, the Sutros sought the assistance not of a priest, but of a Catholic convert who was one of Priscilla's favourite writers.

Out of the blue one evening at the Sutros' flat in 26 Belgrave Square, Graham Greene said: 'The only thing I envy John is Gillian.' His remark sank in. 'When I am feeling low I think of his words,' wrote Gillian, who later became a neighbour of Greene's on the Côte d'Azur. 'Some people thought he was my lover, which was untrue. I was not his type. Ours was a platonic friendship, almost the only one I have had with a heterosexual. When in trouble I always turn to him.' She did so now over Priscilla, who had included Greene's classic novel about mortal sin and adultery, *The Heart of the Matter*, on a handwritten list entitled 'Books to be taken in case of shipwreck on desert island'.

Gillian had met Greene in 1947 in Rome, where John Sutro was producing *Her Favourite Husband*; yet their friendship took another decade to bloom. In April 1958, Greene arrived early at a cocktail party that the Sutros were throwing in London, but decided to leave before it started. 'I was upset,' Gillian wrote. 'He said he was in a nervous state and did not feel like meeting people. After brooding a minute or two, he said "I'll stay if you let me spank you." I was wearing tight tangerine silk Gucci pants, which I suppose may have given him ideas. "OK," I said, turning around. "Spank!" He gave me a couple of sharp wallops on my buttocks. "Now I feel better," he said. "I'll stay." I knew Graham Greene's moods and how to deal with them.'

In 1963, Greene dedicated his book of stories, *A Sense of Reality*, to the Sutros. He prized his friendship with them for their 'shepherd's pie evenings' at Belgrave Square. Right up until Greene left England in 1966, he walked over to their flat from his rooms in Albany, arriving on the stroke of 8 p.m. and disappearing at 11 p.m. He refused the offer of any fourth guest, preferring the three of them. Gillian sensed that he appreciated the privacy and lack of fuss, so much of his life being spent in hotels. 'He liked to be able to relax and talk openly about all sorts of things, which is not possible in a noisy restaurant, where he always thought he was being overheard.'

The ritual of these evenings did not vary. First the martini. He never enjoyed a starter, saying it blunted his appetite for the main dish. This was cooked by Gillian using lots of butter. Greene unfailingly took two big helpings. 'He was dithyrambic over my shepherd's pie. Other women would try and do the same, but he would say dolefully: "There's nothing wrong with your pies, but they haven't got the flavour of Gillian's. Hers is unique."'

The meal at which they discussed Priscilla was washed down with two bottles of 1950 Cheval Blanc which Greene had sent round the day before, so that any sediment could settle.

On that evening in December 1965, to their immense regret, he being their favourite guest, Greene informed the Sutros of his irrevocable decision to take up residence in France. He was leaving England early in the New Year. 'We shall terribly miss our dear friend,' Gillian wrote.

After treating Greene to her raspberry fool, Gillian broached the subject of her other dear friend, Priscilla, who became, in absentia, the fourth at their table.

Gillian was confident of pricking Greene's interest. 'For years, I was the recipient of his love problems to which I listened with patience.' She intrigued him about Priscilla by saying: 'She had a rather a rackety life during the Occupation.'

Greene had known Priscilla's father in Brighton and Oxford. He had not met Priscilla, but no subject was dearer to his heart than her spiritual predicament as outlined by Gillian, who revealed that Priscilla had 'become haunted by the idea that she is living in perpetual sin'. Greene was packing up Albany for his departure to France, but he promised to help find Priscilla a priest.

On 14 December, Gillian gave him a nudge: 'Dearest Graham, You kindly said I was to remind you to let me know the name of the Jesuit priest who might perhaps be of help to my girl friend. You thought there was someone at Farm Street who would be just right for her.' Two days later, in one of his last acts before quitting England, Greene wrote to Father Dermot Mills at Stonyhurst. Unfortunately, Father Mills had left the school six years earlier and there is no record that he received Greene's letter.

'Dear Dermot, I have been asked to find a sympathetic priest at Farm Street for a rather difficult case and since your departure and Philip's and the death of Martindale I know nobody. The case is of a young woman who married a Catholic and became a genuine Catholic as a result after the marriage.' Greene explained that Priscilla had since remarried a non-Catholic. 'She is in a very melancholy and nervy condition. She is a friend of a friend and I don't know her personally but I did explain to her friend that there was nothing that could be done to regularise her position, but I thought it might be of great help to her if she started once again going regularly to Mass and perhaps had a few conversations with a sympathetic priest – not from the point of view of getting anything done but from the point of view of simple encouragement to keep her foot in the door.

'Apparently her husband is very jealous of the church and this also causes difficulty. You would have been the ideal person to call on, but alas you are far away. I would be most grateful for any counsel which I could pass on to my friend.

'Affectionately, Graham.'

Timothy Radcliffe, a senior Dominican priest once tipped for the papacy, believed that Father Mills would have been in a position to calm Priscilla's worries.

Graham Greene, Evelyn Waugh, Priscilla – Radcliffe observed of such converts how often their attraction was to the drama of Catholicism, to living on 'the dangerous edge of things'. At the same time, they clung to their interpretation of a consoling, unshifting certainty. Cradle-born Catholics, by contrast, said Radcliffe, are accustomed to living in a muddle and in a world where no one is unforgivable. 'I do not think that anyone is ever "beyond the pale" and it is deeply sad that she thought so. It was not even the case that her position could not have been regularised officially. Since her second marriage was to a man who was divorced then it would not have been recognised as a sacramental marriage by the Church, and so she would not have needed to "fix" it. Anyway, human beings have a tendency to get into messes, which is why we believe in the incarnation. God shared our mess, however deep the shit. A few minutes with a sympathetic priest would have set her mind at rest.'

The outcome of Greene's intercession is unclear. Priscilla never spoke of it, although she wrote to my mother in 1980, after learning that we had met Greene in Sintra: 'I love all his books. He lives near my great chum Gill Sutro. She knows him well and is always nattering about him.' Greene, too, preserved the secret of the confessional, not mentioning it when I spent a day with him in Antibes in 1988, for a profile in the *Telegraph* magazine – even though, unknown to me, Gillian was keeping an eye on us, asking Greene if we had talked about Priscilla ('does not recollect') and writing to him on 29 September: 'He is the nephew of my late childhood friend Priscilla (the converted Catholic with 2 marriages and a drink problem, I told you about her).' But through

Greene or Father Mills, or off her own bat, Priscilla did meet a sympathetic clergyman.

Fred Cate was the verger at Chichester cathedral, a small, lean, wrinkled man who shuffled down the aisles like a tortoise. He died before Tracey told me about him. She said that whenever Priscilla was in Chichester she found an excuse to slip off and see Cate, and that Raymond never knew.

Cate had worked as a porter at the station. A former Dean described him as a country person, a man of the soil, practical, humble, understanding, able to keep a secret. 'If you could confide in someone, you could confide in him.' One of Cate's jobs was to fill the cathedral's large cast-iron stoves, each the height of a man. The Dean recalled Cate standing before a stove which he had finished stoking, saying approvingly: 'He's the hottest one in the cathedral.' I like to imagine him fuelling a similar warmth in my aunt.

In June 1966, less than a year after her breakdown, Priscilla wrote to Raymond. She was almost fifty.

'Darling, As we are soon to celebrate our 18th wedding anniversary I wanted to tell you how happy you have made me over the years. You have such a capacity to cherish and protect and I will never forget the last few months. You have saved me from myself and I have taken on a new lease of life as you know. Thank you, I love you, Priscilla.'

It is her only letter to Raymond which survives.

37.
DETONATIONS FROM THE PAST

'Always, everywhere, there is some voice crying from a tower,' wrote Graham Greene.

Despite the affection in her letter to Raymond, her first husband had not faded into the background. He remained a steady presence.

Priscilla once listed the noises that she heard from her window at Church Farm. 'Hooter – six times a day. Boiler alarm. Electric saw. Tractor. Turning machine. Men cutting up wood and hammering (mending boxes).' She broke off and for a moment she was back in Boisgrimot.

She had returned in 1947, at the tail-end of her holiday with Gillian, when she had met Raymond. While a captivated Raymond booked telephone call after telephone call to speak with her at Gillian's deserted Paris apartment, Priscilla was making a pilgrimage to Robert's chateau.

Nine years later, Priscilla submitted a description of that day to her tutor at the Fleet Street School in High Holborn; in a despairing final gesture, she had enrolled for a six-month correspondence course in freelance authorship and journalism.

'At last I found the long avenue which led up to the house. I walked slowly towards it with a feeling of unreality. The trees which had been on either side had disappeared, as had the German soldiers who had been camping there when last I saw it.

'From a distance the chateau looked as I remembered it: a long, rectangular building without much claim to beauty. As I got nearer I noticed an air of complete dilapidation: all the windows had been blown in, the roof had caved in and the façade was scarred with shrapnel and bullet wounds. Nearby farmers had stored their hay and straw in what had once been the rather grandiose sitting-room.

'I turned and fled.'

At the time of her visit to Boisgrimot, Robert was in Paris, where he lived for the rest of his life. She imagined him asleep or praying in his chair, or alone in his narrow bed. The man of gloom, unconsoled, the Prince of Aquitaine, his tower in ruins. 'He became very, very sombre after the divorce,' said Zizi Carer, the steward's daughter.

One June day in 1948, Priscilla stubbed out her cigarette and telephoned him.

'Why did you ring me?' he asked.

'Because I wanted to tell you myself of my remarriage. I didn't want you to hear it from someone else.'

His reply ended a long silence. 'I suppose I ought to wish you happiness. But I don't want you to be happy with anyone else.'

This wasn't a question of selfishness, he said; it was how he felt.

Priscilla's final identity was Mrs Raymond Thompson, Church Farm, East Wittering. But her past did not go away. It kept on detonating.

In her bedroom, in the garden, wherever she was, she was conscious of Raymond: moody when bills came in, listening to the weather forecasts, going out late at night to regulate the temperatures or stoke the boiler, with frosted fingers harvesting the mushrooms, each one having to be picked up individually and twisted. He was never far away. His first wife had run off with his best man. He was not going to let that happen again. He found it hard to tether his jealousy, though. 'Anybody who got close to her,' Vivien said, 'Raymond was awful to.' His jealousy extended to Priscilla's family, friends, former lovers – even to her God. Only with her first husband did he, out of some unexplained motive, slacken the rein.

Maybe Raymond sensed that he was being over-restricting and that in this one area – which anyway posed no threat – he had little choice but to relent. I am not certain how else to explain his decision, after they had been married ten years, to allow Priscilla to meet up with Robert in Paris.

My parents were among the few members of Priscilla's family whom Raymond could tolerate. When we moved to Paris in the late 1950s, Raymond and Priscilla came over each summer to stay. Tracey was living with us in Rue Jean Nicot, and she remembered how during their visits, from which I retain a clear and evocative image of my aunt sunbathing on our roof terrace, Priscilla would take the opportunity to go off and see someone: 'There was always that one person, "the friend".'

Robert wrote to Priscilla only once following her remarriage – in 1958, twelve years after their divorce. 'Give me a sign when you're coming in June. I'd be happy to see you again for a few moments.'

Half a century after we left Paris, I accompanied my father back to France to stir up memories of his days there, first as a student immediately after the war, then as a teacher, next as a journalist and latterly as a diplomat. He had not visited the city since 1961. Images from his past slowed his step from the moment we arrived at the Gare du Nord.

We were crossing Pont Alexandre III, when my father pointed towards the right bank. The quay was deserted; these days no private boats were permitted to tie up. He was gazing down to where his twenty-eight-year-old self had jumped from a deck, holding a rope.

'Raymond had a state-of-the-art motor-cruiser, and on one memorable occasion in 1958 he invited me, an agile young man then, for a crossing of the Channel to help with locks between the mouth of the Seine and Paris.' *Vulture* was a converted motor torpedo boat with a speed of 20 knots. A plaque in the wheel-house saluted her role at Dunkirk.

'We moored there, directly below the Grand Palais. And Robert came on board for a drink one evening.'

The person who my father recalls stepping into the saloon was a tall, slim, distinguished-looking man, elegantly dressed and rather gentle, and much older than Priscilla. 'He could have been her father. He was plainly pleased to see Priscilla, whom he regarded still as his wife. And it was clear in a way I didn't understand that Priscilla felt she was still married to him. It was the only time I ever got a hint of her Catholicism, because she never discussed religion. Raymond was putting up with it, tolerantly in the background. The two of them chatted amicably for an hour and that was it.'

But their 'few moments' together reignited something.

My mother told me: 'I remember Priscilla saying she met Robert every year, always with Raymond, and they always had lunch.'

In the fields around Boisgrimot, mines and anti-tank rockets continued to maim farmers and children. In a drought year, a Wehrmacht helmet, a belt buckle, a Mauser and the turret of a German tank were discovered in the moat. As late as 2002 bodies were being unearthed from the ditches, giving flesh to the idea that Normandy had been martyred to save the rest of France.

Robert died in October 1978, aged seventy-nine. He was buried in Sainteny churchyard next to his brother Guy, whom he had outlived by two years. Priscilla was not at the funeral, even had she been told about it. But she had never ceased to think of him.

'To be beautiful, one has to suffer,' he told her more than once.

Robert was not the only person from her past who kept surfacing. Whenever in later life Priscilla waited for someone, she caught herself half-hoping to see a man with the initials PD embroidered on his Sulka shirt. Gillian knew how she felt. 'The only man she was in love with was Pierre.'

Priscilla's heart when she thought of Pierre, the sheen of his voice in a blacked-out bedroom, flailed around inside her like a hooked fish.

He had returned to his wife, but he never let go of Priscilla. 'I love you, Pris of my heart, I love you piercingly,' he wrote from his desk in Annemasse. 'You know that I love you most in all the world – yes, you know – and you know also that my greatest joy will be to see you again.'

Then, on 16 April 1946, three months before her divorce and one year and six months before she met Raymond, a thunderbolt: 'My love, How dearly I would like to say that "our" daughter has been born, but this was not fate's wish. And so I'm writing to tell you that on 13 April at 11.40 p.m. Carole Duboyon "my" daughter made her entry into the world. You can imagine my joy at having a girl, and you can see how, in wanting her to be part of my happiness, I have given her the same name which we chose for our child. Her birth was the simplest and easiest one in the world.'

Carole had Priscilla's clear, bright blue gaze. 'Her hair is a little sparse at the moment, but she promises to grow into a very sympathetic blonde. When I catch her looking at me, I recognise the same soft and sly expression that I love to see in your eyes.'

His daughter's birth in Croix did not stop Pierre from pursuing Priscilla to London the following month. 'I place you first before everyone, Pris dear.' In May, and again in July, they met at the Esplanade Hotel in Warwick Avenue. Before their second encounter, Pierre imagined himself coming back into her room, 'and I am naked like the last time . . . and you are offering me what belongs to me, that is to say, your lips, your body, your soul. I kiss you every-where EVERYWHERE EVERYWHERE. PIERRE.'

But Priscilla was going mad, leading a life incomprehensible even to herself. After her turbulent years in France and divorced at last, she was crying out for permanence. She wanted to settle down. She wanted a home. She loved Pierre, but these snatched visits left her stricken. When he kissed Priscilla goodbye, he was returning to be with the daughter they had talked about having. To the end of her life, this conversation would dart out from behind a rock and swim up.

Their love affair played itself out during a business trip which Pierre made to Bradford in January 1947. He telephoned again and again from his hotel, panicking when Priscilla failed to answer. Could she have forgotten his arrival? Enshrouded in a northern fog that limited his vision to a hundred metres, he 'exteriorised' his fear of losing her. 'For the first time I feel alone, terribly alone. I have the impression that I've been abandoned.'

His instinct was correct. Once Priscilla had accepted Raymond Thompson's proposal, she wrote to Pierre requesting that he not contact her.

Priscilla had been married to Raymond for four years when Pierre sent her a short handwritten letter, dated 7 November 1952. Her chest thudded as she read it. 'My dear Pris, I'm writing to you with some very sad news: the death of my sister Simone Vernier.' She had died on 31 October after a short illness. 'I know that you loved her, and that's why I've overcome my emotions to send you these quick lines.'

The death of her 'double' during the Occupation moved Priscilla to break her silence. Her condolence message elicited one further piece of correspondence. It was the last love letter that she kept – possibly the last she received.

'Pris darling, Thanks for your letter. Thanks for your telegram. I was so sad not to be able to write to you on your birthday on 12 July. I thought of you a lot on that day and I abided by your wish expressed in your letter before last: not to write to you again.' But if Priscilla could see a way to be in London on Saturday 13 December, he would be overjoyed to spend a moment with her. 'I hug you hard, hoping to be able to tell you very soon "Me too". Pierre.' Priscilla felt dizzy. She had recovered from her heart-break. And yet, and yet . . . she did want to see Pierre again – 'just once'. She wrote back to say that she was prepared to come by the Esplanade Hotel in Warwick Avenue. But she dared not tell Raymond, who was bound to be furious. He was already aware of her unfortunate passion – 'Do you still think of Pierre?' he had once asked out of the blue. And then whispered, before she had time to formulate a reply, holding her close, 'You won't ever leave me, darling, will you?' 'Of course not, you old silly,' and she kissed him fondly.

Even so, guilt crept over her. While Raymond never articulated his passion like Pierre, he had given her far more devotion. When the day arrived, she wrote a note to Pierre. She had changed her mind. They had missed their chance, there was no going back. She took a taxi to Warwick Avenue and handed the note to the porter.

But Priscilla did see Pierre again. Later that very same morning she joined Raymond at Paddington station. Just when she hoped to have put Pierre behind her, Priscilla had a rush of blood to her head and felt her face burning at the sight of him standing next to the ticket collector. He had grown stout and his hair had thinned. He wore a dark grey suit and a subdued tie. 'His thick white silk shirt had his initials engraved in blue.'

Raymond had been buying a newspaper. He took her arm and urged her towards the train. Priscilla was abreast of Pierre and kept her eyes to the ground. Her heart roaring in her ear, she passed through the gates, almost touching him, and walked in quick steps down the platform, without glancing back.

She sat with Raymond in a carriage that they had to themselves.

Raymond looked at her with a concerned expression and patted her knee. 'You look pale, darling. Are you tired?'

Priscilla nodded. At last, the train began to move. She looked out of the window. There was Pierre, staring at her from the platform.

38.
THE END

Raymond had concealed Priscilla's illness from her family. Osteomyelitis, which had stopped her from dancing in Paris, had again erupted in her right leg. And then one day she threw up blood.

'I'm afraid that my news is *not* too cheerful,' Priscilla wrote to Gillian on 18 May 1978. 'Tomorrow I go into hospital for an operation (next week) on my gullet (gosier?) CANCER ... Don't fret or worry too much – they say I shall be as good as new in 6 weeks or two months time! Meanwhile, naturally I shall be in pain, but I've felt so bloody awful for 4 or 5 months that I couldn't care less.'

Vivien took a week off to be with her. On the last morning, she asked the surgeon: 'What are the prospects for my sister? I gather not awfully bright.' The surgeon replied angrily: 'I have cured your sister' – Priscilla could go home. But she had a hell of a time recuperating, Vivien told me. 'When she swallowed food, it shot back. Raymond kept taking her abroad. He needed her. He was frightened she might run away and hauled her off, a crime when she was unwell. "Oh for God's sake pull yourself together. You know you're cured."'

Few understood at the time why Raymond denied Priscilla's illness, or why he insisted on taking her sailing to Elba and Menton. I discovered the explanation only much later. In the summer after her operation, a policeman had found sixty-seven-year-old Raymond wandering around the centre of Chichester unable to remember who he was. That night, his farm manager received a call. 'We've got someone here who we think is Raymond Thompson. Could you come and identify him?' Raymond had suffered a nervous break-down after losing a substantial sum when experimenting with his mushroom business. In one calamitous experiment, he had spread tons of shredded paper on top of the compost.

Raymond's doctor ordered him to go abroad for six months. With Pris-cilla's help, Raymond improved. But his breakdown impeded her recovery. On a trip with him to Vieux Roquebrune, they stayed in an apartment which no taxi could reach and had to lug their baggage along the road. Priscilla lifted a suitcase and ripped something in her eye.

Gillian was worried. 'Priscilla is not in good shape, alas,' she wrote to Harold Acton in October 1979. 'She had a nasty gullet operation last year and now faces on her return to England a cataract operation. I must say, when sorrows come ... I feel very sorry for her as she can't drive any more. She's got cataracts in *both* eyes.'

Priscilla could not see to read, she stumbled when walking, she was unable to speak properly. But Raymond was intransigent. A concerned Imogen kept calling to be updated on her sister's health, only to be deflected. 'Oh, she's fine,' Raymond said. 'Thanks for ringing.'

Stuck up in her bedroom without company, without books, only the television, Priscilla sought relief in half-bottles of Krug.

In the end, it all happened quickly. On Saturday 13 March 1982, Raymond had to go with Tracey to his brother-in-law's funeral at Farley Mount. Tracey put her foot down – they could not leave Priscilla on her own. 'I said for goodness sake, this was a perfect time for Imogen to come. So he gave in on this day and Imogen was alone with Priscilla all that afternoon.'

Tracey and Raymond had already left when Imogen arrived at 11.30 a.m. 'The housekeeper let me in. I went upstairs to Pris's bedroom, the Holy of Holies – I'd never been in there before. I found Pris pretty ill in bed, and obviously fading.'

Imogen had brought along one of SPB's early books. 'I'd chosen it carefully because I wanted it to be about before we arrived on the scene, Mummy and Lalage and me. I wanted it to be pre-us.'

She asked Priscilla: 'Would you like me to read Daddy's book?'

Priscilla nodded and closed her eyes. SPB had died seven years before – on his own, bankrupt and heartbroken, after Winnie left him and married the novelist who had first proposed to her when she was seventeen.

Imogen sat on Priscilla's bed and began to read aloud. As she remembered it, the passage described their father going into a church.

'I was in the middle of reading to her when she opened her eyes and looked up and gazed into space, on the track of what Daddy had written. Her mind went off into what the future would be. Suddenly, it impinged on her. Having converted, she was still a Catholic, and what had happened between her and Raymond was not of significance.'

Then Priscilla turned her head and looked at Imogen. 'Maybe I've never really been married to Raymond. Maybe I was always married to Robert.'

She was finding it harder to speak. From the telephone beside the bed, Imogen rang the Penina Hotel in the Algarve, catching my mother in the middle of a diplomatic function.

'You need to talk to Priscilla.'

Priscilla's voice was very faint. 'I think I'm going. I want to say goodbye.'

My mother burst into tears.

Priscilla's last words to her were: 'Don't worry, I'm living on champagne.'

Two days later, Raymond, who could not cope with her dying and had hidden in the mushroom shed, finally sat down at the end of the dining-room table and wrote to Gillian Sutro. 'Priscilla died last night of a malignant brain tumour. She died peacefully with *no* pain. Although you were for very many years her closest friend, she did not want me to tell you that she was dying. Love, Raymond.'

She was sixty-five.

39.
AN UNSENT LETTER

Priscilla never realised two desires. She did not publish a book. She failed to bear a child. Her life is a reflection of how hard it was to be fulfilled as a woman, even until recently. The two things she had wanted to do, she could do today, without the help of a man: she could have told her story honestly, and she could have had a child out of wedlock.

In death, Priscilla was denied a third wish. She had requested a Catholic funeral, according to Vivien. 'She said to our common mother: "If I look as if I'm dying, I must have the last rites."'

But Raymond refused to summon a priest. He had Priscilla cremated in Chichester.

Imogen was Priscilla's only sister – and blood relation – to attend the service. She said: 'The impression was given by Raymond that Pris had not been "religious" and the sooner it was over the better.'

Raymond rushed in and rushed out, not pausing to speak to anyone. He was so upset that he had not bothered to register Priscilla's death. 'I had to register it,' Tracey said. 'When we asked him about flowers, he wanted a bunch of red roses loose on the coffin. The undertakers warned that they would blow away, so the roses had to be stuck down with tape.'

A small reception was held afterwards at a nearby hotel. My mother could not reach the service because she was in Portugal, and is terrified of flying. Gillian was conspicuous by her absence. With Priscilla's death half of her had died. Completely distraught, she could not face the funeral of a friend she had adored since childhood.

When Tracey turned eighteen, Priscilla wrote her a letter, but then decided for some reason not to send it. I discovered it folded away in the padded chest. Tracey was sixty-eight when she read this letter for the first time. Priscilla had been dead for almost thirty years.

'My darling child,

'As you very well know you are not strictly speaking my daughter, but as far as I am concerned you might just as well be. I have brought you up from an early age with all the love and affection that I would have given to my own child, had I had one. I believe that your childhood has been a happy one. Certainly far happier than my own.

'It is now my duty to teach you about life as I have found it. I sincerely hope that you won't grow up thinking that divorce is an easy solution to any troubles that may occur. Believe me, it is not. It is a wicked and terrible thing, especially if there are children concerned. Nevertheless, I would urge you, when the time comes, to take marriage very seriously. It is not easy to spend one's life with one man to the exclusion of all others and as time goes by there seem to be more temptations rather than less. I would suggest that you should not consider marriage before you are 21, and if possible leave it until you are 24 or 25. Then you should know your own mind. Not before. Of course, if you fall in love before then you will think, as we all do, that it will last for a lifetime, but we all change as we grow older and it is impossible to know exactly what we want at an early age.

'Next there is the question of money. You happen to have parents who are both well off and can give you much in life. It will be difficult for you to find a young man who can keep you in the luxury to which you have become accustomed. It is very important in this life to gradually better one's position. Don't believe people who talk about "love in a cottage". It rarely succeeds. I don't mean by this that you should be mercenary. God forbid! But don't ever let any man marry you for your money, and make quite sure that he is capable of keeping you, if not in luxury, at least in comfort.

'Now my last point is a tricky and extremely delicate one. It is a question of morality. Nowadays young girls have a lot of freedom and many of them lead immoral lives. Many marriages are brought about by the fact that the girl is pregnant. Please whatever you do, don't marry for this reason. It is a bad basis for a marriage. If ever you are in trouble of any sort you must come to me and ask my advice. I don't know what I shall say to you because there is no easy way out, but I do know that I shall do my utmost to stop you marrying for such a reason.

'Should you not come to see me, you might try and find your own solution and here you must beware of upsetting your health. Young and ignorant girls have often lived to regret a hasty decision.

'Drinking and smoking are to be taken seriously too. Both your father and I and all our friends do both, if not to excess, at least too much.

'One other thing I would like to mention before I end this letter. Whatever you do in life try not to hurt anybody or you will pay for it in the end. Don't play with people's feelings and don't whatever you do leave your husband for somebody else. It is never worth it.'

ACKNOWLEDGEMENTS

This book could not have been written without the assistance of Tracey Maitland, who gave me unrestricted access to Priscilla's papers. For their recollections and encouragement, I am also indebted to Carleton Thompson, my parents John and Lalage Shakespeare, my aunt Imogen Vignoles, and my late aunt Vivien Van Dam. I cannot adequately thank them for their unstinting support. In no instance was there pressure put on me to remove or alter anything that I uncovered about Priscilla's life.

For access to Priscilla's police file and related material in the Musée de la Préfecture de Police archives in Paris, I would like to thank Béatrice Le Fur.

For access to collections of Gillian Sutro's papers and related material, I would like to thank Bryan Ward-Perkins and the Fellows of Trinity College Oxford; Colin Harris of the Special Collections Department at the Bodleian.

For access to collections of S. P. B. Mais's papers, I would like to thank Alison McCann at the West Sussex Records Office in Chichester; Laura Russo at the Howard Gotlieb Archival Research Center in Boston; Jeff Walden at the BBC Written Records Centre in Caversham; Rachel Hassall at Sherborne College; Alexander Waugh. For access to Intelligence reports on Alois Miedl at the National Archives and Records Administration in Washington, I would like to thank Eric Van Slander and Rebecca L. Collier.

For access to reports on British internees in France at the National Archives in Kew, I would like to thank Neil G. Cobbett.

For access to his private collection of papers about the women's internment camp at Besançon, and for his patience in answering umpteen questions, I would like to thank James A. Fox; for the recollections of their internment, I would like to thank Rita Harding and Shula Troman. As well, and for permission to use her unpublished diaries and memoir, I would like to thank Yvette Goodden.

For permission to quote from his letters to Priscilla, I would like to thank the estate of the late Robert Doynel de la Sausserie.

For permission to quote from Henri Johanet's letters to Priscilla, I would like to thank Gisèle Levrat.

For access to his father's unpublished memoir and related material, I would like to thank Quentin Tiberghien and his family.

For permission to quote from Robert Donat's letters to Priscilla, I would like to thank Brian Donat and his family.

For permission to use the sound recording of Jacqueline Grant's interview at the Imperial War Museum, I would like to thank Stephen Walton.

For permission to quote from 'To Your Daughter' in Alec Waugh's *Resentment* (Richard, 1918), and from Alec's letters to Arthur Waugh, I would like to thank Peter Waugh.

For permission to quote from Graham Greene's letter to Dermot Mills (© 2013, Verdant SA), I would like to thank the estate of Graham Greene and David Higham Associates. For permission to quote from Greene's *The Quiet American* (© 1955), I would like to thank Random House.

For permission to quote from Geoffrey Wansell's letter to Priscilla, I would like to thank the estate of Geoffrey Wansell and the Sayle Literary Agency.

For permission to quote from Jean D'Ormesson's *At God's Pleasure* (© 1977), tr. Barbara Bray, I would like to thank the author and Harvill Secker, Random House.

For permission to quote from Joseph Kessel's *Belle de Jour* (© 2007), tr. Geoffrey Wagner, I would like to thank Gerald Duckworth & Co.

For permission to quote from Rosemary Say's *Rosie's War* (© 2011), I would like to thank Noel Holland and Michael O'Mara Books.

For permission to quote from Antonia Hunt's *Little Resistance* (© 1982), I would like to thank the estate of Antonia Hunt and Leo Cooper/Pen & Sword Books.

For permission to quote from Hanna Diamond's *Women and the Second World War in France, 1939–48: Choices and Constraints* (© 1999), I would like to thank the author and Longman.

For permission to quote from Michael Bar-Zohar's *The Phantom Conspiracy* (© 1981), I would like to thank the author and Orion Publishing Group.

For permission to quote from Antony Beevor's *D-day: The Battle for Normandy* (© 2010), I would like to thank the author and Penguin Books.

For permission to quote from Elisabeth Furse's *Dream Weaver* (© 1993), I would like to thank the estate of Elisabeth Furse and Ann Barr.

For permission to quote from Martha Gellhorn's *The Honeyed Peace* (© 1953), I would like to thank the estate of Martha Gellhorn and Penguin Books.

For permission to quote from P. G. Wodehouse's *Performing flea, a self-portrait in letters* (© 1954), I would like to thank the estate of P. G. Wodehouse. Reproduced by permission of the author c/o Rogers, Coleridge & White Ltd.

For permission to quote from George Orwell's 1945 broadcast 'In Defense of P. G. Wodehouse', anthologized in *The Orwell Reader* (© 1978), ed. Peter Davison, I would like to thank the estate of George Orwell c/o A. M. Heath and Houghton Mifflin Harcourt Publishing Company.

I would like to express my gratitude to the following: Gillon Aitken, Brian Aldiss, Elisabeth Barillé, Francesca Barrie, Vicky Bassadone, John Bevington, Maurice Bezard, Jennifer Booth, Carmen Callil, Joseph Carer, Zizi Carer, Peter and Louise Cawthra, Jacques and Marie-Ange Chabert, Maria Corelli, Judy Daulton, Eric Daviatte, Brian Donat, Serge Doubrovsky, Richard and Adeline Doynel de la Sausserie, Heinz Fehlauer, Jean-Michel Fouquet, Didier Gamerdinger, Robert Girardi, Michael Goodden, Jacqueline Hodey, Annette Howard, Robert Irving, Phyllis Jeffery, Adrianne Joseph, Michael Kerr, Katherine Lack, Christophe Lafaye, Patrick Langlade, Gisèle Levrat, Christopher

MacLehose, Angela Mclean, Bryan Magee, Tracey and Tim Maitland, Rüdiger von Maltzahn, Jean-Paul Pitou, Priscilla Pessey, Sue Procopio, Timothy Radcliffe OP, Maisie Robson, Claudius Schonenberger, Gitta Sereny, Michael Sheringham, Jon Stallworthy, Priscilla Thiriez-Andre, Susie Thompson, Ariel Tiberghien, Arnaud and Christiane Tiberghien, Didier Tiberghien, Gael Tiberghien, Jean-Loup Tiberghien, Pierre-Yves and Susan Tiberghien, Quentin Tiberghien, Peter Waugh, Michaël Yannaghas, Nancy Yeide, Sofka Zinovieff.

I would like to thank the staff of the Codrington Library and Taylorian Library in Oxford; the Fondation Ledig-Rowohlt and staff of Château de Lavigny in Switzerland, where part of this book was written.

All writers depend on the input of others. I would like to thank Antony Beevor for his generous nit-picking; my editor Liz Foley for her calm guidance; Clare Alexander, Gillian Johnson, Nicholas Robinson and Peter Washington for reading early drafts and for their comments. In particular, I would like to thank John Hatt for his time and patience, and for lessons in punctuation.

SOURCES

Abbreviations used in source sections:

PT: Priscilla Thompson papers

SPB: S. P. B. Mais papers, West Sussex Records Office, Chichester

GS: Gillian Sutro papers, Special Collections, Bodleian Library, Oxford

IWM: Imperial War Musem, Lambeth

NA: National Archives, Kew

BBC: BBC Written Archives Centre, Caversham

MPP: Musée de la Préfecture de Police archives, Paris

ANF: Archives Nationale de France, Paris

AM: Archives départementales de la Manche, Saint-Lô

AC: Archives départementales du Calvados, Caen

HGA: Howard Gotlieb Archival Research Center, Boston

NARA: National Archives and Records Administration, Washington DC

Literature on the Occupation would fill the two libraries in Oxford where I wrote much of this book, and every day fresh archival material appears online. For help in understanding the background to Priscilla's life in France, I am grateful to a number of writers, whose works are listed below. Like any student of this period, I am indebted to the pioneering scholarship of Robert Paxton, Julian Jackson, Philippe Burrin, Patrick Buisson, Robert Gildea, Antony Beevor, Allan Mitchell, Hanna Diamond, Ian Ousby and Richard Vinen.

PART ONE

Based on conversations with Vicky Bassadone, Peter Cawthra, Maria Corelli, Judy Daulton, Annette Howard, Phyllis Jeffery, Tracey Maitland, John and Lalage Shakespeare, Carleton and Susie Thompson, Vivien Van Dam.

Unpublished sources: MPP; PT; SPB; Vivien Van Dam memoir; 'Venal Vera', published anonymously (although attributed to Canadian war correspondent Quentin Reynolds).

Newspapers: *Nursing Times, Chichester Observer.*

Books: *All the Days of My Life*, by S. P. B. Mais (Hutchinson, 1937); *Buffets and Rewards*, by S. P. B. Mais (Hutchinson, 1952); *The Happiest Days of My Life*, by S. P. B. Mais (Max Parish, 1953).

PART TWO

Based on conversations with Maurice Bezard, Joseph Carer, Zizi Carer, Richard and Adeline Doynel de la Sausserie, Jacqueline Hodey, Robert Irving, Bryan Magee, Jean-Paul Pitou, Sue Procopio, Michel Lepourry, Jon Stallworthy, Shula Troman, Vivien Van Dam, Michaël Yannaghas.

Unpublished sources: PT; GS; SPB; IWM; BBC; NA; IWM; AC; AM; Rossall School archives.

Newspapers: *The Times, News of the World, Daily Mirror, Daily Express, Daily Telegraph, Bonnier's, Vogue, London Gazette, L'Ouest Éclair.*

Books and articles: *A French Officer's Diary: 23 August 1939–1 October 1940*, by D. Barlone, tr. L. V. Cass (Cambridge, 1942); *The Private Diaries of Paul Baudouin*, tr. Charles Petrie (Eyre & Spottiswoode, 1948); *BBC Handbook 1941* (BBC, 1941); *Fireworks at Dusk: Paris in the Thirties*, by Olivier Bernier (Little, Brown, 1993); *Strange Defeat*, by Marc Bloch (Oxford, 1949); *Myths of War*, by Marie Bonaparte (Imago, 1947); *Voices from the Dark Years: The Truth about Occupied France, 1940–45*, by Douglas Boyd (Sutton, 2007); *The Thirty-nine Steps*, by John Buchan (Blackwood, 1915); *Living with Defeat: France under the German Occupation, 1940–44*, by Philippe Burrin tr. Janet Lloyd (Arnold, 1996); *The Road to Bordeaux*, by Douglas Cooper & C. Denis Freeman (Cresset, 1942); *Looking for Trouble*, by Virginia Cowles (Hamish Hamilton, 1941); *Généalogie de la Maison Doynel*, by Colonel Doynel de La Sausserie, in 'Héraldique et généalogie', 1986, pp. 392–401; *Paris Diary 1932–33*, by Edward Gordon Craig, ed. Colin Franklin (Bird & Bull Press, 1982); *An American in Paris*, by Janet Flanner (Simon & Schuster, 1940); *Marching to Captivity: the War Diaries of a French Peasant 1939–45*, by Gustave Folcher, tr. Christopher Hill (Brassey's, 1966); *The Thirties: an Intimate History*, by Juliet Gardiner (Harper Press, 2010); *Memoirs of Montparnasse*, by John Glassco (Oxford, 1970); *Brighton Rock*, by Graham Greene (Heinemann, 1938); *Holy Deadlock*, by A. P. Herbert (Methuen, 1934); *The Ayes Have It; the Story of the Marriage Bill*, by A. P. Herbert (Methuen, 1937); *Front Line*, by Clare Hollingworth (Cape, 1990); *A Strange Eventful History: the Dramatic Lives of Ellen Terry, Henry Irving and their Remarkable Families*, by Michael Holroyd (Chatto & Windus, 2008); *Memories of Occupied France*, by Agnès Humbert, tr. Barbara Mellor (Bloomsbury, 2008); *The Fall of France: 1940*, by Julian Jackson, (Oxford, 2003); *France: the Dark Years 1940–1944*, by Julian Jackson (Oxford, 2001); *Report on France*, by Thomas Kernan (John Lane, 1942); *Belle de Jour*, by Joseph Kessel (Gallimard, 1928; Duckworth, 2007, tr. Geoffrey Wagner); *Scum of the Earth*, by Arthur Koestler (Cape, 1941); *De Gaulle: the Rebel 1890–1944; De Gaulle: the Ruler 1945–70*, by Jean Lacouture, tr. Alan Sheridan (Harvill, 1992); *The Leopard*, by Giuseppe di Lampedusa (Collins, 1960); *If Britain had Fallen*, by Norman Longmate (Greenhill, 2004); *Shadows Lengthen*, by Clara Longworth de Chambrun (Scribner, 1949); *Loose ends*, by Arnold Lunn (Hutchinson, 1919); by S. P. B. Mais : *A Public School in Wartime* (John Murray 1916); *Interlude* (Chapman & Hall, 1917); *Rebellion* (Richards, 1917); *A Schoolmaster's Diary* (Richards, 1918); *Education of a Philanderer* (Richards, 1919); *An English Course for Everybody* (Richards, 1921); *Oh! To be in England* (Richards, 1922); *Delight in Books* (Wheaton, 1931); *See England first* (Richards, 1932); *This Unknown Island* (Putnam, 1932); *These I Have Loved* (Putnam, 1933); *S.O.S.: Talks on Unemployment* (Putnam, 1933); *A Modern Columbus* (Rich & Cowan, 1934); *Time to Spare: What Unemployment Means*, ed. Felix Greene (Allen & Unwin, 1935); *The Writing of English* (Chapman & Hall, 1935); *England's Character* (Hutchinson, 1936); *The Three-Coloured Pencil* (Eyre & Spottiswoode, 1937); *The English Scene Today* (Rockliff, 1938); *Raven Among the Rooks* (Eyre & Spottiswoode, 1939); *Listen to the Country* (Hutchinson, 1939); *Diary of a Public Schoolmaster* (Lutterworth, 1940); *Diary of a Citizen* (Lutterworth, 1941); *Caper Sauce* (Hutchinson, 1948); *I Return to Switzerland* (Christopher Johnson, 1948); *Wodehouse: a Life*, by Robert McCrum (Viking, 2004); *Hitchcock and the Making of Marnie*, by Tony Lee Moral (Manchester University Press, 2002); *Suite Française*, by Irène Némirovsky, tr. Sandra Smith (Chatto & Windus, 2004); *At God's Pleasure*, by Jean D'Ormesson, tr. Barbara Bray (Harvill, 1978); *Occupation: The Ordeal of France 1940–1944*, by Ian Ousby (John Murray, 1997); *A Pacifist's War: Diaries 1939–45*, by Frances Partridge (Phoenix, 1999); *Occupied Territory*, by Polly Peabody (Cresset, 1941); *Bluebell: the Authorized Biography of Margaret Kelly, Founder of the Legendary Bluebell Girls*, by George Perry (Pavilion, 1986); *The Life of Irène Némirovsky*, by Olivier Philipponnat and Patrick Lienhardt, tr. Euan Cameron (Chatto & Windus, 2010); *Death and Tomorrow*, by Peter de Polnay (Secker & Warburg, 1944); *Pages d'atelier, 1917–1982*, by Francis Ponge (Gallimard, 2005); *An Unrepentant Englishman: The life of S. P. B. Mais, Ambassador of the Countryside*, by Maisie Robson (King's England Press, 2005); *Wodehouse at War*, by Iain Sproat (Ticknor & Fields, 1981); *Histoire généalogique de la maison de Chivré, 1096–1987: Maine, Anjou, Normandie, Drôme, Avignon*, Gérard de Villeneuve avec la collaboration de Paul Doynel de La Sausserie et de René de Chivré, (Versailles, 1988); *The Loom of Youth*, by Alec Waugh (Richards, 1917); *Resentment: Poems*, by Alec Waugh, (Richards, 1918); *The Eye of the Storm*, by Patrick White (Cape, 1973); *Devon Holiday*, by Henry Williamson (Cape, 1935); *At the Blue Moon Again*, by D. B. Wyndham Lewis (Methuen, 1925); *On straw and other conceits*, by D. B. Wyndham Lewis (Methuen, 1927); *The Stuffed Owl: an Anthology of Bad Verse*, selected by D. B. Wyndham Lewis and Charles Lee (Dent, 1930); *Performing Flea, a Self-Portrait in Letters*, by P. G. Wodehouse (Herbert Jenkins, 1953).

PART THREE

Based on conversations with Eric Daviatte, Colonel Jean-Michel Fouquet, James Fox, Yvette Goodden, Christophe Lafaye, Patrick Langlade, Rita Harding, Shula Troman.

Unpublished sources: PT; GS; SPB; BBC; IWM: Jacqueline Powell (Sound ref. 8854/5); memoirs of M. Bayliss (96/49/1), Sister Patricia McGauley (99/82/1); James Fox; Caserne Vauban archive, Besançon; archives of the 19th Régiment du Génie, Besançon; 'More Reminiscences of Frontstalag 142', by Yvette Goodden; Stella Gumuchian Collection of drawings.

Newspapers: Hansard, *L'Est Républicain*, *Telegraph* magazine.

Films: *Two Thousand Women* (1944), dir. Frank Launder.

Books and articles: *Nor Iron Bars a Cage*, by W. H. Aston (Macmillan, 1946); *La Seconde Guerre mondiale en Franche-Comté Besançon*, by Colonel Robert Dutriez, (Cêtre, 1984); *Fantastic Interlude*, by Claire Fauteux (Vantage Press, 1961); *Food Facts for the Kitchen Front* (Collins, 1941); *Dream Weaver*, by Elisabeth Furse and Ann Barr (Chapmans, 1993); *Little Resistance: a Teenage English girl's Adventures in Occupied France*, by Antonia Hunt (Leo Cooper, 1982); *Curfew in Paris, a Record of the German Occupation*, by Ninette Jucker (Hogarth Press, 1960); *Frontstalag 142: the Internment Diary of an English Lady*, by Katherine Lack (Amberley, 2010); *Continental Coach Tour Holiday*, by S. P. B. Mais and Gillian Mais (Alvin Redman, 1960); *Nineteen Eighty-Four*, by George Orwell (Secker & Warburg, 1949); *Frontstalag 142: Rosie's War: an Englishwoman's Escape from Occupied France*, by Rosemary Say & Noel Holland (Michael O'Mara, 2011); *The House Near Paris*, by Drue Tartière with M. R. Werner (Victor Gollancz, 1947); *Divided Loyalties: a Scotswoman in Occupied France*, by Janet Teissier du Cros (Hamish Hamilton, 1962); *The Bonfire of the Vanities*, by Tom Wolfe (Cape, 1988); *Red Princess: a Revolutionary Life*, by Sofka Zinovieff (Granta, 2007).

PART FOUR

Based on conversations with Elisabeth Barillé, Antony Beevor, Martine Brunelle, Carmen Callil, Robert Girardi, Yvette Goodden, Rita Harding, Joseph Carer, Jacqueline Hodey, Gisèle Levrat, Rüdiger von Maltzahn, Jean-Paul Pitou, Gitta Sereny, Ariel Tiberghien, Arnaud Tiberghien, Didier Tiberghien, Gael Tiberghien, Jean-Loup Tiberghien, Quentin Tiberghien, Pierre-Yves Tiberghien, Shula Troman, Vivien Van Dam, Michaël Yannaghas.

Unpublished sources: PT; GS; SPB; BBC; NARA (Safehaven Reports 148, 229; M-1782); NA (FO 371/28277-85; FO 916/141; FO 916/2594; FO 369/2960; FO 916/352; FO 916/627; FO 916/635); MPP (77w359-162191; 77w1927-305315; 77w1074-9340252); ANF (AJ40-930); Cabinet of the Prince's Palace, Monaco; *Envolés*, private memoir by Alain Tiberghien; Yvette Goodden, diary; 'Memories of Vichy: The Papon Trial', BA dissertation by John Warlow.

Newspapers: *Telegraph* magazine; *L'Ouest Éclair*.

Films: Interview with Vincent Malle about *Lacombe, Lucien* (1974), dir. Louis Malle, on DVD of Louis Malle Collection Vol.2 (2006); *The Raven* (1943), dir. Henri-Georges Clouzot.

Books and articles: *Nazi Looting: the Plunder of Dutch Jewry During the Second World War*, by Gerard Aalders (Berg, 2004); *More Memoirs of an Aesthete*, by Harold Acton (Hamish Hamilton, 1986); *An American Heroine in the French*

Resistance: the Diary and Memoir of Virginia d'Albert-Lake, ed. Judy Barrett Litoff (Fordham University Press, 2006); *Nazi Plunder: Great Treasure Stories of World War II,* by Kenneth D. Alford (Cambridge, 2001); *Histoire de l'épuration,* by Raymond Aron (Fayard, 1969–75); *Outwitting the Gestapo,* by Lucie Aubrac, tr. Konrad Bieber (Lincoln, 1993); *Tu trahiras sans vergogne, histoire de deux collabos, Bonny et Lafont,* by Philippe Aziz (Fayard, 1969); *The Phantom Conspiracy,* by Michael Bar-Zohar (Weidenfeld & Nicolson, 1981); *The Letters of Sylvia Beach,* ed. Keri Walsh (Colombia, 2010); *The Letters of Samuel Beckett, 1941–56,* ed. by George Craig, Martha Dow Fehsenfeld, Dan Gunn & Lois More Overbeck (Cambridge, 2012); *The Second World War,* by Antony Beevor (Weidenfeld & Nicolson, 2012); *D-day: the Battle for Normandy,* by Antony Beevor (Viking, 2009); *Paris after the Liberation,* by Antony Beevor and Artemis Cooper (Hamish Hamilton, 1994); *Les policiers français sous l'Occupation: d'après les archives inédites de l'épuration,* by Jean-Marc Berlière (Perrin, 2001); *Journal: Hélène Berr,* tr. David Bellos (MacLehose, 2008); *Colonel Henri's story: the War Memoirs of Hugo Bleicher, former German Secret Agent,* by Hugo Ernst Bleicher (W. Kimber, 1954); *L'étrange Monsieur Joseph,* by Alphonse Boudard (Laffont, 1998); *1940–45 années érotiques: Vichy ou les infortunes de la vertu,* by Patrick Buisson (Albin Michel, 2008); *Bad Faith: a Forgotten History of Family and Fatherland,* by Carmen Callil (Cape, 2006); *Invasion – They're Coming! The German Account of the Allied Landings and the 80 Days Battle for France,* by Paul Carell (Harrap, 1962); *The Song Before it is Sung,* by Justin Cartwright (Bloomsbury, 2007); *Chanel: an Intimate Life,* by Lisa Chaney (Fig Tree, 2011); *The Resistance: the French Fight Against the Nazis,* by Matthew Cobb (Simon & Schuster, 2009); *Is Paris Burning?* by Larry Collins and Dominique Lapierre (Victor Gollancz, 1965); *Joseph Kessel ou sur la piste du lion,* by Yves Courrière (Plon, 2003); *Bolter's Grand-Daughter,* by Angela Culme Seymour (Writersworld, 2003); *Hidden Faces,* by Salvador Dali (Peter Owen, 1973); *The French against the French: Collaboration and Resistance,* by Milton Dank (Cassell, 1978); *A Square of Sky: Memoirs of a Wartime Childhood,* by Janina David (Eland, 1992); 'Le Musée 39–45 "Message Verlaine" ou la guerre des ondes a bien eu lieu à Tourcoing,' by Francis Delannoy and Gaston

Delau (*De Raton Six*, 7/4/1992); *Trafics et crimes sous l'Occupation*, by Jacques Delarue (Fayard, 1968); *The Gestapo: a History of Horror*, by Jacques Delarue, tr. Mervun Savill (Frontline, 2008); *Women and the Second World War in France, 1939–48: Choices and Constraints*, by Hanna Diamond (Longman, 1999), *Wartime Notebooks*, by Marguerite Duras, tr. Linda Coverdale (MacLehose, 2008); *Les Comptesses de la Gestapo*, by Cyril Eder (Grasset, 2006); *Monuments Men: Allied heroes, Nazi thieves and the Greatest Treasure Hunt in History*, by Robert M. Edsel (Preface, 2009); *The Love Charm of Bombs: restless lives in the Second World War*, by Laura Feigel (Bloomsbury, 2013); *The Lost Museum*, by Hector Feliciano (BasicBooks, 1997); *We Will Wait: Wives of French Prisoners of War, 1940–45*, by Sarah Fishman (Yale, 1992); *Sylvia Beach And The Lost Generation: A History of Literary Paris in the Twenties and Thirties*, by Noel Fitch (Souvenir Press, 1983); *Noah's Ark*, by Marie-Madeleine Fourcade (Dutton and Co., New York, 1974); *Surrender on Demand*, by Varian Fry (Atlantic, 1999); *Journal, 1940–1950*, by Jean Galtier-Boissière (Quai Voltaire, 1992); *Journals: 1889–1949*, by André Gide (Penguin, 1967); *Marianne in Chains: Daily Life in the Heart of France during the German Occupation*, by Robert Gildea (Macmillan, 2002); *The Demons Tormenting Untersturmführer Hans Otto Graebner*, by Robert Girardi (Delta, 1999); *Americans in Paris*, by Charles Glass (Harper Press, 2009); *Deserter: the Last Untold Story of the Second World War*, by Charles Glass (Harper Press, 2013); *L'affaire Joinovici: collaborateur, résistant, et bouc émissaire*, by André Goldschmidt (Privat, 2002); *Collaborationism in France During the Second World War*, by B. Gordon (Cornell, 1980); *The Lost Masters: the Looting of Europe's Treasure Houses*, by Peter Harclerode (Orion, 1999); *England's Last War against France*, by Colin Harris (Orion, 2010); *All Hell Let Loose: The World at War 1939–45*, by Max Hastings (Harper Press, 2011); *The Philosopher of Auschwitz: Jean Améry and Living with the Holocaust*, by Irène Heidelberger-Leonard tr. Anthea Bell (I. B. Tauris, 2010); *La Bande Bonny-Lafont*, by Serge Jacquemard (Fleuve Noir, 1992); *Palace of Sweet Sin*, by Fabienne Jamet (W. H. Allen, 1977); *Carousel*, by J. Robert Janes (Constable, 1992); *Occupied France : Collaboration and Resistance, 1940–1944*, by H. R. Kedward (Blackwell, 1985); *The Liberation of*

France: Image and Event, ed. H. R. Kedward and Nancy Wood (Berg, 1995); *Army of Shadows*, by Joseph Kessel (Cresset, 1944); *Koestler*, by Marke Levene (Wolff, 1984); *Return to Malaya*, by Robert Hamilton Bruce Lockhart (Putnam, 1936); *The Man Who Made Vermeers*, by Jonathan Lopez (Mariner, 2009); *The Fall of Paris June 1940*, by Herbert R. Lottman (Harper Collins, 1992); *The People's Anger: Justice and Revenge in Post-Liberation France*, by Herbert R. Lottman (Hutchinson, 1986); *The White Rabbit, from the Story as Told to Him by Wing Commander F. F. E. Yeo-Thomas G.C. M.C.*, by Bruce Marshall (Evans, 1952); *A Question of Loyalties*, by Allan Massie (Hutchinson, 1989); *Looted Treasure: Germany's Raid on Art*, by George Mihan (Alliance Press, 1944); *The Desert Fox in Normandy: Rommel's Defense of Fortress Europe*, by Samuel W. Mitcham Jr (Cooper Square Press, 2001); *Nazi Paris: the History of an Occupation, 1940–1944*, by Allan Mitchell (Berghahn Books, 2008); *The Devil's Captain: Ernst Jünger in Nazi Paris, 1941–1944*, by Allan Mitchell (Berghahn Books, 2011); *Ernst Jünger and Germany: into the Abyss, 1914–1945*, by Thomas R. Nevin (Duke University Press, 1996); *The Rape of Europa: the Fate of Europe's Treasures in the Third Reich and the Second World War*, by Lynn H. Nicholas (Macmillan, 1994); *Goering: Hitler's Iron Knight*, by Richard Overy (I. B. Tauris, 2012); *Double Agent: Mathilde Carré*, by Lauran Paine (Hale, 1986); *Vichy France: Old Guard and New Order, 1940–1944*, by Robert Paxton (Barrie & Jenkins, 1972); *Paris Under the Occupation*, by Gilles Perrault and Pierre Azema (Vendome, 1989); *Götz von Berlichingen*, by Jean-Claude Perrigault and Rolf Meister (Heimdal, 2004); *The Faustian Bargain: the Art World in Nazi Germany*, by Jonathan Petropoulos (Oxford, 2000); *Paris in the Third Reich: a History of the German Occupation, 1940–1944*, by David Pryce-Jones (Harper Collins, 1981); *La police de Vichy: les forces de l'ordre françaises au service de la Gestapo, 1940–1944*, by Maurice Rajsfus (Cherche-Midi, 1995); *The Longest Day*, by Cornelius Ryan (Coronet, 1959); *Koestler: the Indispensable Intellectual*, by Michael Scammell (Faber, 2011); *The Price of Glory*, by Henriette von Schirach (Muller, 1960); *The German Trauma: Experiences and Reflections 1938–2001*, by Gitta Sereny (Penguin, 2000); *Repatriation of Art from the Collecting Point in Munich after World War*

II : *Background and Beginnings with Reference especially to the Netherlands,* by Craig Hugh Smyth (Maarssen, 1988); *The Shameful Peace: how French Artists and Intellectuals Survived the Nazi Occupation,* by Frederic Spotts (Yale, 2008); *While Berlin burns: the Diary of Hans-Georg von Studnitz, 1943–1945* (Weidenfeld & Nicolson, 1964); *Villa Air-Bel: World War II, Escape, and a House in Marseille,* by Rosemary Sullivan (Harper, 2007); *Reclaimed: Paintings from the Collection of Jacques Goudstikker,* by Peter C. Sutton (Yale, 2008); *Choices in Vichy France: the French under Nazi Occupation,* by John F. Sweets (Oxford, 1986); *Le front de l'art: défense des collections françaises, 1939–1945,* by Rose Valland (Plon, 1961); *The Silence of the Sea,* by Vercors (Berg, 1991); *The Battle of Silence,* by Vercors (Collins, 1968); *The Unfree French: Life under the Occupation,* by Richard Vinen (Allen Lane, 2006); *Paris under the Occupation,* by Gérard Walter (Orion, 1960); *The Last Days of Paris: a Journalist's Diary,* by Alexander Werth (Hamish Hamilton, 1940); *Not That Sort of Girl,* by Mary Wesley (Macmillan, 1987); *Battle for Saint-Lô,* by Peter Yates (Sutton, 2004).

PART FIVE

Based on conversations with Brian Aldiss, Karen Andrews, John Bevington, Maria Corelli, Serge Doubrovsky, Annette Howard, Tracey Maitland, Priscilla Pessey, Timothy Radcliffe OP, Lalage and John Shakespeare, Michael Sheringham, Jon Stallworthy, Carleton Thompson, Ariel Tiberghien, Arnaud Tiberghien, Gael Tiberghien, Pierre-Yves Tiberghien, Quentin Tiberghien, Sheila Troman, Vivien Van Dam, Peter Waugh.

Unpublished sources: PT; GS; SPB (S. P. B. Mais memoir, *All Change*; Gillian Mais memoir, *Never Look Back*); HGA (Alec Waugh papers, Box 42, SPB to Arthur Waugh, 30 January 1917; Box 34: SPB to Alec Waugh, 18 October 1917; 20 May 1965; 1 June 1965; 20 August 1965; Jill Mais to Alec Waugh, 4 June 1975); Sherborne College archive; Alexander Waugh papers.

Newspapers: *Telegraph* magazine; Mushroom Growers' Newsletter

Books and articles: *Demobbed: Coming Home after the Second World War*, by Alan Allport (Yale, 2009); *Mr Chips: the life of Robert Donat*, by Kenneth Barrow (Methuen, 1985); *In Love and War: A Letter to My Parents*, by Maria Corelli (Short Books, 2001); *An Introductory History of British broadcasting*, by Andrew Crisell (Routledge, 1997); *Laissé pour conte*, by Serge Doubrovsky (Grasset, 1999); *The Honeyed Peace*, by Martha Gellhorn (Doubleday, 1953); *Prince Rainier of Monaco: his Authorised and Exclusive Story*, by Peter Hawkins (Kimber, 1966); by S. P. B. Mais: *I Return to Scotland* (Christopher Johnson 1947); *It isn't Far from London* (Richards, 1930); *The Riviera: New Look & Old* (Christopher Johnson, 1949); *Austrian Holiday* (Alvin Redman, 1952); *Literature or Life*, by Jorge Semprún (Viking, 1997); *Once Upon a Time: the Story of Princess Grace, Prince Rainier and Their Family*, by J. Randy Taraborrelli (Sidgwick & Jackson, 2003); *Robert Donat: a Biography*, by J. C. Trewin, (Heinemann, 1968); *Island in the Sun*, by Alec Waugh (Farrar, Straus & Cudahy 1955); *The Early Years of Alec Waugh*, by Alec Waugh (Cassell, 1962); *The Best Wine Last: An Autobiography Through the Years, 1932–1969*, by Alec Waugh (Allen, 1978); *Fathers and Sons*, by Alexander Waugh (Headline, 2004); *Borges: a Life*, by Edwin Williamson (Viking, 2004).

A note on names: My grandmother was known to us as Jill or Gillian, but to avoid confusion with Gillian Sutro I have called her Winnie, the name by which she was christened. Out of consideration for their relatives still living, I have changed the names of two further characters.

PICTURE CREDITS

TM = Tracey Maitland
PC = Peter Cawthra
GS = Gillian Sutro papers, Special Collections
Department, Bodleian Library, Oxford
MPP = Musée de la Préfecture de Police
archives, Paris
NARA = National Archives and Records
Administration, Washington DC
NS = author
SG/JF = Stella Gumuchian collection,
courtesy of James Fox archive

Cover [TM]
Endpapers – Boisgrimot Avenue [Jacqueline Hodey]
p. viii Frontispiece – Pris in Occupied France [TM]

PART ONE
p.10 Pris portrait by Vertés 1939 [TM]
p.14 Pris obituary 1982 [Chichester Observer]
p.16 Pris & Hermès handbag [TM]
p.20 Pris & cup 1940 [TM]
p. 23 Padded chest [NS]
p. 25 Swimmer & eel 1940 [TM]
p. 28 Box of documents [NS]

PART TWO
p.34 Doris Mais 1919 [PC]
p.39 Doris & Mrs Snow [TM]
p.42 Pris & Vivien on Brighton beach [PC]
p.47 Gillian Sutro [TM]
p.51 Boo Wyndham-Lewis [PC]
p.52 Boo with face scratched [TM]
p.53 Pris's scrapbook [TM]
p.55 Gillian & Pris 1932 [GS]
p.57 Pris & Doris [PC]
p.59 SPB & Pris on Brighton beach [PC]
p.63 Pris, Doris & Vivien in Paris 1932 [PC]
p.70 Pris pregnant 1937 [TM]
p.76 Pris passport photo 1937 [TM]
p.76 Robert Doynel passport photo 1937 [TM]
p.93 Boisgrimot [Jean-Paul Pitou]
p.95 Monsieur Carer's buggy [NS]
p.97 Boisgrimot Avenue [Jacqueline Hodey]
p.113 Pris wedding day 1938 [TM]
p.114 Pris & Robert wedding 1938 [TM]
p.121 Marcel Vertès [GS]
p.127 Zoë Temblaire [TM]
p.137 Pris milking cow 1940 [TM]
p.139 Ted 1940 [TM]

p.140 Daniel Vernier 1940 [TM]
p.166 Gillian & John Sutro wedding 1940 [TM]

PART THREE
p.183 SPB book [NS]
p.186 Lavabos [SG/JF]
p.187 Batiment C [SG/JF]
p.189 B.71? [NS]

PART FOUR
p.217 Gillian's red notebook [NS, GS]
p.218 Pris & Daniel 1941 [TM]
p.221 Signing in [NS, Caserne Vauban archive]
p.232 Emile Cornet 1942 [TM]
p.238 Pris's police folder 1942 [NS, MPP]
p.242 Le Meur's report 1942 [NS, MPP]
p.246 Priscilla with Emile's associate [TM]
p.248 Max Stocklin [NS, MPP]
p.255 Pris in fur coat 1941/2 [TM]
p.263 Pris in La Roque Gageac 1942 [TM]
p.278 Gillian [TM]
p.283 Otto Graebener 1943 [TM]
p.298 Alois Miedl [NARA]
p.307 Otto in spats [TM]
p.314 Callipyge [NS, Arnaud Tiberghien]
p.320 8 Avenue de la Marne [Arnaud Tiberghien]
p.326 Pris in barn 1944 [TM]
p.341 Harold Acton [GS]

PART FIVE
p.349 Robert Donat [TM]
p.352 Donat letter [TM]
p.357 Gillian notebook [NS, GS]
p.358 Pris in Morocco 1948 [TM]
p.361 Pris & Gillian in Saint-Maxime 1947 [GS]
p.363 Pris & Raymond wedding 1948 [TM]
p.369 Pris's Vogue audition 1945 [TM]
p.374 Rejection letters 1944–1957 [NS, TM]
p.384 Pris, Vivien & Winnie [PC]
p.394 Robert in trilby [Zizi Carer]
p.395 Boisgrimot gutted 1944 [Jacqueline Hodey]
p.397 Author's father in Paris 2011 [NS]
p.407 Pris back in England 1944 [GS]

ABOUT THE AUTHOR

Nicholas Shakespeare was born in 1957. His novels have been translated into twenty languages. They include *The Vision of Elena Silves*, a winner of the Somerset Maugham Award, and *The Dancer Upstairs*, which was chosen by the American Library Association in 1997 as the year's best novel, and in 2001 was made into a film of the same name by John Malkovich. *Bruce Chatwin*, Shakespeare's biography of the British novelist, was published in 2000 to widespread critical acclaim. Shakespeare is married with two sons and currently lives in Oxford.

Environs de Carent
Avenue et Château
de Boisgrimot